THE
DEVELOPMENT
OF
SECONDARY
EDUCATION

Frederick M. Raubinger
Harold G. Rowe
Donald L. Piper
Charles K. West

THE MACMILLAN COMPANY

THE DEVELOPMENT OF SECONDARY EDUCATION

COLLIER-MACMILLAN LIMITED / LONDON

First Printing

Library of Congress catalog card number: 69-16490

THE MACMILLAN COMPANY
COLLIER-MACMILLAN CANADA, LTD., TORONTO, ONTARIO

PRINTED IN THE UNITED STATES OF AMERICA

PREFACE

During the past ten years there has been a frantic pace in education. Hundreds of projects have been carried on, and hundreds of proposals have been made for improving the schools. Some are contradictory of others in both direction and purpose. What is most urgently needed now is a period of calm reflection, objective appraisal, and evaluation. If the Educational Policies Commission was correct in stating in 1944 that we must create a secondary school system for all American youth—and we believe it was—then how are we progressing toward that goal? And what is yet required if that goal is to be reached? How should such schools be organized, and how should they be taught? What are the uses of subject matter, and how do we relate it to or use it for the achievement of purposes and goals? What *are* the purposes? What are the needs of youth, and what part should the schools play in meeting these needs? Such questions as these, raised again and again in earlier reports, are still valid and call for re-examination.

Conditions of society have changed, but the roots of the changes lie deep in the past. The same questions about secondary schools asked several generations ago recur today.

Two fundamental misconceptions about the secondary schools of the United States seem to be prevalent among many who today are making judgments about them. The first is that the concept and the development of the universal secondary school, that is, a school which embraces and seeks to provide meaningful educational experiences for all youth, go far back in our history.

This is not so. As recently as forty years ago no more than half of the boys and girls of secondary school age were in school, and as recently as that, many influential persons argued with considerable vigor that it was folly to think of a secondary school open to all.

The second misconception is that awareness of such problems as the high school drop-out, the educational disadvantages suffered by the children of the urban and rural poor, the lack of opportunity for the Negro, and the irrelevance of the curriculum for many pupils, is characteristic only of the thinking about schools which has been generated during recent years.

The judgment of Santayana comes to mind. "Those who cannot remember the past are condemned to repeat it." The development of secondary education is revealed in the reports and recommendations contained in this book. They serve to remind us that there is a past that can add necessary perspective to those who today think and write about and make pronouncements and recommendations concerning the schools.

Some of the reports reprinted here are becoming difficult to find on library shelves. By assembling them under one cover, we hope to provide a ready reference to a literature that in significant degree has influenced the transformation of the secondary school over the past seventy-five years. As one rereads the reports he is struck by their timeliness now.

We gratefully acknowledge permission to publish the several reports. It is our hope that, by making them available, those who influence policies for secondary education for the future may be helped in arriving at wise judgments.

We especially acknowledge our debt to Fred Wilhelm, who wrote the text for *Background for Choice-Making in Secondary Education,* National Committee Paper Number One of the National Committee on Secondary Education of the National Association of Secondary School Principals. Mr. Wilhelm was at that time associate secretary of the association. It was this publication that led to our decision to prepare this book. We are grateful for permission to quote liberally from Mr. Wilhelm's material. However, the full responsibility for the contents and arrangement of *The Development of Secondary Education* rests with ourselves.

F. M. R.
H. G. R.
D. L. P.
C. K. W.

CONTENTS

1   *Introduction*   *1*

2   *Secondary School Studies and Reading List for English*   *25*

Reports by the Committee of Ten, the Conference on English, and about the Carnegie Unit

3   *Reorganization of Secondary Education*   *97*

Reports by the Committee of Nine, the Committee on College Entrance Requirements, and including the Cardinal Principles of Secondary Education

4   *Issues and Functions of Secondary Education*   *131*

Reports by the Committee on the Reorientation of Secondary Education

5   *Relation of School and College*   *159*

Portions of the Eight-Year Study by the Progressive Education Association

6   *Youth Tell Their Story*   *203*

Excerpts from a Survey by the American Youth Commission

7   *Character and Cost of Public Education*   *265*

Selections from the Regents' Inquiry in the State of New York

8 *Education for All American Youth*　　　*303*
Reports of the Educational Policies Commission and the
Harvard Committee

9 *Epilogue*　　　*355*

Bibliography　　　*369*

THE
DEVELOPMENT
OF
SECONDARY
EDUCATION

INTRODUCTION

 *This book contains studies and reports of various important committees and commissions on public secondary education in the United States, beginning with the Report of the Committee of Ten, issued in 1893, and continuing with those issued over a period of approximately fifty years. The period covered ends with the beginning of the 1950's.*

Taken together, these reports provide historical insight into the development of that unique institution, the American free public high school. Reports, studies, criticisms, and recommendations made during the period beginning roughly with the post-Sputnik era are not included, although reference will be made to this period in the Epilogue.

DEVELOPMENT OF THE FREE PUBLIC
SECONDARY SCHOOL

The public school system of America did not evolve as an integrated whole, with elementary school, secondary school,

1

college, and university making parallel progress toward public acceptance and support. Its parts grew separately and unevenly, and the progress toward integration of the various levels into a unified system reaching from kindergarten through university is a fairly recent development, even now not complete.

The early struggle to achieve free tax-supported publicly controlled schools centered around the elementary school, and it was not until the last quarter of the nineteenth century that this battle was won. The common school, used in the sense that it was to be free and open to all, was the elementary school.

Here, in the vision of some of the founders of the Republic, the citizenry would become literate and thus able to inform themselves. Here the people would learn the principles of self-government. In the common school distinctions of class and differences between the rich and poor would be minimized. In the common school children would learn to read and write and figure, thus preparing themselves to take their places in commerce and industry. Here they would learn the principles of the great experiment that began with the Declaration of Independence and the laws and forms and ideals of the Republic.

Such were the arguments and justifications advanced for the common school. It was primarily to establish and consolidate this common school that Horace Mann in Massachusetts, Henry Barnard in Connecticut, Newton Bateman in Illinois, and similar leaders in other states strove, and for which they pressed for public support and acceptance. The success of the efforts that had persisted since the opening of the nineteenth century, and before, is indicated by the fact that by 1870 the number enrolled in the common schools was just under 7,000,000, and by 1890 had increased to 12,500,000. The public high schools, by contrast, enrolled only 80,000 in 1870, and by 1890 only 203,000 were enrolled. It can hardly be argued that the American secondary school was in any significant degree a common school, open to all, in 1890 at the time the Committee of Ten was preparing its report on the curriculum of the secondary school. With only 203,000 enrolled, there were almost 3,000,000 boys and girls who were not enrolled. Even if allowance is made for those attending private schools and academies, it is probable that more than two and a half million of those of high school age were not in secondary school, either public or private, even though some of the high school age group were no doubt still retained in the elementary schools.

The National Teachers' Association, forerunner of the National Education Association, was organized in 1857. The programs of its annual conventions in succeeding years included hundreds of topics bearing on the work of the common schools and the normal schools in which teachers for the common schools were being prepared. Yet it was not until 1877 that a specific reference to the public secondary school was made on a convention program.

The Association adopted plans in 1870 for organizing departments at the same time that the name was changed to the National Educational Association. The program of the 1870 convention was divided among the new departments which included elementary education, normal schools and higher education; a department of secondary education was not added until 1885.

Actually, secondary schools had been established early in the history of this country, but they were neither free to all nor were they intended to be. The colonists brought with them the European concept of a class system of education, by which one kind of education was considered to be the prerogative of the upper classes and quite another believed to be appropriate for the masses. The early Latin grammar schools were designed to provide instruction in Latin and Greek for a select few as preparation for entrance to the colonial colleges, where the study of the two languages and their literature dominated the course of study.

A publication of The American Council on Education described the colonial secondary schools as follows:

The secondary schools established by the early American colonies followed the pattern of the secondary schools of Europe, which had been the dominant educational institutions of all the Western European countries since the medieval period. The colonial secondary schools were variously known as "Latin schools," "grammar schools," or "Latin grammar schools." The chief item in their curriculum as indicated by their name, was the Latin language. They were distinct from the schools which served the sons and daughters of the common people. The schools for ordinary boys and girls limited their instruction to teaching how to read the vernacular—the Latin schools prepared for college. The pupils of these Latin schools were a small select group of boys who were looking forward to careers in the professions; at first, in the ministry, later, in the law, and still later, in medicine.[1]

Nor did most of the founding fathers of the Republic think of secondary education as being universal or free to all. Thomas Jefferson, for example, although showing remarkable foresight for his time concerning the need for and the purposes of education in the new nation,

---

[1] American Council on Education. *What the High Schools Ought to Teach.* Washington, D.C.: 1940, pp. 1–2.

nevertheless thought of education beyond the common school as highly selective.

As a member of the Virginia legislature Jefferson, in 1799, introduced a bill for a state system of schools. In his explanatory statement he outlined the principal provisions.

This bill proposes to lay off every county into small districts of five or six miles square, called hundreds, and in each of these establish a school for teaching reading, writing, and arithmetic. The tutor to be supported by the hundred, and every person in it entitled to send their children three years gratis, and as much longer as they please paying for it. These schools to be under a visitor, who is annually to choose the boy of most genius in the school, of whose parents are too poor to give them further education, and to send him forward to one of the grammar schools, of which twenty are proposed to be erected in different parts of the country, for teaching of Greek, Latin, geography, and the higher branches of numerical arithmetic. Of the boys sent in any one year, trial is to be made at the grammar schools one or two years; and the best genius of the whole selected and continued six years, and the residue dismissed. By this means twenty of the best geniuses will be raked from the rubbish annually, and be instructed, at the public expense, so far as the grammar schools go. At the end of six years instruction, one half are to be discontinued . . . ; and the other half, who are to be chosen for the superiority of their parts and disposition, are to be sent and continued three years . . . at William and Mary College . . . the ultimate result of the whole scheme of education would be the teaching of all the children of the state reading, writing and common arithmetic: turning out ten annually of superior genius, well taught in Greek, Latin, geography and the higher branches of arithmetic: turning out ten others annually, of still superior parts, who to those branches of learning, shall have added such of the science as their genius shall have led them to: the furnishing to the wealthier part of the people convenient schools, at which their children may be educated, at their own expense.

The first public high school was established in Boston in 1821, when the Boston school committee created a three-year English Classical School which soon became known as the English High School.[2] Entrance was at age twelve and was by way of examination. Other public high schools were organized in succeeding decades, but they were principally to be found in the cities. Portland, Maine, Worcester, Massachusetts, and New York City followed closely on the example of

---

[2] The Boston Latin School, organized in 1635, continued after the English High School was established. From 1815–1861 the average number per year prepared for college by the Latin School was fewer than thirteen. This number may be put in perspective when it is seen that the population of Boston in 1861 was 178,000, and the enrollment in the common schools of Boston was 28,000.

Boston. *The first public high school in Philadelphia was founded in 1838; in Cincinnati, in 1847; and in Chicago, in 1856.*[3] *It has been estimated that by 1860 there were 300 public high schools in the country, but most of them were small and in most instances admission was selective. Even by 1890, when approximately 6,000 schools were operating under the name of public high schools, the average enrollment would have been less than 40; and, considering the larger size of some of the city schools, the enrollment in many of the remainder must have been very small indeed.*

Nevertheless, in the middle decades of the nineteenth century the idea of a publicly controlled, tax-supported secondary school had taken root. The principle itself was bitterly contested in state after state, and the legality of the right of government to tax for the support of a public high school was not determined beyond reasonable doubt until the Kalamazoo decision in 1874, and a series of other state supreme court cases which soon followed in other states. In the Kalamazoo case the Supreme Court of Michigan upheld the right of a school district to provide at public expense instruction in subjects above those of the elementary schools. The court took the position that public elementary schools had already been established, that public universities had also been established, and that there was no good reason why the intermediate link between the two, the high school, should not likewise be established and supported.

However, it was the twentieth century that was to see the concept of the common school extended to include the public high school. From 1900 until 1930 the enrollments doubled every ten years, and the proportion of those of high school age who were in high school increased from slightly more than one in ten to one of every two.

By 1960, the enrollment of public secondary schools exceeded eight million, and 87 per cent of the age group was in high school. It is predicted that the 1970 census will show the enrollment to be in excess of eleven million, with better than 90 per cent of the age group in high school.

To speak intelligently about the modern school, it is necessary to understand how recent the expansion of the American public secondary school is as well as the phenomenal increase in the school age

---

[3] According to a report of the superintendent of schools of Chicago in 1857, the high school, built to accommodate 320 pupils, had a first-year enrollment of 151, of whom 50 were in the Classical department, 79 in the English course, and 22 in the Normal department, the latter being those being prepared to teach in the common schools. At that time Chicago had a total population of approximately 108,000 and a common school enrollment of 8,577.

population enrolled in the public high school during the expansion period. An awareness of these facts is also essential to an understanding of the various studies and reports included in this book.

Two currents of thought that ran through the early perceptions of secondary schools in America came together as those schools moved toward becoming part of the common school system, open to all, tax supported, publicly controlled.

The first type of school has already been described in part in the preceding account. Its curriculum, originally designed for the few, was selective and "classical" in that it placed heavy emphasis on the study of Latin in particular and, to a lesser extent, Greek, especially in the earlier period.

The Committee on the Reorientation of Secondary Education, reporting in 1918, paid its respects to the fact that secondary education in America was provided so early in the history of the country. The Committee pointed out, however, that only a few pupils in only a few places had access to secondary education, and that what was provided was a relic from Europe, outmoded even while it was being imitated in America and ill suited to the needs of the New World. Worse still, the Committee said, was the fact that this early institution for a long while prevented educators from using their imagination to devise a kind of secondary education suited to those needs.

The other current had its source in the thoughts of Benjamin Franklin who almost alone among the political geniuses of his time, saw the need for a different and broader conception of secondary education than that offered by the classical pattern.

A tract written by Franklin, first printed in Philadelphia in 1749, was titled "Proposals Relating to the Education of Youth in Pennsylvania."

Franklin urged that public spirited citizens apply for a charter ". . . in which they may be incorporated, with power to erect an academy for the education of youth. . . ." It would be good, Franklin said, ". . . if the students could be taught everything that is useful, and everything that is ornamental: but art is long and their time is short. It is therefore proposed that they learn those things that are likely to be most useful and most ornamental. Regard being had to the several professions for which they are intended."

The students should be taught to write legibly, clearly, and concisely; to speak well; to draw; to learn arithmetic and accounts and some of the first principles of geometry and astronomy. The history of men and nations, especially Britain and the colonies, was to be read in English; as well as the history of commerce, arts, manufacture, and trade. The concept was close to that which much later became known as the social studies and embraced attention to political science, geography, the history of religions, and morality.

Natural science was to receive attention so that merchants and mechanics would know more about the commodities and materials of their trades.

One proposal called for practical experience in agriculture, and it was recommended that students plant and tend gardens and observe farming by means of trips to farms.

Franklin's proposals paid respect to the classical tradition and advocated the study of Latin and Greek for those who were preparing for professions in which these languages were used.

Franklin had ideas about how the trustees of the academy should relate to the students. They would, he hoped, ". . . look on the students as in some sort of their children, treat them with familiarity and affection, and when they have behaved well and gone through their studies, and are to enter the world, zealously write, and make all interest that can be made to establish them, whether in business, offices, marriage, or any other thing for their advantage, preferably to all other persons of equal merit."

The school, he said, should be a pleasant place, with a garden and orchard and fields. It would have books, maps, globes, scientific instruments, and machines.

Health was not to be neglected, and he proposed wrestling, running, leaping, and swimming as ways to build strong bodies.

Butts and Cremin summarized the Proposals as follows:

Franklin's real hope was to enlarge and make respectable an education for civil and occupational life that would not need to rest upon religious instruction or the classics. He hoped his academy would have an English school that would be on a level of equality and even more valuable than its classical school.[4]

In 1751 Franklin wrote "Idea of the English School" which was an extension of his original argument. He concluded as follows:

Thus instructed, youth will come out of this school fitted for learning any business, calling or profession, except such wherein languages are required; and though unacquainted with any ancient or foreign tongue, they will be masters of their own, which is of more immediate or general use; and withal will have attained many other valuable accomplishments; the time usually

---

[4] R. Freeman Butts, and Lawrence Cremin, *A History of Education in American Culture.* New York: Henry Holt and Co., 1953, p. 79.

spent in acquiring those languages, often without success, being here employed in laying such a foundation of knowledge and ability as, properly improved, may qualify them to pass through and execute the several offices of civil life with advantage to themselves and country.

Franklin's proposals received wide attention and support from influential persons. His academy was established, but his ideas proved to be generations ahead of his time. Later on, Franklin complained that the "Latinists" within the school had succeeded in building their part of the academy at the expense of the English school. His disappointment at this was such that he demanded that the English school be split away, the stock of the corporation divided, and the corporation itself dissolved.

The ideas behind Franklin's proposals, however, were not to die. They were incorporated in the thousands of academies established in the first three-quarters of the nineteenth century. Later, they were to merge with the purposes of the public high schools when these institutions were forced to adapt themselves to becoming the schools for all of the children of all the people.

Little more than 25 years after the publication of Franklin's Proposals, two brothers, Samuel and John Phillips, provided an endowment and drew up a constitution for an academy at Andover, Massachusetts, ". . . for the purpose of instructing youth, not only in English and Latin grammar, writing, arithmetic, and those sciences wherein they are commonly taught; but more especially to learn them the GREAT END AND REAL BUSINESS OF LIVING."

English, Latin, Greek, writing, arithmetic, music, the art of speaking, geometry, and logic were to be taught in the academy. Special attention was to be given to health. The pupils were to perform manual labor, such as gardening. Special attention was to be given to moral training for ". . . although goodness without knowledge (as it respects others) is weak and feeble; yet knowledge without goodness is dangerous. . . ."

The Phillips Andover Academy was founded in 1778 and incorporated in 1780, the first chartered academy in New England. It had a self-perpetuating board of trustees, and it charged tuition. John Phillips endowed another academy at Exeter which was incorporated in 1781 and opened in 1783.

The idea of the academy took hold rapidly and spread to all parts of the country. Both in number of schools and in the number enrolled, the academy became the dominant institution of secondary education until well past the close of the Civil War. By 1850 it is estimated that 6,000 academies were in existence. Some were chartered, some were purely proprietary and unincorporated. Among them they offered a wide variety of types of instruction. These academies were local in character and existed side-by-side with the common school. But they were not under public control, they were not free, and although some received subsidies from government sources—often land on which to erect buildings—they were not tax supported in the same way as the common schools or the emerging public high schools.

Even though the academy moved a long way toward providing useful and practical secondary education it still failed to meet certain purposes. One was that with all its expansion, and with all the students it served, there were still large groups of youngsters whose parents could not afford to pay tuition. Increasingly arguments pointed to the paradox of a common school system attempting to provide genuine equality of educational opportunity to all and a secondary school system open only to those who could pay began to achieve results.[5]

The age of the academies had begun to draw to a close shortly after the Civil War, and the public high school began to emerge as the institution that the people of the United States would choose for the education of their adolescents. By 1890, this was rather clearly discernible. Although at the time not many proponents of the public high school envisioned the secondary school as intended for or even suited to more than a small fraction of the boys and girls. On the contrary, even though many secondary schools opened in all sections of the country were supported by taxation and controlled by the citizens of the communities through their elected boards of education, the schools were small; only a few of the many boys and girls legally eligible to attend were enrolled. The era of the universal public high school had not arrived, and it is doubtful if any of the leaders of the time sensed that it was so near that in each of the four succeeding decades the secondary enrollments would double.

THE COMMITTEE ON SECONDARY

SCHOOL STUDIES

This was the state of affairs when the Committee on Secondary School Studies, more often referred to as the Committee of Ten, was appointed by the National Education Association in 1892.

[5] *Ibid.* p. 262.

This may be a good place to digress, for in the development of secondary schools, 1890 was a watershed. Much had been accomplished. The struggle to establish the common school was won. The legality of the public high school had been upheld. The academies, which had made great contributions to secondary education were yielding to the public high school, whose program they influenced so beneficially. But it is well for anyone inclined to look nostalgically to the good old days to remember that in 1890, in addition to the fact that most boys and girls of the high school age group were not in school, the average length of the school term was 135 days and the average number of days attended per student enrolled was 86. Total expenditures on public education were only $140,000,000.

In a nation of 62,622,250, the number of students in colleges and universities was only 157,000.

Against this background one can understand the work of the Committee of Ten which is the first of the series of reports to appear in this book. It is unlikely that the views of this committee reflected what George Boutwell, onetime governor of Massachusetts and secretary of the State Board of Education, had in mind when in 1859, he spoke of the public high school.

The distinguishing difference between the advocates of endowed schools and free schools is this: those who advocate the system of endowed academies go back in their arguments to one foundation, which is, that in the education of higher grades the great mass of people are not to be trusted. And those who advocate a system of free education in high schools put the matter where we have put the rights of property and liberty, where we put the institutions of law and religion, upon the public judgment.[6]

The Committee was dominated by men from the colleges who were primarily interested in the secondary school as an institution from which the students in their colleges were to be obtained. A reading of the full report leads to this conclusion even though, in a paradoxical section, the Committee maintained that the course of study it proposed was to be the same for all, whether or not college was the destination, and that, as a matter of fact, preparation for college was not the predominant purpose of the high school.

It is doubtful if the people who were supporting the public high schools in 1890 or the boards of education through whom public control was exercised had any influence over the report by the Committee of Ten. Nor was there any good reason why views of the public or

[6] Quoted in Butts and Cremin, *op. cit.*, p. 208.

public officials would be solicited or volunteered. In 1890 secondary schools did not touch the lives of the great majority of boys and girls. The time when the secondary school belonged to all, open to all, lay ahead.

The report, nevertheless, had considerable impact on secondary education. Its specification of subjects to be studied and valued, and specific content to be covered, its pronouncements on the time to be allotted to the various subjects, its underlying belief in the faculty psychology upon which its recommendations were based affected the program, the design and structure, and the rationale for secondary schools for generations. Even now, these influences and the point of view behind them play no small part in the continuing debates and discussions about the proper function of the public high schools, how their program shall be arranged, and how they shall be taught.

The Committee of Ten were more in tune with traditions of the past than with questions of the future. The first two reports of conferences on the subject fields were for Latin and Greek. For the former, a minimum of four years of study, five times a week, not less than forty-five minutes at a time, was recommended. The study of Latin should be treated in the same way whether students intended to go to college, scientific school, or to neither, it declared. Higher "standards" were urged and the example set in England and on the Continent was praised.

The learning of Latin as a tool for the professions no longer being necessary, it was argued that the end of reading Latin was to gain ". . . an insight into the thought and feeling of people who have contributed very largely to make the life of the civilized world what it is today."

Greek, it was recommended, should be studied for three years, five recitations per week the first year and four in the last two years. Somewhat reminiscent of proposals being made presently about how much subject matter pupils can "go through," the Conference on Greek reported approvingly on the statement of an unnamed headmaster who said that ". . . some years ago his classes read three books of Homer in the senior year; as he received pupils better trained and secured better instruction, the amount read was increased to five books; then to eight; and he hopes in the same way to increase the amount read still further." [7]

The table of time-allotments shown in the first section of this book

[7] Report of the Committee of Ten on Secondary School Studies. New York: Published for the National Education Association by the American Book Company, 1894. Reports on the Conferences on Latin and Greek, pp. 60–86.

reveals the provision for these subjects and others specified for the four-year high school curriculum. It can scarcely be described as broad or flexible or suited to the needs of the new high school that lay just beyond the horizon.

By 1900, the public high school enrollment was more than double the 1890 figure. In 1910 the 1900 enrollment figure had been doubled. In the years intervening since the Report of the Committee of Ten there was evident a stir and a ferment among leaders of the secondary schools. Reports appeared which indicated that the schools were chafing under the domination of the colleges; that they believed they had a mission of their own, related to in a degree but not dependent on or subservient to the mission of the colleges. Signs were clear that the restricted curriculum could not contain the needs of the pupils coming into the schools. The seams of the curriculum pattern proposed by the Committee were coming apart.

Forces that could not be denied were exerting influences which would eventually lead to the creation of a secondary school which was accepted everywhere as a legitimate and necessary part of the common school system. These influences led to a broadening of the curriculum; they affected methods of teaching and gradually led to a view of the secondary school as youth's own institution, the only institution created by society embracing almost the total population of school age. This latter view of the secondary school, often honored more in the breach, even now, came slowly and gradually, and was accepted by many grudgingly or reluctantly.

What forces combined to influence the schools in this direction? The Second Industrial Revolution was radically changing work patterns and opportunities. The country was moving from predominantly rural to urban. The development of commerce and industry as well as changes in methods of agriculture demanded new knowledge and skills. Laws were passed regulating child labor, eliminating many from the work force who would previously have left school to go to work at an early age. The passage of compulsory attendance laws, with the permissive age for leaving school raised progressively in state after state kept the older adolescent in school. These laws were based on mixed motives. The aim of providing more years of education for all was certainly one motive. Equally important, probably, was the intention to limit the number who would be entering the labor force. Whatever the reasons, the immediate result was to channel large numbers into the schools, children who would not have gone there had it not been for laws that compelled attendance.

It was also becoming recognized that the secondary school age group had many and widespread capacities which could be given opportunity to grow and develop provided three things: that the school curriculum was broad and flexible enough to accommodate them; that those who managed and taught the schools were willing to broaden their own vision sufficiently to encompass all the possibilities; and further, that citizens, through their taxes, would procure the funds necessary to bring the vision to reality.

Other influences came from psychology with its new insights about how people learned and from philosophers with their fresh view of the dynamics of democracy and their belief in the values of broadened educational opportunities for all as a way to strengthen and vitalize democratic processes in all areas of life, including government.

The growth of secondary schools brought along with it a new kind of administrator and educational leader—the high school principal— many of whom had studied in emerging departments or colleges of education which had been created in a number of universities. Those principals were becoming familiar with newer psychology and newer educational philosophy; also, some had studied with men who were redefining the role of the principalship itself and attempting to provide for it a professionalism which went beyond management to the heart of the educative process.

COMMISSION ON THE REORGANIZATION OF SECONDARY EDUCATION

It was primarily members of this new group, principals and professors, who joined together to study issues and bring these to their counterparts in schools and colleges and to the public in the form of reports and recommendations. It was such a combination of persons that made up the Commission on the Reorganization of Secondary Education which in 1918 issued the Cardinal Principles of Secondary Education.

Forty years after the Cardinal Principles appeared, this group was to be labeled the Establishment, connoting a kind of closed fraternity. Whatever justification there may have been for this later judgment, which itself is not without bias, the fact is that the early principals, faced as they were with the day-to-day encounter with pupils and public, undoubtedly reflected public attitudes and aspirations for a new kind of secondary school.

The changes referred to briefly above led to a point of view about secondary schools noticeably different from the earlier Report of the Committee of Ten. The first paragraph of the Report of the Commis-

sion on the Reorganization of Secondary Education signalled the change.

Secondary education should be determined by the needs of the society to be served, the character of the individuals to be educated, and the knowledge of educational theory and practice available. These factors are by no means static. Society is always in process of development; the character of the secondary school population undergoes modification; and the sciences on which educational theory and practice depend constantly furnish new information. Secondary education, however, like any other established agency of society, is conservative and tends to resist modification. Failure to make adjustments when the need arises leads to the necessity for extensive reorganization at irregular intervals. The evidence is strong that such a comprehensive reorganization of secondary education is imperative at the present time.[8]

Previous reports had centered on subjects to be offered—on the processes *of education. The Cardinal Principles set first things first and concentrated on the* purposes *or objectives of secondary education, listing seven: health, command of fundamental processes, worthy home membership, vocation, civic education, worthy use of leisure time, and ethical character.*

Subject matter was considered to be a means to these ends and not an end in itself. From the time of this report to the present, recommendations about the schools have been influenced by the belief that it is necessary to define and agree upon purposes, objectives, and goals before it is practicable to explore means. Purpose precedes process.

The Report on the Reorganization of Secondary Education was issued as World War I drew to a close.

With the entry of the United States into World War I the nation, like it or not, became a recognized great power and was drawn into international affairs on a scale hardly imagined a generation earlier, an involvement that was to grow in complexity and intensity in the decades to follow.

One manifestation came less than a score of years after the appearance of the Cardinal Principles. The United States found itself sinking into the depths of the Great Depression, an economic failure worldwide in scope. Abroad, in the Thirties, ideologies alien to the democratic way of life drew allegiance from peoples and nations. The growth of Communism, Nazism, Fascism abroad led to searching questions here at home. Democracy was apparently not a condition that would evolve

8 Commission on the Reorganization of Secondary Education, *Cardinal Principles of Education.* Washington, D.C.: U.S. Government Printing Office, 1918, p. 7.

by some kind of historical predetermination until it was accepted and embraced by all peoples. Education, it was discovered, could be used to further the ends of authoritarian dictatorship as well as it could be used to advance the cause of democracy.

The decade of the Thirties was one of soul searching in American education.

As the Thirties opened, the people of the United States could look back upon an astonishing increase in the number enrolled in the secondary schools and on an even more astonishing increase in the percentage of secondary school age youth enrolled. Even so, the end of the increase in both numbers and percentage was not then in sight (see Table 1).

TABLE 1   Percentage of Youth 14–17 Years Enrolled in Secondary Schools

Year	Percentage	Number Enrolled
1890	6.7	203,000
1900	11.4	519,000
1910	15.4	915,000
1920	32.3	2,200,000
1930	51.4	4,400,000

"Background for Choice-Making in Secondary Education," which is Committee Paper Number One of the National Committee on Secondary Education of the National Association of Secondary School Principals, issued in 1966, contains comments on the era.[9]

Going back three decades takes us into the middle thirties. It was a time of questioning, a time of vivid ideas. Perhaps it was the way the great depression had shaken old certainties within our own land. Perhaps it was the shock of Communism, Fascism, and Nazism in Europe plunging mankind into a brutality long considered a thing of the past, and threatening the very foundations of democracy. Something drove men to face up to fundamental questions and enabled them to dream of a great reconstruction.

Nowhere was the ferment more active than in education. The Progressive Education Association was at its zenith. But its members were by no means alone in their drive. Even though it was a time of vigorous debate on specifics, there was a basic consensus in the land. The Cardinal Principles of Secondary Education had become almost an unspoken standard of the way to conceptualize educational purposes. And educators everywhere were dominated by

9 The National Association of Secondary School Principals, *Background for Choice-Making in Secondary Education.* Washington, D.C.: 1961, p. 7.

concern for people and their problems along with zeal for the development of a truly democratic society.
Especially striking was the number of major educational ventures which had their beginnings in those middle thirties . . . their chief characteristic was a searching for a coherent set of purposes by which to guide the whole enterprise.

Studies of secondary education during the Thirties were originated and carried out by a variety of groups, acting under a wide range of sponsorship. Yet all in one way or another represented attempts to state coherent purposes, to clarify goals and to provide statements of objectives to guide the schools. Most of the studies revealed gaps between what the schools professed to believe and do and what they were doing; between philosophy and practice; between purposes and processes. This search for purpose had its antecedent in the statement of the Cardinal Principles, but in the Thirties the search gained new momentum and was intensified.

THE COMMITTEE ON REORIENTATION OF SECONDARY EDUCATION

The Committee on the Reorientation of Secondary Education, appointed by the National Association of Secondary School Principals, made two reports. The first, in 1936, attempted to define the issues with which the secondary schools should be concerned. The second, in 1937, was a statement of the functions the secondary school should perform.

THE EIGHT-YEAR STUDY

The Commission on the Relation of School and College of the Progressive Education Association was created in 1930. In spite of the acknowledged advances already accomplished in secondary education, the Commission reflected dissatisfaction with much that was being done. It believed the conventional curriculum was far removed from the needs of youth, the traditional curriculum had lost much of its vitality and significance, appreciation of the American heritage was neglected, many teachers ". . . lacked full knowledge of the nature of youth—of physical, intellectual and emotional drives and growth."

The secondary school suffered from lack of "clearcut, central purpose." The guidance of youth left much to be desired.

The Commission recognized that significant modifications of the curriculum, securing better ways of teaching, and a definition of broader purpose would be impeded unless a better articulation between school and college could be achieved, and more specifically, until the schools could be freed to a great degree from the type of requirements imposed upon them by the colleges. Hence, the Commission, with the cooperation of a great number of colleges, launched an eight-year experiment to determine whether students could succeed in college if their high school curriculum were permitted to depart from the traditional subject patterns, time requirements, and the like. The study, begun in 1933 and concluded in 1941, upheld the belief and hope of the Commission that students who departed from the conventional subject patterns could achieve as well in college as those whose preparation followed traditional practice.

Five volumes, under the general title, Adventure in American Education *contain the history and results of the experiment. The summary is found in the first volume,* The Story of the Eight-Year Study.

THE AMERICAN YOUTH COMMISSION

The year 1935 marked the beginning of yet another study that had significant relationship to secondary education. The American Council on Education appointed a commission of seventeen persons, selected for the most part from the public at large, to become known as the American Youth Commission. The Commission carried out a number of studies but the most celebrated was that in the state of Maryland, published under the title, Youth Tell Their Story.

The following account gives a brief description of what the study revealed.

Taken together with other data being gathered at the same time, this cogent, colorful report drawn directly from interviews with a sample of some 13,000 Maryland youth, was a shocker. It presented a stark picture of educational inequality, with many youth cut off from schooling by economic need. It challenged the reality of free public secondary education accessible to all. It revealed thousands of young people wandering aimlessly, out of school and without a job—or in jobs of a poor sort (a situation exacerbated, of course, by the depression, but with a familiar ring today). Furthermore, the book painted a disquieting picture of the sterile use of leisure. And it revealed a dismaying meagerness in the young persons' personal and civil ideals. This aspect of the report may not have caught as much attention as the economic sector did, but the gap between what the schools thought they were teaching about citizenship and the actual civic attitudes and functioning of young people has never been more glaringly apparent.[10]

THE REGENTS' INQUIRY

The Board of Regents of the State of New York launched a broad investigation of the schools of that state in 1935, the same year the Educational Policies Commission was established. The Regents' Inquiry, carried out at a cost of a million dollars, gathered a tremendous amount of information about the schools of New York. Those in charge of the study went to schools, to students and parents, to cross sections of the population, to leaders in business, labor, and civic life to obtain facts and opinion which would be helpful in drawing conclusions about the schools. These showed the lack of adaptability of the schools to changing conditions in society, a failure to meet the needs of the expanding population of the secondary schools, the need for more effective education for citizenship, and a lack of clear and generally recognized and accepted goals.

THE EDUCATIONAL POLICIES COMMISSION

The National Education Association and the American Association of School Administrators [11] joined, in 1935, to establish the Educational Policies Commission. The Commission has been described as "a unique agency within the profession of education . . . an autonomous, deliberative body which examines major issues in education and makes recommendations for dealing with them. [It] enjoys autonomous status in order that it may act as an independent voice on behalf of education. Speaking for itself only, the Commission examines educational issues in an atmosphere free from pressures involved in satisfying a constituency or meeting periodic deadlines." [12]

The Commission was in existence from 1935 to 1967. Its membership changed from time to time, but over the years it included twenty-three

10 *Ibid.,* pp. 15–16.
11 Originally the Department of Superintendence.
12 From a statement describing the EPC, made by the National Education Association.

classroom teachers, seventeen superintendents of schools, twenty-eight
university officials, thirteen staff members of professional educational
organizations, ten state and federal education officials, seventeen uni-
versity professors, ten other types of educational administrators, thirty-
two presidents of the National Education Association, and a like
number of presidents of the American Association of School Adminis-
trators. In addition, the Commission was assisted by a large number of
advisers selected to secure a representative cross section from all levels
of education.

At the general session of the National Education Association on
February 26, 1936, a member of the Educational Policies Commission
described the reasons for its creation, and the circumstances that had
brought the schools to crisis.

Up to the onset of the so-called depression, public education in
America had expanded almost without interruption. This expansion
occurred both with respect to areas served and with respect to number
of persons affected by these services. This era of prosperity and progress
was so long and so uninterrupted that it created in the public mind a
comfortable matter-of-fact attitude toward the schools, their financial
support, their control, their management, and their fixed place among
the indispensable services of government. Schools were a matter of
course, like the air we breathe. Proposals affecting them were dismissed
as of minor consequence or as affecting only insignificant aspects of
the school program. Our people regarded public education in America
as so safely and securely established as to be beyond the slightest possibility of serious impairment or curtailment.

With catastrophic suddenness, the economic depression dealt our
schools a staggering, paralyzing blow. Without significantly reducing
the faith of our people in the desirability, even the necessity, for free,
universal agencies of public education and without so much as raising
the question of the significant implications of public education as a
means of social progress, millions of our citizens have been compelled
to stand helplessly by and see their schools steadily retreat before the
implacable forces of economic necessity.

For a time there was comfort in the assurance that when the low
point of the economic crisis had passed and economic recovery had set
in, the benefits thereof would be reflected in increased financial support, and the schools would be restored to their former status. You are
well aware that now, although economic recovery is reputed to be well
advanced, recovery and resumption of normal functioning for the
agencies of public education are as yet illusionary. Indeed, there is

conclusive evidence that, in a great majority of the states and in count-less thousands of school districts, such resumption is impossible of ac-complishment under existing conditions. Furthermore, there is no basis whatsoever for an assumption that these limiting factors will be cor-rected or improved by any amount of economic recovery or any degree of so-called prosperity, except as there is definite planning for the specific purpose of establishing and maintaining a program of public education compatible with our national needs. Once again, America faces the age-old challenge inherent in the very nature of a democracy —that its citizens must, by social cooperation, prepare themselves and their children to accept their responsibilities as citizens, to discharge the duties which citizenship implies, and to guide the destiny of that democracy. At other times, great leaders have appeared to guide the nation in the adjustments necessary to meet the challenge. Today, the National Education Association and the Department of Superin-tendence join together in a cooperative effort to plan a long-term pro-gram of public education for America, and to attempt to arouse to action those agencies essential to the implementation of the program.

The first and most essential accomplishment will be that of releasing to the service of the public schools of America the most able, the most consecrated, and the most courageous lay and professional leadership available. To this end, the Educational Policies Commission will first address its efforts. It can, in fact, do little more than operate as an agency to reflect the steps necessary for the accomplishment of desired ends, and appeal to you and to others to undertake the duties and obligations involved in their completion. The Commission will pro-ceed democratically in an attempt to formulate plans and policies, seek-ing advice, counsel, cooperation, suggestion, and direction. The result depends upon you and upon thousands of others—how seriously you regard the present crisis; how conscious you are of the implications of past and impending changes and readjustments; how much of time, thought, and effort you, as an individual, are willing to contribute to this task of placing public education in its proper status as an essen-tial service of government in this democratic society. With all the sincerity of purpose and wholehearted consecration to the responsi-bilities imposed, that the individual members of the Commission pos-sess, they solicit your unreserved enlistment in the cause for the duration of the campaign. The Commission has no illusions; it does not underestimate the greatness of the task; it expects a long and diffi-cult program with all too many discouraging incidents, defeats, and disappointments. Its invitation to you is a call to strenuous duty, in an effort to advance the cause of public education in America.

The task ahead, in the opinion of the Commission, is that of evolving well-considered and effective plans and policies. We are of the opinion that the preliminary steps in the solution of our problems have been completed by the collection of data, the survey of conditions, the measurement of need, and the tentative determination of the kind and type of educational agencies essential for the objective realization of an effective program of public education. The Commission proposes not to repeat these studies and investigations but rather to utilize them in evaluating proposed procedures toward educational progress and improvement. Thousands of pages of reports, studies, pronouncements, recommendations, and conclusions of inestimable value in the intelligent administration of public education have been forgotten or ignored during the past decade of economic and social confusion. The best work of the wisest educational leadership in America stands dust covered in government archives or on the shelves of research bureaus, while the children of America suffer for that educational opportunity which these pronouncements would, if applied, provide for them.

There are certain critical issues of immediate portent on which the Commission must act immediately. Two are selected as typical: first, the financing of public education in the light of demands for, and trends toward, federal participation; second, the control of public education in the light of present trends to establish new educational agencies to serve large numbers of youth and then to remove them from the custody of the organized agencies of public education and to establish for them new institutions and new practises in such fields as preschool and adult education, and even deep into the secondary and college levels.

It does not seem that it should be necessary to emphasize the significance of trends of such importance, and their probable influence upon the future of the program of public education in America. It is obvious that policies which will shape these trends, and which will guide them toward their full objective realization as potent agencies of educational influence in America, are to be evolved around hundreds of conference tables thruout the length and breadth of America in the months that are ahead. From the standpoint of the Commission, it seems important and essential that those who represent public education, that those who are concerned about public education, who have an understanding of its needs, and who are guided in their thinking by sound principles, shall be present at these councils, and shall influence plans and policies pertaining thereto.

While the issues suggested above are the larger issues, others of equal importance are under consideration thruout the nation. What should be the relationship of education to social reconstruction? How shall the social income be allocated to the various services of government, of which education is admittedly one of the more important? How shall we establish and maintain conditions of social and economic security for our teaching profession, adequate to their needs and of such a character as will guarantee the effectiveness of their teaching? How shall we organize and unify the teaching profession to the end that it may exert its influence toward the furtherance of an adequate program of public education? What can the schools contribute to the solution of problems of unsocial behavior, crime, and delinquency? How can lay groups of unquestioned influence and power be enlisted in support of a program of public education? Why is it that hundreds of thousands of children in rural communities are without educational opportunities, and how may this condition be corrected?

In the opinion of the Commission, the next five years should be a period of great significance in the rebuilding of our structure of public education; of reestablishing, in the minds of our citizens, those great purposes to which public education was originally dedicated; of recreating public enthusiasm for the American ideal, not only in education, but with regard to all matters pertaining to social progress. It would be unfortunate if the educational leadership of this nation, if members of this great teaching profession, should stand idly upon the sidelines while this great contest for the survival of the agencies of social progress is waged before their very eyes. . . .[13]

The titles of some of the publications give an indication of the questions with which the Commission wrestled. The first document, issued in 1937, was The Unique Function of Education in American Democracy. *Written in great part by the historian Charles Beard, it remains a classic statement, and although its contents do not come strictly within the purview of this book, it nevertheless can be read with profit by those who seek to get their bearings in this present era of uncertainty and change. This was followed by* The Structure and Administration of Education in American Democracy *and* The Purposes of Education in American Democracy.

In 1939, the Commission published Educational Policies for Occupational Adjustment *and* Toward More Effective Education for Civic Responsibility. *The following year saw the publication of* Learning the Ways of Democracy, *a reporting of practices in the schools as seen by skilled observers, and* Education and Economic Well-Being in Amer-

13 *Proceedings*, NEA, 1936, pp. 463–67.

ican Democracy. *In 1941,* The Education of Free Men in American Democracy *appeared.*

The reports of the EPC covered a wide range, and although almost all had relevance to secondary education only a few bore directly and exclusively on the secondary schools. Included in a later section of this book are extensive excerpts from Education For All American Youth, *which was published in 1944, and which was aimed squarely at the high schools.*

During the years of World War II the Commission turned its attention to the demands of the war effort on the schools and to considerations of postwar adjustment. The reports of the 1950's and the early 1960's were largely concerned with specialized issues.

SECONDARY SCHOOL STUDIES AND READING LIST FOR ENGLISH

2

Reports by the Committee of Ten, the Conference on English, and about the Carnegie Unit

*The report of the Committee on Secondary School Studies, known as The Report of the Committee of Ten, is interesting and significant for a number of reasons. It came at a time when the public high school was emerging as the principal institution of secondary education and at the close of the period of the academies. It was probably the first report on public secondary schools that could be considered nationwide in its scope and influence. As such, for a generation it set the pattern of secondary education in the United States and provided a rationale of philosophy and psychology in support of its recommendations that persisted as a source of controversy long after the pattern of course offerings it was designed to support had been broken. The report was a successful effort on the part of colleges and universities, with notable leadership from the private Eastern universities, to determine to a large degree the purpose of the secondary schools and what should be taught in them. It was an example*

25

of the influence a few men of prestige could exert on the public school, both because of their own prestige and their energetic propagandizing through important magazines and educational journals to which they had access by virtue of their positions. Taken by itself, the report is of historical importance to those who are interested in the ferment of an age that is gone. Yet there are other reasons it may be examined with profit more than three-quarters of a century later. The ideas of those who wrote the report, their views of the functions and purposes of the p⋅blic schools, the methods they used to make their views prevail, provided a theme that has run through subsequent discussions about what the public schools should do, how their purposes should be determined, and how they should be controlled.

The Committee of Ten was appointed July 9, 1892, at the meeting of The National Educational Association held in Saratoga, New York.[1]

[1] To understand the circumstances which led to the appointment of the Committee, it is useful to examine briefly the history and organization of the National Education Association. In 1856, Daniel B. Hagar, president of the Massachusetts Teachers' Association, issued at the suggestion of T. W. Valentine, president of the New York Teachers' Association, an invitation to ". . . all practical teachers in the North, the South, the East, the West, who are willing to unite in a general effort to promote the general welfare of our country by concentrating the wisdom and power of numerous minds and by distributing among all the accumulated experiences of all; who are ready to devote their energies and their means to advance the dignity, respect, ability, and usefulness of their calling." The following year, on August 26, 1857, a small group of men responded to the invitation and met in Philadelphia to organize the National Teachers' Association, to draft a constitution and to elect officers. The reservoir upon which the new organization was to draw in the beginning included twenty-three state teachers' associations, the American Institute of Instruction, which had been organized in New England in 1830, and the American Association for the Advancement of Education, organized in 1850 under the leadership of Horace Mann, among others.

The first constitution as drafted defined eligibility for membership as " . . . any gentleman who is regularly occupied in teaching in a public or private elementary school, college or university, or who is regularly employed as a private tutor, as the editor of an educational journal, or as a superintendent of schools." The constitution of the organization was amended in 1870, and the name changed to the National Educational Association. The eligibility for membership was amended to include ". . . any person in any way connected with the work of education." The Association was reorganized into four departments: School Superintendence, Normal Schools, Elementary Schools, and Higher Instruction, and provision was made for the inclusion of other departments.

Acting under the permissive provision, other departments were organized, the first two being the Department of Higher Education and the Department of Primary or Elementary Instruction. The Industrial Department was added in 1875, and as stated above, the National Council of Education in 1880. It is a significant commentary upon the late development of public secondary education that the Department of Secondary Education was not added until 1885. The

It was, however, an offspring of a department of the Association known as the National Council of Education. The Council was organized in 1880. It had a constitution of its own. Its membership was limited to 60, chosen from the membership of the Association, with staggered terms to insure continuity. Its work was carried on through 12 standing committees of five members each, the committees being those on State School Systems, City School Systems, Higher Education, Secondary Education, Elementary Education, Normal Education, Technological Education, Pedagogics, Moral Education, School Sanitation, Hygiene and Physical Training; Psychological Inquiry, and Educational Reports and Statistics.

As noted in the Introduction, the mention of secondary education in the Constitution of the National Council on Education was one of the earliest references made to secondary schools in the history of the proceedings of the National Educational Association. The object of the Council was, according to the Preamble of its constitution, "The consideration and discussion of educational questions of general interest and public importance, and the presentation, through printed reports, of the substance of the discussions, and the conclusions formulated." The Council met concurrently with the National Association.

In its purpose, and activities, the National Council may well be considered to be the forerunner of the Educational Policies Commission, which was established in 1935 and which, until it was discontinued in 1967, performed much the same kind of function as the Council.

In 1891 a Committee of the National Council which had been appointed the previous year under the chairmanship of Joseph H. Baker, the principal of the Denver High School made a report to the Council on the general subject of school program and college admission requirements. The Committee were continued and requested to arrange a conference on the subject at the meeting of the Council in 1892 which would include representatives of colleges and secondary schools. Such a conference was held July 7, 8, 9, 1892, in Saratoga, New York, and it was reported that there were between 20 and 30 delegates in attendance.

The conference then sent to the Council, which was in session, the following recommendations:

National Association of Secondary School Principals was founded in 1916. In 1928, the name was changed to The Department of Secondary School Principals of the National Education Association of the United States. In 1939, the organization reverted to its earlier name adopted in 1916. The name of the National Educational Association was changed to the National Education Association in 1907.

1. *That it is expedient to hold a conference of school and college teachers
of each principal subject which enters into the programs of secondary
schools in the United States and into the requirements for admission to
college—as, for example, of Latin, of geometry, or of American history—
each conference to consider the proper limits of its subject, the best methods
of instruction, the most desirable allotment of time of the subject, and the
best methods of testing the pupils' attainments therein, and each conference to represent fairly the different parts of the country.*
2. *That a Committee be appointed with authority to select the members of
these conferences and to arrange their meetings, the results of all the conferences to be reported to this Committee for such action as it may deem
appropriate, and to form the basis of a report to be presented to the Council
by this Committee.*
3. *That this Committee consist of the following gentlemen:*
   *Charles W. Eliot, President of Harvard University, Cambridge, Mass., Chair-
   man.*
   William T. Harris, Commissioner of Education, Washington, D.C.
   James B. Angell, President of the University of Michigan, Ann Arbor, Mich.
   *John Tetlow, Head Master of the Girls' High School and the Girls' Latin
   School, Boston, Mass.*
   James M. Taylor, President of Vassar College, Poughkeepsie, N.Y.
   Oscar D. Robinson, Principal of the High School, Albany, N.Y.
   James H. Baker, President of the University of Colorado, Boulder, Colo.
   Richard H. Jesse, President of the University of Missouri, Columbia, Mo.
   *James C. MacKenzie, Head Master of the Lawrenceville School, Lawrence-
   ville, N.J.*
   Henry C. King, Professor in Oberlin College, Oberlin, Ohio.
   These recommendations of the conference were adopted by the National
Council of Education on the 9th of July; and the Council communicated the
recommendations to the Directors of the National Educational Association,
with the further recommendation that an appropriation not exceeding $2,500
be made by the Association towards the expenses of these conferences. On the
12th of July the Directors adopted a series of resolutions under which a sum
not exceeding $2,500 was made available for this undertaking during the aca-
demic year 1892–93.[2]

*The driving force behind the report of the Committee on Secondary
School Studies was Charles W. Eliot, the chairman. It was he who organized the conferences, urged the completion of their work, and edited
the final draft and sent it to the printer. Not to be overlooked as a
prime mover in the enterprise was Nicholas Murray Butler, professor*

[2] *Report of the Committee of Ten on Secondary Studies*, New York: Published
for the National Educational Association by The American Book Company, 1894,
pp. 1–4.

of philosophy at Columbia, who, although not a member of the Committee, was active in shaping opinions and was a principal propagandizer for the findings of the Report in the years following its publication. It was Butler who selected the membership of the Committee. Although the subject of the conference was primarily the public high school, representatives from these schools were a minority of the Committee.

The conditions of the times undoubtedly called for an attempt to bring some kind of order out of a somewhat chaotic condition that prevailed in secondary education during the final decades of the nineteenth century.

For most of the century, education beyond the elementary level had been provided to a great degree by the academies, quasi-public institutions, sometimes chartered by the state but financed principally by tuition, or in the case of a favored few, in part by income from endowment. Barnard estimated that in 1850 the more than 6,000 academies in operation enrolled more than a quarter of a million pupils. Among them, they offered a wide variety of courses from those of a college preparatory nature to others which had a more immediate and practical aim or which in some cases were little more than an extension of elementary offerings. Some courses were as brief as six weeks in length; others ran for as long as a full term.

In their day, the academies made a great contribution to the country. Nineteenth century America was predominantly a rural nation. As late as 1900, the total population was only 76,000,000, and 46,000,000 of these lived in communities of fewer than 2,500 inhabitants. The sparsity of population lent itself to the boarding-school academy more than to the public high school. But in the last quarter of the nineteenth century changes began to be apparent. More urban centers became established, ways of making a living changed as industrialization made headway, and by 1880 it was estimated that enrollment in public high schools for the first time exceeded that in the academies. Soon, except for a few which were strong enough to survive, the age of the academies was to come to a close and the era of the universal public secondary school was to begin.

It was in this crucial time of transition that the Report of the Committee of Ten was issued.

The time was one of change for colleges and universities, also. New institutions were coming into existence, notably the land-grant institutions, and for both the older established universities and colleges as well as those that were emerging, the time-honored classical curriculum was giving way to the broadening pressures of science and the applied technology which was the handmaiden of industrialization.

The universities and colleges had for some time been unable to depend on the academies to provide a sufficient number of students equipped to be admitted; many had created preparatory departments of their own in which students were enrolled in order to fit them for entrance. Established as an expedient, these preparatory departments were far from satisfactory, and for this reason among others the institutions of higher education welcomed the attempt of the Committee of Ten to improve conditions in the secondary schools as these related to college admission.

Viewed in another perspective, too, the nature of the Report should not be surprising.

In 1890, the "common" school, that is, the public school that enrolled a large proportion of the age group, was the elementary school. Grades kindergarten through eight enrolled twelve-and-a-half million pupils. On the other hand, the public high schools in 1890 enrolled only 203- 000 pupils, or only 6.7 per cent of the age group 14–17. A decade earlier, in 1880, only 110,000 were enrolled in the public high schools. Perhaps it is not surprising that the Committee of Ten thought of this group principally as recruits for the colleges and universities, and fashioned their curriculum, their time allotments, and their theories of learning accordingly. Even here, however, there were surprising paradoxes in the Report. Having devised a program for the secondary schools which seemed clearly aimed at those who would continue their education, the Committee inserted this comment toward the end of the report: "The secondary schools of the United States, taken as a whole, do not exist for the purpose of preparing boys and girls for college. Only an insignificant percentage of the graduates of these schools go to colleges or scientific schools. Their main function is to prepare for the duties of life that small proportion of all the children in the country—a proportion small in number, but very important to the welfare of the nation—who show themselves able to profit by an education prolonged to the eighteenth year, and whose parents are able to support them while they remain so long in school . . . a secondary school program intended for national use must therefore be made for those children whose education is not to be pursued beyond the secondary school. The preparation of a few pupils for college or scientific school should in the ordinary secondary school be the incidental, and not the principal object." [3]

Although the public high school in the latter part of the nineteenth century grew out of the aspirations of the citizens and the willingness

[3] *Ibid.* pp. 51–2.

of the people and their elected representatives to tax themselves for their support, it cannot be said that the curriculum proposals of the Committee of Ten had a similar origin. They were, on the other hand, the work of the men who fashioned them, and mirrored their ideas and opinions. Their beliefs about curriculum were anchored to the belief in the theory of mental discipline. The subjects they advocated were to be taught the same way, for the same time to all students, whether or not it was their aim to continue their education. To these men, education for all was a matter of the intellect alone, and they had faith in the subjects they chose as the proper vehicles for strengthening the mental faculties.

The report was the subject for sharp and sometimes acrimonious debate in the two decades after its publication. Some of the debate was "in the family," so to speak, between those who favored more or less time to the study of Greek, for example. Other controversy, however, went to the heart of the premises upon which the Report was based.

For two and a half decades the report had a profound effect on educational thinking and on secondary school practice. Its effect was diminished as the secondary schools doubled in enrollment in each succeeding decade, bringing into the schools many thousands for whom the curriculum held little of relevance or value, and as social and economic conditions changed. These changes were brought into focus with the publication, in 1918, of the Cardinal Principles of Education, and were foreshadowed even earlier in the Report of the Committee of Nine, presented in 1911.

Yet, as stated earlier, the ideas and beliefs of the Committee of Ten were not to die, even though the school changed. Echoes were heard in the post-Sputnik furore about the schools, and traces of the earlier report were to be found in the writings of yet another president of Harvard, James B. Conant, who, like Eliot, issued his own reports on secondary education.

What subjects to teach?—goes one refrain. And as counterpoint, others ask what are the goals and how can they best be reached?

REPORT OF THE COMMITTEE OF TEN

To the National Council of Education.

Every gentleman named on the Committee of Ten accepted his appointment; and the Committee met, with every member present, at Columbia College, New York City, from the 9th to the 11th of November, 1892, inclusive.

In preparation for this meeting, a table had been prepared by means of a prolonged correspondence with the principals of selected secondary schools in various parts of the country, which showed the subjects taught in forty leading secondary schools in the United States, and the total number of recitations, or exercises, allotted to each subject. Nearly two hundred schools were applied to for this information; but it did not prove practicable to obtain within three months verified statements from more than forty schools. This table proved conclusively, first, that the total number of subjects taught in these secondary schools was nearly forty, thirteen of which, however, were found in only a few schools; secondly, that many of these subjects were taught for such short periods that little training could be derived from them; and thirdly, that the time allotted to the same subject in the different schools varied widely. Even for the older subjects, like Latin and algebra, there appeared to be a wide diversity of practice with regard to the time allotted to them. Since this table was comparative in its nature,—that is, permitted comparisons to be made between different schools,—and could be easily misunderstood and misapplied by persons who had small acquaintance with school programs, it was treated as a confidential document; and was issued at first only to the members of the Committee of Ten and the principals of the schools mentioned in the table. Later, it was sent—still as a confidential paper—to the members of the several conferences organized by the Committee of Ten.

Questions for the Conferences

The Committee of Ten, after a preliminary discussion on November 9th, decided on November 10th to organize Conferences on the following subjects: 1. Latin; 2. Greek; 3. English; 4. Other Modern Languages; 5. Mathematics; 6. Physics, Astronomy, and Chemistry; 7. Natural History (Biology, including Botany, Zoölogy, and Physiology); 8. History, Civil Government, and Political Economy; 9. Geography (Physical Geography, Geology, and Meteorology). They also decided that each Conference should consist of ten members. They then proceeded to select the members of each of these Conferences, having regard in the selection to the scholarship and experience of the gentlemen named, to the fair division of the members between colleges on the one hand and schools on the other, and to the proper geographical distribution of the total membership. After selecting ninety members for the nine Conferences, the Committee decided on an additional number of names to be used as substitutes for persons originally chosen who should decline to serve, from two to four substitutes being selected for each Conference. In the selection of substitutes the Committee found it difficult to regard the geographical distribution of the persons selected with as much strictness as in the original selection; and, accordingly, when it became necessary to call on a considerable number of substitutes, the accurate geographical distribution of membership was somewhat impaired. The lists of the members of the several Conferences were finally adopted at a meeting of the Committee on November 11th; and the Chairman and Secretary of the Committee were then empowered to fill any vacancies which might occur.

The Committee next adopted the following list of questions as a guide for the discussions of all the Conferences, and directed that the Conferences be called together on the 28th of December:

1. In the school course of study extending approximately from the age of six years to eighteen years—a course including the periods of both elementary and secondary instruction—at what age should the study which is the subject of the Conference be first introduced?

2. After it is introduced, how many hours a week for how many years should be devoted to it?

3. How many hours a week for how many years should be devoted to it during the last four years of the complete course; that is, during the ordinary high school period?

4. What topics, or parts, of the subject may reasonably be covered during the whole course?

5. What topics, or parts, of the subject may best be reserved for the last four years?

6. In what form and to what extent should the subject enter into college requirements for admission? Such questions as the sufficiency of translation at sight as a test of knowledge of a language, or the superiority of a laboratory examination in a scientific subject to a written examination on a text-book, are intended to be suggested under this head by the phrase "in what form."

7. Should the subject be treated differently for pupils who are going to college, for those who are going to a scientific school, and for those who, presumably, are going to neither?

8. At what stage should this differentiation begin, if any be recommended?

9. Can any description be given of the best method of teaching this subject throughout the school course?

10. Can any description be given of the best mode of testing attainments in this subject at college admission examinations?

11. For those cases in which colleges and universities permit a

division of the admission examination into a preliminary and
a final examination, separated by at least a year, can the best
limit between the preliminary and final examinations be approximately defined?

The Committee further voted that it was expedient that the Conferences on Latin and Greek meet at the same place. Finally, all further
questions of detail with regard to the calling and the instruction of the
Conferences were referred to the Chairman with full power.

Composition of the Conferences

During the ensuing six weeks, the composition of the nine Conferences was determined in accordance with the measures adopted by the
Committee of Ten. Seventy persons originally selected by the Committee accepted the invitation of the Committee, and sixty-nine of these
persons were present at the meetings of their respective Conferences
on the 28th of December. Twenty substitutes accepted service, of whom
twelve were persons selected by the Committee of Ten, and eight were
selected under the authority granted to the Chairman and Secretary
of the Committee in emergencies. One of these eight gentlemen was
selected by a Conference at its first meeting. Two gentlemen who accepted service—one of the original members and one substitute—
absented themselves from the meetings of their respective Conferences
without giving any notice to the Chairman of the Committee of Ten,
who was therefore unable to fill their places. With these two exceptions,
all the Conferences met on December 28th with full membership.

The ninety members of the Conferences were divided as follows:
forty-seven were in the service of colleges or universities, forty-two in
the service of schools,[4] and one was a government official formerly in
the service of a university. A considerable number of the college men,
however, had also had experience in schools. Each Conference, in accordance with a recommendation of the Committee of Ten, chose its
own Chairman and Secretary; and these two officers prepared the
report of each Conference. Six of the Chairmen were college men,
and three were school men; while of the Secretaries, two were college
men and seven school men. The Committee of Ten requested that the
reports of the Conferences should be sent to their Chairman by the
1st of April, 1893—three months being thus allowed for the preparation of the reports. Seven Conferences substantially conformed to this
request of the Committee; but the reports from the Conferences on

4 Only 15 of these, however, were representatives of *public* schools.

Natural History and Geography were delayed until the second week in July. The Committee of Ten, being of course unable to prepare their own report until all the reports of the December Conferences had been received, were prevented from presenting their report, as they had intended, at the Education Congress which met at Chicago July 27th–29th.

Unanimity of the Conferences

All the Conferences sat for three days; their discussions were frank, earnest, and thorough; but in every Conference an extraordinary unity of opinion was arrived at. The nine reports are characterized by an amount of agreement which quite surpasses the most sanguine anticipations. Only two Conferences present minority reports, namely, the Conference on Physics, Astronomy, and Chemistry, and the Conference on Geography; and in the first case, the dissenting opinions touch only two points in the report of the majority, one of which is unimportant. In the great majority of matters brought before each Conference, the decision of the Conference was unanimous. When one considers the different localities, institutions, professional experiences, and personalities represented in each of the Conferences, the unanimity developed is very striking, and should carry great weight.

Before the 1st of October, 1893, the reports of the Conferences had all been printed, after revision in proof by the chairmen of the Conferences respectively, and had been distributed to the members of the Committee of Ten, together with a preliminary draft of a report for the Committee. With the aid of comments and suggestions received from members of the Committee a second draft of this report was made ready in print to serve as the ground-work of the deliberations of the Committee at their final meeting. This meeting was held at Columbia College from the 8th to the 11th of November, 1893, inclusive, every member being present except Professor King, who is spending the current academic year in Europe. The points of view and the fields of work of the different members of the Committee being fortunately various, the discussions at this prolonged meeting were vigorous and comprehensive, and resulted in a thorough revision of the preliminary report. This third revise having been submitted to the members of the Committee, a cordial agreement on both the form and the substance of the present report, with the exceptions stated in the minority report of President Baker, was arrived at after a correspondence which extended over three weeks. The report itself embodies the numerous votes and resolutions adopted by the Committee.

Professor King, having received in Europe the Conference reports, the two preliminary drafts of the Committee's report, and the third revise, desired to have his name signed to the final report.

Number and Variety of Changes Urged

The Council and the public will doubtless be impressed, at first sight, with the great number and variety of important changes urged by the Conferences; but on a careful reading of the appended reports it will appear that the spirit of the Conferences was distinctly conservative and moderate, although many of their recommendations are of a radical nature. The Conferences which found their tasks the most difficult were the Conferences on Physics, Astronomy, and Chemistry; Natural History; History, Civil Government, and Political Economy; and Geography; and these four Conferences make the longest and most elaborate reports, for the reason that these subjects are today more imperfectly dealt with in primary and secondary schools than are the subjects of the first five Conferences. The experts who met to confer together concerning the teaching of the last four subjects in the list of Conferences all felt the need of setting forth in an ample way what ought to be taught, in what order, and by what method. They ardently desired to have their respective subjects made equal to Latin, Greek, and Mathematics in weight and influence in the schools; but they knew that educational tradition was adverse to this desire, and that many teachers and directors of education felt no confidence in these subjects as disciplinary material. Hence the length and elaboration of these reports. In less degree, the Conferences on English and Other Modern Languages felt the same difficulties, these subjects being relatively new as substantial elements in school programs.

The Committee of Ten requested the Conferences to make their reports and recommendations as specific as possible. This request was generally complied with; but, very naturally, the reports and recommendations are more specific concerning the selection of topics in each subject, the best methods of instruction, and the desirable appliances or apparatus, than concerning the allotment of time to each subject. The allotment of time is a very important matter of administrative detail; but it presents great difficulties, requires a comprehensive survey of the comparative claims of many subjects, and in different parts of the country is necessarily affected by the various local conditions and historical developments. Nevertheless, there will be found in the Conference reports recommendations of a fundamental and far-reaching character concerning the allotment of program time to each subject.

Time-Allotment by Subject

It might have been expected that every Conference would have demanded for its subject a larger proportion of time than is now commonly assigned to it in primary and secondary schools; but, as a matter of fact, the reports are noteworthy for their moderation in this respect—especially the reports on the old and well-established subjects. The Latin Conference declares that "In view of the just demand for more and better work in several other subjects of the preparatory course, it seemed clear to the Conference that no increase in the quantity of the preparation in Latin should be asked for." Among the votes passed by the Greek Conference will be noticed the following: "That in making the following recommendations, this Conference desires that the average age at which pupils now enter college should be lowered rather than raised; and the Conference urges that no addition be made in the advanced requirements in Greek for admission to college." The Mathematical Conference recommends that the course in arithmetic in elementary schools should be abridged, and recommends only a moderate assignment of time to algebra and geometry. The Conference on Geography says of the present assignment of time to geography in primary and secondary schools that "it is the judgment of the Conference that too much time is given to the subject in proportion to the results secured. It is not their judgment that more time is given to the subject than it merits, but that either more should be accomplished, or less time taken to attain it."

Earlier Introduction of Subjects

Anyone who reads these nine reports consecutively will be struck with the fact that all these bodies of experts desire to have the elements of their several subjects taught earlier than they now are; and that the Conferences on all the subjects except the languages desire to have given in the elementary schools what may be called perspective views, or broad surveys, of their respective subjects—expecting that in later years of the school course parts of these same subjects will be taken up with more amplitude and detail. The Conferences on Latin, Greek, and the Modern Languages agree in desiring to have the study of foreign languages begin at a much earlier age than now—the Latin Conference suggesting by a reference to European usage that Latin be begun from three to five years earlier than it commonly is now. The Conference on Mathematics, wish to have given in elementary schools not only a general survey of arithmetic, but also the elements of algebra, and concrete geometry in connection with drawing. The Conference on Physics, Chemistry, and Astronomy urge that these studies should constitute an important part of the elementary school course from the very beginning. The Conference on Natural History wish the elements of botany and zoölogy to be taught in the primary schools. The Conference on History wish the systematic study of history to begin as early as the tenth year of age, and the first two years of study to be devoted to mythology and to biography for the illustration of general history as well as of American history. Finally, the Conference on Geography recommended that the earlier course treat broadly of the earth, its environment and inhabitants, extending freely into fields which in later years of study are recognized as belonging to separate sciences.

In thus claiming entrance for their subjects into the earlier years of school attendance, the Conferences on the newer subjects are only seeking an advantage which the oldest subjects have long possessed. The elements of language, number, and geography have long been imparted to young children. As things now are, the high school teacher finds in the pupils fresh from the grammar schools no foundation of elementary mathematical conceptions outside of arithmetic; no acquaintance with algebraic language; and no accurate knowledge of geometrical forms. As to botany, zoölogy, chemistry, and physics, the minds of pupils entering the high school are ordinarily blank on these subjects. When college professors endeavor to teach chemistry, physics, botany, zoölogy, meteorology, or geology to persons of eighteen or twenty years of age, they discover that in most instances new habits of observing, reflecting, and recording have to be painfully acquired by the students—habits which they should have acquired in early childhood. The college teacher of history finds in like manner that his subject has never taken any serious hold on the minds of pupils fresh from the secondary schools. He finds that they have devoted astonishingly little time to the subject; and that they have acquired no habit of historical investigation, or of the comparative examination of different historical narratives concerning the same period of events. It is inevitable, therefore, that specialists in any of the subjects which are pursued in the high schools or colleges should earnestly desire that the minds of young children be stored with some of the elementary facts and principles of their subject; and that all the mental habits, which the adult student will surely need, begin to be formed in the child's mind before the age of fourteen. It follows, as a matter of course, that all the Conferences except the Conference on Greek, make strong suggestions concerning the programs of primary and grammar schools—

generally with some reference to the subsequent programs of secondary schools. They desire important changes in the elementary grades; and the changes recommended are all in the direction of increasing simultaneously the interest and the substantial training quality of primary and grammar school studies.

Correlation of Subjects

If anyone feels dismayed at the number and variety of the subjects to be opened to children of tender age, let him observe that while these nine Conferences desire each their own subject to be brought into the courses of elementary schools, they all agree that these different subjects should be correlated and associated one with another by the program and by the actual teaching. If the nine Conferences had sat all together as a single body, instead of sitting as detached and even isolated bodies, they could not have more forcibly expressed their conviction that every subject recommended for introduction into elementary and secondary schools should help every other; and that the teacher of each single subject should feel responsible for the advancement of the pupils in all subjects, and should distinctly contribute to this advancement.

On one very important question of general policy which affects profoundly the preparation of all school programs, the Committee of Ten and all the Conferences are absolutely unanimous. Among the questions suggested for discussion in each Conference were the following:

1. Should the subject be treated differently for pupils who are going to college, for those who are going to a scientific school, and for those who, presumably, are going to neither?
2. At what age should this differentiation begin, if any be recommended?

A Simplification of Programs

The first question is answered unanimously in the negative by the Conferences, and the second therefore needs no answer. The Committee of Ten unanimously agree with the Conferences. Ninty-eight teachers, intimately concerned either with the actual work of American secondary schools, or with the results of that work as they appear in students who come to college, unanimously declare that every subject which is taught at all in a secondary school should be taught in the same way and to the same extent to every pupil so long as he pursues it, no matter what the probable destination of the pupil may be, or at what point his education is to cease. Thus, for all pupils who study Latin, or history, or algebra, for example, the allotment of time and the method of instruction in a given school should be the same year by year. Not that all the pupils should pursue every subject for the same number of years; but so long as they do pursue it, they should all be treated alike. It has been a very general custom in American high schools and academies to make up separate courses of study for pupils of supposed different destinations, the proportions of the several studies in the different courses being various. The principle laid down by the Conferences will, if logically carried out, make a great simplification in secondary school programs. It will lead to each subject's being treated by the school in the same way by the year for all pupils, and this, whether the individual pupil be required to choose between courses which run through several years, or be allowed some choice among subjects year by year.

Teachers More Highly Trained

Persons who read all the appended reports will observe the frequent occurrence of the statement that, in order to introduce the changes recommended, teachers more highly trained will be needed in both the elementary and the secondary schools. There are frequent expressions to the effect that a higher grade of scholarship is needed in teachers of the lower classes, or that the general adoption of some method urged by a Conference must depend upon the better preparation of teachers in the high schools, model schools, normal schools, or colleges in which they are trained. The experienced principal or superintendent in reading the reports will be apt to say to himself, "This recommendation is sound, but cannot be carried out without teachers who have received a training superior to that of the teachers now at my command." It must be remembered, in connection with these admissions, or expressions of anxiety, that the Conferences were urged by the Committee of Ten to advise the Committee concerning the best possible—almost the ideal—treatment of each subject taught in a secondary school course, without, however, losing sight of the actual condition of American schools, or pushing their recommendations beyond what might reasonably be considered attainable in a moderate number of years. The Committee believe that the Conferences have carried out wisely the desire of the Committee, in that they have recommended improvements, which, though great and seldom to be made at once and simultaneously, are by no means unattainable. The existing agencies for giving instruction to teachers already in service are numerous; and the normal schools and the colleges are capable of making prompt and successful efforts to supply the better trained and equipped teachers for whom the reports of the Conferences call.

Many recommendations will be found to be made by more than one

Conference. Thus, all the Conferences on foreign languages seem to agree that the introduction of two foreign languages in the same year is inexpedient; and all of them insist on practice in reading the foreign language aloud, on the use of good English in translating, and on practice in translating the foreign language at sight, and in writing it. Again, all the Conferences on scientific subjects dwell on laboratory work by the pupils as the best means of instruction, and on the great utility of the genuine laboratory notebook; and they all protest that teachers of science need at least as thorough a special training as teachers of languages or mathematics receive. In reading the reports, many instances will be noticed in which different Conferences have reached similar conclusions without any consultation, or have followed a common line of thought.

Recommendations Summarized

Your Committee now proceed to give summaries of the most important recommendations made by the Conferences as regards topics and methods, reserving the subject of time-allotment. But in so doing, they desire to say that the reading of these summaries should not absolve anyone interested in the general subject from reading with care the entire report of every Conference. The several reports are so full of suggestions and recommendations concisely and cogently stated that it is impossible to present adequate abstracts of them.

1. LATIN

An important recommendation of the Latin Conference is the recommendation that the study of Latin be introduced into American schools earlier than it now is. They recommend that translation at sight form a constant and increasing part of the examinations for admission to college and of the work of preparation. They next urge that practice in writing Latin should not be dissociated from practice in reading and translating; but, on the contrary, that the two should be carried on with equal steps. The Conference desire the schools to adopt a greater variety of Latin authors for beginners, and they give good reasons against the exclusive use of Caesar's Gallic War. They object to the common practice of putting the teaching of beginners into the hands of the youngest teachers, who have the slenderest equipment of knowledge and experience. They dwell on the importance of attending to pronunciation and reading aloud, to forms, vocabulary, syntax, and order, and to the means of learning to understand the Latin before translating it; and they describe and urge the importance of a higher ideal in translation than now prevails in secondary schools. The formal recommendations of the Conference, fourteen in number, will be found concisely stated in numbered paragraphs at the close of their report.

2. GREEK

The Conference on Greek agree with the Conference on Latin in recommending the cultivation of reading at sight in schools, and in recommending that practice in translation into the foreign language should be continued throughout the school course. They urge that three years be the minimum time for the study of Greek in schools; provided that Latin be studied four years. They would not have a pupil begin the study of Greek without a knowledge of the elements of Latin. They recommend the substitution of portions of the Hellenica for two books of the Anabasis in the requirements for admission to college, and the use of some narrative portions of Thucydides in schools. They urge that Homer should continue to be studied in all schools which provide instruction in Greek through three years, and they suggest that the Odyssey is to be preferred to the Iliad. They regret "that so few colleges through their admission examinations encourage reading at sight in schools." Like the Latin Conference, the Greek Conference urge that the reading of the text be constantly practiced by both teacher and pupil, "and that teachers require from their pupils no less intelligent reading of the text than accurate translation of the same." The Greek Conference also adopted a vote "to concur with the Latin Conference as to the age at which the study of Latin should be begun." The specific recommendations of the Conference will be found in brief form in the paragraphs at the head of the eleven numbered sections into which their report is divided.

3. ENGLISH

The Conference on English found it necessary to deal with the study of English in schools below the high school grade as well as in the high school. Their opening recommendations deal with the very first years of school, and one of the most interesting and admirable parts of their report relates to English in the primary and the grammar schools.

The Conference are of the opinion that English should be pursued in the high school during the entire course of four years; but in making this recommendation the Conference have in mind both study of literature and training in the expression of thought. To the study of rhetoric they assign one hour a week in the third year of the high school course. To the subject of historical and systematic grammar they assign one hour a week in the fourth year of the high school course. The intelligent reader of the report of this Conference will find described in it the means by which the study of English in secondary schools is to be made the equal of any other study in disciplinary or developing power. The Conference claim for English as much time as the Latin Conference claim for Latin in secondary schools; and it is clear that they intend that the study shall be in all respects as serious and informing as the study of Latin. One of the most interesting opinions expressed by the Conference is "that the best results in the teaching of English in high schools cannot be secured without the aid given by the study of some other language; and that Latin and German, by reason of their fuller inflectional system, are especially suited to this end." In the case of high schools, as well as in schools of lower grade, the Conference declare that every teacher, whatever his department, should feel responsible for the use of good English on the part of his pupils. In several passages of this report the idea recurs that training in English must go hand in hand with the study of other subjects. Thus the Conference hope for the study of the history and geography of the English-speaking people, so far as these illustrate the development of the English language. They mention that "the extent to which the study of the sources of English words can be carried in any school or class will depend on the acquaintance the pupils possess with Latin, French, and German." They say that the study of words should be so pursued as to illustrate the political, social, intellectual, and religious development of the English race; and they urge that the admission of a student to college should be made to depend largely on his ability to write English, as shown in his examination books on other subjects. It is a fundamental idea in this report that the study of every other subject should contribute to the pupil's training in English; and that the pupil's capacity to write English should be made available, and be developed, in every other department. The very specific recommendations of the Conference as to English requirements for admission to colleges and scientific schools are especially wise and valuable.

4. OTHER MODERN LANGUAGES

The most novel and striking recommendation made by the Conference on Modern Languages is that an elective course in German or French be provided in the grammar school, the instruction to be open to children at about ten years of age. The Conference made this recommendation "in the firm belief that the educational effects of modern language study will be of immense benefit to all who are able to pursue it under proper guidance." They admit that the study of Latin presents the same advantages; but living languages seem to them better adapted to grammar school work. The recommendations of this Conference with regard to the number of lessons a week are specific. They even construct a table showing the time which should be devoted to modern languages in each of the last four years of the elementary schools and in each year of the high school. They plead that "all pupils of the same intelligence and the same degree of maturity be instructed alike, no matter whether they are subsequently to enter a college or scientific school, or intend to pursue their studies no farther." The Conference also state with great precision what in their judgment may be expected of pupils in German and French at the various stages of their progress. An important passage of the report treats of the best way to facilitate the progress of beginners: pupils should be lifted over hard places; frequent reviews are not to be recommended; new texts stimulate interest and enlarge the vocabulary. Their recommendations concerning translation into English, reading aloud, habituating the ear to the sounds of the foreign language, and translating into the foreign language, closely resemble the recommendations of the Conferences on Latin, Greek, and English regarding the best methods of instruction in those languages. In regard to college requirements, the Conference agree with several other Conferences in stating "that college requirements for admission should coincide with the high school requirements for graduation." Finally, they declare that "the worst obstacle to modern language study is the lack of properly equipped instructors; and that it is the duty of universities, states, and cities to provide opportunities for the special preparation of modern language teachers."

5. MATHEMATICS

The form of the report of the Conference on Mathematics differs somewhat from that of the other reports. This report is subdivided under five headings: 1st, General Conclusions; 2nd, the Teaching of Arithmetic; 3rd, the Teaching of Concrete Geometry; 4th, the Teaching of Algebra; 5th, the Teaching of Formal or Demonstrative Geometry.

The first general conclusion of the Conference was arrived at unanimously. The Conference consisted of one government official and university professor, five professors of mathematics in as many colleges, one principal of a high school, two teachers of mathematics in endowed schools, and one proprietor of a private school for boys. The professional experience of these gentlemen and their several fields of work were various, and they came from widely separated parts of the country; yet they were unanimously of opinion "that a radical change in the teaching of arithmetic was necessary." They recommend "that the course in arithmetic be at once abridged and enriched; abridged by omitting entirely those subjects which perplex and exhaust the pupil without affording any really valuable mental discipline, and enriched by a greater number of exercises in simple calculation, and in the solution of concrete problems." They specify in detail the subjects which they think should be curtailed, or entirely omitted; and they give in their special report on the teaching of arithmetic a full statement of the reasons on which their conclusion is based. They map out a course in arithmetic which, in their judgment, should begin about the age of six years, and be completed at about the thirteenth year of age.

The Conference next recommend that a course of instruction in concrete geometry with numerous exercises be introduced into the grammar schools; and that this instruction should, during the earlier years, be given in connection with drawing. They recommend that the study of systematic algebra should be begun at the age of fourteen; but that, in connection with the study of arithmetic, the pupils should earlier be made familiar with algebraic expressions and symbols, including the method of solving simple equations. "The Conference believe that the study of demonstrative geometry should begin at the end of the first year's study of algebra, and be carried on by the side of algebra for the next two years, occupying about two hours and a half a week." They are also of opinion "that if the introductory course in concrete geometry has been well taught, both plane and solid geometry can be mastered at this time." Most of the improvements in teaching arithmetic which the Conference suggest "can be summed up under the two heads of giving the teaching a more concrete form, and paying more attention to facility and correctness in work. The concrete system should not be confined to principles, but be extended to practical applications in measuring and in physics."

In regard to the teaching of concrete geometry, the Conference urge that while the student's geometrical education should begin in the kindergarten, or at the latest in the primary school, systematic instruction in concrete or experimental geometry should begin at about the age of ten for the average student, and should occupy about one school hour a week for at least three years. From the outset of this course, the pupil should be required to express himself verbally as well as by drawing and modelling. He should learn to estimate by the eye, and to measure with some degree of accuracy, lengths, angular magnitudes, and areas; to make accurate plans from his own measurements and estimates; and to make models of simple geometrical solids. The whole work in concrete geometry will connect itself on the one side with the work in arithmetic, and on the other with elementary instruction in physics. With the study of arithmetic is therefore to be intimately associated the study of algebraic signs and forms, of concrete geometry, and of elementary physics. Here is a striking instance of the interlacing of subjects which seems so desirable to every one of the nine Conferences.

Under the head of teaching algebra, the Conference set forth in detail the method of familiarizing the pupil with the use of algebraic language during the study of arithmetic. This part of the report also deals clearly with the question of the time required for the thorough mastery of algebra through quadratic equations. The report on the teaching of demonstrative geometry is a clear and concise statement of the best method of teaching this subject. It insists on the importance of elegance and finish in geometrical demonstration, for the reason that the discipline for which geometrical demonstration is to be chiefly prized is a discipline in complete, exact, and logical statement. If slovenliness of expression, or awkwardness of form, is tolerated, this admirable discipline is lost. The Conference therefore recommend an abundance of oral exercises in geometry—for which there is no proper substitute—and the rejection of all demonstrations which are not exact and formally perfect. Indeed throughout all the teaching of mathematics the Conference deem it important that great stress be laid by the teacher on accuracy of statement and elegance of form as well as on clear and rigorous reasoning. Another very important recommendation in this part of the report is to be found in the following passage, "As soon as the student has acquired the art of rigorous demonstration, his work should cease to be merely receptive. He should begin to devise constructions and demonstrations for himself. Geometry cannot be mastered by reading the demonstrations of a textbook; and while there is no branch of elementary mathematics in which purely receptive work, if continued too long, may lose its interest more completely, there is also none in which independent work can be made more attractive and stimulating." These observations are entirely in accordance with the recent practice of some colleges in setting admission examination papers in geometry which demand of the candidates some capacity to solve new problems, or rather to make new application of familiar principles.

6. PHYSICS, CHEMISTRY, AND ASTRONOMY

The Conference on this subject were urgent that the study of simple natural phenomena be introduced into elementary schools; and it was the sense of the Conference that at least one period a day from the first year of the primary school should be given to such study. Apparently the Conference entertained the opinion that the present teachers in elementary schools are ill prepared to teach children how to observe simple natural phenomena; for their second recommendation was that special science teachers or superintendents be appointed to instruct the teachers of elementary schools in the methods of teaching natural phenomena. The Conference were clearly of opinion that from the beginning this study should be pursued by the pupil chiefly, though not exclusively, by means of experiments and by practice in the use of simple instruments for making physical measurements. The report dwells repeatedly on the importance of the study of things and phenomena by direct contact. It emphasizes the necessity of a large proportion of laboratory work in the study of physics and chemistry, and advocates the keeping of laboratory notebooks by the pupils, and the use of such notebooks as part of the test for admission to college. At the same time the report points out that laboratory work must be conjoined with the study of a textbook and with attendance at lectures or demonstrations; and that intelligent direction by a good teacher is as necessary in a laboratory as it is in the ordinary recitation or lecture room. The great utility of the laboratory notebook is emphatically stated. To the objection that the kind of instruction described requires much time and effort on the part of the teacher, the Conference reply that to give good instruction in the sciences requires of the teacher more work than to give good instruction in mathematics or the languages; and that the sooner this fact is recognized by those who have the management of schools the better for all concerned. The science teacher must regularly spend much time in collecting materials, preparing experiments, and keeping collections in order; and this indispensable labor should be allowed for in programs and salaries. As regards the means of testing the progress of the pupils in physics and chemistry, the Conference were unanimously of opinion that a laboratory examination should always be combined with an oral or written examination, neither test taken singly being sufficient. There was a difference of opinion in the Conference on the question whether physics should precede chemistry, or chemistry physics. The logical order would place physics first; but all the members of the Conference but one advised that chemistry be put first for practical reasons which are stated in the majority report. A subcommittee of the Conference has prepared lists of experiments in physics and chemistry for the use of secondary schools,—not, of course, as a prescription, but only as a suggestion, and a somewhat precise indication of the topics which the Conference had in mind, and of the limits of the instruction.

7. NATURAL HISTORY

The Conference on Natural History unanimously agreed that the study of botany and zoölogy ought to be introduced into the primary schools at the very beginning of the school course, and be pursued steadily, with not less than two periods a week, throughout the whole course below the high school. In the next place they agreed that in these early lessons in natural science no textbook should be used; but that the study should constantly be associated with the study of literature, language, and drawing. It was their opinion that the study of physiology should be postponed to the later years of the high school course; but that in the high school, some branch of natural history proper should be pursued every day throughout at least one year. Like the report on Physics, Chemistry, and Astronomy, the report on Natural History emphasizes the absolute necessity of laboratory work by the pupils on plants and animals; and would have careful drawing insisted on from the beginning of the instruction. As the laboratory notebook is recommended by the Conference on Physics, so the Conference on Natural History recommend that the pupils should be made to express themselves clearly and exactly in words, or by drawings, in describing the objects which they observe; and they believe that this practice will be found a valuable aid in training the pupils in the art of expression. They agree with the Conference on Physics, Chemistry, and Astronomy that science examinations should include both a written and a laboratory test, and that the laboratory notebooks of the pupils should be produced at the examination. The recommendations of this Conference are therefore very similar to those of the sixth Conference, so far as methods go; but there are appended to the general report of the Conference on Natural History subreports which describe the proper topics, the best order of topics, and the right methods of instruction in botany for schools below the high school, and for the high school itself, and in zoölogy for the secondary schools. Inasmuch as both the subject matter and the methods of instruction in natural history are much less familiar to ordinary school teachers than the matter and the methods in the languages and mathematics, the Conference believed that descriptive details were necessary in order to give a clear view of the intentions of the Conference. In another subreport the Conference give their reasons for recommending the postponement to the latest possible time of the study of physiology and hygiene. Like the sixth Conference, the Conference on Natural History protest that no person should be regarded as qualified to teach natural science who has not had special training for this work—a preparation at least as thorough as that of their fellow teachers of mathematics and the languages.

8. HISTORY, CIVIL GOVERNMENT, AND POLITICAL ECONOMY

The Conference on History, Civil Government, and Political Economy had a task different in some respects from those of other Conferences. It is nowadays admitted that language, natural science, and mathematics should each make a substantial part of education; but the function of history in education is still very imperfectly apprehended. Accordingly, the eighth Conference were at pains to declare their conception of the object of studying history and civil government in schools, and their belief in the efficiency of these studies in training the judgment, and in preparing children for intellectual enjoyments in after years, and for the exercise at maturity of a salutary influence upon national affairs. They believed that the time devoted in schools to history and the allied subjects should be materially increased; and they have therefore presented arguments in favor of that increase. At the same time, they state strongly their conviction that they have recommended "nothing that was not already being done in some good schools, and that might not reasonably be attained wherever there is an efficient system of graded schools." This Conference state quite as strongly as any other their desire to associate the study of their particular subject with that of other subjects which enter into every school program. They declare that the teaching of history should be intimately connected with the teaching of English; that pupils should be encouraged to avail themselves of their knowledge of ancient and modern languages; and that their study of history should be associated with the study of topography and political geography, and should be supplemented by the study of historical and commercial geography, and the drawing of historical maps. They desire that historical works should be used for reading in schools, and that subjects of English composition should be drawn from the lessons in history. They would have historical poems committed to memory, and the reading of biographies and historical novels encouraged. While they are of opinion that political economy should not be taught in secondary schools, they urge that, in connection with United States history, civil government, and commercial geography, instruction should be given in the most important economic topics. The Conference would therefore have the instruction in history made contributory to the work in three other school departments, namely, English, geography, and drawing. The subject of civil government they would associate with both history and geography.

They would introduce it into the grammar school by means of oral lessons, and into the high school by means of a textbook with collateral reading and oral lessons. In the high school they believe that the study of civil government may be made comparative—that is, that the American method may be compared with foreign systems.

Although the Conference was made up of very diverse elements, every member of the Conference was heartily in favor of every vote adopted. This remarkable unanimity was not obtained by the silence of dissentients, or the withdrawal of opposition on disputed points. It was the natural result of the strong conviction of all the members, that history, when taught by the methods advocated in their report, deserves a position in school programs which would give it equal dignity and importance with any of the most favored subjects, and that the advantages for all children of the rational study of history ought to be diffused as widely as possible. On one point they made a clearer declaration than any other Conference; although several other Conferences indicate similar opinions. They declared that their interest was chiefly "in the school children who have no expectation of going to college, the larger number of whom will not even enter a high school," and that their "recommendations are in no way directed to building up the colleges, or increasing the number of college students." Like every other Conference, they felt anxious about the qualifications of the teachers who are to be entrusted with the teaching of history, and they urged that only teachers who have had adequate special training should be employed to teach history and civil government. In their specific recommendations they strongly urge that the historical course be made continuous from year to year, and extend through eight years, and in this respect be placed upon the same footing with other substantial subjects.

The answers of this Conference to the questions contained in the memorandum sent to the Conferences by the Committee of Ten were specific and clear. They will be found in an appendix to the report of the Conference.

In regard to the time to be devoted to history in school programs, this Conference ask for not less than three periods a week throughout a course of eight years; and they suggest that some of this time can be found by contracting the course in arithmetic, and using for history a part of the time now given to political geography and to language study. Of these eight years they suggest that four should be in the high school and four in the grammar school. They "especially recommend such a choice of subjects as will give pupils in the grammar schools an opportunity of studying the history of other countries, and to the high schools one year's study on the intensive method."

A large portion of the report is necessarily taken up with the description of what the Conference consider the most suitable historical topics and the best methods of teaching history. This portion of the report does not admit of any useful presentation in outline; it must be read in full.

With regard to examinations in history for admission to college, the Conference protest "against the present lax and inefficient system," and seem to sum up their own desires on this subject in the statement that "the requirements for college ought to be so framed that the methods of teaching best adapted to meet them will also be best for all pupils."

Like the Conferences on scientific subjects the Conference on History insist on notebooks, abstracts, special reports, and other written work, as desirable means of teaching. If the recommendations of the nine Conferences should be carried out in grammar and high schools, there would certainly be at least one written exercise a day for every pupil—a result which persons interested in training children to write English deem it important to accomplish.

The observations of the Conference on geographical training in connection with history are interesting and suggestive, as are also the recurring remarks on the need of proper apparatus for teaching history, such as maps, reference libraries, historical pictures, and photographs. It is not the natural sciences alone which need school apparatus.

9. GEOGRAPHY

Considering that geography has been a subject of recognized value in elementary schools for many generations, and that a considerable portion of the whole school time of children has long been devoted to a study called by this name, it is somewhat startling to find that the report of the Conference on Geography deals with more novelties than any other report; exhibits more dissatisfaction with prevailing methods; and makes, on the whole, the most revolutionary suggestions. This Conference had but nine members present at its sessions; and before the final revision of its report had been accomplished, one of the most valued of its members died. Seven members sign the majority report, and the minority report is presented by one member. The dissenting member, however, while protesting against the views of the majority on many points, concurs with the majority in some of the most important conclusions arrived at by the Conference.

It is obvious on even a cursory reading of the majority and minority reports that geography means for all the members of this Conference something entirely different from the term geography as generally used in school programs. Their definition of the word makes it embrace not only a description of the surface of the earth, but also the elements of botany, zoölogy, astronomy, and meteorology, as well as many considerations pertaining to commerce, government, and ethnology. "The physical environment of man" expresses as well as any single phrase can the Conference's conception of the principal subject which they wish to have taught. No one can read the reports without perceiving that the advanced instruction in geography which the Conference conceive to be desirable and feasible in high schools cannot be given until the pupils have mastered many of the elementary facts of botany, zoölogy, geometry, and physics. It is noteworthy also that this ninth Conference, like the seventh, dealt avowedly and unreservedly with the whole range of instruction in primary and secondary schools. They did not pretend to treat chiefly instruction in secondary schools, and incidentally instruction in the lower schools; but, on the contrary, grasped at once the whole problem, and described the topics, methods, and apparatus appropriate to the entire course of twelve years. They recognized that complete descriptions would be necessary in all three branches of the subject—topics, methods, and equipment; and they have given these descriptions with an amplitude and force which leave little to be desired. More distinctly than any other Conference, they recognized that they were presenting an ideal course which could not be carried into effect everywhere or immediately. Indeed at several points they frankly state that the means of carrying out their recommendations are not at present readily accessible; and they exhibit the same anxiety which is felt by several other Conferences about training teachers for the kind of work which the Conference believe to be desirable. After the full and interesting descriptions of the relations and divisions of geographical science, as the Conference define it, the most important sections of their report relate to the methods and means of presenting the subject in schools, and to the right order in developing it. The methods which they advocate require not only better equipped teachers, but better means of illustrating geographical facts in the schoolroom, such as charts, maps, globes, photographs, models, lantern slides, and lanterns. Like all the other Conferences on scientific subjects, the ninth Conference dwell on the importance of forming from the start good habits of observing correctly and stating accurately the facts observed. They also wish that the instruction in geography may be connected with the instruction in drawing, history, and English. They believe that meteorology may be taught as an observational study in the earliest years of the grammar school, the scholars being even then made familiar with the use of the thermometer, the wind vane, and the rain gauge; and that it may be carried much farther in the high school years, after physics has been studied, so that the pupils may then attain a general understanding of topographical maps, of pressure and wind charts, of isothermal charts, and of such complicated subjects as weather prediction, rainfall and the distribution of rain, storms, and the seasonal variations of the atmosphere. Their conception of physiography is a very comprehensive one. In short, they recommend a study of physical geography which would embrace in its scope the elements of half-a-dozen natural sciences, and would bind together in one sheaf the various gleanings which the pupils would have gathered from widely separated fields. There can be no doubt that the study would be interesting, informing, and developing, or that it would be difficult and in every sense substantial.

Time Demands of the Conferences

It already appears that the nine Conferences have attended carefully to three out of the five subjects which it was the intention of the National Council of Education that they should examine. They have discussed fully the proper limits of the several subjects of instruction in secondary schools, the best methods of instruction, and the best methods of testing pupils' attainments. The Conferences were equally faithful in discussing the other two subjects committed to them by the Council, namely, the most desirable allotment of time for each subject, and the requirements for admission to college.

The next subject which the Committee of Ten, following the guidance of the Conferences, desire to present to the Council is, therefore, the allotment of school time among the various subjects of study. It is the obvious duty of the Committee, in the first place, to group together in tabular form the numerous suggestions on this subject made by the Conferences. Having exhibited the program-time suggestions of the Conferences, it will remain for the Committee to construct a flexible and comprehensive schedule of studies, based on the recommendations of the Conferences.

The preceding table exhibits the demands for program time made by all the Conferences. It will be seen at once that this table does not yield, without modification, a practical program. The nine Conferences acted separately, and were studying each their own needs, and not the comparative needs of all the subjects. It was not for them to balance the different interests, but for each to present strongly one interest. It

TABLE 1 *

Subject	Elementary Grades—Primary and Grammar School								Secondary School—High School or Academy			
	1st Year, Age 6–7	2d Year, 7–8	3d Year, 8–9	4th Year, 9–10	5th Year, 10–11	6th Year, 11–12	7th Year, 12–13	8th Year, 13–14	9th Year, 14–15	10th Year, 15–16	11th Year, 16–17	12th Year, 17–18
1. LATIN	Reasons given for beginning Latin earlier than is now the custom.								5p. a wk.	5p. a wk.	5p. a wk.	5p. a wk.
2. GREEK						Latin to be begun a year before Greek.				5p. a wk.	4p. a wk.	4p. a wk.
3. ENGLISH	Pupils to reproduce orally stories told them, to invent stories and describe objects.		Supplementary reading begun—and continued through all the grades. Composition begun—writing narratives and descriptions—oral and written exercises on forms and the sentence.				From this grade no reader to be used.	Grammar, 3p. a wk.	Literature, 3p. a wk. Composition, 2p. a wk.	Literature, 3p. a wk. Composition, 2p. a wk.	Literature, 3p. a wk. Composition, 1p. a wk. Rhetoric, 1p. a wk.	Literature, 3p. a wk. Composition, 1p. a wk. Grammar, 1p. a wk.
4. MODERN LANGUAGES					Elective German or French, 5p. a wk.	Elective German or French, 4p. a wk.	Elective German or French, 3p. a wk. at least.	Elective German or French, 3p. a wk. at least.	The language begun below, 4p. a wk.	The same language, 4p. a wk. Second language, 4p. a wk.	The same language, 4p. a wk. Second language, 4p. a wk.	The same language, 4p. a wk. Second language, 4p. a wk.

TABLE 1 (*Continued*)

Subject											
5. MATHEMATICS	Arithmetic during first eight years, with algebraic expressions and symbols and simple equations—no specific number of hours being recommended.			Concrete Geometry, 1p. a wk.	Concrete Geometry, 1p. a wk.	Concrete Geometry, 1p. a wk.	Concrete Geometry, 1p. a wk.	Algebra, 5p. a wk.	Algebra or Bookkeeping and Commercial Arithmetic, 2½p. a wk. Geometry, 2½p. a wk.	Algebra or Bookkeeping and Commercial Arithmetic, 2½p. a wk. Geometry, 2½p. a wk.	Trigonometry and higher Algebra for candidates for scientific schools.
6. PHYSICS, CHEMISTRY, AND ASTRONOMY	Study of natural phenomena 5p. a wk. through first eight years by experiments, including physical measurements and the recommendations of Conferences 7 and 9.							Elective Astronomy, 5p. a wk. 12 wks.	Chemistry, 5p. a wk.	Physics, 5p. a wk.
7. NATURAL HISTORY	Through first eight years 2p. a wk., of not less than 30 minutes each, devoted to plants and animals; the instruction to be correlated with language, drawing, literature, and geography.							One yr. (which yr. not specified) for botany or zoölogy. Half-yr. (late in course) anatomy, physioloy, and hygiene, 5p. a wk.		5p. a wk.
8. HISTORY			Biography & Mythology, 3p. a wk.		American History and elements of civil government, 3p. a wk.	Greek and Roman History, 3p. a wk.	French History, 3p. a wk.	English History, 3p. a wk.	American History, 3p. a wk.	A special period intensively, and civil government, 3p. a wk.
9. GEOGRAPHY	Time alloted in first eight years to equal that given to number work. The subject—the earth, its environment and inhabitants, including the elements of astronomy, meteorology, zoölogy, botany, history, commerce, races, religions, and governments. Physical Geography.						(Physiography, geology, or meteorology at some part of the high school course. Possibly more than one of these where election is allowed.)	English History, 3p. a wk.	Elective Meteorology, ½ this year or next.	Elective geology or physiography, ½ yr.

* Abbreviations: p. = a recitation period of 40–45 minutes; wk. = week; yr. = year.

55

will further be noticed that some of their demands are not specific—that is, they do not call for any specified number of recitation periods for a definite number of weeks during a stated number of years. The Conferences on Languages and History are the most definite in their recommendations, the Conferences on Mathematics and the Sciences being much less definite. Table 1 is therefore not a program, but the materials from which serviceable programs may be constructed.

The Committee of Ten deliberately placed in this one table the recommendations of the Conferences for the elementary grades and the recommendations for secondary schools, in order that the sequence of the recommendations for each subject might be clearly brought out. The recommendations made for the secondary schools presuppose in many cases that the recommendations made for the elementary schools have been fulfilled; or, at least, in many cases the Conferences would have made different recommendations for the secondary schools, if they had been compelled to act on the assumption that things must remain just as they are in the elementary schools.

Proper Secondary School Subjects

At this point it is well to call attention to the list of subjects which the Conferences deal with as proper for secondary schools. They are: 1. languages—Latin, Greek, English, German, and French, (and locally Spanish); 2. mathematics—algebra, geometry, and trigonometry; 3. general history, and the intensive study of special epochs; 4. natural history—including descriptive astronomy, meteorology, botany, zoölogy, physiology, geology, and ethnology, most of which subjects may be conveniently grouped under the title of physical geography; and 5. physics and chemistry. The Committee of Ten assent to this list, both for what it includes and for what it excludes, with some practical qualifications to be mentioned below.

Total Instruction Recommended

Table 2 exhibits the total amount of instruction (estimated by the number of weekly periods assigned to each subject) to be given in a secondary school during each year of a four years' course, on the supposition that the recommendations of the Conferences are all carried out.

Number of Weekly Recitation Periods

The method of estimating the amount of instruction offered in any subject by the number of recitation periods assigned to it each week

TABLE 2

1st Secondary School Year		
Latin	5	p.
English Literature, 3 p. ⎫ Composition, 2 p. ⎭ ⋯	5	p.
German or French	4	p.
Algebra	5	p.
History	3	p.
	22	p.

2nd Secondary School Year		
Latin	5	p.
Greek	5	p.
English Literature, 3 p. ⎫ Composition, 2 p. ⎭ ⋯	5	p.
German	4	p.
French	4	p.
Algebra,* 2½ p. ⎫ Geometry, 2½ p. ⎭	5	p.
Astronomy (12 weeks)	5	p.
Botany or Zoölogy	5	p.
History	3	p.
	37½	p.

3rd Secondary School Year		
Latin	5	p.
Greek	4	p.
English Literature, 3 p. ⎫ " Composition, 1 p. ⎬ ⋯ Rhetoric, 1 p. ⎭	5	p.
German	4	p.
French	4	p.
Algebra *	2½	p.
Geometry	2½	p.
Chemistry	5	p.
History	3	p.
	35	p.

4th Secondary School Year		
Latin	5	p.
Greek	4	p.
English Literature, 3 p. ⎫ " Composition, 1 p. ⎬ ⋯ " Grammar, 1 p. ⎭	5	p.
German	4	p.
French	4	p.
Trigonometry, 2 p. ½ yr. ⎫ Higher Algebra, 2 p. ½ yr. ⎭ ⋯	2	p.
Physics	5	p.
Anatomy, Physiology, and Hygiene ½ yr.	5	p.
History	3	p.
Geology or Physiography, ⎫ 3 p. ½ yr. ⎬ ⋯ Meteorology, 3 p. ½ yr. ⎭	3	p.
	37½	p.

* Option of bookkeeping and commercial arithmetic.

for a given number of years or half years is in some respects an inadequate one, for it takes no account of the scope and intensity of the instruction given during the periods; but so far as it goes, it is trustworthy and instructive. It represents with tolerable accuracy the proportional expenditure which a school is making on a given subject, and therefore the proportional importance which the school attaches to that subject. It also represents roughly the proportion of the pupil's entire school time which he can devote to a given subject, provided he is free to take all the instruction offered in that subject. All experience shows that subjects deemed important get a large number of weekly periods, while those deemed unimportant get a small number. Moreover, if the program time assigned to a given subject be insufficient, the value of that subject as training cannot be got, no matter how good the quality of the instruction.

Every one of these years, except the first, contains much more instruction than any one pupil can follow; but, looking at the bearing of the table on the important question of educational expenditure, it is encouraging to observe that there are already many secondary schools in this country in which quite as many subjects are taught as are mentioned in this table, and in which there are more weekly periods of instruction provided for separate classes than are found in any year of the table. In some urban high schools which provide from five to nine different courses of three to five years each, and in some endowed secondary schools which maintain two or three separate courses called Classical, Latin-scientific, and English, or designated by similar titles, the total number of weekly periods of unrepeated instruction given to distinct classes is even now larger than the largest total of weekly periods found in Table 2. The annual expenditure in such schools is sufficient to provide all the instruction called for by Table 2. The suggestions of the Conferences presuppose that all the pupils of like intelligence and maturity in any subject study it in the same way and to the same extent, so long as they study it at all—this being a point on which all the Conferences insist strongly. No provision is made, therefore, for teaching Latin, or algebra, or history to one portion of a class four times a week, and to another portion of the same class only thrice or twice a week. Such provisions are very common in American schools; but the recommendations of the Conferences, if put into effect, would do away with all expenditures of this sort.

One Quarter of School Time for Science

It clearly appears from Table 2 that the recommendations of the Conferences on scientific subjects have been moderate so far as the proposed allotment of time to them is concerned. The Conferences on Physics, Chemistry and Astronomy, Natural History, and Geography held one combined session in Chicago, and passed a resolution that one fourth of the whole high school course ought to be devoted to natural science, their intention doubtless being that each pupil should devote one quarter of his time to science; yet if all the time asked for in secondary schools by the scientific Conferences be added together, it will appear, first, that the rare pupil who should take all the scientific instruction provided would need for it only one quarter of his time, and secondly, that less than one sixth of the whole instruction to be given in accordance with the combined recommendations of all the Conferences is devoted to subjects of natural science. The first year of the secondary school course according to Table 2 will contain no science at all; and it is only in the last year of the secondary school that the proportion of natural science teaching rises to one fourth of the whole instruction.

In studying these two tables which result from the recommendations of the Conferences, the Committee of Ten perceived at once, that if the recommendations are to be carried out, so far as offering the instruction proposed is concerned, a selection of studies for the individual pupil must be made in the second, third, and fourth years of the secondary school course. This selection will obviously be made in different ways in different schools. Any school principal may say, "With the staff at my command I can teach only five subjects out of those proposed by the Conferences in the manner proposed. My school shall therefore be limited to these five." Another school may be able to teach in the thorough manner proposed five subjects, but some or all of these five may be different from those selected by the first school. A larger or richer school may be able to teach all the subjects mentioned, and by the methods and with the apparatus described. In the last case, each pupil, under the supervision of the teachers, and with the advice of parents or friends, may make choice between several different four years' courses arranged by the school; or, if the school authorities prefer, the pupil may be allowed to make year by year a carefully guided choice among a limited number of subjects; or these two methods may be combined. Selection for the individual is necessary to thoroughness, and to the imparting of power as distinguished from information; for any large subject whatever, to yield its training value, must be pursued through several years and be studied from three to five times a week, and if each subject studied is thus to claim a considerable fraction of the pupil's school time, then clearly the individual pupil can give attention to only a moderate number of subjects.

In Table 2, the number of weekly periods assigned to a single subject varies from two to five, about half of the assignments being made for five periods a week. There is an obvious convenience in the number five because it ordinarily gives one period a day for five days in the week; but there is also an obvious disadvantage in making too free use of the number five. It practically limits to three or, at most, four, the number of subjects which the individual pupil may pursue simultaneously; and this limit is inexpedient in a four years' program.

Recommendations of the Conferences Modified

The Committee have therefore prepared the following modification of Table 2, using four as the standard number of weekly periods, except in the first year of a new language, and in the few cases in which the Conferences advise a number smaller than four. By this means the total number of periods is somewhat reduced, except in the first year, and the numbers of periods allotted to different subjects are made more consonant, each with the others. The result is only a correlation and adjustment of the recommendations of the Conferences, no judgment or recommendation of the Committee being expressed in it.

TABLE 3

1st Secondary School Year	
Latin	5 p.
English Literature, 2 p. ⎱	
" Composition, 2 p. ⎰	4 p.
German or French	5 p.
Algebra	4 p.
History of Italy, Spain, and France	3 p.
Applied Geography (European political—continental and oceanic flora and fauna)	4 p.
	25 p.

2nd Secondary School Year	
Latin	4 p.
Greek	5 p.
English Literature, 2 p. ⎱	
" Composition, 2 p. ⎰	4 p.
German, continued	4 p.
French, begun	5 p.
Algebra,* 2 p. ⎱	
Geometry, 2 p. ⎰	4 p.
Botany or Zoölogy	4 p.
English History to 1688	3 p.
	33 p.

3rd Secondary School Year	
Latin	4 p.
Greek	4 p.
English Literature, 2 p. ⎱	
" Composition, 1 p. ⎬	4 p.
Rhetoric, 1 p. ⎰	
German	4 p.
French	4 p.
Algebra,* 2 p. ⎱	
Geometry, 2 p. ⎰	4 p.
Physics	4 p.
History, English and American ..	3 p.
Astronomy, 3 p. 1st ½ yr. ⎱	
Meteorology, 3 p. 2nd ½ yr. ⎰ ...	3 p.
	34 p.

4th Secondary School Year	
Latin	4 p.
Greek	4 p.
English Literature, 2 p. ⎱	
" Composition, 1 p. ⎬	4 p.
" Grammar, 1 p. ⎰	
German	4 p.
French	4 p.
Trigonometry ⎱	
Higher Algebra ⎰	2 p.
Chemistry	4 p.
History (intensive) and Civil Government	3 p.
Geology or Physiography, 4 p. 1st ½ yr. ⎱	
Anatomy, Physiology, and Hygiene, 4 p. 2nd ½ yr. ⎰ ...	4 p.
	33 p.

* Option of bookkeeping and commercial arithmetic.

The adoption of the number four as the standard number of weekly periods will not make it impossible to carry into effect the fundamental conception of all the Conferences, namely, that all the subjects which make part of the secondary school course should be taught consecutively enough and extensively enough to make every subject yield that training which it is best fitted to yield—provided that the proposed correlation and association of subjects are carried out in practice. With regard to the arrangement or sequence of subjects, the Committee follow in this table the recommendations of the Conferences with only slight modifications. They insert in the first year applied geography, using the term in the sense in which it is used by the Conference on Geography; and they make this insertion in order that natural science may be represented in the program of that year, and that a complete break of continuity, as regards science subjects, between the eighth grade and the second year of the secondary school may be avoided. They have felt obliged to put physics into the third year, and chemistry into the fourth, in order that the subject of physics may precede meteorology and physiography; and they have slightly increased the number of lessons in astronomy. With regard to the proportions of school time to be devoted to the different subjects, Table 3 reduces somewhat the proportional time devoted to Latin, English, and mathematics, and increases the proportional time to be devoted to natural science. In a secondary school which teaches all the subjects recommended by the Conferences, and to the extent contemplated in Table 3, nearly one fifth of the whole instruction given will be devoted to natural science.

The Source of Various Programs

The Committee regard Table 3 not, of course, as a feasible program, but as the possible source of a great variety of good secondary school programs. It would be difficult to make a bad program out of the materials contained in this table, unless indeed the fundamental principles advocated by the Conferences should be neglected. With some reference to Table 1, excellent six years' and five years' programs for secondary schools can readily be constructed by spreading the subjects contained in Table 3 over six or five years instead of four, of course with some changes in the time-allotment.

The details of the time-allotment for the several studies which enter into the secondary school program may seem to some persons mechanical, or even trivial—a technical matter to be dealt with by each superintendent of schools, or by each principal of a secondary school, acting on his own individual experience and judgment; but such is not the opinion of the Committee of Ten. The Committee believe that to establish just proportions between the several subjects, or groups of allied subjects, on which the Conferences were held, it is essential that each principal subject shall be taught thoroughly and extensively, and therefore for an adequate number of periods a week on the school program. If twice as much time is given in a school to Latin as is given to mathematics, the attainments of the pupils in Latin ought to be twice as great as they are in mathematics, provided that equally good work is done in the two subjects; and Latin will have twice the educational value of mathematics. Again, if in a secondary school Latin is steadily pursued for four years with four or five hours a week devoted to it, that subject will be worth more to the pupil than the sum of half a dozen other subjects, each of which has one sixth of the time allotted to Latin. The good effects of continuous study in one subject will be won for the pupil through the Latin, and they will not be won through the six other subjects among which only so much time as is devoted to the single language has been divided. If every subject studied at all is to be studied thoroughly and consecutively, every subject must receive an adequate time-allotment. If every subject is to provide a substantial mental training, it must have a time-allotment sufficient to produce that fruit. Finally, since selection must be exercised by or on behalf of the individual pupil, all the subjects between which choice is allowed should be approximately equivalent to each other in seriousness, dignity, and efficacy. Therefore they should have approximately equal time-allotments. The Conferences have abundantly shown how every subject which they recommend can be made a serious subject of instruction, well fitted to train the pupil's powers of observation, expression, and reasoning. It remains for makers of school programs to give every subject the chance of developing a good training capacity by giving it an adequate time-allotment.

The schedule of studies contained in Table 3 permits flexibility and variety in three respects. First, it is not necessary that any school should teach all the subjects which it contains, or any particular set of subjects. Secondly, it is not necessary that the individual pupil should everywhere and always have the same number of periods of instruction per week. In one school the pupils might have but sixteen periods a week, in another twenty; or in some years of the course the pupils might have more periods a week than in other years. Within the schedule many particular arrangements for the convenience of a school, or for the welfare of an individual pupil would be possible. Thirdly, it is not necessary that every secondary school should begin its work at the level which is assumed as the starting point of secondary instruction in Tables 1, 2, and 3. If in any community the high school has no such grammar school foundation beneath it as is imagined in Table 1, it will simply have to begin its work lower down in the table. The sequence of studies recommended by the Conferences would still serve as a guide; but the demarcation between the elementary schools and the high school would occur in that community at a lower point. From this point of view, Tables 1, 2, and 3 may be considered to set a standard towards which secondary schools should tend; and not a standard to which they can at once conform.

The adoption of a program based on Table 3 would not necessarily change at all the relation of a school to the colleges or universities to which it habitually sends pupils. Any such program would lend itself either to the examination method of admission to college, or to the certificate method; and it could be slightly modified in such a way as to meet the present admission requirements of any college in the country. Future changes in admission requirements might fairly be made with a view to the capabilities of programs based on Table 3.

Specimen Programs

As samples of school programs constructed within the schedules of Table 3, the Committee present the following working programs, which they recommend for trial wherever the secondary school period is limited to four years. All four combined might, of course, be tabulated as one program with options by subject.

These four programs taken together use all the subjects mentioned in Table 3, and usually, but not always, to about the amounts there indicated. History and English suffer serious contraction in the Classical program. All four programs conform to the general recommendations of the Conferences, that is—they treat each subject in the same way for all pupils with trifling exceptions; they give time enough to each subject to win from it the kind of mental training it is fitted to supply; they put the different principal subjects on an approximate equality so far as time-allotment is concerned; they omit all short information courses; and they make sufficiently continuous the instruction in each of the main lines, namely, language, science, history and mathematics. With slight modifications, they would prepare the pupils for admission to appropriate courses in any American college or university on the existing requirements; and they would also meet the new college requirements which are suggested below.

Prolonging the Secondary School Period

In preparing these programs, the Committee were perfectly aware that it is impossible to make a satisfactory secondary school program, limited to a period of four years, and founded on the present elementary school subjects and methods. In the opinion of the Committee, several subjects now reserved for high schools—such as algebra, geometry, natural science, and foreign languages—should be begun earlier than now, and therefore within the schools classified as elementary; or, as an alternative, the secondary school period should be made to begin two years earlier than at present, leaving six years instead of eight for the elementary school period. Under the present organization, elementary subjects and elementary methods are, in the judgment of the Committee, kept in use too long.

The most striking differences in the four programs will be found, as is intimated in the headings in Table 4, in the relative amounts of time given to foreign languages. In the Classical program the foreign languages get a large share of time; in the English program a small share. In compensation, English and history are more developed in the English program than in the Classical.

Many teachers will say, at first sight, that physics comes too early in these programs and Greek too late. One member of the Committee is firmly of the opinion that Greek comes too late. The explanation of the positions assigned to these subjects is that the Committee of Ten attached great importance to two general principles in program making: In the first place they endeavored to postpone till the third year the grave choice between the Classical course and the Latin-Scientific. They believed that this bifurcation should occur as late as possible, since the choice between these two roads often determines for life the youth's career. Moreover, they believed that it is possible to make this important decision for a boy on good grounds, only when he has had opportunity to exhibit his quality and discover his tastes by making excursions into all the principal fields of knowledge. The youth who has never studied any but his native language cannot know his own capacity for linguistic acquisition; and the youth who has never made a chemical or physical experiment cannot know whether or not he has a taste for exact science. The wisest teacher, or the most observant parent, can hardly predict with confidence a boy's gift for a subject which he has never touched. In these considerations the Committee found strong reasons for postponing bifurcation, and making the subjects of the first two years as truly representative as possible. Secondly, inasmuch as many boys and girls who begin the secondary school course do not stay in school more than two years, the Committee thought it important to select the studies of the first two years in such a way that linguistic, historical, mathematical, and scientific subjects should all be properly represented. Natural history being represented by physi-

TABLE 4

Year	Classical — Three foreign languages (one modern)		Latin-Scientific — Two foreign languages (one modern)	
1.	Latin	5 p.	Latin	5 p.
	English	4 p.	English	4 p.
	Algebra	4 p.	Algebra	4 p.
	History	4 p.	History	4 p.
	Physical Geography	3 p.	Physical Geography	3 p.
		20 p.		20 p.
2.	Latin	5 p.	Latin	5 p.
	English	2 p.	English	2 p.
	German or French begun *	4 p.	German or French begun	4 p.
	Geometry	3 p.	Geometry	3 p.
	Physics	3 p.	Physics	3 p.
	History	3 p.	Botony or Zoölogy	3 p.
		20 p.		20 p.
3.	Latin	4 p.	Latin	4 p.
	Greek *	5 p.	English	3 p.
	English	3 p.	German or French	4 p.
	German or French	4 p.	Mathematics { Algebra 2 / Geometry 2 }	4 p.
	Mathematics { Algebra 2 / Geometry 2 }	4 p.	Astronomy ½ yr. & Meteorology ½ yr.	3 p.
		20 p.	History	2 p.
				20 p.
4.	Latin	4 p.	Latin	4 p.
	Greek	5 p.	English { as in Classical 2 / additional 2 }	4 p.
	English	2 p.	German or French	3 p.
	German or French	3 p.	Chemistry	3 p.
	Chemistry	3 p.	Trigonometry & Higher Algebra or History	3 p.
	Trigonometry & Higher Algebra or History	3 p.	Geology or Physiography and Anatomy, Physiology & Hygiene ½ yr.	3 p.
		20 p.		20 p.

* In any school in which Greek can be better taught than a modern language, or in which local public opinion or the history of the school makes it desirable to teach Greek in an ample way, Greek may be substituted for German or French in the second year of the Classical program.

TABLE 4 (*continued*)

YEAR	Modern Languages *Two foreign languages* *(both modern)*		English *One foreign language* *(ancient or modern)*	
1.	French or German begun ...	5 p.	Latin, or German, or French	5 p.
	English	4 p.	English	4 p.
	Algebra	4 p.	Algebra	4 p.
	History	4 p.	History	4 p.
	Physical Geography	3 p.	Physical Geography	3 p.
		20 p.		20 p.
2.	French or German	4 p.	Latin, or German, or	
	English	2 p.	French ...... 5 or	4 p.
	German or French begun ...	5 p.	English ...... 3 or	4 p.
	Geometry	3 p.	Geometry	3 p.
	Physics	3 p.	Physics	3 p.
	Botany or Zoölogy	3 p.	History	3 p.
			Botany or Zoölogy	3 p.
		20 p.		20 p.
3.	French or German	4 p.	Latin, or German, or French	4 p.
	English	3 p.	English $\begin{cases} \text{as in others } 3 \\ \text{additional} \quad 2 \end{cases} \cdots$	5 p.
	German or French	4 p.		
	Mathematics $\begin{cases} \text{Algebra} \quad 2 \\ \text{Geometry } 2 \end{cases}$.	4 p.	Mathematics $\begin{cases} \text{Algebra} \quad 2 \\ \text{Geometry } 2 \end{cases}$.	4 p.
	Astronomy ½ yr. &		Astronomy ½ yr. &	
	Meteorology ½ yr.	3 p.	Meteorology ½ yr.	3 p.
	History	2 p.	History $\begin{cases} \text{as in the Latin-} \\ \quad \text{Scientific} \quad 2 \\ \text{additional} \quad 2 \end{cases} \cdots$	4 p.
		20 p.		
				20 p.
4.	French or German	3 p.	Latin, or German, or French	4 p.
	English $\begin{cases} \text{as in Classical 2} \\ \text{additional} \quad 2 \end{cases} \cdots$	4 p.	English $\begin{cases} \text{as in Classical 2} \\ \text{additional} \quad 2 \end{cases} \cdots$	4 p.
	German or French	4 p.	Chemistry	3 p.
	Chemistry	3 p.	Trigonometry & Higher	
	Trigonometry & Higher		Algebra	3 p.
	Algebra 3 or History	3 p.	History	3 p.
	Geology or Physiography and		Geology or Physiography	
	Anatomy, Physiology, &		½ yr. and	
	Hygiene ½ yr.	3 p.	Anatomy, Physiology, &	
			Hygiene ½ yr.	3 p.
		20 p.		20 p.

cal geography, the Committee wished physics to represent the inorganic sciences of precision. The first two years of any one of the four programs presented above will, in the judgment of the Committee, be highly profitable by themselves to children who can go no farther.

Although the Committee thought it expedient to include among the four programs, one which included neither Latin nor Greek, and one which included only one foreign language (which might be either ancient or modern), they desired to affirm explicitly their unanimous opinion that, under existing conditions in the United States as to the training of teachers and the provision of necessary means of instruction, the two programs called respectively Modern Languages and English must in practice be distinctly inferior to the other two.

Explanation of the Sample Programs

In the construction of the sample programs the Committee adopted twenty as the maximum number of weekly periods, but with two qualifications, namely, that at least five of the twenty periods should be given to unprepared work, and that laboratory subjects should have double periods whenever that prolongation should be possible.

The omission of music, drawing, and elocution from the programs offered by the Committee was not intended to imply that these subjects ought to receive no systematic attention. It was merely thought best to leave it to local school authorities to determine, without suggestions from the Committee, how these subjects should be introduced into the programs in addition to the subjects reported on by the Conferences.

The Committee were governed in the construction of the first three programs by the rule laid down by the language Conferences, namely, that two foreign languages should not be begun at the same time. To obey this rule is to accept strict limitations in the construction of a four years' Classical program. A five years' or six years' program can be made much more easily under this restriction. The Committee were anxious to give five weekly periods to every foreign language in the year when it was first attacked; but did not find it possible to do so in every case.

Economy of the Programs—Missing Subjects

The four programs can be carried out economically in a single school; because, with a few inevitable exceptions, the several subjects occur simultaneously in at least three programs and with the same number of weekly periods.

Numerous possible transpositions of subjects will occur to every experienced teacher who examines these specimen programs. Thus, in some localities it would be better to transpose French and German; the selection and order of science subjects might be varied considerably to suit the needs or circumstances of different schools; and the selection and order of historical subjects admit of large variety.

Many subjects now familiar in secondary school courses of study do not appear in Table 3 or in the specimen programs given above; but it must not be supposed that the omitted subjects are necessarily to be neglected. If the recommendations of the Conference were carried out, some of the omitted subjects would be better dealt with under any one of the above programs than they are now under familiar high school and academy programs in which they figure as separate subjects. Thus, drawing does not appear as a separate subject in the specimen programs; but the careful reader of the Conference reports will notice that drawing, both mechanical and freehand, is to be used in the study of history, botany, zoölogy, astronomy, meteorology, physics, geography, and physiography, and that the kind of drawing recommended by the Conferences is the most useful kind, namely, that which is applied to recording, describing, and discussing observations. This abundant use of drawing might not prevent the need of some special instruction in drawing, but it ought to diminish the number of periods devoted exclusively to drawing. Again, neither ethics nor economics, neither metaphysics nor aesthetics appear in the programs; but in the large number of periods devoted to English and history there would be some time for incidental instruction in the elements of these subjects. It is through the reading and writing required of pupils, or recommended to them, that the fundamental ideas on these important topics are to be inculcated. Again, the industrial and commercial subjects do not appear in these programs; but bookkeeping and commercial arithmetic are provided for by the option for algebra designated in Table 3; and if it were desired to provide more amply for subjects thought to have practical importance in trade or the useful arts, it would be easy to provide options in such subjects for some of the science contained in the third and fourth years of the "English" program.

Saturday Work-Assistants

The Committee of Ten think much would be gained if, in addition to the usual program hours, a portion of Saturday morning should be regularly used for laboratory work in the scientific subjects. Laboratory work requires more consecutive time than the ordinary period of recitation affords; so that an hour and a half is about the shortest advantageous period for a laboratory exercise. The Committee venture to suggest further that, in addition to the regular school sessions in the morning, one afternoon in every week should be used for out-of-door instruction in geography, botany, zoölogy, and geology, these after-noon and Saturday morning exercises being counted as regular work for the teachers who conduct them. In all laboratory and field work, the Committee believe that it will be found profitable to employ as assistants to the regular teachers—particularly at the beginning of laboratory and field work in each subject—recent graduates of the secondary schools who have themselves followed the laboratory and field courses; for at the beginning the pupil will need a large amount of individual instruction in the manipulation of specimens, the use of instruments, and the prompt recording of observations. One teacher without assistants cannot supervise effectively the work of thirty or forty pupils, either in the laboratory or in the field. The laboratory work on Saturday mornings could be maintained throughout the school year; the afternoon excursions would of course be difficult, or impossible, for perhaps a third of the school year.

In general, the Committee of Ten have endeavored to emphasize the principles which should govern all secondary school programs, and to show how the main recommendations of the several Conferences may be carried out in a variety of feasible programs.

Requirements for Admission to College

One of the subjects which the Committee of Ten were directed to consider was requirements for admission to college; and particularly they were expected to report on uniform requirements for admission to colleges, as well as on a uniform secondary school program. Almost all the Conferences have something to say about the best mode of testing the attainments of candidates at college admission examinations; and some of them, notably the Conferences on History and Geography, make very explicit declarations concerning the nature of college examinations. The improvements desired in the mode of testing the attainments of pupils who have pursued in the secondary schools the various subjects which enter into the course will be found clearly described under each subject in the several Conference reports; but there is a general principle concerning the relation of the secondary schools to colleges which the Committee of Ten, inspired and guided by the Conferences, feel it their duty to set forth with all possible distinctness.

The secondary schools of the United States, taken as a whole, do not exist for the purpose of preparing boys and girls for colleges. Only an insignificant percentage of the graduates of these schools go to colleges or scientific schools. Their main function is to prepare for the duties of life that small proportion of all the children in the country—a proportion small in number, but very important to the welfare of the nation—who show themselves able to profit by an education prolonged to the eighteenth year, and whose parents are able to support them while they remain so long at school. There are, to be sure, a few private or endowed secondary schools in the country, which make it their principal object to prepare students for the colleges and universities; but the number of these schools is relatively small. A secondary school program intended for national use must therefore be made for those children whose education is not to be pursued beyond the secondary school. The preparation of a few pupils for college or scientific school should in the ordinary secondary school be the incidental, and not the principal object. At the same time, it is obviously desirable that the colleges and scientific schools should be accessible to all boys or girls who have completed creditably the secondary school course. Their parents often do not decide for them, four years before the college age, that they shall go to college, and they themselves may not, perhaps, feel the desire to continue their education until near the end of their school course. In order that any successful graduate of a good secondary school should be free to present himself at the gates of the college or scientific school of his choice, it is necessary that the colleges and scientific schools of the country should accept for admission to appropriate courses of their instruction the attainments of any youth who has passed creditably through a good secondary school course, no matter to what group of subjects he may have mainly devoted himself in the secondary school. As secondary school courses are now too often arranged, this is not a reasonable request to prefer to the colleges and scientific schools; because the pupil may now go through a secondary school course of a very feeble and scrappy nature—studying a little of many subjects and not much of any one, getting, perhaps, a little information in a variety of fields, but nothing which can be called a thorough training. Now the recommendations of the nine Conferences, if well carried out, might fairly be held to make all the main subjects taught in the secondary schools of equal rank for the purposes of admission to college or scientific school. They would all be taught consecutively and thoroughly, and would all be carried on in the same spirit; they would all be used for training the powers of observation, memory, expression, and reasoning; and they would all be good to that end, although differing among themselves in quality and substance. In preparing the programs of Table 4, the Committee had in mind that the requirements for admission to colleges might, for schools which adopted a program derived from that table, be simplified to a considerable extent, though not reduced. A college might say, "We will accept for admission any groups of studies taken from the secondary school program, provided that the sum of the studies in each of the four years amounts to sixteen, or eighteen, or twenty periods a week—as may be thought best—and provided, further, that in each year at least four of the subjects presented shall have been pursued at least three periods a week, and that at least three of the subjects shall have been pursued three years or more." For the purposes of this reckoning, natural history, geography, meteorology, and astronomy might be grouped together as one subject. Every youth who entered college would have spent four years in studying a few subjects thoroughly; and, on the theory that all the subjects are to be considered equivalent in educational rank for the purposes of admission to college, it would make no difference which subjects he had chosen from the program—he would have had four years of strong and effective mental training. The Conferences on Geography and Modern Languages make the most explicit statement to the effect that college requirements for admission should coincide with high school requirements for graduation. The Conference on English is of opinion "that no student should be admitted to college who shows in his English examination and his other examinations that he is very deficient in ability to write good English." This recommendation suggests that an ample English course in the secondary school should be required of all persons who intend to enter college. It would of course be possible for any college to require for admission any one subject, or any group of subjects, in the table, and the requirements of different colleges, while all kept within the table, might differ in many respects; but the Committee are of opinion that the satisfactory completion of any one of the four years' courses of study embodied in the foregoing programs should admit to corresponding courses in colleges and scientific schools. They believe that the close articulation between the secondary schools and the higher institutions would be advantageous alike for the schools, the colleges, and the country.

Every reader of this report and of the reports of the nine Conferences will be satisfied that to carry out the improvements proposed more highly trained teachers will be needed than are now ordinarily to be found for the service of the elementary and secondary schools. The Committee of Ten desire to point out some of the means of procuring these better trained teachers. For the further instruction of teachers in actual service, three agencies already in existence may be much better utilized than they now are. The Summer Schools which many universities now maintain might be resorted to by much larger numbers of teachers, particularly if some aid, such as the payment of tuition fees and travelling expenses, should be given to teachers who are willing to devote half of their vacations to study, by the cities and towns which these teachers serve. Secondly, in all the towns and cities in which colleges and universities are planted, these colleges or universities may usefully give stated courses of instruction in the main subjects used in the elementary and secondary schools to teachers employed in those towns and cities. This is a reasonable service which the colleges and universities may render to their own communities. Thirdly, a superintendent who has himself become familiar with the best mode of teaching any one of the subjects which enter into the school course can always be a very useful instructor for the whole body of teachers under his charge. A real master of any one subject will always have many suggestions to make to teachers of other subjects. The same is true of the principal of a high school, or other leading teacher in a town or city. In every considerable city school system the best teacher in each department of instruction should be enabled to give part of his time to helping the other teachers by inspecting and criticising their work, and showing them, both by precept and example, how to do it better.

Getting Teachers More Highly Trained

In regard to preparing young men and women for the business of teaching, the country has a right to expect much more than it has yet obtained from the colleges and normal schools. The common expectation of attainment for pupils of the normal schools has been altogether too low the country over. The normal schools, as a class, themselves need better apparatus, libraries, programs, and teachers. As to the colleges, it is quite as much an enlargement of sympathies as an improvement of apparatus or of teaching that they need. They ought to take more interest than they have heretofore done, not only in the secondary, but in the elementary schools; and they ought to take pains to fit men well for the duties of a school superintendent. They already train a considerable number of the best principals of high schools and academies; but this is not sufficient. They should take an active interest, through their presidents, professors, and other teachers, in improving the schools in their respective localities, and in contributing to the thorough discussion of all questions affecting the welfare of both the elementary and the secondary schools.

Uniform Dates for Admission Examinations

Finally, the Committee venture to suggest, in the interest of secondary schools, that uniform dates—such as the last Thursday, Friday, and Saturday, or the third Monday, Tuesday, and Wednesday of June and September—be established for the admission examinations of colleges and scientific schools throughout the United States. It is a serious inconvenience for secondary schools which habitually prepare candidates for several different colleges or scientific schools that the admission examinations of different institutions are apt to occur on different dates, sometimes rather widely separated.

The Committee also wish to call attention to the service which Schools of Law, Medicine, Engineering, and Technology, whether connected with universities or not, can render to secondary education by arranging their requirements for admission, as regards selection and range of subjects, in conformity with the courses of study recommended by the Committee. By bringing their entrance requirements into close relation with any or all of the programs recommended for secondary schools, these professional schools can give valuable support to high schools, academies, and preparatory schools.

Charles W. Eliot,
William T. Harris,
James B. Angell,
John Tetlow,
James M. Taylor,
Oscar D. Robinson,
James H. Baker,
Richard H. Jesse,
James C. Mackenzie,
Henry C. King.

4 December, 1893.

Minority Report

President Baker signs the above report, but adds the following statement:

TO THE NATIONAL COUNCIL OF EDUCATION:

I beg leave to note some exceptions taken to parts of the Report of the Committee of Ten. Had the Committee not been limited in time, doubtless fuller discussion would have resulted in modifying some statements embodied in the report. The great value of the reports of the Conferences upon the subjects referred to them, as to matter, place, time, methods, adequate and continuous work for each subject, and identity of work in different courses, and the masterly summary and tabulation of their recommendations, made by the Chairman of the

Committee of Ten, can but invite cordial commendation. Objections are raised to parts of the special work of the Committee.

1. I cannot endorse expressions that appear to sanction the idea that the choice of subjects in secondary schools may be a matter of comparative indifference. I note especially the following sentences, referring the reader to their context for accurate interpretation.

"Any school principal may say: 'With the staff at my command I can teach only five subjects out of those proposed by the Conferences in the manner proposed. My school shall, therefore, be limited to these five.' Another school may be able to teach in the thorough manner proposed five subjects, but some or all of these five may be different from those selected by the first school."

"If twice as much time is given in a school to Latin as is given to mathematics, the attainments of the pupils in Latin ought to be twice as great as they are in mathematics, provided that equally good work is done in the two subjects; and Latin will have twice the educational value of mathematics."

"The schedule of studies contained in Table 3 permits flexibility and variety in three respects. First, it is not necessary that any school should teach all the subjects which it contains, or any particular set of subjects."

"Every youth who entered college would have spent four years in studying a few subjects thoroughly; and on the theory that all the subjects are to be considered equivalent in educational rank for the purpose of admission to college, it would make no difference which subjects he had chosen from the program—he would have had four years of strong and effective mental training."

All such statements are based upon the theory that, for the purposes of general education, one study is as good as another—a theory which appears to me to ignore Philosophy, Psychology, and Science of Education. It is a theory which makes education formal and does not consider the nature and value of the content. Power comes through knowledge; we can not conceive of observation and memory in the abstract. The world which offers to the human mind several distinct views is the world in which our power that comes through knowledge is to be used, the world which we are to understand and enjoy. The relation between the subjective power and the objective—or subjective—knowledge is inseparable and vital. On any other theory, for general education, we might well consider the study of Egyptian hieroglyphics as valuable as that of physics, and Choctaw as important as Latin. Secondary school programs can not well omit mathematics, or science, or history, or literature, or the culture of the ancient classics. An education which gives a view in all directions is the work of elementary and secondary schools. Such an education is the necessary preparation for the special work of the university student. If I rightly understood, the majority of the

Committee rejected the theory of equivalence of studies for general education.

Studies vary in value for the training of the different powers, and for this additional reason the choice can not be regarded as a matter of indifference.

The training of "observation, memory, expression and reasoning" (inductive) is a very important part of education, but is not all of education. The imagination, deductive reasoning, the rich possibilities of emotional life, the education of the will through ethical ideas and correct habit, all are to be considered in a scheme of learning. Ideals are to be added to the scientific method.

The dilemma which appears on an examination of the time demands of the various conferences offers to the program-maker the alternatives of omitting essential subjects and of a rational adjustment of the time element, while retaining all essential subjects. Reason and experience point toward the latter alternative. By wise selection of matter within the lines of study adequate and consecutive time can be given to each.

2. The language of the second paragraph following Table 2 might be misconstrued to mean that the Committee favor the multiplication of courses with a loss of the thoroughness attainable when the teaching force is devoted to one or two courses. Intension rather than extension of effort, both in respect to the number of courses and in respect to the number of studies or topics under each principal subject, is to be strongly recommended.

3. It may seem trivial to offer criticism of the specimen programs made by the Committee, and yet I believe that each member felt that with ample deliberation results somewhat different would have been reached. Note for instance that in some of the programs history is entirely omitted in the second year, and physics is given only three hours per week—no more time than is allowed for botany or zoölogy. There are many symmetrical secondary school programs in actual operation today which furnish continuous instruction in all important subjects throughout the four years, allowing to each an amount of time adequate to good results. For most high schools the first, the Classical program, and the last program, the one offering one foreign language, will commend themselves because they are economical, and they combine a good finishing course with adequate college preparation.

4. On the basis of the tabulated results of the Conferences I believe that by earnest scientific examination a scheme of work can be formulated that will meet the views of the members of the Committee and of most educators. As an afterthought it may be an occasion for regret that the strength of the discussion was not devoted to Table 3. Instead of considering the work of the Committee as ended, I would recommend that the National Council hold itself responsible for further examination of the data furnished by the Conferences. I have not presumed to offer a substitute report, because I believe that the importance of the work demands further effort of an entire Committee.

THE READING LIST FOR ENGLISH (*PROPOSED BY THE CONFERENCE ON ENGLISH OF THE COMMITTEE OF TEN*)

It is illuminating to examine the source of some of the practices carried on in the secondary schools long after the source has become obscured. The Conference on the Study of English in the High School reported by the Committee of Ten is a good illustration.

One of the specific recommendations was as follows: "That the reading of certain masterpieces of English literature, not fewer in number than those at present assigned by the Commission of New England Colleges, should be required." [4]

The list to which the Report referred was adopted on June 2, 1888 by the Commission of Colleges in New England on Admission Examinations. It was made up of the following: Addison, Sir Roger de Coverley Papers; Austin, Pride and Prejudice; Coleridge, Ancient Mariner; Eliot, George, Scenes from Clerical Life, Silas Marner; Gray, Elegy Written in a Country Churchyard; Hawthorne, House of the Seven Gables; Irving, Alhambra; Johnson, Lives of Swift and Gray; Longfellow, Courtship of Miles Standish, Evangeline; Macaulay, Essay on Lord Clive, Second Essay on the Earl, Chatham; Scott, Marmion, Old Mortality, Quentin Durward, Rob Roy, Talisman; Shakespeare, As You Like it, Julius Caesar, Merchant of Venice, Midsummer Night's Dream; Swift, Gulliver's Travels; Thackeray, English Humorists; Webster, First Bunker Hill Oration.

The books listed persisted as required study in secondary school English courses as necessary reading of "classics" long after the origin of the list had been obliterated by the passage of time. Indeed, many of the works continue today as objects of study and are not infrequently justified by the erroneous belief that they are required reading for admission to college.

The Committee of Ten, through its recommendations about subjects to be taught, attempted to standardize the curriculum of the secondary schools. Not long afterward, in 1909, the Carnegie unit was imposed upon the schools, as described in the following excerpt from a study made in 1954.

---

[4] Report of the Committee of Ten on Secondary School Studies. *Op cit.,* p. 93.

THE HISTORY OF THE CARNEGIE UNIT [5]

The Carnegie Unit is a device for measuring high school work in terms of credits based on time spent in the classroom. This device was imposed on the high schools by efforts of the colleges and universities to standardize admission procedures.

Its historical setting divides into three chronological parts. The first, extending from 1873 to 1908, may be characterized as a period of growing dissatisfaction with college admission practices and numerous attempts to formulate and implement a solution to acknowledged and acute problems of high school-college articulation.

The second part, 1908 to 1910, deals with the proposal of a standard high school unit and its introduction to actual day-to-day educational procedure. The third period, from 1910 to the present, includes the development of the Carnegie Unit, its widespread growth, its effect on secondary and higher education, and the slowly evolving evaluation of its effect.

This chapter does not present the historical background of the Carnegie Unit as outlined above, because that would require a greater number of pages than the entire report. Therefore, the history of the Carnegie Unit begins first with certain essential definitions and facts, and then proceeds to analyses of influences and conditions.

Some First Questions

WHAT IS THE CARNEGIE UNIT?

It is a unit representing a year's study in any major subject in a secondary school, constituting approximately a quarter of a full year's work. Under ordinary circumstances, it assumes that a satisfactory year's work in any major subject cannot be accomplished in less than *120 sixty-minute hours,* or their equivalent.

WHAT WAS ITS ORIGINAL PURPOSE?

To afford a standard of measurement for the work done in secondary schools and thereby to facilitate transfer of credits between schools and colleges. It took the 4-year high school as a basis and assumed (1) that the length of the school year was from 36 to 40 weeks, (2) that a period

[5] Ellsworth Tompkins and Walter H. Gaumnitz, *The Carnegie Unit: Its Origin, Status, and Trends.* Washington, D.C.: U.S. Department of Health, Education, and Welfare, Bulletin, No. 7, 1954, pp. 4–19.

was from 40 to 60 minutes long, and (3) that a subject was studied for 4 or 5 periods a week.

WHAT WAS ITS ORIGINAL FUNCTION?

To recognize a well-ordered high school course and to provide a means for calculating college entrance requirements quantitatively.

WHEN AND BY WHOM WAS IT FIRST STATED?

In 1909 by the Carnegie Foundation for the Advancement of Teaching. It was approved by the College Entrance Examination Board in November 1909.

IS THAT WHY IT IS CALLED THE CARNEGIE UNIT?

Yes, but the term was never officially adopted or approved. Both the Carnegie Foundation and the College Entrance Examination Board described it only as a "standard unit." The term "Carnegie Unit" arose because of popular usage, and is no more than an easily understood label.

WAS THE CARNEGIE UNIT A FORWARD STEP IN EDUCATION IN 1909?

Yes, to overcome at least 7 sources of confusion existing prior to 1909:

1. Confusion regarding *admission requirements to college.* The general practice was for each college or university to establish its own requirements without regard to those established by other institutions. This was true of specific subject requirements and total requirements.
2. Confusion regarding *the time-allotment of subject-matter fields in secondary schools.* Frequently, one subject would be offered 5 days a week in one high school and the same subject offered 2 days a week in another school, yet many colleges would recognize the work as equal in weight.
3. Confusion concerning *the function and scope of the high school.* A great many colleges maintained high school departments as part of their organization. Other colleges taught high school subjects along with college subjects. High school youth were often admitted to college before they had completed high school.
4. Confusion regarding *preparation of students for college.* To prepare students for particular colleges, high schools had to offer a wider variety of subjects than they could justifiably defend. For example. one college required a study of Sallust, another Livy

not Sallust, and another neither Sallust nor Livy but Roman and Greek history not required by the first two colleges.

5. Confusion concerning *competition for students.* In the latter half of the 19th century, American colleges, both established and newly started, began to compete keenly for students and place great emphasis on size of student body. The best institution was often regarded as synonymous with the largest one. In this quest for students, many new colleges came into being. For example, in 1907, 85 colleges had yearly incomes ranging from $1,000 to $10,000; and 144 others had incomes ranging from $10,000 to $25,000. Furthermore, paid advertising by colleges was common practice: Harvard initiated this practice in February 1870 when it bought a page in the Atlantic Monthly. More important, however, was the effect of competition for students on relaxation of entrance standards.

6. Confusion about *waiving college admission requirements* to attract the admission of a greater number of freshmen. Some colleges had no entrance requirements; others had extremely limited entrance requirements; still others announced formal requirements but allowed alternative methods of admission. Many colleges maintained their own preparatory schools—not as preparatory schools, but as part of the higher institution. Very few colleges announced high entrance requirements and lived up to them. For example, Harvard, Princeton, and Yale in September 1908 admitted the following percentage of conditional (*i.e.,* deficient in preparation) students to the freshmen class: 49 per cent, 53 per cent, and 58 per cent, respectively.

7. Confusion regarding *lack of sensible continuity in the educational system.* Elementary schools and universities were established institutions before the public high school was developed, with the result that an orderly articulation between the three parts of the educational system was for many years if not impossible at least unknown. Colleges tended, therefore, to conduct their own institutions as separate units rather than as factors in a general system of education.

DID THE CARNEGIE UNIT SUCCEED IN RESOLVING SOME OF THESE CONFUSIONS?

Yes, for 1, 2, 3, 4; partially, for 5; no, for 6 and 7. The Carnegie Foundation for the Advancement of Teaching played a major role in obtaining consensus and compliance among colleges and secondary schools on the use of their standard unit measure of high school work.

It did so in an amazingly short time. The definition of the amount of preparation which colleges ought to demand of entering students was widely accepted both by colleges and high schools shortly after it was stated by the Foundation and endorsed by the College Entrance Examination Board in 1909.

DID OTHER COMMISSIONS AND ORGANIZATIONS ALSO PLAY A MAJOR ROLE?

A large role, but not necessarily a major one. From 1873 to 1909 numerous inquiries into school-college articulation called attention to the serious problems involved in improving college admission policies, for example, Harvard Faculty Discussions (1873–1887); the Report of the Committee of Ten (1891–94); the Report of the NEA Committee on College Entrance Requirements (1895–99); the annual reports of the College Entrance Examination Board (1900–1910); and the reports published by regional, state, and university accrediting agencies. In general, the effect of these reports was to alert the education profession to the complexity of the problems in college admissions requirements. But since their recommendations and resolutions were addressed to the profession generally, they failed of significant implementation.

HOW DID THE CARNEGIE FOUNDATION ACHIEVE AGREEMENT AMONG COLLEGES SO QUICKLY?

In brief, it was a case of "money talks." Andrew Carnegie in 1905 gave $10,000,000 to the trustees of the Carnegie Foundation for the Advancement of Teaching, the income from which was to provide retiring allowances for college professors in the United States, Canada, and Newfoundland. The trustees decided that these retiring allowances, or pensions, should be paid to the institution rather than to the person. In order to tell whether an institution could qualify to receive funds for their professors, the trustees had to define "a college," and in doing this, they found it necessary to define "a high school." Thus, from its beginning, the Carnegie Foundation for the Advancement of Teaching, *whose function was the dispensing of pensions to college professors,* acquired an equally important function of determining, and in a sense, compelling acceptance of "educational standards." It announced that if a college could not qualify as a college according to the definition provided by the Carnegie Foundation, it could not receive retiring allowances for its professors. Since few colleges by 1905 had their own pensions or annuity funds, it was financially imperative for many of them to qualify to receive the income of the Carnegie fund for their retired and retiring professors.

DID THE CARNEGIE FOUNDATION DEFINE A HIGH SCHOOL AND COLLEGE?

Yes, in both cases. It proposed that 14 units constitute the minimum amount of preparation to be interpreted as "4 years of academic or high school preparation." (A unit here was defined as a college entrance subject studied 5 periods weekly for the school year.) Also, the Carnegie Foundation defined a high school as a 4-year preparatory institution *not* connected with, or part of, a college or university.

It proposed that an institution be ranked as a college if it (1) had at least 6 professors giving their entire time to college and university work, (2) had a course of 4 full years in liberal arts and sciences, and (3) required for admission not less than the usual 4 years of academic or high school preparation, in addition to the pre-academic or grammar school studies.

In commenting on these definitions, the Carnegie Foundation's First Report (1905) stated:

The terms college and university have as yet no fixed meaning on this continent. It is not uncommon to find flourishing high schools which bear one or another of these titles. To recognize institutions of learning without some regard for this fact would be to throw away whatsoever opportunity the Foundation has for the exertion of educational influence.

WAS THE CARNEGIE FOUNDATION MAINLY RESPONSIBLE FOR THE ESTABLISHMENT OF THE CARNEGIE UNIT IN HIGH SCHOOLS?

Yes, largely so. There were two phases of its influence. (1) In the period from 1905 to 1908, the Foundation acted persistently to separate preparatory or high school departments from the college program, and to gain professional acceptance of the 4-year high school as the standard high school. (2) The definition and adoption of the (Carnegie) Unit as a measure of high school work occurred in 1909; it had an almost immediate effect on education at both college and high school levels. Within a short time after 1909, practically all high schools measured their work in terms of the Unit defined by the Carnegie Foundation and approved by the College Entrance Examination Board. The action of regional accrediting associations in approving the Unit encouraged its wide adoption.

WAS THERE ANY COMPULSION IN THE WIDE ACCEPTANCE OF THE CARNEGIE UNIT?

Not forcible compulsion; but to receive income from the Carnegie Foundation, colleges had to comply with the rules as established by the trustees of the Foundation. The President of the Foundation, Henry S. Pritchett made it clear that he would permit no relaxation of regulations. To that extent, therefore, the Carnegie Foundation "compelled" colleges either to alter their policies and procedures or fail to gain and retain status. And the colleges compelled the high schools. However, a college was under no compulsion to apply for Carnegie Foundation retiring allowances. The fact is that a great many institutions did so. Consequently, the Carnegie Foundation became an accrediting educational agency.

A statement in the Second Annual Report of the Carnegie Foundation (1906) (2a) stated:

> The true task of this Board is not to pass upon the merits of individuals but of colleges; to decide upon such educational standards as seem fair and wise, and then to proceed to admit to the system of retiring allowances such institutions as, complying with these standards, come within the provisions of the charter and the deed of gifts. In a word the Carnegie Foundation for the Advancement of Teaching must be first an educational agency before it can act wisely in awarding retiring allowances.

WHO WERE SOME OF THE TRUSTEES OF THE CARNEGIE FOUNDATION?

The first board appointed by Mr. Carnegie consisted of 25 members, 22 of whom were college presidents and 3 bankers. Among the first group were Woodrow Wilson, Charles W. Eliot, Arthur T. Hadley, Nicholas Murray Butler, David Starr Jordan, Jacob Gould Schurman, William Rainey Harper, and Henry S. Pritchett. As the years passed, the Board of Trustees continued to attract an equally distinguished group of leaders. This fact in itself was a persuasive influence.

WHY DID THE CARNEGIE FOUNDATION ORIGINALLY SPECIFY COMPLETION OF THE 4-YEAR HIGH SCHOOL AS THE COMMON BASIS FOR COLLEGE ENTRANCE?

Because it was the prevailing type of high school organization at the time. Practically all of the 10,213 public secondary schools reporting enrollments to the Office of Education in 1909–10 were of the 4-year type. In the Report for 1906, the Carnegie Foundation had adopted the definition of a college patterned after the one stated in the revised ordinances of the State of New York:

> An institution to be ranked as a college must have at least six professors giving their entire time to college and university work, a course of 4 full years in liberal arts and sciences, and should *require for admission not less*

than the usual 4 years of academic or high school preparation, or its equivalent, in addition to the pre-academic or grammar school studies.

In the Sixth Annual Report (1911) (2b), the Foundation stated: "The movement for the colleges to relate more directly to 4-year high schools and articulate with them is a mark of educational progress."

Although the Committee of Ten (1893) suggested that high schools should be 6-year institutions—grades 7–12—the recommendation was not widely accepted at the time. And the initial stage of development of the junior high school occurred after 1910. (The first junior high schools, incorporated in a 6–3–3 organization, were developed at Berkeley, Calif. and Columbus, Ohio, in 1909.) In passing, the number of secondary schools of the 4-year type increased from about 2,526 in 1890 to 6,005 in 1900 and thence to 10,213 in 1910. Thus the reason for the specification of the 4-year high school by the Carnegie Foundation appears to have been the fact that it was the customary type of secondary school organization in the first decade of this century.

DID THE CARNEGIE FOUNDATION EXPECT THAT THE UNIT
RECOMMENDED IN 1909 WOULD BE WIDELY ADOPTED BY
COLLEGES AND SECONDARY SCHOOLS?

Probably so. The Foundation had worked closely with colleges, the College Entrance Examination Board, and other professional groups; it had reason to believe that with the endorsement of these agencies and their leaders the unit of work recommended would be widely adopted. For example, in the Third Annual Report (1907) (2a) President Pritchett reported:

The time has now come when the efforts which have been made independently in various parts of the country may be crystallized into one standard which shall be national in scope. We have passed through an experimental epoch out of which we should seek principles and conclusions which shall be practical and national.

And in the Fourth Annual Report (1909) (2a), he stated:

A large percentage of the colleges and universities in all parts of the country have now stated their requirements for admission in terms of such units. The College Entrance Examination Board in April of the present year adopted the Foundation's numerical valuation of each of the subjects in which the board holds examinations. Similarly, the Association of Colleges and Preparatory Schools of the Southern States voted at its meeting (1909) in Chattanooga to adopt the unit as defined by the Foundation.

WHY DID THE CARNEGIE FOUNDATION SET THE STANDARD OF 14
TOTAL UNITS FOR A COMPLETED 4-YEAR HIGH SCHOOL COURSE?

It based this minimum standard on accepted practice in high schools recognized for their preparation of college-bound students.

In the Second Annual Report (1907) (2a):
The better high schools require pupils to recite on the average 4 studies daily 5 times a week. Assuming a study pursued for 1 year with recitations 5 times weekly as a unit, the ordinary high school would furnish in 4 years 16 such units. . . . Taking into consideration the need for reviews, for possibility of changes of study and other conditions likely to arise, 14 such units seem a fair measure of the work of the high school, and this is the standard which the board of trustees of this Foundation has adopted in its definition of a college. If a college requires 14 units for admission, it is maintaining the proper distinction between the work of the college and the work of the high school.

The element of time is not the sole criterion of the value of the unit. Each subject is valued at a certain specific number of units if the proper time has been devoted to its preparation, but its value cannot rise above that number of units no matter how much time the student has given to it. For example, no amount of time spent on plane geometry in excess of 1 year will give to that subject a higher standard than one unit.

The principle of measurement rested upon the fact that during each of 4 years in high school a student could pursue steadily 3 or 4 years' studies at one time, and would accumulate on the average 14 such units during a 4-year course. The chief advantage of using 14 units at the time lay in the fact that after their acceptance by the various colleges, they formed a common means of estimating the high school curriculum. It was a common measure for comparing work done in one high school with the work done in another.

Influences and Criticisms

DID THE CARNEGIE FOUNDATION RECOGNIZE THE RESPONSIBILITY OF
THE COLLEGE TO STRENGTHEN THE HIGH SCHOOL?

The Foundation early called the attention of colleges to their rightful responsibility toward the high schools but chiefly with reference to fitting youth for college.

A section of the Fifth Annual Report (1910) (2b) is given to a consideration of this matter:

. . . the college has an enormous influence upon the development of the secondary school and may contribute markedly to its improvement by wise action . . . the hope for the college for the future lies in this improvement.

In no other country of the world do the higher institutions of learning expend such prodigious effort on material not yet ready for their teaching as in America.

The report goes on to say that there are three practical steps for colleges to take in strengthening secondary schools:

1. They can try to articulate better with the high schools in the State and region in which they are located. "Articulation with the secondary school system of the State is so evidently the duty of the college that it would seem unnecessary to argue it."
2. They can extend to the secondary school a larger measure of freedom. "The college must . . . accept the judgment of the secondary school as to what is best for the girl or boy to study. The real question in which a college is interested is not, What prescribed studies are taught? but rather, Is the school a place where boys learn to think?"
3. They can substitute for the present highly varied and technical admission requirements simple tests which touch the knowledge of fundamental subjects and the possession of intellectual power, and then live up to these tests. "Hitherto entrance requirements have tended to promote . . . a cramming process hurtful alike to secondary school and college. What sort of test can be devised which will try the student's general knowledge of fundamental subjects and his ability to use his mind? . . . Students entering Oxford or Cambridge undergo no such detailed examinations as are exacted of students entering Harvard, Princeton, or Columbia. Their examinations are of such a sort that they cannot be met by a few months of cramming. . . . The practical question arises in the choice of fundamental studies, and in framing an examination that will test the mastery of a subject and not the efficiency of the coaching process. If the college wishes to secure this result, it must find some test of high school performance other than mere acceptance of a certificate or the passing of detailed examinations in which a large proportion of conditions is allowed."

DID THE CARNEGIE FOUNDATION MAKE ANY EARLY PRONOUNCEMENTS REGARDING SUBJECT-MATTER CONTENT IN THE HIGH SCHOOL?

No. At the time the Carnegie Foundation proposed the Unit measure, it made no substantial comment on the content of subjects offered for college preparation. However, agreement with the subject outlines of the College Entrance Examination Board was indicated. The two great educational committee reports in the 1890's made detailed recommendations on the scope and content of these major subjects offered in secondary schools:

Latin	Modern Language	Natural History
Greek	Mathematics	History and Government
English	Science	Geography

These recommendations are contained in the Reports of the NEA Committee of Ten (1893) and the NEA Committee on College Entrance Requirements (1899).

IS IT TRUE THAT THE CARNEGIE FOUNDATION WAS MORE CONCERNED WITH HIGHER EDUCATION THAN SECONDARY SCHOOLS?

Directly, yes. Twenty-two of the 25 original trustees of the Carnegie Foundation for the Advancement of Teaching were college presidents. The endowment of the Foundation was intended to be used to provide retiring allowances for professors in colleges and universities. And on the whole the educational interest of the Foundation was first and primarily concerned with higher education. But in defining what a college was, the trustees found it necessary to define first what a high school was. Also, in discussing college-high school articulation, they frequently expressed salient points of view regarding the function and the program of the high school. Indirectly, therefore, the Foundation dealt with many aspects of secondary school development, although the primary interest to which it addressed itself was higher education. The fact that college presidents are so highly regarded by American educators gave their ideas and suggestions great weight.

HAVE THE CARNEGIE FOUNDATION'S RECOMMENDATIONS AFFECTED HIGHER EDUCATION MORE THAN SECONDARY EDUCATION?

Probably the reverse is true when one considers the educational influences of the Foundation for the period from 1906 to the present. In the early part of that period, the Foundation's impact on colleges and universities was great. But college administration has through the years been free to make alterations in admission requirements because the colleges attracted leaders who were willing and able to assert their freedom, while secondary school administration has not had so high a degree of freedom. In the four and a half decades since 1909 there has been little change in the high school's use of the Unit measure. From the high school's point of view, therefore, even today the influence upon secondary education of the Carnegie Unit is far from weak.

DID THE CARNEGIE FOUNDATION RECOGNIZE THE POTENTIALLY RESTRICTIVE INFLUENCE OF THE UNIT IT RECOMMENDED?

The evidence is that it did so on several counts. It realized that it might be accused of dictating to the colleges, of standardizing educational procedures, of imposing a standard unit on secondary education. The following excerpts from annual reports of the Carnegie Foundation indicate that the trustees recognized the danger and how they felt toward potential criticisms:

1. The question now is whether without sacrifice of elasticity we can bring into orderly communication the several parts into which our educational system is broken up. Must an endowed university like Harvard or Vanderbilt, for example, look to special fitting schools, or employ special methods to get its clientele, or can it become part of an organization making towards a common end without surrender of individuality? . . . To establish such comity, we require a simple language which will convey a few fundamental facts. The unit used by the Carnegie Foundation aims to be such a symbol as between colleges, whether State or endowed institutions, and high schools, private or public. It is not mere mechanical standardization. It involves no limitation upon the freedom of the secondary school or the college. It is simply the effort to find a "counter." . . . The only part the Foundation has had in this effort has been to express in concrete form the actual usages of the colleges themselves together with the admirable results of the College Entrance Examination Board in unifying these usages. (Third Annual Report, 1908) (2a)

2. It is clear that the use of some such unit or counter is an almost inevitable consequence of the acceptance of the 4-year high school as a basis of preparation for college. . . . In whatever way it is approached, the fact remains that the basis of the college preparation rests upon some 15 units of study which the high school can hope to furnish, and that any rigidity or mechanical standardization which ensues will arise not out of this fundamental fact, but out of the requirements of the colleges with respect to prescribed subjects for admission. (Third Annual Report, 1908) (2a)

3. The practical question, therefore, is to choose such a unit as will fairly represent the secondary school work whether the school be in one section of the country or another. Such a unit enables the colleges to compare secondary schools, but it in no way hampers either the college or the secondary school. Its use will simply express uniformly and correctly that which is now expressed under many notations, a fact which renders difficult the comparison of one secondary school with another. (Third Annual Report, 1908) (2a)

4. Such a unit being once accepted, the process of calculating in its terms college entrance requirements is natural and easy and, once more, involves no artificial restrictions upon the subjects chosen or the manner of their study. The number of units indicates clearly and at once the relation of the college to the high school, and the numerical value of each indicates its relation to the total high school scheme. (Third Annual Report, 1908) (2a)

5. Of various agencies now endeavoring . . . to coordinate, strengthen, and differentiate our educational institutions, the Carnegie Foundation is only one. It is important that such agencies should be open to frank criticism. They are capable of harm as well as good. Large sums of money may be unwisely used; excessive centralization may bring evils quite as serious as excessive dispersion.

There is no present reason to be apprehensive. . . . The funds of the Carnegie Foundation represent only about 2 per cent of the collected endowments of the colleges and universities in the United States. The only financial advantage which a college can receive is in the form of retiring allowances for its professors.

Something has been said of the standardizing value of such an agency. The word is not a happy one. There is a vast difference between standardizing and standard making. The Carnegie Foundation has not undertaken to furnish standards to the colleges—that would be standardizing. What it has done is to make clear the standards of the colleges themselves and to throw light on the deviations from the standards they themselves have set up. In the present educational confusion the danger that some subtle standardizing process will take the place of the colleges as standard makers and bring about a level of mediocrity is an extremely remote danger.

There is equally little danger of undue centralization. The Foundation has no direct coercive power. Its influence depends primarily upon rational persuasion. The trustees perceive that heretofore educational forces have been almost wholly centrifugal and individualistic. There is a distinct need at this juncture for an agency interested in organization, in coordination, in differentiation of parts, and in the definition of true standards. (Fourth Annual Report, 1909) (2a)

6. In the effort to deal with these problems (college entrance requirements), the Foundation adopted the 4-year high school as the only common basis upon which colleges were likely to unite as a means for preparing for college, and it introduced a simple method (units) of estimating the contents of the high school curriculum. . . .

The units have now served their main purpose. *They were never intended to constitute a rigid form of college admission, but merely a means of comparison.* Already the process in this matter has been so satisfactory that the general conception of college admission no longer contemplates a certain number of units, but the completion of a satisfactory 4-year high school course. (Seventh Annual Report, 1912) (2b)

7. With the actual choice or enforcement of college standards, the Carnegie Foundation has little to do. These standards are set up and administered by the college faculties. . . . The Foundation has never attempted to dictate to any college what its standards of admission ought to be. It has not hesitated, however, to call attention to the wide discrepancy which existed between standards of admission in the catalog and those enforced in practice.

The public in one way or another has come to believe that the Foundation has laid down certain arbitrary standards which it is seeking to force upon the colleges of the country. Mr. Carnegie has been sharply attacked for inventing the Carnegie Units, which with a diabolical ingenuity and clever use of money he is urging upon the universities. A committee of the NEA on normal schools at its last meeting "viewed with alarm" the efforts of the Foundation to control the educational standards of the country.

The setting up of objective standards lies wholly–or almost wholly–in the hands of school and college faculties. It is impossible to conduct schools and colleges without them. . . . As for the word "standardizers," let us drop it from our educational discussion. Uniformity sometimes makes for freedom, sometimes not. But nobody in American education is in the standardizing business, and no educational trust is seeking to control education in the United States. (Seventh Annual Report, 1912) (2b)

WAS THE CARNEGIE UNIT CRITICIZED IN THE EARLY YEARS, 1909–1914?

There was a moderate amount of adverse criticism during these years because of a feeling that the Foundation was seeking to exert control over college and high school standards. For example, President Jacob Gould Schurman of Cornell speaking before the National Association of State Universities in 1909 said:

An irresponsible, self-perpetuating board, whose business is to dispense money, necessarily tends to look at every question from the pecuniary point of view; it wants its money's worth; it demands immediate and tangible results. Will not its large powers and enormous influence . . . tend to develop in it an attitude of patronage and meddling? I make no exception of the Carnegie Foundation for the Advancement of Teaching . . . and speak with no prejudice, as I regard that endowment as the best thing any benefactor has ever done for higher education in America, and I have the honor of being one of the trustees. But I look with concern and anxiety on the influence of such corporations on the free and independent life of our institutions of learning and research.[6]

The authors have not been able to find evidence that any criticism came from representatives of secondary education during the early period.

DO MOST HIGH SCHOOLS AND COLLEGES STILL USE THE
CARNEGIE UNIT?

Data presented in Improving Transition from School to College,[7] a recent survey of college admission practices, indicate that the majority of high schools and colleges still subscribe to the provisions of the Carnegie Unit as defined in 1909 by the Carnegie Foundation for the Advancement of Teaching.

Further, they indicate that approximately 60 per cent of the colleges and 63 per cent of the high schools still use the Unit method of

[6] Report of the U.S. Commissioner of Education, 1908. Washington: U.S. Government Printing Office, 1908.
[7] Arthur E. Traxler, and Agatha Townsend, *Improving Transition From School to College*. New York: Harper and Bros., 1953, 165 pp.

evaluating pupils' work in high school. About half of the secondary schools enter no objection to a continuation of the Carnegie Unit. And about a third of the colleges report that they have actually abandoned its use.

There are geographical differences reported in the use of the Carnegie Unit. "In the East and South, 70 per cent or more of the high schools find most colleges requiring the Carnegie Unit descriptions." In the North Central and Northwest regions, half and less than half of the high schools, respectively, find that they are required by the colleges to use the Carnegie Unit method.

On the whole, there is more opposition toward the use of Carnegie Unit on the part of high schools than there is on the part of colleges. But as yet, no large proportion of high schools is pressing for some type of credit counting other than the Carnegie Unit.

Comments of a college admissions officer, quoted by Traxler and Townsend: "We prefer this method, as convenient and in wide usage but with no notion that mere accumulation of units indicates adequate preparation." And comments by a dean of students in a preparatory school for boys, "The system (Carnegie Unit), convenient to the colleges though it may be in the mass production situation, is for our purposes far less desirable than one which accepts the school's judgment as to the pupil's readiness to do work at the level required by the individual college."

WHY DO SO MANY HIGH SCHOOLS AND COLLEGES STILL USE THE
CARNEGIE UNIT?

One of the main reasons is that a satisfactory substitute has not been clearly defined and agreed on. Another is that the Carnegie Unit has been administratively convenient and therefore easy to operate. Many teachers and administrators believe that certain kinds of objective measures of achievement will eventually replace "the concept of serving time in the classroom," which is an essential feature of the Carnegie Unit. The practical problems faced in implementing this belief cannot be solved theoretically. The development of satisfactory tests and suitable norms to indicate pupil progress toward major educational objectives is by no means easy, and it cannot be assumed that such tests are likely to be accepted by parents, pupils, and community without question, even when their development is farther along than now.

Tests that measure broad abilities of individual pupils in reading speed and comprehension, language use, problem-solving, spatial relations, and so forth, have been in process of development for many years. They do not have to be developed from scratch. But the difficulty is that many of these tests have been used experimentally or as a supplement to more traditional marking policies, and they have not gained widespread acceptance as criteria for judging the effectiveness of a pupil's high school education.

Another reason is the confusion resulting from misunderstanding the function of the Carnegie Unit. It is and always has been a quantitative, not a qualitative, measure. It is entirely possible that immediate removal of the Carnegie Unit from educational practice would help very little toward establishing qualitative measures of a high school education. As a matter of fact, no school now using the Unit is prevented from developing better qualitative measures of student progress. To claim that such measures cannot be developed until the Carnegie Unit is done away with completely is not reasonable. This is not to say that the Carnegie Unit aids in the development of qualitative criteria; it does not, but there is little logic to the point of view that the Carnegie Unit is a scapegoat. It does not *prevent* qualitative measures from being developed.

Still another reason is the lack of compelling force demanding a change. In 1909 the Carnegie Foundation, by its adoption of the Unit measure, buttressed as it was by disbursements for retiring allowances to college professors, actually galvanized schools and colleges to action. Today no such force is at work. There is no special motivation offered for agreement on a substitute for the Unit and for adoption of that substitute. The regional accrediting associations have produced no consistent leadership to effect a recasting of the role of the Carnegie Unit. Individual State and regional leaders have suggested improvements and there has been considerable discussion of the problems involved, but no action programs have been launched. Therefore, progress toward a substitute involves the slowest sort of approach—that of seeking common areas of agreement regarding a substitute for the Unit on the part of colleges and secondary schools accustomed to unilateral action.

DOES THE RAPID INCREASE OF HIGH SCHOOL ENROLLMENT SINCE 1909 SEEM TO ARGUE AGAINST THE CONTINUING USE OF THE CARNEGIE UNIT?

Logically one might believe so. Actually it is doubtful if increasing enrollments alone have caused any great change in the continuing use of the Carnegie Unit by high schools. It is probable that other factors operate to outweigh the factor of enrollment growth.

The proportion of youth going to public high school (grades 7–12) has increased from about 915,000 in 1910 to over 7,500,000 in 1952, while the total population 14–17 years of age has increased from 7 million to only 8 million during the same period. In 1910 high schools reported to the Office of Education offerings in 20 major subjects or subject areas, while in 1949 they reported 52 such subjects or subject areas.

Diversification of subject offerings, like the tremendous growth and changes in enrollment, would appear to urge a reconsideration of the role of the Carnegie Unit by American high schools. To a slight extent some reexamination and reconsideration have occurred, but the Unit pattern persists strongly even in the face of marked educational change.

WHAT MEANS SUPPLEMENTARY TO THE CARNEGIE UNIT HAVE BEEN
USED BY COLLEGES IN ASSESSING CANDIDATES FOR ENTRANCE?

Traditionally there have been two: (1) entrance by examination and (2) entrance by certificate (high school diploma). In 1910 the College Entrance Examination Board conducted a study on 2,000 students who took its examinations. Findings showed that more than half of these applicants were not able to be rated as high as 50 per cent and that one fifth failed to the extent of about 1 year of high school work. Of course, through the years the College Entrance Examinations have been revised to meet new conditions. In the early days students were examined in a large number of individual subjects. Later on a new plan for reducing the number of subject fields was devised so that a candidate for college entrance might take four comprehensive examinations instead of 16 or 17 separate subject examinations. In the 1940's this plan was replaced by a combination of objective achievement and aptitude tests, which represent current practice today.

Entrance by certificate: Data prepared by the Carnegie Foundation in 1909 revealed that a large percentage of students admitted to college by certificate had failed to fulfill the requirements set forth by institutions of higher learning. Under this system the efficiency or inefficiency of the student's preparation for college is not tested with exactness, the reports of the Foundation say.

State-supported colleges and universities increasingly have supported the plan of admission by certificate of high school completion. However, they often managed to maintain certain controls by seeing to it that high schools within the State offered specified subjects in their college-preparatory curriculum. Such high schools would then be approved by the State institution of higher education or State department of education. Furthermore, candidates having subject-matter deficiencies might be admitted, but would have to make up their deficiencies after admission. Although State institutions have found it frequently necessary to admit all graduates of accredited high schools within the State, they have not generally been required to keep the students if they cannot do the college work satisfactorily. Thus a rigorous selection procedure commonly occurred during the freshman year.

Admission of students to college by examination and by certificate did not avoid use of the Carnegie Unit for subjects completed in the high school course, but these procedures were frequently used as supplementary to the Unit measure.

CURRENT COMMENT ON AND CRITICISM OF THE CARNEGIE UNIT

There is today a great deal of comment on and criticism of the Carnegie Unit, mainly by representatives of secondary education. They point out that the effect of this Unit has been to restrict and hinder the development of a functional high school program. Though complaints against the use of the Carnegie Unit have been made by educational writers and associations with increasing frequency, few of them have described the type of substitute that would work. An example of the criticism found in one textbook on secondary education declares:

There is ground for disturbance in the fact that a means for standardizing colleges (viz, the Carnegie Unit) should have come to be so significant in the organization of the curriculum in the schools below and in some ways a cramping influence on it. This cramping influence is found partly in the necessity of administering the curriculum in counters of *equal* magnitude as measured by the time expended. The hindrance involved did not become so apparent while education was thought of as merely subject matter to be learned; but school workers have grown increasingly aware of it as they have endeavored to administer instruction in terms of the needs of life and living, which we may be sure will not . . . break conveniently into units of equal magnitude. The hindrance extends also to efforts to effect a satisfactory and desirable integration of experiences, which often calls for disruption of conventional subject-matter boundaries. It is certain that the inflexible Carnegie Unit must give way to some method of measuring progress more in harmony with emerging concepts and practices.[8]

Examination of the practices based upon the Carnegie Unit reveals certain fallacies. For example, 16 Units earned at a given high school are generally looked upon as representing much the same scholastic achievements as those earned at another high school. It is obvious that the level of achievement represented by diplomas earned in different

[8] L. V. Koos, J. M. Hughes, P. W. Hutson, and W. C. Reavis, *Administering the Secondary School*. New York: American Book Company, 1940, p. 23.

schools or by different students in the same school on a quantitative basis cannot be qualitatively comparable.

Increasingly the diploma means only that a pupil has attended high school for 4 years, and that classes have met a certain number of minutes per day, periods per week, and days per year. The course content is likely to be different, the quality of instruction depends largely on the individual teachers, and the achievements of the various pupils vary with their scholastic abilities and personal qualities. The actual work covered and the scholastic achievements represented by the same time allotments vary greatly. All this casts grave doubts upon the high school diploma and the Carnegie Units upon which it is based. Without other specific and supplementary information, neither the colleges or employers of a high school graduate can know what he has learned or what his competencies are merely by inspecting his diploma or rank in class.

The trouble with the Carnegie Unit, therefore, is that it interferes with good education. Some of the ways that it adversely affects secondary education are indicated briefly:

1. It lends prestige to those subjects acceptable to college in terms of entrance Units, and discriminates against other subjects excellent in their own right but as yet unacceptable for Unit measure.
2. It considers of equal magnitude *all* subjects for which classes meet an equal number of minutes per semester, provided outside pupil preparation is required. Five periods of English is equal to 5 periods of mathematics, etc.
3. It tends to make inflexible the daily and weekly time schedules of the school, for the Carnegie Unit nourishes the idea that a class should meet one period a day five times a week.
4. It restricts the development of a more functional curriculum based upon students' abilities, interests, and life-needs, because it has been difficult for the high school to obtain units of credit acceptable to the colleges in certain more functional subjects.
5. It measures quantitatively experiences in different subjects and in different schools and counts them as similar in outcome.
6. It ranks pupils in graduating class despite the fact that few of them ever have exactly the same program of studies and despite the fact that seldom are all the years in school counted in the ranking of the pupil.
7. It measures a high school education (and diploma) in terms of *time* served and credits earned by the pupil.

Many educational leaders are alert to the restrictive influences of the Carnegie Unit. They are aware of the difficult problems growing out of widespread use of the Unit today. They recognize that the influence of the Carnegie Unit has resulted in a devotion to *quantitative* measurement of high school work, with less attention to *qualitative* appraisal. As a consequence, the role of qualitative evaluation in assessing high school work will have to be given much more emphasis and adequate time will have to be devoted to its implementation.

Certain high schools have found and are discovering ways to circumvent in part the rigid time requirements of the Carnegie Unit and to place the educational development of pupils *above* the quantitative requirements of time serving.

REORGANIZATION
OF SECONDARY
EDUCATION

*Reports by the Committee of Nine,
the Committee on College Entrance
Requirements, and including the
Cardinal Principles of Secondary
Education*

 *It will be recalled that in 1890 at about
the time the work of the Committee of
Ten was in progress the number of
pupils in the public secondary schools
was only 203,000, representing about one of every 15 in the age
groups 14–17. Even though this number was more than twice
as many as those enrolled in 1880, it is doubtful that those who
heard the presentation of President Eliot at the convention of
the National Education Association in Saratoga had any conception of the phenomenal growth in enrollments that was to
be recorded in each of the six decades ahead. Only two decades
later, in 1910, the secondary enrollment had more than quad-
rupled. More than 900,000 boys and girls were in the secondary
schools, and the proportion of the age group in the high schools
had gone from one of every 15 to better than one of seven.*

*The Committee of Nine on the Articulation of High School
and College, a committee of the Department of Secondary Education of the National Education Association, was appointed*

in 1910, following introduction of resolutions aimed pretty squarely at the earlier recommendations of the Committee of Ten. It was requested, by resolution, for example, that colleges "discontinue the entrance requirements of two foreign languages and recognize as electives all subjects taught well in the high school." [1] *(Italics added.)*

The Committee reported in 1911. Although its purpose was ostensibly to persuade colleges to relax some of their entrance requirements, the report was threaded with references to broader purposes. Education for citizenship, for vocation, the call for more flexibility of program, an enriched curriculum, attention to the needs of those who did not expect to continue their education beyond the high school, were concerns that ran through the report, as the following section, Some Preliminary Considerations on the Field and Function of Education in the High School,[2] reveals:

1. Dr. Henry S. Pritchett, in his Annual Report as president of the Carnegie Foundation, finds that American education, from elementary school to college, is suffering from the attempt to teach too many subjects to the same student at the same time. He believes that students taking the newer subjects should not be required to carry all the older subjects. He states emphatically that this is no argument against the enriched curriculum of the high school; but that, on the contrary, the high school must go on still further enriching its curriculum, and that it is the duty of the college to adjust itself to the high school thus broadened.

2. It is the duty of the tax-supported high school to give every student instruction carefully designed to return to society intelligent, able-bodied, and progressive citizens. To this end certain work should be included in the course of every student, whether or not he contemplates entering a higher institution. The responsibility of the high school in this matter cannot be delegated to the college because there is no guarantee that the particular student will actually go to college.

3. It is coming to be recognized that in a democratic society the high school has a distinct function. The high school period is the testing time, the time for trying out different powers, the time for forming life purposes. Consequently, the opportunity should be provided for the student to test his capacity in a fairly large number of relatively diverse kinds of work.

In the high school the boy or girl may very properly make a start along the line of his chosen vocation, but a final choice should not be forced upon him at the beginning of that career. If he makes a provisional choice early in the course, there should be ample opportunity for readjustment later in the high school. For this reason the requirement of four years of work in any

1 *Addresses and Proceedings*, National Educational Association, July 11, 1911, p. 559.
2 *Ibid.* p. 560.

particular subject, as a condition of admission to a higher institution, unless that subject be one that may properly be required of all high-school students, is illogical and should, in the judgment of this committee, be immediately discontinued.

4. Not only is it the duty of the high school to lay the foundations of good citizenship and to help in the wise choice of a vocation, but it is equally important that the high school should make specific contribution to the efficiency of the individual along various broad lines. In our industrial democracy the development of individual aptitudes and unique gifts is quite as important as the development of the common elements of culture. Moreover, hard work is to be secured not by insistence upon uniformity of tastes and interests, but by the encouragement of special effort along lines that appeal to the individual. Our education would gain in power and in virility if we made more of the dominant interest that each boy and girl has at the time. It would seem that some have come to believe the oft-repeated statement that the liberal should precede the vocational; but an organic conception of education demands the early introduction of training for individual usefulness, thereby blending the liberal and the vocational; for only then does the liberal receive its social significance and importance. In other words, the boy who pursues both the liberal and the vocational sees the relation of his own work to the work of others and to the welfare of society; whereas the liberal without the vocational leaves him a mere spectator in the theater of life, and the boxes in this theater are already overcrowded.

5. Mechanic arts, agriculture, or household science should be recognized as rational elements in the education of all boys and girls, and especially of those who have not as yet chosen their vocation. Under the authority of the traditional conception of the best preparation for a higher institution, many of our public high schools are today responsible for leading tens of thousands of boys and girls away from the pursuits for which they are adapted and in which they are needed, to other pursuits for which they are not adapted and in which they are not needed. By means of exclusively bookish curricula false ideals of culture are developed. A chasm is created between the producers of material wealth and the distributors and consumers thereof.

The high school should in a real sense reflect the major industries of the community which supports it. The high school, as the local educational institution, should reveal to boys and girls the higher possibilities for more efficient service along the lines in which their own community is industrially organized.

Our traditional ideals of preparation for higher institutions are particularly incongruous with the actual needs and future responsibilities of girls. It would seem that such high school work as is carefully designed to develop capacity for and interest in the proper management and conduct of a home should be regarded as of importance at least equal to that of any other work. We do not understand how society can properly continue to sanction for girls high school curricula that disregard this fundamental need, even though such curricula are planned in response to the demand made by some of the colleges for women.

The Committee of Nine included high school principals from Brooklyn, St. Louis, East Orange, N.J., Philadelphia, and Denver; a superintendent of schools from Cincinnati; a professor of education of the University of Chicago; the dean of faculties of the University of California at Berkeley; and the deputy commissioner of education of Massachusetts.

At the same 1911 convention the Committee on College-Entrance Requirements made a progress report. This, too, reflected a restlessness on the part of the secondary schools and efforts to break the mold of subject requirements established earlier by the colleges and reflected in the Report of the Committee of Ten. The high schools were beginning to see the need for a broader definition of mission. The Committee reported:

> It has been our aim to make our plea general for the granting to preparatory schools greater freedom in planning their courses of study to fit local needs, and to develop interests, tastes, and abilities of their students whom they serve.[3]

It may be that the Committee of Nine was made up of unusually perceptive men, or maybe the Committee caught the spirit of change that was abroad in America and articulated it in such a way that those in the schools saw how it applied to their work. It was probably some of both. Whatever the reason, the seeds sown in the Committee statement came to fruit in another report issued in 1918, a report that was one of the landmarks in secondary education.

In this year the Commission on the Reorganization of Secondary Education brought forth "The Cardinal Principles of Secondary Education"; and with its issuance and dissemination thinking about the secondary schools, the boys and girls they were to serve and the mission of the school was changed in a fundamental way. The key word in the 1918 report was reorganization, and the emphasis was on ends to be reached, on purposes and goals.

With the publication of The Cardinal Principles a new way of looking at the secondary schools was opened, and a fresh vision of its possibilities was revealed.

Although the work of the Commission on the Reorganization of Secondary Education is usually associated with the 1918 report, its activities began in 1913. Through 16 committees, the commission sponsored studies of various topics and subject fields: the organization and administration of secondary education, the articulation of high school and college, vocational guidance, agriculture, art, business education,

[3] *Ibid.,* p. 729.

classical languages, English, household arts, industrial arts, mathematics, modern languages, music, physical education, sciences, and social studies.

Separate reports were completed by the Commission between 1913 and 1918 and were issued as bulletins of the U.S. Bureau of Education. These became The Reorganization of Secondary Education, *containing: preliminary statements by the chairmen of the various committees, 1913; "The Teaching of Community Civics," 1915; "The Social Studies in Secondary Education," 1915; "Reorganization of English in Secondary Schools," 1917; "Physical Education in Secondary Schools," 1917; "Vocational Guidance in Secondary Schools," 1918.*

A shift in the type of membership first noted in the Committee of Nine was evident in the Commission on Reorganization of Secondary Education. The Commission was composed of 26 members, 16 of whom were chairmen of the various committees and ten of whom were members at large. The general chairman was the state high school supervisor of Massachusetts, who had also chaired the Committee of Nine. The development of secondary education as a field of university study was reflected in the membership, which included such names as Thomas A. Briggs, of Teachers College, Columbia University; Alexander Inglis of Harvard; Joseph S. Stewart of the University of Georgia; Charles Hughes Johnston of the University of Illinois; Otis Caldwell, director of Lincoln School and professor at Teachers College. The United States Commissioner of Education was a member, along with two specialists from his staff. High school principals, state supervisors, extension specialists from the land-grant institutions, subject teachers from the secondary schools were also on the commission.

The 26 members of the Commission served as a reviewing committee for the separate reports referred to above. As this work went along, the reviewing committees decided that ". . . in addition to its task of criticizing reports, it seemed desirable that the reviewing committee itself should outline in a single brief report those fundamental principles that would be most helpful in directing secondary education."

The work of preparing such a report was begun in 1915 and was concluded three years later with the publication of the Cardinal Principles.

The report of the Commission took into account the changes required in the secondary schools by virtue of the increasing numbers enrolled. But this single fact did not stand alone as justification for reorganization. The schools were facing the fact that education did not have holding power. The Commission reported that only one third of the pupils who entered the first year of elementary school reached

*the four-year high school, a third left before the second year began.
Half left before the beginning of the third year. Fewer than one third
were graduated.*

*The old curriculum was failing the new numbers. New insights had
been gained from psychology, the Commission asserted. Fuller attention must be given to individual differences in capacities and attitudes.
The old conception of "general values," such as mental discipline,
needed to be reassessed and revised, and this in turn required reexamination and reinterpretation of subject values and teaching methods.
Knowledge must be relevant to the learner and applicable to the activities of life, rather than considering the demands of any subject primarily as logically organized science.*

*Education in America was education in and for democracy, and this
required a nice balance. "It is the ideal of democracy that the individual and society may find fulfillment in each other. Democracy sanctions
neither the exploitation of the individual by society, nor the disregard
of the interests of society by the individual."* [4] *The Commission then
proceeded to analyze the activities of the individual. On this analysis
and within the boundaries of a democratic society, the Commission set
down the main objectives of secondary education. The report in its
entirety follows. Even though educational thought in the years following has ebbed and flowed, the basic issues explored in the report of the
Commission on the Reorganization of Secondary Education have a
meaning and timeliness that transcend their era.*

CARDINAL PRINCIPLES OF
SECONDARY EDUCATION

I. The Need for Reorganization

Secondary education should be determined by the needs of the society
to be served, the character of the individuals to be educated, and the
knowledge of educational theory and practice available. These factors
are by no means static. Society is always in process of development; the
character of the secondary school population undergoes modification;
and the sciences on which educational theory and practice depend
constantly furnish new information. Secondary education, however,
like any other established agency of society, is conservative and tends to
resist modification. Failure to make adjustments when the need arises

[4] *Cardinal Principles of Secondary Education,* Bureau of Education Bulletin, No.
35. Washington, D.C.: Department of the Interior, 1918, p. 9.

leads to the necessity for extensive reorganization at irregular intervals. The evidence is strong that such a comprehensive reorganization of secondary education is imperative at the present time.

1. CHANGES IN SOCIETY

Within the past few decades changes have taken place in American life profoundly affecting the activities of the individual. As a citizen, he must to a greater extent and in a more direct way cope with problems of community life, State and National Governments, and international relationships. As a worker, he must adjust himself to a more complex economic order. As a relatively independent personality, he has more leisure. The problems arising from these three dominant phases of life are closely interrelated and call for a degree of intelligence and efficiency on the part of every citizen that can not be secured through elementary education alone, or even through secondary education unless the scope of that education is broadened.

The responsibility of the secondary school is still further increased because many social agencies other than the school afford less stimulus for education than heretofore. In many vocations there have come such significant changes in the substitution of the factory system for the domestic system of industry; the use of machinery in place of manual labor; the high specialization of processes with a corresponding subdivision of labor; and the breakdown of the apprentice system. In connection with home and family life have frequently come lessened responsibility on the part of the children; the withdrawal of the father and sometimes the mother from home occupations to the factory or store; and increased urbanization, resulting in less unified family life. Similarly, many important changes have taken place in community life, in the church, in the State, and in other institutions. These changes in American life call for extensive modifications in secondary education.

2. CHANGES IN THE SECONDARY SCHOOL POPULATION

In the past 25 years there have been marked changes in the secondary school population of the United States. The number of pupils has increased, according to Federal returns, from one for every 210 of the total population in 1889–90, to one for every 121 in 1899–1900, to one for every 89 in 1909–10, and to one for every 73 of the estimated total population in 1914–15. The character of the secondary school population has been modified by the entrance of large numbers of pupils of widely varying capacities, aptitudes, social heredity, and destinies in life. Further, the broadening of the scope of secondary education has brought to the school many pupils who do not complete the full course but leave at various stages of advancement. The needs of these pupils cannot be neglected, nor can we expect in the near future that all pupils will be able to complete the secondary school as full-time students.

At present only about one third of the pupils who enter the first year of the elementary school reach the four-year high school, and only about one in nine is graduated. Of those who enter the seventh school year, only one half to two thirds reach the first year of the four-year high school. Of those who enter the four-year high school about one third leave before the beginning of the second year, about one half are gone before the beginning of the third year, and fewer than one third are graduated. These facts can no longer be safely ignored.

3. CHANGES IN EDUCATIONAL THEORY

The sciences on which educational theory depends have within recent years made significant contributions. In particular, educational psychology emphasizes the following factors:

Individual differences in capacities and aptitudes among secondary school pupils. Already recognized to some extent, this factor merits fuller attention.

The reexamination and reinterpretation of subject values and the teaching methods with reference to "general discipline." While the final verdict of modern psychology has not as yet been rendered, it is clear that former conceptions of general values must be thoroughly revised.

Importance of applying knowledge. Subject values and teaching methods must be tested in terms of the laws of learning and the application of knowledge to the activities of life, rather than primarily in terms of the demands of any subject as a logically organized science.

Continuity in the development of children. It has long been held that psychological changes at certain stages are so pronounced as to overshadow the continuity of development. On this basis secondary education has been sharply separated from elementary education. Modern psychology, however, goes to show that the development of the individual is in most respects a continuous process and that, therefore, any sudden or abrupt break between the elementary and the secondary school or between any two successive stages of education is undesirable.

The foregoing changes in society, in the character of the secondary school population, and in educational theory, together with many other considerations, call for extensive modifications of secondary education. Such modifications have already begun in part. The present need is for the formulation of a comprehensive program of reorganization, and its adoption, with suitable adjustments, in all the secondary schools of the Nation. Hence it is appropriate for a representative body like the National Education Association to outline such a program. This is the task entrusted by that association to the Commission on the Reorganization of Secondary Education.

II. The Goal of Education in a Democracy

Education in the United States should be guided by a clear conception of the meaning of democracy. It is the ideal of democracy that the individual and society may find fulfillment each in the other. Democracy sanctions neither the exploitation of the individual by society, nor the disregard of the interests of society by the individual. More explicitly—

The purpose of democracy is so to organize society that each member may develop his personality primarily through activities designed for the well-being of his fellow members and of society as a whole.

This ideal demands that human activities be placed upon a high level of efficiency; that to this efficiency be added an appreciation of the significance of these activities and loyalty to the best ideals involved; and that the individual choose that vocation and those forms of social service in which his personality may develop and become most effective. For the achievement of these ends democracy must place chief reliance upon education.

Consequently, education in a democracy, both within and without the school, should develop in each individual the knowledge, interests, ideals, habits, and powers whereby he will find his place and use that place to shape both himself and society toward ever nobler ends.

III. The Main Objectives of Education

In order to determine the main objectives that should guide education in a democracy it is necessary to analyze the activities of the individual. Normally he is a member of a family, of a vocational group, and of various civic groups, and by virtue of these relationships he is called upon to engage in activities that enrich the family life, to render important vocational services to his fellows, and to promote the common welfare. It follows, therefore, that worthy home membership, vocation, and citizenship demand attention as three of the leading objectives.

Aside from the immediate discharge of these specific duties, every individual should have a margin of time for the cultivation of personal and social interests. This leisure, if worthily used, will recreate his powers and enlarge and enrich life, thereby making him better able to meet his responsibilities. The unworthy use of leisure impairs health, disrupts home life, lessens vocational efficiency, and destroys civic mindedness. The tendency in industrial life, aided by legislation, is to decrease the working hours of large groups of people. While shortened hours tend to lessen the harmful reactions that arise from prolonged strain, they increase, if possible, the importance of preparation for leisure. In view of these considerations, education for the worthy use of leisure is of increasing importance as an objective.

To discharge the duties of life and to benefit from leisure, one must have good health. The health of the individual is essential also to the vitality of the race and to the defense of the Nation. Health education is, therefore, fundamental.

There are various processes, such as reading, writing, arithmetical computations, and oral and written expression, that are needed as tools in the affairs of life. Consequently, command of these fundamental processes, while not an end in itself, is nevertheless an indispensable objective.

And, finally, the realization of the objectives already named is dependent upon ethical character, that is, upon conduct founded upon right principles, clearly perceived and loyally adhered to. Good citizenship, vocational excellence, and the worthy use of leisure go hand in hand with ethical character; they are at once the fruits of sterling character and the channels through which such character is developed and made manifest. On the one hand, character is meaningless apart from the will to discharge the duties of life, and, on the other hand, there is no guarantee that these duties will be rightly discharged unless principles are substituted for impulses, however well intentioned such impulses may be. Consequently ethical character is at once involved in all the other objectives and at the same time requires specific consideration in any program of national education.

This commission, therefore, regards the following as the main objectives of education: 1. Health. 2. Command of fundamental processes. 3. Worthy home membership. 4. Vocation. 5. Citizenship. 6. Worthy use of leisure. 7. Ethical character.

The naming of the above objectives is not intended to imply that the process of education can be divided into separated fields. This can not be, since the pupil is indivisible. Nor is the analysis all inclusive. Nevertheless, we believe that distinguishing and naming these objectives will aid in directing efforts; and we hold that they should constitute the principal aims in education.

IV. The Role of Secondary Education in Achieving

These Objectives

The objectives outlined above apply to education as a whole—elementary, secondary, and higher. It is the purpose of this section to consider specifically the role of secondary education in achieving each of these objectives.

For reasons stated in Section X, this Commission favors such reorganization that secondary education may be defined as applying to all pupils of approximately 12 to 18 years of age.

1. HEALTH

Health needs can not be neglected during the period of secondary education without serious danger to the individual and the race. The secondary school should therefore provide health instruction, inculcate health habits, organize an effective program of physical activities, regard health needs in planning work and play, and cooperate with home and community in safeguarding and promoting health interests.

To carry out such a program it is necessary to arouse the public to recognize that the health needs of young people are of vital importance to society, to secure teachers competent to ascertain and meet the needs of individual pupils and able to inculcate in the entire student body a love for clean sport, to furnish adequate equipment for physical activities, and to make the school building, its rooms and surroundings, conform to the best standards of hygiene and sanitation.[5]

2. COMMAND OF FUNDAMENTAL PROCESSES

Much of the energy of the elementary school is properly devoted to teaching certain fundamental processes, such as reading, writing, arithmetical computations, and the elements of oral and written expression. The facility that a child of 12 or 14 may acquire in the use of these tools is not sufficient for the needs of modern life. This is particularly true of the mother tongue. Proficiency in many of these processes may be increased more effectively by their application to new material than by the formal reviews commonly employed in grades seven and eight. Throughout the secondary school, instruction and practice must go hand in hand, but as indicated in the report of the

[5] For the outlines of a health program, see a report of this Commission issued by the Bureau of Education as Bulletin, 1917, No. 50, "Physical Education in Secondary Schools."

Committee on English,[6] only so much theory should be taught at any one time as will show results in practice.

3. WORTHY HOME MEMBERSHIP

Worthy home membership as an objective calls for the development of those qualities that make the individual a worthy member of a family, both contributing to and deriving benefit from that membership.

This objective applies to both boys and girls. The social studies should deal with the home as a fundamental social institution and clarify its relation to the wider interests outside. Literature should interpret and idealize the human elements that go to make the home. Music and art should result in more beautiful homes and in greater joy therein. The coeducational school with a faculty of men and women should, in its organization and its activities, exemplify wholesome relations between boys and girls and men and women.

Home membership as an objective should not be thought of solely with reference to future duties. These are the better guaranteed if the school helps the pupils to take the right attitude toward present home responsibilities and interprets to them the contribution of the home to their development.

In the education of every high school girl, the household arts should have a prominent place because of their importance to the girl herself and to others whose welfare will be directly in her keeping. The attention now devoted to this phase of education is inadequate, and especially so for girls preparing for occupations not related to the household arts and for girls planning for higher institutions. The majority of girls who enter wage-earning occupations directly from the high school remain in them for only a few years, after which home making becomes their lifelong occupation. For them the high school period offers the only assured opportunity to prepare for that lifelong occupation, and it is during this period that they are most likely to form their ideals of life's duties and responsibilities. For girls planning to enter higher institutions—

our traditional ideals of preparation for higher institutions are particularly incongruous with the actual needs and future responsibilities of girls. It would seem that such high school work as is carefully designed to develop capacity for, and interest in, the proper management and conduct of· a home should be regarded as of importance at least equal to that of any other work. We do not understand how society can properly continue to sanction for girls

6 Bureau of Education, Bulletin, 1917, No. 2, "Reorganization of English in Secondary Schools."

high school curriculums that disregard this fundamental need, even though such curriculums are planned in response to the demands made by some of the colleges for women.[7]

In the education of boys, some opportunity should be found to give them a basis for the intelligent appreciation of the value of the well-appointed home and of the labor and skill required to maintain such a home, to the end that they may cooperate more effectively. For instance, they should understand the essentials of food values, of sanitation, and of household budgets.

4. VOCATION

Vocational education should equip the individual to secure a livelihood for himself and those dependent on him, to serve society well through his vocation, to maintain the right relationships toward his fellow workers and society, and, as far as possible, to find in that vocation his own best development.

This ideal demands that the pupil explore his own capacities and aptitudes, and make a survey of the world's work, to the end that he may select his vocation wisely. Hence, an effective program of vocational guidance in the secondary school is essential.[8]

Vocational education should aim to develop an appreciation of the significance of the vocation to the community, and a clear conception of right relations between the members of the chosen vocation, between different vocational groups, between employer and employee, and between producer and consumer. These aspects of vocational education, heretofore neglected, demand emphatic attention.

The extent to which the secondary school should offer training for a specific vocation depends upon the vocation, the facilities that the school can acquire, and the opportunity that the pupil may have to obtain such training later. To obtain satisfactory results those proficient in that vocation should be employed as instructors and the actual conditions of the vocation should be utilized either within the high school or in cooperation with the home, farm, shop, or office. Much of the pupil's time will be required to produce such efficiency.

5. CIVIC EDUCATION

Civic education should develop in the individual those qualities whereby he will act well his part as a member of neighborhood, town

[7] Report of the Committee on the Articulation of High School and College, 1911.

[8] For a comprehensive program of vocational guidance see a report of this Commission issued as Bureau of Education Bulletin, 1918, No. 19, "Vocational Guidance in Secondary Schools."

or city, State, and Nation, and give him a basis for understanding international problems.

For such citizenship the following are essential: A many sided interest in the welfare of the communities to which one belongs; loyalty to ideals of civic righteousness; practical knowledge of social agencies and institutions; good judgment as to means and methods that will promote one social end without defeating others; and as putting all these into effect, habits of cordial cooperation in social undertakings.

The school should develop the concept that the civic duties of men and women, while in part identical, are also in part supplementary. Differentiation in civic activities is to be encouraged, but not to the extent of loss of interest in the common problems with which all should cope.

Among the means for developing attitudes and habits important in a democracy are the assignment of projects and problems to groups of pupils for cooperative solution and the socialized recitation whereby the class as a whole develops a sense of collective responsibility. Both of these devices give training in collective thinking. Moreover, the democratic organization and administration of the school itself, as well as the cooperative relations of pupil and teacher, pupil and pupil, and teacher and teacher, are indispensable.

While all subjects should contribute to good citizenship, the social studies—geography, history, civics, and economics—should have this as their dominant aim. Too frequently, however, does mere information, conventional in value and remote in its bearing, make up the content of the social studies. History should so treat the growth of institutions that their present value may be appreciated. Geography should show the interdependence of men while it shows their common dependence on nature. Civics should concern itself less with constitutional questions and remote governmental functions, and should direct attention to social agencies close at hand and to the informal activities of daily life that regard and seek the common good. Such agencies as child welfare organizations and consumers' leagues afford specific opportunities for the expression of civic qualities by the older pupils.

The work in English should kindle social ideals and give insight into social conditions and into personal character as related to these conditions. Hence the emphasis by the committee on English on the importance of a knowledge of social activities, social movements, and social needs on the part of the teacher of English.

The comprehension of the ideals of American democracy and loyalty to them should be a prominent aim of civic education. The pupil should feel that he will be responsible, in cooperation with others, for keeping the Nation true to the best inherited conceptions of democracy, and he should also realize that democracy itself is an ideal to be wrought out by his own and succeeding generations.

Civic education should consider other nations also. As a people we should try to understand their aspirations and ideals that we may deal more sympathetically and intelligently with the immigrant coming to our shores, and have a basis for a wiser and more sympathetic approach to international problems. Our pupils should learn that each nation, at least potentially, has something of worth to contribute to civilization and that humanity would be incomplete without that contribution. This means a study of specific nations, their achievements and possibilities, not ignoring their limitations. Such a study of dissimilar contributions in the light of the ideal of human brotherhood should help to establish a genuine internationalism, free from sentimentality, founded on fact, and actually operative in the affairs of nations.[9]

6. WORTHY USE OF LEISURE

Education should equip the individual to secure from his leisure the re-creation of body, mind, and spirit, and the enrichment and enlargement of his personality.

This objective calls for the ability to utilize the common means of enjoyment, such as music, art, literature, drama, and social intercourse, together with the fostering in each individual of one or more special avocational interests.

Heretofore the high school has given little conscious attention to this objective. It has so exclusively sought intellectual discipline that it has seldom treated literature, art, and music so as to evoke right emotional response and produce positive enjoyment. Its presentation of science should aim, in part, to arouse a genuine appreciation of nature.

The school has failed also to organize and direct the social activities of young people as it should. One of the surest ways in which to prepare pupils worthily to utilize leisure in adult life is by guiding and directing their use of leisure in youth. The school should, therefore, see that adequate recreation is provided both within the school and by other proper agencies in the community. The school, however, has a unique opportunity in this field because it includes in its membership

[9] For a further discussion of civic education, see the reports of this commission on "The Teaching of Community Civics" and "Social Studies in Secondary Education," issued as Bureau of Education Bulletins, 1915, No. 23, and 1916, No. 28, respectively.

representatives from all classes of society and consequently is able through social relationships to establish bonds of friendship and common understanding that can not be furnished by other agencies. Moreover, the school can so organize recreational activities that they will contribute simultaneously to other ends of education, as in the case of the school pageant or festival.

7. ETHICAL CHARACTER

In a democratic society ethical character becomes paramount among the objectives of the secondary school. Among the means for developing ethical character may be mentioned the wise selection of content and methods of instruction in all subjects of study, the social contacts of pupils with one another and with their teachers, the opportunities afforded by the organization and administration of the school for the development on the part of pupils of the sense of personal responsibility and initiative, and, above all, the spirit of service and the principles of true democracy which should permeate the entire school—principal, teachers, and pupils.

Specific consideration is given to the moral values to be obtained from the organization of the school and the subjects of study in the report of this Commission entitled, Moral Values in Secondary Education.[10] That report considers also the conditions under which it may be advisable to supplement the other activities of the school by offering a distinct course in moral instruction.

V. Interrelation of the Objectives in

Secondary Education

This Commission holds that education is essentially a unitary and continuous process, and that each of the objectives defined above must be recognized throughout the entire extent of secondary education. Health needs are evidently important at all stages; the vocational purpose and content is coming properly to be recognized as a necessary and valuable ingredient even in the early stages and even when specific preparation is postponed; citizenship and the worthy use of leisure, obviously important in the earlier stages, involve certain phases of education that require maturity on the part of the pupil and hence are indispensable also in the later stages of secondary education.

Furthermore, it is only as the pupil sees his vocation in relation to his citizenship and his citizenship in the light of his vocation that he will be prepared for effective membership in an industrial democracy. Consequently, this commission enters its protest against any and all

---

[10] Bureau of Education Bulletin, 1917, No. 51.

plans, however well intended, which are in danger of divorcing vocation and social-civic education. It stands squarely for the infusion of
vocation with the spirit of service and for the vitalization of culture by
genuine contact with the world's work.

VI. Recognition of the Objectives in

Reorganizing High School Subjects

Each subject now taught in high schools is in need of extensive
reorganization in order that it may contribute more effectively to the
objectives outlined herein, and the place of that subject in secondary
education should depend upon the value of such contribution. In
Section IV of this report various references have been made to needed
changes. For fuller treatment the reader is referred to reports of this
Commission dealing with the several subjects. These reports indicate
important steps in such modifications. In each report the Commission
attempts to analyze the aims in terms of the objectives; to indicate
the adaptation of methods of presentation to the aims accepted; and
to suggest a selection of content on the basis of aims and methods.

VII. Education as a Process of Growth

Education must be conceived as a process of growth. Only when so
conceived and so conducted can it become a preparation for life. In so
far as this principle has been ignored, formalism and sterility have
resulted.

For example, civic education too often has begun with topics remote
from the pupil's experience and interest. Reacting against this formalism, some would have pupils study only those activities in which they
can engage while young. This extreme, however, is neither necessary
nor desirable. Pupils should be led to respond to present duties and,
at the same time, their interest should be aroused in problems of adult
life. With this interest as a basis, they should be helped to acquire the
habits, insight, and ideals that will enable them to meet the duties and
responsibilities of later life. Similarly in home-making education, to
neglect present duties and responsibilities toward the family of which
the pupil is now a member, is to court moral insincerity and jeopardize
future right conduct. With present duties as a point of departure, home-
making education should arouse an interest in future home-making
activities and with that interest as a basis give the training necessary.

VIII. Need for Explicit Values

The number of years that pupils continue in school beyond the
compulsory school age depends in large measure upon the degree to
which they and their parents realize that school work is worthwhile

for them and that they are succeeding in it. Probably in most communities doubt regarding the value of the work offered causes more pupils to leave school than economic necessity. Consequently, it is important that the work of each pupil should be so presented as to convince him and his parents of its real value.

IX. Subordination of Deferred Values

Many subjects are now so organized as to be of little value unless the pupil studies them for several years. Since a large proportion of pupils leave school in each of the successive years, each subject should be so organized that the first year of work will be of definite value to those who go no further; and this principle should be applied to the work of each year. Courses planned in accordance with this principle will deal with the simpler aspects, or those of more direct application, in the earlier years and will defer the refinements for later years when these can be better appreciated. The course as a whole will then be better adapted to the needs both of those who continue and of those who drop out of school.

X. Division of Education Into Elementary

and Secondary

Individual differences in pupils and the varied needs of society alike demand that education be so varied as to touch the leading aspects of occupational, civic, and leisure life. To this end curriculums [11] must be organized at appropriate stages and the work of pupils progressively differentiated.

To accomplish this differentiation most wisely the pupil should be assisted ordinarily at about 12 or 13 years of age to begin a preliminary survey of the activities of adult life and of his own aptitudes in connection therewith, so that he may choose, at least tentatively, some field of human endeavor for special consideration. Following the period of preliminary survey and provisional choice, he should acquire a more intimate knowledge of the field chosen, including therewith an appreciation of its social significance. Those whose schooling ends here should attain some mastery of the technique involved. The field chosen will be for some as sharply defined as a specific

---

[11] The term "curriculum" is used by this Commission to designate a systematic arrangement of subjects, and courses in those subjects, both required and elective, extending through two or more years and designed for a group of pupils whose common aims and probable careers may properly differentiate a considerable part of their work from that of other groups in the school.

trade; for others, it will be but the preliminary choice of a wider domain within which a narrower choice will later be made.

These considerations, reenforced by others, imply, in the judgment of this Commission, a redivision of the period devoted to elementary and secondary education. The eight years heretofore given to elementary education have not, as a rule, been effectively utilized. The last two of these years in particular have not been well adapted to the needs of the adolescent. Many pupils lose interest and either drop out of school altogether or form habits of dawdling, to the serious injury of subsequent work. We believe that much of the difficulty will be removed by a new type of secondary education beginning at about 12 or 13. Furthermore, the period of four years now allotted to the high school is too short a time in which to accomplish the work above outlined.

We, therefore, recommend a reorganization of the school system whereby the first six years shall be devoted to elementary education designed to meet the needs of pupils of approximately 6 to 12 years of age; and the second six years to secondary education designed to meet the needs of pupils of approximately 12 to 18 years of age.

XI. Division of Secondary Education Into Junior

and Senior Periods

The six years to be devoted to secondary education may well be divided into two periods which may be designated as the junior and senior periods. In the junior period emphasis should be placed upon the attempt to help the pupil to explore his own aptitudes and to make at least provisional choice of the kinds of work to which he will devote himself. In the senior period emphasis should be given to training in the fields thus chosen. This distinction lies at the basis of the organization of junior and senior high schools.

In the junior high school there should be the gradual introduction of departmental instruction, some choice of subjects under guidance, promotion by subjects, prevocational courses, and a social organization that calls forth initiative and develops the sense of personal responsibility for the welfare of the group.

In the senior high school a definite curriculum organization should be provided by means of which each pupil may take work systematically planned with reference to his needs as an individual and as a member of society. The senior high school should be characterized by a rapidly developing social consciousness and by an attitude of self-reliance based upon clearly perceived objectives.

Under ordinary circumstances the junior and senior periods should each be three years in length so as to realize their distinctive purposes. In sparsely settled communities where a senior high school can not be maintained effectively, the junior high school may well be four years in length, so that the pupils may attend school nearer to their homes for one more year.

The Commission is not unmindful of the desirability, when funds permit, of extending secondary education under local auspices so as to include the first two years of work usually offered in colleges, and constituting what is known as the "junior college," but it has seemed unwise for the Commission to attempt to outline the work of this new unit.

XII. Articulation of Secondary Education With

Elementary Education

Admission to high school is now, as a rule, based upon the completion of a prescribed amount of academic work. As a result many over-age pupils either leave school altogether or are retained in the elementary school when they are no longer deriving much benefit from its instruction. Should a similar conception of the articulation of the two schools continue after the elementary program has been shortened to six years, similar bad results will persist. Experience in certain school systems, however, shows that the secondary school can provide special instruction for over-age pupils more successfully than the elementary school can. Consequently we recommend that secondary schools admit, and provide suitable instruction for, all pupils who are in any respect so mature that they would derive more benefit from the secondary school than from the elementary school.

XIII. Articulation of Higher Education With

Secondary Education

In view of the important role of secondary education in achieving the objectives essential in American life, it follows that higher institutions of learning are not justified in maintaining entrance requirements and examinations of a character that handicap the secondary school in discharging its proper functions in a democracy.

As stated in Section XII of this report, the secondary school should admit all pupils who would derive greater benefit from the secondary than from the elementary school. With the demand of democratic society for extended liberal and vocational education for an ever increasing number of persons, the higher institutions of learning, taken as a whole, are under a similar obligation with reference to those whose needs are no longer met by the secondary school and are disposed to continue their education. The conception that higher education should be limited to the few is destined to disappear in the interests of democracy.

The tradition that a particular type of education, and that exclusively nonvocational in character, is the only acceptable preparation for advanced education, either liberal or vocational, must therefore give way to a scientific evaluation of all types of secondary education as preparation for continued study. This broader conception need not involve any curtailment of opportunities for those who early manifest academic interest to pursue the work adapted to their needs. It does, however, mean that pupils who, during the secondary period, devote a considerable time to courses having vocational content should be permitted to pursue whatever form of higher education, either liberal or vocational, they are able to undertake with profit to themselves and to society.

XIV. Recognition of the Objectives in Planning Curriculums

No curriculum in the secondary school can be regarded as satisfactory unless it gives due attention to each of the objectives of education outlined herein.

Health, as an objective, makes imperative an adequate time assignment for physical training and requires science courses properly focused upon personal and community hygiene, the principles of sanitation, and their applications. Command of fundamental processes necessitates thorough courses in the English language as a means of taking in and giving forth ideas. Worthy home membership calls for the redirection of much of the work in literature, art, and the social studies. For girls it necessitates adequate courses in household arts. Citizenship demands that the social studies be given a prominent place. Vocation as an objective requires that many pupils devote much of their time to specific preparation for a definite trade or occupation, and that some pursue studies that serve as a basis for advanced work in higher institutions. The worthy use of leisure calls for courses in literature, art, music, and science so taught as to develop appreciation. It necessitates also a margin of free electives to be chosen on the basis of personal avocational interests.

Due recognition of these objectives will provide the elements of distribution and concentration which are recognized as essential for a well-balanced and effective education.

XV. The Specializing and Unifying Functions of Secondary Education

1. THEIR SIGNIFICANCE

The ideal of a democracy, as set forth in Section II of this report, involves, on the one hand, specialization whereby individuals and groups of individuals may become effective in the various vocations and other fields of human endeavor, and, on the other hand, unification whereby the members of that democracy may obtain those common ideas, common ideals, and common modes of thought, feeling, and action that make for cooperation, social cohesion, and social solidarity.

Without effective specialization on the part of groups of individuals there can be no progress. Without unification in a democracy there can be no worthy community life and no concerted action for necessary social ends. Increasing specialization emphasizes the need for unification, without which a democracy is a prey to enemies at home and abroad.

2. THE SPECIALIZING FUNCTION

Secondary education in the past has met the needs of only a few groups. The growing recognition that progress in our American democracy depends in no small measure upon adequate provision for specialization in many fields is the chief cause leading to the present reorganization of secondary education. Only through attention to the needs of various groups of individuals as shown by aptitudes, abilities, and aspirations can the secondary school secure from each pupil his best efforts. The school must capitalize the dominant interest that each boy and girl has at the time and direct that interest as wisely as possible. This is the surest method by which hard and effective work may be obtained from each pupil.

Specialization demands the following provisions in secondary education:

A wide range of subjects. In order to test and develop the many important capacities and interests found in pupils of secondary school age, the school should provide as wide a range of subjects as it can offer effectively.

Exploration and guidance. Especially in the junior high school the pupil should have a variety of experience and contacts in order that he may explore his own capacities and aptitudes. Through a system of educational supervision or guidance he should be helped to determine his education and his vocation. These decisions should not be imposed upon him by others.

Adaptation of content and methods. The content and teaching methods of every study should be adapted to the capacities, interests, and needs of the pupils concerned. In certain studies these factors may differ widely for various groups of pupils, e.g., chemistry should emphasize different phases in agricultural, commercial, industrial, and household arts curriculums.

Flexibility of organization and administration. Flexibility should be secured by "election" of studies or curriculum, promotion by subjects from the beginning of the junior high school, possible transfer from curriculum to curriculum, provision for maximum and minimum assignments for pupils of greater and less ability, and, under certain conditions, for the rapid or slow progress of such pupils.

Differentiated curriculums. The work of the senior high school should be organized into differentiated curriculums. The range of such curriculums should be as wide as the school can offer effectively. The basis of differentiation should be, in the broad sense of the term, vocational, thus justifying the names commonly given, such as agricultural, business, clerical, industrial, fine arts, and household arts curriculums. Provision should be made also for those having distinctively academic interests and needs. The conclusion that the work of the senior high school should be organized on the basis of curriculums does not imply that every study should be different in the various curriculums. Nor does it imply that every study should be determined by the dominant element of that curriculum. Indeed any such practice would ignore other objectives of education just as important as that of vocational efficiency.

3. THE UNIFYING FUNCTION

In some countries a common heredity, a strongly centralized government, and an established religion contribute to social solidarity. In America, racial stocks are widely diversified, various forms of social heredity come into conflict, differing religious beliefs do not always make for unification, and the members of different vocations often fail to recognize the interests that they have in common with others. The school is the one agency that may be controlled definitely and consciously by our democracy for the purpose of unifying its people. In this process the secondary school must play an important part because the elementary school with its immature pupils can not alone develop the common knowledge, common ideals, and common interests essential to American democracy. Furthermore, children of immigrant parents attend the secondary school in large and increasing numbers; secondary education comes at a stage in the development of boys and girls when social interests develop rapidly; and from the secondary school the majority of pupils pass directly into participation in the activities of our society.

The unifying function calls for the following provisions in secondary education:

(a) Studies of direct value for this purpose, especially the social studies and the mother tongue, with its literature.

(b) The social mingling of pupils through the organization and administration of the school.

(c) The participation of pupils in common activities in which they should have a large measure of responsibility, such as athletic games, social activities, and the government of the school.

4. SPECIALIZATION AND UNIFICATION AS SUPPLEMENTARY FUNCTIONS

With increasing specialization in any society comes a corresponding necessity for increased attention to unification. So in the secondary school, increased attention to specialization calls for more purposeful plans for unification. When there was but little differentiation in the work within the secondary school, and the pupils in attendance were less diversified as to their heredity and interests, social unification in the full sense of the term could not take place.

The supplementary character of these functions has direct bearing upon the subjects to be taken by secondary school pupils. To this end the secondary school should provide the following groups of studies:

Constants. To be taken by all or nearly all pupils. These should be determined mainly by the objectives of health, command of fundamental processes, worthy home membership, citizenship, and ethical character.

Curriculum variables. Peculiar to a curriculum or to a group of related curriculums. These should be determined for the most part by vocational needs, including, as they frequently do, preparation for advanced study in special fields.

Free electives. To be taken by pupils in accordance with individual aptitudes or special interests, generally of a nonvocational nature. These are significant, especially in preparation for the worthy use of leisure.

The constants should contribute definitely to unification, the curriculum variables to specialization, and the free electives to either or both of these functions.

In the seventh year, that is the first year of the junior high school, the pupil should not be required to choose at the outset the field to which he will devote himself. For those who do not at this time have a definite purpose, opportunity should be given to gain some experience with several significant types of work, such as some form of industrial arts, gardening or other agricultural activity, typewriting or problems drawn from business, household arts for girls, and for at least a part of the pupils some work in a foreign language. It may be found feasible to organize several such subjects or projects into short units and to arrange the schedule so that every pupil may take several of them. The work thus offered may and should be of real educational value, in addition to its exploratory value.

In the two following years of the junior high school, some pupils should continue this trying-out process, while others may well devote one fourth to one half of their time to curriculum variables. Pupils who will probably enter industry at the end of the ninth grade may well give as much as two thirds of their time to vocational preparation, but they must not be permitted to neglect preparation for citizenship and the worthy use of leisure.

In the senior high school the relative proportion of these three groups of subjects will vary with the curriculum. Pupils who are to enter a gainful occupation before the completion of the senior high school may well devote a large proportion of their time to the curriculum variables, especially during their last year in school.

In brief, the greater the time allowed for curriculum variables, the more purposeful should be the time devoted to the constants in order that the school may be effective as an agency of unification. Above all, the greater the differentiation in studies, the more important becomes the social mingling of pupils pursuing different curriculums.

The supplementary character of the specializing and unifying functions has a direct bearing also upon the type of high school best suited to the needs of democratic society, as discussed in the next section.

XVI. The Comprehensive High School as the Standard Secondary School

The comprehensive (sometimes called composite, or cosmopolitan) high school, embracing all curriculums in one unified organization, should remain the standard type of secondary school in the United States.

Junior high schools must be of the comprehensive type, whatever policy be adopted for the senior high schools, since one of the primary purposes of the junior high school is to assist the pupil through a wide variety of contacts and experiences to obtain a basis for intelligent choice of his educational and vocational career. In the judgment of the commission senior high schools and four-year high schools of the older organizations should, as a rule, be of the comprehensive type for the following reasons:

1. FOR EFFECTIVENESS OF VOCATIONAL EDUCATION

When effectively organized and administered the comprehensive high school can make differentiated education of greater value to the individual and to society, for such value depends largely upon the extent to which the individual pursues the curriculum best suited to his needs. This factor is of prime importance, although frequently ignored in discussions regarding the effectiveness of vocational and other types of differentiated education.

In a system of special-type schools many influences interfere with the wise choice of curriculum. Thus many pupils choose the high school nearest to their homes, or the school to which their friends have gone or are going, or the school that provides the most attractive social life or has the best athletic teams. Still others are unwisely influenced by the notions of neighbors and friends of the family. After entering a special-type school, many pupils drop out because the work is not adapted to their needs, while comparatively few transfer to another school.

In a comprehensive school the influences interfering with a wise choice of curriculum may be reduced to a minimum. When an unwise choice has been made the pupil may be greatly aided in discovering a curriculum better adapted to his needs because he can see other work in the school, talk with school companions, and confer with teachers who are able to give him expert advice regarding such curriculums. When such a pupil has found a curriculum better adapted to his needs, he can be transferred to it without severance of school relationships and, what seems to him, the sacrifice of school loyalty.

Moreover, pupils in comprehensive schools have contacts valuable to them vocationally, since people in every vocation must be able to deal intelligently with those in other vocations, and employers and employees must be able to understand one another and recognize common interests. Similarly, teachers in comprehensive schools have a better opportunity to observe other curriculums and are thereby better able to advise pupils intelligently.

Summarizing under this head, the well-organized comprehensive school can make differentiated education of greater value than can the special-type school, because it aids in a wise choice of curriculum, assists in readjustments when such are desirable, and provides for wider contacts essential to true success in every vocation.

2. FOR UNIFICATION

When administered by a principal who himself recognizes the social value of all types of secondary education and inspires a broad spirit of democracy among teachers and pupils, the comprehensive high school is a better instrument for unification. Through friendships formed with pupils pursuing other curriculums and having vocational and educational goals widely different from their own, the pupils realize that the interests which they hold in common with others are, after all, far more important than the differences that would tend to make them antagonistic to others. Through school assemblies and organizations they acquire common ideas. Through group activities they secure training in cooperation. Through loyalty to a school which includes many groups they are prepared for loyalty to State and Nation. In short, the comprehensive school is the prototype of a democracy in which various groups must have a degree of self-consciousness as groups and yet be federated into a larger whole through the recognition of common interests and ideals. Life in such a school is a natural and valuable preparation for life in a democracy.

3. FOR OBJECTIVES OTHER THAN VOCATION

A comprehensive high school can provide much more effectively for health education, education for the worthy use of leisure, and home making education than a number of smaller special-type schools can.

The most effective health education requires adequate equipment and instructors competent to diagnose health needs and direct health activities. Expenses and difficulties of duplication of such facilities in every smaller special-type school are almost prohibitive. Preparation for the worthy use of leisure is best achieved when there is a wide variety of activities from which pupils may select, such as arts and crafts clubs, literary and debating societies, and musical organizations. All of these require for their success enthusiastic leadership such as can best be secured from a large faculty. Girls in all curriculums should have the advantages of work in household arts under efficient directors and with adequate equipment. Such conditions are most readily provided in the comprehensive school where there is a strong department of household arts.

With the establishment of a special-type high school it frequently happens that various important phases of education are neglected or minimized in the other schools of that system.

4. FOR ACCESSIBILITY

In cities large enough to require more than one high school it is desirable to have each school so located as to serve a particular section of the city, thereby reducing the expense and loss of time involved in travel on the part of pupils. The proximity of the school to the homes results also in greater interest in education on the part of pupils and parents, and consequently increases the drawing and holding power of the school.

5. ADAPTATION TO LOCAL NEEDS

In recommending the comprehensive high school as the standard secondary school the commission recognizes that in large cities where two or more high schools are needed it is not always possible to provide every curriculum in each high school, such a practice being precluded by the fact that certain curriculums would thereby enroll in the several schools too few pupils to permit economical organization and administration. In such cases a few curriculums may well appear in selected comprehensive schools or even in a single school only, while other curriculums appear in every school.

The Commission also recognizes the impracticability of offering every curriculum in every small rural high school. In such cases it is desirable that a curriculum for which the number of pupils does not warrant such duplication should be offered in selected schools, and that pupils needing that curriculum should go to those schools. This plan is substantially the same as that recommended for the large city.

6. EFFECTIVE ORGANIZATION OF CURRICULUM IN COMPREHENSIVE HIGH SCHOOLS

Finally, the Commission recognizes that in the past relatively ineffective instruction has been afforded in some comprehensive schools. This has been due in part to the fact that everywhere vocational education has been passing and is still passing through a period of experimentation. The Commission believes, however, that the most serious defect in vocational education in the comprehensive high school has been due to a lack of proper organization and administration. Effective vocational education can not be secured when administered like so many accidental groupings of subjects. To remedy this situation the Commission recommends that each curriculum, or group of closely related curriculums, in the large comprehensive high school be placed under the supervision of a director whose task it shall be to organize that curriculum and maintain its efficiency. The curriculum directors must work under the general direction of the principal, who must be the coordinator of all the activities of the school. Especially it is necessary that each director shall be selected with the same care that would be exercised in choosing the principal of a special-type school enrolling as many pupils as are enrolled in the curriculum or curriculums under his direction. In medium sized high schools unable to employ directors for the various curriculums, the teachers should be organized into committees to consider the problems of the various curriculums, all working under the direction of the principal.

Unless the various curriculums are effectively organized and administered, and unless the democratic spirit pervades the school, the comprehensive high school is in danger of failure; with these factors present, it has every promise of success.

XVII. Recognition of the Objectives in

Organizing the School

The objectives must determine the organization, or else the organization will determine the objectives. If the only basis upon which a high school is organized is that of the subjects of study, each department being devoted to some particular subject, there will result an over valuation of the importance of subjects as such, and the tendency will be for each teacher to regard his function as merely that of leading the pupils to master a particular subject, rather than that of using the subjects of study and the activities of the school as means for achieving the objectives of education. The departmental organization is desirable but needs to be supplemented. The two following methods are suggested:

1. THE PRINCIPAL'S COUNCIL

The principal may select from his teachers a council, each member of which shall be charged with the responsibility of studying the activities of the school with reference to a specific objective. Plans for realizing these objectives should be discussed by the principal and the council. Without impairing in any way the ultimate responsibility of the principal, it will, as a rule, increase the efficiency of the school if the principal encourages initiative on the part of these council members and delegates to them such responsibilities as he finds they can discharge. The members of such a council and their duties are suggested as follows:

Health director. This council member should seek to ascertain whether the health needs of the pupils are adequately met. For this purpose he should consider the ventilation and sanitation of the building, the provisions for lunch, the posture of pupils, the amount of home work required, the provisions for physical training, and the effects of athletics. He should find out whether the pupils are having excessive social activities outside of school, and devise means for gaining the cooperation of parents in the proper regulation of work and recreation. He may well see whether the teaching of biology is properly focused upon hygiene and sanitation.

Citizenship director. The citizenship director should determine whether the pupils are developing initiative and the sense of personal responsibility. He should foster civic mindedness through the school paper, debating society, and general school exercises, and give suggestions for directing the thinking of the pupils to significant problems of the day.

Curriculum directors. As discussed in Section XVI of this report, for each important group of vocations for which the school offers a curriculum, or group of curriculums, there should be a director to study the needs of these vocations and find out the respects in which the graduates are succeeding or failing in meeting legitimate vocational demands. With the knowledge thus gained he should strive to improve the work offered by the school.

One of these curriculum directors should have charge of preparation for colleges and normal schools. He should obtain the records of graduates attending those schools and find out the strong and weak points in their preparation. He will advise with pupils intending to enter these institutions as to the work that they should take in the high school.

Director of vocational and educational guidance. This member of the council should collect data regarding various vocational and educational opportunities and the qualifications needed. If the school is small, he may help individual pupils in acquiring an intelligent attitude toward the choice of a vocation or of a higher education; but if the school is large, he must train others who can know the pupils more intimately, to assist in this service, always holding himself ready to give advice.

Director of preparation for leisure. This council member should, so far as possible, see that the pupils are developing interests that will assist them in later life to use their leisure wisely. He should consider especially the musical organizations, the school library, the art clubs and classes, and the various ways in which pupils are spending their leisure.

The large school may have need for additional directors to deal with other vital phases of education.

2. BY COMMITTEES

The principal may appoint committees of teachers each of which would be charged with duties similar to those described. An advantage of the committee plan is that a larger number of teachers will be stimulated to acquire a broad educational point of view.

Theoretically, it is possible for the principal himself to supervise the teaching and direct all the activities of the school. Practically, however, the majority of administrators tend to become absorbed in a few aspects of education. In fact, intensive creative work along any one line on the part of the principal leads naturally to at least a temporary neglect of the other aspects of education. Consequently, either a principal's council or committees of teachers seem essential in order that none of the objectives may be neglected.

It is not intended that the council or the committees should in any way lessen the ultimate responsibility of the principal, but that by this means the cooperation of the entire teaching body may be secured and all the objectives held in view.

XVIII. Secondary Education Essential for all Youth

To the extent to which the objectives outlined herein are adopted as the controlling aims of education, to that extent will it be recognized that an extended education for every boy and girl is essential to the welfare, and even to the existence, of democratic society. The significance of these objectives is becoming more and more apparent under modern conditions in our democracy. These conditions grow out of increased knowledge of science with its rapidly extending applications to all the affairs of life, keener competition with its attendant dangers, closer contacts of peoples of varied racial and religious types, and greater assertiveness of all men and women in the control of their own destinies. These and many other tendencies increase the significances of health, worthy home membership, vocation, citizenship, the worthy use of leisure, and ethical character.

Each of these objectives requires for its realization not only the training and habit formation that the child may secure, but also the intelligence and efficiency that can not be developed before adolescence. In fact, their realization calls for the full period allotted to both the junior and senior high schools.

Consequently, this commission holds that education should be so reorganized that every normal boy and girl will be encouraged to remain in school to the age of 18, on full time if possible, otherwise on part time.

XIX. Part-Time Schooling as a Compulsory

Minimum Requirement

As stated in Section I of this report, only one American youth in about three reaches the first year of the four-year high school, and only one in about nine remains in school to the end of the high school course. This condition is, in the last analysis, due principally to four causes: First, the limited range of instruction commonly offered by secondary schools; second, the failure on the part of the school adequately to demonstrate to young people and their parents the value of the education offered; third, the lure of employment, together with the desire for increased economic independence on the part of young persons; and fourth, economic pressure in the family, real or imagined.

The first of these causes is rapidly disappearing through the introduction of curriculums with rich vocational content. The second may be removed by subordinating deferred values and reorganizing instruction so as to make the values more evident to the learner, as discussed in Sections VIII and IX. The third may be diminished in its effect by greater virility in school work. Economic pressure will continue until social conditions can be materially improved.

In the meantime, a sound national policy dictates the urgent need for legislation whereby all young persons, whether employed or not, shall be required to attend school not less than eight hours in each week that schools are in session until they reach the age of 18.

Attendance for eight hours in each week will make possible important progress not only in vocational efficiency but also in the promotion of health, preparation for worthy home membership, civic intelligence and efficiency, the better utilization of leisure, and ethical development. All these objectives are evidently as important for the young worker as for those who remain in full-time attendance at school.

The value of part-time instruction, if properly organized, is out of all proportion to the time involved, because it can utilize as a basis the new experiences of the young worker and his new social and civic contacts. Moreover, continued attendance at school will afford an intellectual stimulus too often lacking to these young persons under the modern subdivision of labor.

Consequently, this Commission recommends the enactment of legislation whereby all young persons up to the age of 18, whether employed or not, shall be required to attend the secondary school not less than eight hours in each week that the schools are in session.

In some States it may be held to be impracticable at the outset to require such part-time attendance beyond the age of 16 or 17, but the Commission holds that the imperative needs of American democracy can not be met until the period is extended to 18.

To make this part-time schooling effective it will be necessary to adapt it specifically to the needs of the pupils concerned. Moreover, teachers must be trained for this new type of work. Without such provisions there is great danger of failure and a consequent reaction against this most valuable extension of secondary education.

In view of the importance of developing a sense of common interests and social solidarity on the part of the young worker and those of his fellows who are continuing in full-time attendance at school, it appears to this commission that this part-time education should be conducted in the comprehensive secondary school rather than in separate continuation schools, as is the custom in less democratic societies. By this plan the part-time students and the full-time students may share in the use of the assembly hall, gymnasium, and other equipment provided for all. This plan has the added advantage that the enrollment of all pupils may be continuous in the secondary school, thus furthering employment supervision on the one hand and making easier a return to full-time attendance whenever the lure of industry or the improvement of economic conditions in the family makes such a return inviting and feasible.

The part-time attendance for eight hours a week of all persons between 14 and 18 who are not now in school will require a large increase in the teaching force in secondary schools. No other single piece of educational legislation could, however, do more to raise the level of intelligence and efficiency and to insure the welfare of democracy.

XX. Conclusion

In concluding this report on the cardinal principles of secondary education the Commission would call attention to its 17 other reports in which the principles herein set forth are applied to the various aspects of secondary education. The reports now available are listed on the last page of this bulletin, and others are nearly ready for publication. One report will consider in detail the application of these principles to the organization and administration of secondary schools. Thirteen reports deal with the aims, methods, and content of the various subjects of study and curriculums in the light of these principles. Three others discuss vocational guidance, physical education, and the moral values that should be derived from secondary school organization and instruction.

It is becoming increasingly apparent that the problems of secondary education merit much more serious attention than they have received heretofore. The study of the best methods for adapting secondary education to the needs of modern democratic life is but begun. The physical, intellectual, emotional, and ethical characteristics of young people are still but vaguely comprehended. Such knowledge of social needs and educational theory and practice as is already available has been seriously studied by comparatively few administrators and teachers. Progress will depend very largely upon adequate professional training of teachers both before and after entering upon service. Plans must be adopted for pooling the results of successful experimentation on the part of individual teachers. To make the reorganization effective, competent supervision and constructive leadership must be provided in the various fields of secondary education.

It is the firm belief of this commission that secondary education in the United States must aim at nothing less than complete and worthy living for all youth, and that therefore the objectives described herein must find place in the education of every boy and girl.

Finally, in the process of translating into daily practice the cardinal principles herein set forth, the secondary school teachers of the United States must themselves strive to explore the inner meaning of the great democratic movement now struggling for supremacy. The doctrine that each individual has a right to the opportunity to develop the best that is in him is reinforced by the belief in the potential, and perchance unique, worth of the individual. The task of education, as of life, is therefore to call forth that potential worth.

While seeking to evoke the distinctive excellencies of individuals and groups of individuals, the secondary school must be equally zealous to develop those common ideas, common ideals, and common modes of thought, feeling, and action, whereby America, through a rich, unified, common life, may render her truest service to a world seeking for democracy among men and nations.

ISSUES AND FUNCTIONS OF SECONDARY EDUCATION 4

Reports by the Committee on the Reorientation of Secondary Education

THE COMMITTEE ON THE
REORIENTATION OF
SECONDARY EDUCATION

 *The Department of Secondary School Principles of the National Education Association meeting in Washington in 1932 authorized the appointment of a Commission "to study and restate the principles and objectives of secondary education." It became known as The Committee on the Reorientation of Secondary Education. Chaired by Thomas H. Briggs, its membership was made up of leaders in secondary school administration. It had been 14 years since the Committee on the Reorganization of Secondary Education had stated the Cardinal Principles. In the meantime social, economic, and political changes that had in part led to the earlier reexamination of the purposes of the high schools had accelerated. The depression had demonstrated the growing interde-*

pendence of all people and all regions of the nation, economically and socially. The stagnation of the economy had emphasized what had for some time begun to be apparent: there were no longer significant employment opportunities for the youth who had left school. By the hundreds of thousands, boys and girls turned to the secondary schools in the 30's as almost their only haven. Political questions had become more complicated, government itself more complex, and the responsibilities of citizenship more demanding. No longer could it be assumed that a span of education terminating with the elementary schools was, for millions of pupils, sufficient preparation for life, work, and responsible citizenship in a changing urbanized society.

It was an awareness of new and emerging needs and the impact of rapidly expanding secondary school population that prompted the establishment of the new Commission, to which should be added the belief that first, the schools had lagged behind the demands of the times and the needs of the pupils, and second, that in spite of a great deal of fact gathering, no clear-cut definition of function and purpose for secondary schools had emerged or been developed.

In presenting the issues, the Committee said:

"It is especially notable in our history that provision was so early made for secondary education. But the pride with which we have celebrated this phenomenon should not blind us to the fact that it was for a long time provided in only a few localities and for a very small number of highly selected boys, that it was frankly and fully imitative of an institution already a relic of largely outgrown needs in a civilization far different from that in America, and that it could have had small significance to the pioneer people. It did prevent learning of a sort from being buried in the grave of our fathers, but at the same time it stifled the imagination of educators and made them content to follow already outworn practices without planning soundly and comprehensively for what the New World needed.

Proposals for improvement and for adaptions to the demands of new conditions were few, spaced at long intervals, and, except for those by Benjamin Franklin in the middle of the eighteenth century, singularly small and lacking in inventiveness to meet new needs. Although the academies made wide curricular experimentation, there was a continuing lack of any attempt to prepare a sound, comprehensive, and long sighted program for secondary education. This lack has continued to the present time. Although the several committees of the National Education Association have made valuable contributions, the need for agreement on fundamental principles and definitions of secondary education in our country is today almost as great as it ever was. This need is especially imperative in light of the many and significant changes that have come in our civilization.[1]

[1] *Issues of Secondary Education:* Report of the Committee on the Reorientation of Secondary Education. Bulletin No. 59, Department of Secondary School Principals of the National Education Association, January, 1936, p. 20.

The Committee on the Reorientation of Secondary Education made its first report in 1936, presenting ten issues facing the secondary schools.

ISSUES OF SECONDARY EDUCATION

1. Shall secondary education be provided at public expense for all normal individuals or for only a limited number?
2. Shall secondary education seek to retain all pupils in school as long as they wish to remain, or shall it transfer them to other agencies under educational supervision when, in the judgment of the school authorities, these agencies promise to serve better the pupils' immediate and probable future needs?
3. Shall secondary education be concerned only with the welfare and progress of the individual, or with these only as they promise to contribute to the welfare and progress of society?
4. Shall secondary education provide a common curriculum for all, or differentiated offerings?
5. Shall secondary education include vocational training, or shall it be restricted to general education?
6. Shall secondary education be primarily directed toward preparation for advanced studies, or shall it be primarily concerned with the value of its own courses, regardless of a student's future academic career?
7. Shall secondary education accept conventional school subjects as fundamental categories under which school experiences shall be classified and presented to students, or shall it arrange and present experiences in fundamental categories directly related to the performance of such functions of secondary schools in a democracy as increasing the ability and the desire better to meet socio-civic, economic, health, leisure time, vocational and preprofessional problems and situations?
8. Shall secondary education present merely organized knowledge, or shall it also assume responsibility for attitudes and ideas?
9. Shall secondary education seek merely the adjustment of students to prevailing social ideals, or shall it seek the reconstruction of society?
10. Granting that education is a "gradual, continuous, unitary process," shall secondary education be presented merely as a phase of such a process, or shall it be organized as a distinct but closely articulating part of the entire educational program, with peculiarly emphasized functions of its own?

The issues were accompanied by historical analysis, by pro and con arguments considered by the Committee, but the position of the Committee on each of the ten issues is made clear. Principles emerged. Secondary education should be universal and not selective.

The Commission rejected the concept of European secondary schools which, it said, ". . . have been definitely planned as schools for the ruling class—the socially, economically, or intellectually elite," a kind of education which ". . . constitutes in European eyes both a special kind of education and the education of a special class of pupils." [2]

The Commission examined reasons inherent in the nature of the characteristic American secondary school which resulted in many boys and girls dropping out of school.

[Their] curricula usually involve sitting on hard chairs four or five hours a day, reading and writing, discussing and reciting, learning the facts of history, grammar, science, mathematics and the like. Tension is created by severe competition in which many children are destined never to succeed, and by high standards of achievement which they can never meet. Normal social communication and cooperation are forbidden. It is no wonder that many children rebel against this regime with almost hysterical violence and drop out of school.[3]

The secondary schools should admit all boys and girls who had been promoted from the elementary schools, as well as those who might not have completed the elementary school, but who seemed likely to benefit from secondary school, assuming that the secondary school modified its program to provide greater flexibility. Boys and girls who had left secondary school should be readmitted if readmission promised both individual and social benefits.

The secondary school would have to broaden its offerings to embrace as many kinds of educational activity as needed to meet the needs and abilities of the pupils. It needed to experiment with programs designed to meet such needs.

A pupil should not be encouraged by the school to leave until he had mastered the minimum essentials and had had the opportunity to try every practicable type of instruction which it was reasonable to believe could be adapted to his needs.

Teachers would need to define competence on the part of pupils in broader ways than mastery of "facts." External motivations, often applied arbitrarily in relation to supposed "standards," and expressed in

[2] *Ibid.,* p. 25.
[3] *Ibid.,* p. 33.

marks and passing and failing grades, needed to be reexamined. Better guidance of pupils should be established. The program of the school should provide both integration, which is to say education common to all, and differentiation, providing leeway for individual capacities and interests. Vocational education should be a respected part of the secondary school program, and the training in skills needed for those who are not going to continue their formal education beyond high school should be provided by the schools and not by other agencies. Adult workers should have the privilege of using vocational facilities of the schools when such use does not conflict with use by secondary school pupils.

The domination of the secondary school program by colleges and universities was examined. The Committee came to the conclusion that the secondary school should be primarily concerned with its own courses, rejecting the idea that a single pattern of courses required by colleges was necessary for success in college.

The Committee came to the conclusion that ". . . in the light of what this Committee considers to be sound educational philosophy applicable to the problem of creating a desirable educational program in our American democracy and on the basis of what experimental psychology has contributed to knowledge of educational methods and procedures, this Committee does not believe that a curriculum utilizing conventional subjects as the categories under which school experiences are organized, presents a defensible method of procedure." More fundamental categories of organization of learning experiences should be developed and used. These would transcend conventional subject-matter lines, and relate learning to the needs of the learner in a more productive manner.

The Committee believed that education is a continuous, unitary process. Even though it is necessary to house different levels of education in separate facilities, it is the task of administration to see the process as a whole and to effect articulation among separate units.

"We must get rid of the idea of one school preparing for another and foster the idea of the schools continuously centering attention on the intellectual and emotional needs of the child. This is particularly needed where emphasis on subject matter fields is prevalent," the Committee stated.

The Committee proposed the issues and the functions of secondary education at a critical period in our history. The country was in a severe economic depression. Money to build schools and to finance a necessary program was difficult to obtain. In the name of economy, critics were demanding cutbacks in program, and were calling for a

*return to the "fundamentals." Some, perhaps many vocal critics raised
doubts about the principle of universal secondary education itself.
Abroad, Nazism in Germany and Fascism in Italy were on the rise.
Doubts about the ability of democracy to survive the economic challenge at home and the political challenge abroad were openly expressed. Some spokesmen were calling on the schools to take the lead in
bringing about a new social order in America. Counts, in a pamphlet
published in 1932, Dare the School Build a New Social Order? took
such a view, and his ideas were widely discussed and debated.*

*The question of whether the schools should aim to ". . . recon-
struct" society or whether they should "adjust" pupils to the prevailing
concepts obviously caused the Committee great difficulty. In the end,
it rejected both extremes. It recognized the dynamics of democracy,
of which change is an inevitable concomitant. "Secondary education
should dispose schools favorably to social change," the Committee
stated, but it "should not plan the reconstruction of society in any
sense that would commit the young to specific changes in the social
order. It may legitimately attempt to foresee the probable course of
events and to prepare youth to deal with it intelligently." Freedom of
inquiry, critical examination of ideas were to be supported. But the
Committee stopped short of general agreement about how far social
criticism in the secondary schools might be allowed to go.*

FUNCTIONS OF SECONDARY EDUCATION

*The second report of the Committee on the Reorientation of Second-
ary Education was presented in 1937 and was titled, Functions of Secondary Education.[4] The ten functions, with introductory summaries,
follow:*

Function I

To continue by a definite program, though in a diminishing degree,
the integration of students. This should be on an increasingly intellectual level until the desired common knowledge, appreciations, ideals,
attitudes, and practices are firmly fixed.

INTRODUCTORY SUMMARY

The aims of social integration can be stated simply. It is an old
axiom that there can be no social progress worthy of the name unless

---

4 *Functions of Secondary Education:* Report of the Committee on the Orientation
of Secondary Education. Bulletin No. 64, Department of Secondary School Principals of the National Education Association. January, 1937, excerpts.

individuals are able and willing to work together—unless they have common backgrounds of experience and culture, common purposes, and the cooperative spirit.

Schools have the function of integrating youths with each other and with society for the excellent reason that no other agency can do the work completely or well. To be sure, just living together may in itself do a great deal to integrate people in common social practices and in the prevailing standards of the time. But a mere emphasis upon the conventionalities ought not to satisfy a dynamic society committed to change. We wish not only to maintain the present standards of life; we wish also to join together in raising them by whatever processes a mature democracy affords. This cannot be done, however, unless people first agree upon what higher standards are desirable and how they should go about getting them. Nor can it be done unless they develop an intelligent popular will that will insist on the appropriate social action. Obviously, the incidental integration arising from our daily intercourse is entirely inadequate for this. A great deal of common education is necessary. Indeed we must depend increasingly upon schools to promote a social integration much more complete and pro-ductive of change than that provided by life itself.

America is beginning to use the secondary school for this purpose. The elementary school must, of course, still carry the peak load of integrating young people, for it has an almost universal spread in its enrollment and deals with children at their most impressionable age. But life is now so complex and the necessity for intelligent collective action so great if democracy is to survive that the elementary schools cannot handle the more intellectual aspects of a fully developed pro-gram of social integration. The secondary school must assume respon-sibility for continuing on a higher level what the elementary school has begun.

In general terms the aim of social integration on the secondary school level—as on all levels—is to enable and encourage individuals to cooperate in using for the welfare of all the knowledges and the skills which they acquire individually. This aim requires that pupils possess certain characteristics of mind and view in common. They should have the scientific, pragmatic habit of mind; mastery over a flexible, effective, as well as standard speech; an understanding and appreciation of the arts; an intelligent attitude toward good health; a common background of social and scholastic experience; maturity in all social relationships; and an accurate mental picture of the world based upon scientific knowledge and an informed social purpose. A school program directed toward integrating pupils along these lines would do much to produce the type of individual whose presence in society in large numbers is the best guarantee of its progress.

Briefly, the aim of a program of social integration is to develop socially-minded, socially-active individuals. Its governing principle is that the subject matter it uses should be deeply rooted in the truth. This is particularly important in presenting the basic ideals of democracy, about which the greatest misapprehension still exists. Superficially the American people may know what democracy means, but they do not understand it thoroughly enough to apply it to those areas in our national life—areas of politics, religion, social relations, economics, and industry—where men are still discriminated against, exploited, or oppressed. From these bonds of ignorance and prejudice, only the truth can make us free.

If the secondary school is really serious about integrating its pupils in the pursuit of higher standards of life, the first thing it should do is to examine its own program to see how it is now serving this function. It can then begin to eliminate the negative elements which retard integration and amplify the positive elements which promote it. New methods of promoting integration may also be added to the school program as the work goes on of defining and popularizing the major aims of society and as investigations are made of the common patterns of thought, emotion, and behavior which by being widely diffused among the people will enable them to attain cooperatively the social aims they may agree to seek. These investigations should provide the school with specific objectives to work for and an opportunity to reorganize itself to eliminate wasted effort and to develop more effectively the attitudes and powers the pupil should possess in order to take his place in a society moving toward better things.

In fact, living and working intelligently together so that all people may enjoy higher standards of life is precisely what social integration means. Secondary education must represent and encourage cooperative action of that kind.

Function II

To satisfy the important immediate and probable future needs of the students in so far as the maturity of the learner permits, guiding the behavior of youth in the light of increasingly remote, but always clearly perceived and appreciated, social and personal values.

INTRODUCTORY SUMMARY

The American people pour annually from the public purse millions of dollars into the support of free schools. Underlying this action is a vague but persistent popular belief that public education is one of the best ways of ministering to an individual's needs. No one imagines, of course, that education taken by itself can satisfy needs in the sense of creating spiritual values or material goods where none existed before; but people are generally united in thinking that education should bestow upon the individual the desire and the power to produce and enjoy them. The schools of America have not fully justified this faith of their supporters, but the principle upon which the people established them is still sound. There is no other defensible reason for educational effort than its ultimate power to serve the needs of mankind.

If educational institutions have failed in the past to meet the needs of individuals, it is not because educators were ignorant of the purpose of education. Rather, the fault of the educator has been in misjudging what the real needs of pupils were. Even when they have seen certain needs clearly, they have been blind to others. The medieval monks, for example, in their preoccupation with spiritual values neglected the material needs of mankind. The humanists exalted the values of language and literature. Neither of them to any significant extent based their instruction upon a balanced view of human needs. Neither dealt in a broad kind of learning that applied to more than a few of the problems of daily life. But the monks and the humanists by no means stood alone in this fault. Many others have erred in exactly the same way.

The modern trend in the schools, however, is very definitely toward bringing education more directly into the service of human needs. Circumstances quite as much as theory have been responsible for the change. The older educational agencies such as the church and the home are no longer as effective as they once were in guiding the individual's development. New educational agencies have arisen—witness the movies and the press—whose influence is not always for the best. These events have forced the school to assume additional obligations in meeting its pupils' needs.

But there are lagging members of the educational profession who are notably unmoved by things happening plainly before their eyes. It requires a great effort to convince them that the school curriculum must be substantially revised before the essential needs of the modern pupil can be satisfactorily met. Therefore the first step that secondary education should take in this respect is to spread the conviction throughout the profession that the needs of young people should be accurately determined and classified and that on this basis the school curriculum should be revised.

The exact determination and classification of the present and probable future needs of young people is, of course, a task that will occupy generations of workers to come. The problem is as broad as the whole range of human activities, it is as deep as the nature of man, and there is no end to it because it keeps renewing itself as fast as people alter their modes of living. But enough is already known about the needs of the individual to give the secondary school plenty to start on. In fact its immediate problem, far from uncovering new needs of the pupil, is to select from the needs it already knows about the particular ones it should attempt to satisfy.

Certain needs are so pressing that their choice requires no deliberation. The maintenance of health, skill in the use of machines, the development of social efficiency, and the like—these are needs so urgent and fundamental that they lie partly within the province of the elementary school. Secondary schools have a responsibility for continuing this work. Beyond that, they should consider carefully what other needs of the pupil they should meet, particularly those more remote from his present requirements but so important to his future that it is right to anticipate them and prepare for them before an individual leaves school. There are limitations, to be sure—limitations with respect to time and money, the maturity of the pupils, the capabilities of teachers, and the principle that education is an investment by society to promote its own interests and not to indulge the purely personal wishes of the individual.

Any wholehearted attempt on the part of the secondary school to organize itself for the purpose of meeting directly the needs of its pupils will involve radical changes in the content of its curriculum, in the methods of its instruction, and in the types of its equipment. No sudden and disturbing revolution is possible or desirable, but there should be steady progress toward breaking down the barriers which the traditional department divisions of the curriculum presents to the full and proper use of subject matter. The quality of instruction should be tested by the outcomes it produces rather than by the amount of material covered, time spent, or facts acquired. Particular courses of study should be offered only to those pupils for whom they function and new courses of greater promise in meeting pupils' needs should be added to the curriculum. In the face of these changes there is grave danger no doubt that the pupil may become even more bewildered than he is now and lose sight of ultimate aims just when it is most important that he perceive them. A form of guidance which recognizes the immaturity of the pupil and his need for help in making wise decisions is therefore an indispensable part of the school's educational service.

But no obstacle should be allowed to stand in the way of enabling the secondary school to discharge its function of meeting the real needs of pupils. The penalty is too great. When education neglects human needs it becomes ineffective and, at the worst, useless to those whom it is expected to serve.

Function III

To reveal higher activities of an increasingly differentiated type in the major fields of the racial heritage of experience and culture, their significant values for social living, the problems in them of contemporary life, the privileges and duties of each person as an individual and as a member of social groups; to make these fields satisfying and desired by those gifted for successful achievement and to give information as to requirements for success in these fields and information as to where further training may be secured.

INTRODUCTORY SUMMARY

So completely dependent is man upon the past that the loss of his cultural inheritance would mean the collapse of civilization. It is to preclude such a possibility as well as to lay the basis for further social progress that schools are established. It is their function to acquaint young people with the materials of living, to represent to them an accepted way of life, and to reveal opportunities for higher activity in the major fields of their heritage of experience and culture.

All educational institutions share this general function. But just as there are particular reasons why the elementary school should bear the main burden of integrating children, there are likewise particular reasons why the task of revealing higher activities should weigh most heavily upon the secondary school. It is usually the period of adolescence that the possibilities of mature living begin to dawn upon the individual. At this age and immediately following it, a youth prepares to enter upon the broad concourse of adult life. He begins now to anticipate the higher activities which older people engage in. It is natural, therefore, that he should turn to the secondary school to give him some inkling of what the higher activities are like.

Unfortunately for its pupils, the secondary school has too often disappointed rather than satisfied the eager mind of youth. It apparently assumed that the revelation of higher activities mattered only with gifted children and would take care of itself in the natural course of events. At any rate, it left the whole problem to the pupil himself or to the chance interest of the teacher. At one stage in the history of American education, this system, or rather this lack of it, may have sufficed. But recent events have forced upon the schools the bitter fruits of their neglect. They now realize that to give to the present school population—made up of all sorts of pupils—some idea of the finer opportunities and the more durable values of life is a problem at once difficult and acute. They have also discovered—and this is the nub of the matter—that they do not possess the essential techniques by which the problem can be solved.

The secondary school can develop the necessary techniques only as it comes to understand the exact nature of its problem. Fundamentally, its problem is to interpret the higher activities to each pupil in terms of his power to engage in them profitably. It is to disclose to pupils new and challenging opportunities for work and study which they can undertake with benefit to themselves and to society. It is to explain clearly to them the condition under which they can enjoy the values which the best forms of experience yield. It is even to bring these experiences into the curriculum itself where pupils can be encouraged to take part in them and to enjoy them. By using every means at its command, the secondary school must help its pupils to cultivate in number, variety and depth the enduring interests which intelligent people develop from their contacts with life.

Important as this function is, the secondary schools cannot be expected to perform it successfully under unfavorable conditions. Although there are conspicuous exceptions, one cannot say, for example, that secondary schools are generally staffed by men and women of high qualifications—persons rich in their interests, stimulating in personality, and masters of their subject field. Nor can one say that secondary schools are commonly places where young people come into contact with the vital issues of their personal and social life, issues which must be faced before many of the higher activities can be truthfully revealed.

Educators should realize, however, that one of the surest ways to remove unfavorable conditions is to combine protests against them with efforts to make the schools as effective as possible under the circumstances that prevail. Much can be done to improve the quality and diversity of the educational program in many localities by reorganizing smaller schools into larger units. Moreover, in interpreting higher activities to pupils, the school need not consider itself the sole source of material nor the only agent of revelation. The home, the community, indeed all areas of the environment should be carefully surveyed for higher activities of a kind that the school cannot directly provide. Pupils can be encouraged to observe and take part in them just as much as if they were a part of the school program.

As in the case of most other problems of the secondary school, the ultimate solution of the problem of revealing higher activities and of differentiating them as the pupil grows older centers around improvements in the curriculum and in the quality of instruction. The responsibility for initiating and sustaining these improvements falls largely upon the institutions which prepare teachers, but it should also be shared by the teachers now in service. Most of them are anxious to share it when permitted to do so. The cooperative study of the secondary school curriculum by the teachers of Virginia gives convincing evidence of the power of teachers to attack educational problems constructively and to raise the standards of their instruction.

Such instances of the readiness of teachers to support constructive movements in education ought to hearten all those who believe that the revelation to pupils of the higher activities of their racial heritage is a part of the basic function of schools. For if secondary school staffs, and through them boards of education and parents, can be brought to share the same belief, the major battle to include this function in the work of the secondary schools can be won.

Function IV

To explore higher and increasingly specialized interests, aptitudes, and capacities of students, looking toward the direction of them into avenues of study and of work for which they have manifested peculiar fitness.

INTRODUCTORY SUMMARY

People generally agree that the individual finds his greatest happiness in placing at the disposal of his fellow men the services which by nature and nurture he is most fitted to perform. To render such services ought to be among the supreme purposes of the individual in life. It is a purpose to which education can be profitably directed and on which the energies of the school can be well spent. Indeed, if secondary schools are to yield the largest possible return from society's investment in public education, they must assume as one of their principal functions the task of helping each pupil to find a place in the world where he can use his energy and talents with profit to society and to himself.

This function of the secondary school is manifestly of the greatest importance. Equally manifest is the general way in which it can be intelligently performed. The secondary school must explore and develop the basic equipment of the individual in terms of his interests, aptitudes, and capacities to attain to and participate successfully in the higher activities which education and other forms of experience reveal.

Why exploration in terms of a pupil's interests? Largely because interests are the dynamics of education. They determine the kind and quality of the things which an individual does. They not only support learning; they perpetuate it. Their very indispensability forbids their neglect. Fortunately interests are not hard to arouse. The natural curiosity of children provides an ample base for developing them. In truth most children come to school with many interests already formed. It is the task of the school in conjunction with the pupil to discover these interests, to develop others, and to press any and all of them into the service of the higher activities of life.

A pupil's aptitudes and capacities are no less important than his interests. As a matter of fact, aptitudes are closely related to interests and to the integration of personality. We are usually interested in what we do successfully, and successful activity is the basis on which we integrate a healthy personality. But the activity must be successful. Schools as a whole are too much concerned with bookish activities, whereas many pupils are not academic in their aptitudes. Since aptitudes nonacademic in nature are so common, they must be given a fair chance to develop and to help the individual adjust himself to life. Capacity, on the other hand, refers to the native endowment of the pupil. Perhaps this cannot be intrinsically improved, but it can be freed from inhibitions and by supplementing intelligence tests with achievement tests, teacher judgments, and exploratory courses, it can be more justly estimated.

As a part of the task of securing the wisest distribution of human talent in the higher activities of life and of guiding the pupil accordingly, the secondary school should be able to tell a pupil and his parents the essential facts about his interests, aptitudes, and capacities. But the school will never be able to give this information unless it develops and puts to good use adequate techniques for the purpose. Reorganization in administration, in the curriculum, and in the functions of teachers will undoubtedly be necessary. The school ought, for example, to devise for use early in a pupil's educational career a limited number of exploratory courses in the major fields of the curriculum. If these courses are weighted with immediate rather than deferred values, their brevity will not preclude substantial benefits to the pupil and they may prove of the greatest service in planning his subsequent program. It is also an essential part of good exploratory techniques to establish a continuous contact between the pupil and some one teacher. It is now recognized that to fully understand the pupil, the teacher must view him in all his relationships, continuously and as a whole. And finally it will be necessary to enlist the cooperation of both the pupil and his parents, for they are precisely the ones on whom the success of the teacher in understanding and helping the pupil ultimately depends. In the last analysis the pupil develops himself, but he does it under the conditions set by the school and the home.

Objections are sometimes raised to the function of exploration because of its alleged costs and its tendency towards over-specialization. But neither argument is conclusive. It is economical to spend a little money to prevent great wastes. The most important costs to consider are the random efforts, the purposeless lives, and the demoralizing driftings of individuals when the function is neglected. The charge of over-specialization, on the other hand, is based upon a misinterpretation of the function. If the function is clearly understood and properly performed, it reveals inadequacies in areas of common knowledge, while determining abilities in special fields.

More disturbing than theoretical objections are the practical difficulties in carrying out the function. But these will gradually yield to effort just as the objections will yield to reason. The problem of differentiating the program of small schools, for example, may be effectively attacked by reorganizing them into larger units, by employing more versatile teachers, and by capitalizing on the opportunity in small schools to establish a more intimate contact between teachers and pupils. Other suggestions for overcoming the rigidity of the curriculum, the over-zealousness of department staffs, the faulty training and selection of teachers, the inadequacy of techniques of evaluation, and the paucity of provisions for personnel work are given in the discussion which follows. The only *sine qua non* to the solution of these problems is an honest recognition of their presence and a readiness on the part of all educators to work together in incorporating the function into the work of the secondary school.

Function V

To systematize knowledge previously acquired or being acquired in course in such ways as to show the significance both of this knowledge and especially of the laws and principles, with understanding of wider ranges of application than would otherwise be perceived.

INTRODUCTORY SUMMARY

The work of systematizing knowledge into forms especially suited to young people must be included among the legitimate functions of the secondary school as long as formal programs of education are used to transmit knowledge and culture to the youth of society. The secondary school should exercise this function, of course, only within its own area. Other institutions exist for the purpose of systematizing knowledge in general for people in general. But the secondary school should not permit such institutions to interfere within its own sphere of activity. It alone has the right to select from established systems of knowledge such portions as it shall use in the education of its pupils. It alone has the task of reconstructing from the portions of knowledge it has selected new systems of special significance to youth.

Secondary schools became interested in this function when traditional systems of knowledge, unmodified, proved unsuited to their use. They found, for example, that systems of knowledge as fixed by academic authorities, who usually have a greater regard for the inner logic of the system than for the variable character of the secondary school population, may serve as convenient compilations of information, but they do not adequately serve the purposes of the school in helping all sorts of pupils to improve their living. Equally inappropriate to the purposes of secondary education are systems of knowledge that aim only at meeting the requirements of admission to college, or that reflect the antiquated notion that certain subjects are exclusively good for disciplining the mind, or that concentrate on limited vocational skills, or that conform to the mechanics of the American system of education with its tendency to substitute credits earned for educational growth attained.

It would be foolish, of course, to dismiss all such systematizations of knowledge as entirely without value to secondary schools. The formal organization of materials into the traditional subjects of the curriculum has, for example, advantages of ease and economy and it may still be appropriate for the intellectually superior students who are well advanced on the long academic road of preparing for the professions. Of even greater importance is the emphasis the traditional systematizations place upon order and coherence in arranging materials and activities—characteristics conspicuously lacking in much of the new elements added to the curriculum. These features of its older practices should not be neglected by the secondary school in making a new approach to the problem of systematization.

This new approach should be principally dominated, however, by a wise regard for the interests and needs of pupils, the laws which govern their learning, and the aims of society in supporting schools. For developing systems of knowledge along these lines, there are many techniques available—some already tested by use. The materials for learning, for example, may be organized into units centering around problems common to many pupils. Another promising method developed in recent experiments is to awaken a pupil's initial interest in his school work by relating his learning to immediate activities and then to systematize his subsequent learning upon a progression of directed interests. Even the older method of moving in logical steps from one segment of subject matter to another has its place in the total scheme, particularly as the higher levels of learning are reached. In fact, every method of systematization appropriate to the circumstances should be called upon at times to promote that inner process by which knowledge is organized and evaluated in the mind of the pupil—the final measure of the school's success in discharging this function.

It is to be expected that the methods of systematizing knowledge adopted by secondary schools will in practice be modified by the individual teacher. The school may select the materials of learning to be used, establish general principles of procedure and define the ends of education, but it must leave in the hands of the teacher the final problem of converting all three into a pupil's educational growth. Hence by training and by native ability, a teacher should be master at adapting knowledge to learning so skilfully that the proper habits, skills concepts, and attitudes will emerge from a pupil's school experiences and modify his subsequent behavior.

Undoubtedly serious obstacles will arise to hamper the secondary school in developing a system of knowledge suitable to the education of all youth. The limited intelligence of many pupils and the difficulty of selecting curriculum material appropriate to their interests and capacities will be the major impediment. The native intelligence of the pupil we know cannot be altered. But the possibilities of adapting the materials of education and of discovering new materials are far from being exhausted. One of the first steps to be taken in this direction is to reconcile the two conflicting theories of learning and curriculum organization which favor controversy at the expense of progress. Educators now tend to divide into those who believe that the nature of subject matter defines the character of education and those who believe, on the contrary, that the character of education is defined by the nature of the child. Each theory has its value—one in rescuing education from the restrictions of individual interest; the other in giving personal significance and purpose to learning. A mature educational theory will harmonize both views, and once this is done the profession will be in a position to remove the remaining obstacles to the discharge of the function by using better guidance procedures, by developing skill in the selection of appropriate subject matter, by simplifying for general consumption the more difficult aspects of the aesthetic arts such as music and literature, by reforming the selection and training of teachers, by relaxing college requirements, and by constantly liberalizing the curriculum, particularly in the vocational field.

Function VI

To establish and to develop interests in the major fields of human activity as means to happiness, to social progress, and to continued growth.

INTRODUCTORY SUMMARY

Interests are the dynamics of education; in a broad sense they are the moving forces of life itself. Every intelligent educator makes them his silent allies in the work of educating children. He knows that interests are necessary to motivate learning and to vitalize it. Interests are equally important outside the classroom. They are indispensable means to happiness at all times and in all places. Without them the individual cannot grow, nor a society of individuals progress. Both for the sake of education itself and for the welfare of the supporting public, the establishment and development in pupils of interests in the major fields of human activity is a legitimate, not to say a paramount, function of the secondary school.

Interests grow out of human needs and endure by proving their power to contribute to the satisfaction of our wants. Therefore as their relationship to needs becomes clearer in the mind, as they become more consistent, more attainable, more social, and more inclusive, they exercise a more beneficent influence upon the individual, enrich his education, and fructify in his living. Interests should be recruited from all areas of human activity—from work, home life, play, politics, religion, the community, and the world of leisure—for the virtue of the educated individual is that he can derive values from a great variety of activities rather than from a few.

This recruiting of interests is obviously a gigantic task, but the school, very fortunately, does not have to start from nothing. Home and community influences awaken the interest of pupils in the most important fields of human activity. It is the work of the school to extend, develop, and redirect these interests in such a way that a pupil grows continuously and harmoniously in his power to live fully and well.

If secondary schools commit themselves to the extension, development and redirection of a pupil's interests, they will, of course, come face to face with new problems or with old ones in new form. By what means, for example, can interests be extended, developed, and redirected, and how can progress toward this objective be estimated? There is no ready made solution to the problem, but the more progressive schools, working on the fundamental principle that a pupil must first be led to express his interests and make them accessible to the school and to himself, are developing practices which hold promise. Once brought out into the open and embodied in written record or in some tangible accomplishment, interests cease to be vague longings but assume a substance and meaning which can be enlarged, refined, reformulated, even measured. The pupil and his counselor can then plan confidently a definite program by which the pupils' interests can be strengthened.

Every resource of the school should be utilized to this end. This immediately raises the question of how the curriculum of the school can best be organized to favor the pursuit and redirection of interests. Changes in curricular organization now in progress offer clues to an ultimate program conducive to the establishment of interests at the same time that other educational values are conserved. Many school systems have successfully introduced into the junior high school grades an integrated course of the "practical problems" type which bring pupils and teachers together for a cooperative venture in making pupils interested, competent, and intellectually at home in each important phase of their present and probable future activities. In the senior high school this course merges into a related course built around the major common interests developed in the lower grades and aiming at refining them until each can serve as the integrating core or center for a program of increasing specialization suited to the pupil as he approaches the end of his secondary school career.

Courses designed to cultivate interests cannot be inserted into the curriculum without overcrowding a pupil's schedule unless the burden of traditional subject matter carried is lightened. It is therefore suggested that elective courses be restricted to two periods daily and that this restriction be governed by the contribution which the established courses make to a development of a pupil's interests. It is highly probable that in such circumstances a great expansion will take place in courses in the arts and in the natural sciences and that the time devoted to the formal study of mathematics, foreign languages, and English will decline.

Some critics will doubtless oppose these shifts, attributing them to whim or caprice and warning against a further loss of values in the educational program. This is a mistaken fear, unmindful of ultimate values. The satisfaction of human needs, the continued growth and happiness of the individual, and the progress of society depend upon the cultivation of interests. If the secondary school neglects them, it does so at its own and society's risk.

Function VII

To guide pupils, on the basis of exploratory and revealing courses and of other information gathered from personnel studies, as wisely as possible into wholesome and worthwhile social relationships, maximum personality adjustment, and advanced study or vocations in which they are most likely to be successful and happy.

INTRODUCTORY SUMMARY

The shift in emphasis in American education from caring for the needs of the few to caring for the needs of the many, from identity of educational opportunity for a limited number to diversity of educational opportunity for all, is eminently desirable. Nevertheless, it has produced in numerous instances a serious maladjustment between a pupil and his educational program. Unintelligent choices of studies, misfitting of pupils, misapplication or lack of effort, inarticulation of subjects, academic and personality failures, retardation, truancy, and even delinquency are evils which follow in the train of education when many pupils and many subjects are promiscuously thrown together.

Maladjustments within school may be further supplemented by other maladjustments outside of school. Here the individual faces an ever more complex series of relationships, social, cultural, vocational, civic, and the like, which require immediate adjustment on his part or an adequate preparation for making adjustments to them in the future.

It is to help the individual respond happily and well to his total environment that the secondary school has the function of guidance. Guidance aims to serve the educative process by individualizing it so effectively that it works for each pupil. To this end, the school must have a sympathetic understanding of the pupil's interests, aptitudes, and abilities and must make a conscious effort to help him to develop them for the satisfaction of his needs, the discharge of his duties and obligations, and the enjoyment of his opportunities. It follows that there should be no attempt in guidance to establish a rigid control over the pupil. On the contrary, the right kind of guidance strives to help pupils help themselves, to make them ultimately as completely independent of formal procedures as they can be—even independent of guidance itself.

If the secondary school is to realize its function of guidance it must see to it that it guides pupils not only in name but in fact. It is an elementary principle that the effectiveness of guidance is limited by the amount of information available concerning the pupils to be helped.

No less important is the converse—the value of the information gathered is limited by the use made of it. In the light of these principles, the school should compile from both objective and subjective sources cumulative records of all the factors which have influenced and are modifying the growth of each pupil. Then it must use the records intelligently—not only to assist the pupil to turn the resources of the school to his educational advantages, but quite as important, to modify the organization and program of the school itself whenever it is desirable and feasible to do so. Sufficient emphasis may have been put upon the value of guidance procedures in directing the development of the pupil, but certainly too little has been put upon their value in directing the development of the school.

When guidance procedures are more widely used to determine needed modifications in the schools themselves, many of the common evils attached to attempts to educate large numbers of individuals can be removed. They will tend to disappear as educational opportunities are made to fit the individual. But it is not enough to diversify the program of studies. Testing, grading, discipline, organization, and administration must all submit alike to the process of individualizing education. Otherwise we will not be allowing each pupil to make the greatest growth of which he is capable nor will we be able to educate both the leaders and followers, both the academically superior and the academically inferior, at one and the same time.

The most immediate task of guidance is, of course, to aid the pupil to make wise choices and decisions. The school does not monopolize this function to the exclusion of the pupil's parents or friends nor does it exercise it irrespective of his need for help. But of all sources of guidance the school is best equipped to provide the pupil with the experience, the information, and the advice which he needs before he can make a decision wisely, or even know that some sort of decision should be made. The error of the school is never in offering guidance, if it be timely, but rather in using a false approach. It must not think of guidance in any corrective or remedial sense, nor yet as a means of making a pupil's program conform to any preconceived notion of his destiny, whether the notion originate with pupil or counsellor. The correct approach is for the school to study the pupil and assist him step by step in enlarging and enriching his life inside the school and out. Then when the time comes, and it will, for the pupil to select a college or vocation, the school should aid him to make a wise choice in the light of the interests, abilities, and prospects which his previous school and extra school experience has revealed.

To discharge its function of guidance with full success, the school must organize itself for that purpose. The exact form which its organization should take will vary according to its resources and needs, but the purposes of its organization are in each case the same. Competent members of the school staff must stand ready to make the resources of the school available to each pupil in ways which will promote his full growth. The objective of the counsellor is always to help the pupil to establish for himself worthy objectives and to achieve them. This should be the attitude of the whole school as well. It must not leave the counsellor to play a lone hand, but must support his position with the services of a guidance department or office where counsellors may be trained and where they may secure the information and techniques which they need. Any school can organize itself for the purpose of guidance, even though at first it be in a small way. Costs may be always a consideration; if they are reasonable they ought never to be a barrier. The best way to prevent the waste of money in education is to use the services of guidance to make education function for each pupil.

Function VIII

To use in all courses as largely as possible methods that demand independent thought, involve the elementary principles of research, and provide intelligent and somewhat self-directed practice, individual and cooperative, in the appropriate desirable activities of the educated person.

INTRODUCTORY SUMMARY

As the institution which brings the formal education of the great majority of people to a close, the secondary school has a very definite responsibility and function. It should see to it that those individuals whose formal education it terminates have in so far as possible reached the point where they can continue their education on an informal and independent basis and are capable of intelligent self-direction in the appropriate and desirable activities of an educated member of society.

This capacity for intelligent self-determination in the light of one's social obligations is a fundamental civic virtue in a democracy. It is also a virtue in personal living. To conceive of intelligent action, to take such action, and to abide by its outcomes means to substitute reason for sheer authority—in civic relations as well as in the daily round of duty. Nor is this all. A sense of having acted intelligently is indispensable to the mental security of a thinking person. Furthermore, if intelligent action eventuates in successful accomplishment, it carries with it the added reward of personal freedom. Freedom should not be thought of as mere release from difficulty; it comes from mastering obstacles by incorporating them into a successful scheme of action.

If the school is to function usefully in a democratic society and in the lives of intelligent individuals, it must by its spirit and its program provide and encourage opportunities for independent thinking and self-directed activity. These terms are neither mutually exclusive, nor are they antagonistic, as some people have thoughtlessly supposed. They are both aspects of the complete unit of behavior and exist in harmony and balance in any truly educative experience. The aspect of "doing" gives a feeling of reality to learning and provides it with drive or purpose; the aspect of "reflective thinking" gives it enriched meaning as well as a sense of security, of achievement, and of freedom to the learner.

Translated into terms of school organization, this view implies that the life of the school should be built around purposeful activities to give it reality, but that reflective thinking should be included as a necessary element in activity to give to school experience rationality, richness, and the promise of personal growth and freedom. In terms of teaching it means that the primary work of the teacher becomes guidance. Inasmuch as the learner is not "plastic clay" to be molded into some predetermined form, but is a "going concern" with needs, desires, and purposes of his own, it is the function of the teacher to help him formulate his purpose in the light of his needs, to reformulate them from time to time, and to choose the most effective activities by which his purposes may be realized.

The construction of the school curriculum around activities selected on the basis of how well they meet the needs and purposes of the learner would mean the abandonment of courses of study as formal, predetermined bodies of facts to be learned, but it would not mean the elimination of subject matter in every sense of the term. Out of the cooperative search of child and teacher for a factual background to the activities of the school would emerge bodies of information, some mainly scientific, others mainly historical, or mathematical, or literary, or social. The fundamental difference is that information would be subordinate to education and placed in proper relation to it. The felt needs of the pupil would be the point of departure for curriculum construction and the learner would participate in planning and evaluating the activities of which the curriculum was composed. The primer of democracy would then replace the manual of authority as the basic text of the school.

When reduced to its bare outline, the argument behind this function of the school is simple and plain. If independent thinking and intelligent self-direction are indispensable elements in the life of a democratic state and in the activities of the educated individual, then from the very logic of these facts secondary education must in the manner suggested provide for its pupils opportunities in which their intelligence may function independently, in which their faith in intelligent action may be strengthened by its good results, their mental security safeguarded, and their sense of freedom through the mastery of difficulties enlarged.

Function IX

To begin and gradually to increase differentiated education on the evidence of capacities, aptitudes, and interests demonstrated in earlier years. Care must be taken to provide previous to and along with differentiation as balanced and extended a general education as is possible and profitable.

INTRODUCTORY SUMMARY

The first concern of the school is to help pupils understand their cultural heritage and participate successfully in the common activities of life. Schools therefore devote a large share of their efforts to providing a "general" education for all. Even in secondary education, as distinguished from elementary education, there is a strong tendency to emphasize the universal rather than the specialized aspects of formal training. This tendency is increasing with the years.

Two principal reasons may be given for the current trend toward more "general" education in the secondary schools. In the first place, modern life exacts so much from the individual that no one of us can be happy or successful without a greater degree of competence in a wide variety of activities than our ancestors thought necessary. In the second place, we have more time to devote to the general aims of education. Most young people are now withheld from remunerative employment so long that there is less need than formerly for an early specialization of individual talents, and greater opportunity is afforded for developing the fundamental skills which all should possess.

It is a mistake to assume, however, that the outcomes desired of education, including those which should be common to all pupils, are at all times best served by offering in the same way an identical program of studies to each pupil. Diversity should characterize the school program if for no other reason than to prepare pupils effectively for the general activities which all are expected to take part in. The contradiction which this principle seems to present may be explained on the basis of individual differences. While all pupils are alike in some respects, they differ in others. Their differences become intensified during the age of adolescence, and the secondary school finds itself dealing with a multitude of pupils who must be educated in a multitude of ways even if similar educational outcomes are envisioned for all.

In addition to its usefulness in adapting the curriculum and methods of instruction to the individual differences of pupils, the principle of differentiation has a place in education in its own right. In cases where the secondary school is the terminal educational institution for a pupil —which is not the exception but the rule—it cannot neglect to provide in the closing years of his schooling for such a development and specialization of his personal talents as will give him competence in the beginning stages of some selected vocational field. Even in cases where the secondary school is preparatory to higher institutions of learning, a degree of differentiation, whether it be always wise or not, is necessitated by the varying requirements for admission prescribed by the colleges, universities, and technical schools. Finally, some differentiation, apart from these considerations, can be justified on the ground of respecting the legitimate interests of the pupil.

There is, therefore, little difficulty in showing that differentiation in education is necessary. The great problem is to determine correctly when differentiation should begin and how much of it should be provided. With respect to this problem we may establish the principle that there should be at least enough differentiation in a pupil's education to enable him, in spite of his differences, to attain to the best of his ability the educational objectives which the school prescribes for all. Beyond this, a differentiated program may be used for the opposite purpose of capitalizing on individuality to yield a varied educational product. The extent and kind of the differentiation provided for this purpose depend upon the pupil's vocational ambition or his plans for higher education as these may be determined from the capacities, aptitudes, and interests he has demonstrated in his previous education. But even here there are definite limits beyond which differentiation in education ought not to go. Schools should determine their ultimate policy with reference to their own resources, the temper of the community, the rival claims of all pupils, the principle that a pupil should first of all possess such competences as the interests of society demand that he have, and finally the best interests of the pupils themselves. To apply these limitations with exactness and justice in the case of each individual is so difficult that the whole problem should be the subject of a never-ending and informed study by the officers of the school. To assist in such a study is perhaps the most important service which a department of guidance can perform.

The greatest limitation upon a wise increase of differentiated education goes back, as most things must, to intangibles. The success of the secondary school in carrying out its function of diversifying its program and methods until the education each pupil receives is suitable to his interests, capacities, and needs must depend ultimately upon the broad training, the social vision, the technical knowledge, and the initiative of educational leaders and teachers. The importance of this dependence of the school upon its staff is plain enough, and has been often pointed out, but it cannot be overemphasized—not, at any rate, until the best minds of the profession have succeeded in making the school program function effectively for every child.

Function X

To retain each student until the law of diminishing returns begins to operate, or until he is ready for more independent study in a higher institution; and when it is manifest that he cannot or will not materially profit from further study of what can be offered, to eliminate him promptly, as wisely as possible directing him into some other school or into work for which he seems most fit.

INTRODUCTORY SUMMARY

In terms of function, every social institution may be said to have the threefold task of selecting the individuals it will serve, of retaining them during the period of its service, and finally of eliminating them when its work is done. The school is no exception to this rule. Ideally, its function of selection is to bring all normal young people under its influence; its function of retention is to keep them in regular attendance while it provides them with the education both individually suitable and socially valuable; and its function of elimination is to discharge them into wholesome employment as soon as they are fully ready for it, or into higher institutions of learning as soon as they can qualify in all essential respects for admission.

In recent years, fundamental economic and social changes in conjunction with the democratic impulses of the people have helped the school to approximate the ideal with respect to the selection and retention of pupils. As everyone knows, the secondary schools of America are now crowded with a larger proportion of youth than has ever been enrolled in the schools of any other country or in any other period of history. As a consequence, the secondary school has been forced to attend to the needs of nearly all boys and girls whether it wanted to or not. Likewise, the problem of retaining pupils, once very difficult, is now largely solved because the virtual impossibility of securing employment at an early age encourages young people to remain in the schools. But at the same time that underlying conditions have tended to solve the problems of selection and retention, they have complicated the problem of elimination by making it very difficult to terminate a pupil's schooling when he fails completely in his studies. The effect is to create a serious dilemma for the educator. In case of complete academic failure, he neither wishes to direct the pupil out of school into an inhospitable world, nor does he know how, with the resources at his command, to give to the pupil the kind of education suited to his needs.

Most educators would naturally prefer to break the impasse by modifying the school until education became profitable to each pupil regardless of his status. But this is clearly impossible unless society is able and willing to provide the funds needed to differentiate the school program to fit the needs of each pupil. Meanwhile the school must frankly face the necessity either of eliminating many pupils prematurely or else of continuing to deceive the public about the effectiveness of education while wasting the taxpayers' money to keep certain pupils in school when, except for the incidental protection schooling affords, it would be better for them and for their fellow students that they be eliminated and, if possible, put to work.

Of the two evils, the lesser is undoubtedly for the school to eliminate all pupils who are no longer making progress in the most suitable program it can offer, and by so doing to remind the public that it is the public's responsibility not the school's to provide for them. Perhaps the public will then respond by seeing that those eliminated are given work to do. But if such pupils are kept on at school, they face immediate discouragement or disillusionment, they retard the progress of other pupils, and they waste time, effort, and money in futile efforts, or lack of efforts, to derive some benefits from their schooling. The ultimate solution to the problem may be found in appropriating enough money to differentiate the school program until it serves all pupils, or in establishing entirely new types of schools, or even in social revolution. But these are options on which the public not the schools must decide. Pending a decision, the school should promptly eliminate a pupil as soon as it becomes perfectly clear that he can no longer profit materially from any program the school can offer. If the school is designed by society for educational rather than custodial purposes, it can in all honesty follow no other course.

There are, of course, many difficulties in eliminating pupils from schools under any circumstances. There is always the difficulty of estimating accurately the ability of the pupil and of reconciling parents to a disposition of their child that differs radically from their own hopes concerning him. Added to these obstacles is the lack of knowledge as to how education, especially in the case of smaller secondary schools, can be made more effective for individuals who do not respond to the old methods and materials of instruction. When these difficulties are considered in connection with the tardiness of the public to understand and support what the schools are trying to do to liberalize the curriculum, it seems likely that educators will find it hard, for a long time to come, to eliminate pupils at the exact time when their education should cease.

Although elimination in the ideal sense of directing pupils into constructive employment or into higher institutions of learning must wait until either one or the other of these opportunities is open to all young people, educators ought not to neglect their present duty. The first step they should take is to agree upon the provisional principle of elimination as here stated and to use it courageously and consistently as a guide to their actions. Then as the people come to see that public education is a social investment and not a benevolence, the necessary funds may be appropriated to fit the school to the needs of all. Otherwise the public will have to care for many young people by other means than schools. Whatever the ultimate decisions rendered, there is one further thing which educators should do. They should learn all they can about the individual pupil, his needs, capacities, interests, and aptitudes, and be prepared to guide him into the most appropriate of all the opportunities for development, in school or out, which society makes available for youth.

RELATION OF
SCHOOL AND
COLLEGE 5

*Portions of the Eight-Year Study
by the Progressive Education
Association*

THE EIGHT-YEAR STUDY

 *It is not the purpose of this book to
describe or analyze the progressive edu-
cation movement in America. It is not
subject to easy definition, since it is reflected in various ways, it has accommodated ideas from many
sources here and abroad, and it has drawn its leadership from
persons of varied backgrounds and motivation.*

*The progressive thought in education was part of a broader
humanitarian movement which emerged shortly after the
Civil War. The agrarian life characteristic of America when
the Declaration of Independence was written and the Constitution drawn up was yielding to the changes brought on by the
Industrial Revolution. Workers moved to the location of machines, cities and towns grew, and a landless class of labor
appeared. In spite of the early establishment of state school
systems, it has been estimated that in 1900, 1,700,000 children
under 16 were working, almost half of whom were in factories,
mines, or tenement sweatshops. Health care for the children of*

the poor was almost nonexistent, and the mortality rate was high. The progressive movement saw demands for legislation governing the employment of children, the establishment of playgrounds, and assistance in child and maternal health. Settlement houses were established, perhaps the most famous being Hull House in Chicago, founded by Jane Addams and Ellen Gates. Boys and girls clubs were organized in the slums and the leaders in the settlement houses carried on aggressive campaigns to improve the lives of those in the tenement districts, particularly the lives of the young.

Workers in order to protect themselves from exploitation were organizing. The muckrakers were uncovering the corruption that pervaded many levels of government and calling for political reform.

The broader progressive movement was rooted in the ideals of government expounded by the founding fathers and represented the attempt to apply these ideals to the changing society that was becoming urban and industrial.

In education, the progressive movement was in the same spirit of general social reform. More specifically, it aimed to reform a sterile school formalism and traditionalism, to relate the schools to the realities and problems of a new kind of society, and to introduce humane considerations into school thought and practice.

The progressive education movement meant, according to Cremin,[1] ". . . broadening the program and function of the school to include direct concern for health, vocation and the quality of family and community life . . . applying in the classroom the pedagogical principles derived from new scientific research in psychology and the social sciences . . . tailoring instruction more and more to the different kinds and classes of children who were being brought within the purview of the school."

It meant these things and much more as those leading the movement attempted to translate their ideas into the organization and programs of the schools.

The Progressive Education Association was formed in 1919, providing the progressive education movement an organization. Its first honorary president was Charles W. Eliot, whose work as chairman of the Committee of Ten seems so far removed in theory and spirit from the spokesmen for the new association.

In its beginning the Progressive Education Association was managed by and supported for the most part by private citizens whose interest

---

[1] Lawrence A. Cremin, *The Transformation of the School.* New York: Alfred A. Knopf, 1961, pp. viii–ix.

lay in creating a different kind of school. Much of the early work was done in private and experimental institutions and was centered primarily at the elementary level. During the latter part of the decade of the 20's and 30's, the Association grew and its influence widened. Its membership came to include leaders of education in public as well as private schools, in secondary education as well as in elementary education, and leaders of educational thought in colleges and universities.

The annual convention of the Progressive Education Association held in April, 1930, had before it the question: "How can the high school improve its service to American youth?"

Every proposal made for improvement in the high school program was met with the objection that changes would jeopardize the chances of students being admitted to college, according to the report of the convention. Then it was proposed that there be established a Commission on the Relation of School and College, "To explore possibilities of better coordination of school and college work and to seek an agreement which would provide the necessary freedom for secondary schools to attempt fundamental reconstruction."

The Commission was appointed in October, 1930. The early work of the Commission, the study which began in 1933 and terminated in 1941, is reported in a series, Adventure in American Education, made up of five volumes: The Story of the Eight-Year Study, Wilford Aikin, 1942, McGraw-Hill Book Company, Inc., a summary; Exploring the curriculum, *Giles, et al., summaries of the work in the schools in the experiment;* Appraising and Recording Student Progress, *Eugene Smith, et al., includes the records and evaluations in the schools;* Did They Succeed in College? *Chamberlin, et al., reports of the follow-up of the secondary graduates through college; Thirty Schools Tell Their Story, accounts by the participating schools of their particular efforts.*

The 26 members of the Commission, included (to use the classification reported in The Story of the Eight-Year Study) high school teachers and principals; college deans, presidents, teachers, and admission officers; evaluation specialists; educational philosophers; and journalists.

After a year of meetings and study the Commission issued a statement about what were considered to be inadequacies in secondary schools.

The next step was to enlist the cooperation of more than 300 colleges and universities in an experiment which was to continue for eight years. (It was originally for a five-year period, but later extended to eight years.) By agreement, the colleges and universities would release a selected group of secondary schools from the usual subject and unit requirements for college admission. Students from the selected secondary schools would be admitted without discrimination in relation to students from other schools who had met the standard admission requirements. A careful evaluation would be made over the course of the study to determine the success of the graduates of those schools for whom standard requirements had been removed.

In 1933, the schools that were to participate in the study were chosen. They included private and public schools, some large, some small, located in different sections of the country. The stated concern of the committee was, "To choose competent schools which were dissatisfied with the work they were doing and eager to inaugurate exploratory studies and changes which could not be undertaken without the freedom granted by the colleges." One of the schools originally chosen, Pelham Manor, withdrew from the study in 1936. The list of schools included the following:

> *Altoona Senior High School, Altoona, Pa.*
> *Baldwin School, Bryn Mawr, Pa.*
> *Beaver Country Day School, Chestnut Hill, Mass.*
> *Bronxville High School, Bronxville, N.Y.*
> *Cheltenham Township High School, Elkins Park, Pa.*
> *Dalton Schools, New York, N.Y.*
> *Denver Senior and Junior High Schools, Denver, Colo.*
> *Des Moines Senior and Junior High Schools, Des Moines, Ia.*
> *Eagle Rock High School, Los Angeles, Calif.*
> *Fieldston School, New York, N.Y.*
> *Francis W. Parker School, Chicago, Ill.*
> *Friends' Central School, Overbrook, Pa.*
> *George School, George School, Pa.*
> *Germantown Friends' School, Germantown, Pa.*
> *Horace Mann School, New York, N.Y.*
> *John Burroughs School, Clayton, Mo.*
> *Lincoln School of Teachers College, New York, N.Y.*
> *Milton Academy, Milton, Mass.*
> *New Trier Township High School, Winnetka, Ill.*
> *North Shore Country Day School, Winnetka, Ill.*
> *Radnor High School, Wayne, Pa.*
> *Shaker High School, Shaker Heights, Ohio*
> *Tower Hill School, Wilmington, Del.*
> *Tulsa Senior and Junior High Schools, Tulsa, Okla.*
> *University of Chicago High School, Chicago, Ill.*
> *University High School, Oakland, Calif.*

University School of Ohio State University, Columbus, Ohio
Winsor School, Boston, Mass.
Wisconsin High School, Madison, Wis.

An exciting eight years followed. The experimental schools, freed from college-imposed restrictions, moved in a variety of ways to modify their programs. The problems the schools encountered, the ways in which they approached their new freedom are parts of the story. During the eight years careful records were maintained and an evaluation procedure was devised.

At the conclusion of the experiment the results of the study were accepted as valid by both the participating schools and the cooperating colleges and universities.

The excerpts which follow are taken from The Story of the Eight-Year Study.[2]

The Commission, in the following section, pay their respects to the advances which had been made in secondary education between 1900–1930 and then describe those areas needing further exploration and improvement.

Also included is the agreement of the colleges and universities to take part in the cooperative experiment by which the usual college entrance requirements would be waived for a selected number of secondary schools.

THE STORY OF THE EIGHT-YEAR STUDY

Areas Needing Improvement

All members of the Commission were conscious of the amazing development of our secondary schools in the first three decades of the century. They realized that the number of boys and girls in high school had grown from less than one million to almost ten millions; that about 70 per cent of all American youth of high school age are in school; that billions had been invested by states, cities, towns, counties, and townships in imposing buildings and modern equipment; that these communities were gladly taxing themselves to pay the salaries of nearly 300,000 high school teachers; and that the faith of the American people in education remained unshaken.

Many in this group had shared in these thirty exciting years of Ameri-

[2] Reprinted by permission from *The Story of the Eight-Year Study,* by Wilford M. Aikin. Copyright 1942 by McGraw-Hill, Inc.

can education. They had seen the limited curriculum consisting chiefly of history, foreign languages, mathematics, science, and English extended to include the social studies, commercial subjects, the arts, home economics, shop work, and other courses of many kinds. They had participated in changing the content of traditional subjects and methods of teaching them. They had encouraged the development of student activities in speech, dramatics, music, athletics, publications, and a score of other fields. They had helped make the high school an orderly place of good feeling between teachers and pupils—a place to which most pupils went gladly because of pleasant association with others and interest in the general life of the school. They had seen the high school diploma become the magic key to doors of social and economic preferment.

These representative educators were vividly aware of the great achievements of our high schools. They shared the people's pride in them, but they were not satisfied. They were conscious of defects and determined, if possible, to correct them. They knew that of six who enter the high school only three graduate; of the three who graduate, only one goes on to college. For five out of six their high school is the end of formal schooling. For these *five* as well as for the *one,* the secondary school years can become a profoundly significant experience, said these educators.

SCHOOLS AND COLLEGES FACE THE FACTS

After more than a year's study the Commission issued a statement setting forth some of the areas which needed exploration and improvement by our schools. It seemed to the Commission that secondary education was clearly inadequate in certain major aspects of its work.

Secondary education in the United States did not have clear-cut, definite, central purpose. It had many goals, not one clear purpose in relation to which all others are of secondary importance. True, the high school diploma led to higher social and economic levels. It was believed that a "high school education" was good for youth but few asked seriously, "Good for what?" Neither society nor education knew certainly what the major purpose of the high school should be. The result was that teachers had no sure sense of direction and that boys and girls had no integrating, deeply satisfying school experience.

Schools failed to give students a sincere appreciation of their heritage as American citizens. The study of the history of the United States usually left students without understanding of the way of life for which we have been striving throughout our history; it seldom aroused enthusiasm and devotion. American youth left high school with diplomas but without insight into the great political, social, and economic problems of our nation.

Our secondary schools did not prepare adequately for the responsibilities of community life. Schools generally were excellent examples of autocratic, rather than democratic organization and living. Since little effort was made to lead youth into a clear understanding of the ideals of democracy, most students left school without principles to guide their action as they sought work and a place in adult life. Not many had developed any strong sense of social responsibility or deep concern for the common welfare.

The high school seldom challenged the student of first-rate ability to work up to the level of his intellectual powers. It was easy for him to "get his lessons," pass his courses. The result was that many a brilliant mind developed habits of laziness, carelessness, superficiality. These habits, becoming firmly established during adolescence, prevented the full development of powers. Even the conscientious student of superior ability did not often find himself seriously involved in a great intellectual enterprise. Seldom was any student "set on fire" intellectually, eager to explore on his own, ready to conquer difficulties and go through whatever drudgery might be necessary to achieve his purpose. The individual and society were both losers.

Schools neither knew their students well nor guided them wisely. Not often did teachers know students as young human beings striving to find their way into adulthood. Personal guidance was futile, usually involving only an occasional friendly chat; vocational guidance was limited to classroom study of occupations; and educational guidance was superficial, consisting chiefly of casual counsel concerning the subjects to be "taken" next semester. Few schools were seriously concerned about those who dropped out before graduation or about what happened to those who did receive diplomas.

Schools failed to create conditions necessary for effective learning. In spite of greater understanding of the ways in which human beings learn, teachers persisted in the discredited practice of assigning tasks meaningless to most pupils and of listening to recitations. The work was all laid out to be done. The teacher's job was to see that the pupil learned what he was supposed to learn. The student's purposes were not enlisted and his concerns were not taken into account. All this was in violation of what had been discovered about the learning process. The classroom was formal and completely dominated by the teacher. Rarely did students and teacher work together upon problems of genuine significance. Seldom did students drive ahead under their own power at tasks which really meant something to them.

Somehow, eagerness to learn grew less year by year as pupils advanced through school. This was not true of all, but it was characteristic of so many that the members of the Commission were seriously disturbed. They recognized that disintegrating and deadening forces outside school were partially responsible for this deplorable result, but they were quite sure that the content and organization of the curriculum had something to do with it.

The Commission was conscious, also, of the fact that the creative energies of students were seldom released and developed. Students were so busy "doing assignments," meeting demands imposed upon them, that they had little time for anything else. When there was time, they were seldom challenged or permitted to carry on independent work involving individual initiative, fresh combination of thought, invention, construction, or special pursuits. Although the creative urge may express itself in any field of endeavor, the arts, which afford unusual opportunity in this respect, were looked upon as "fads and frills," nonexistent in many schools, inadequately taught in most others. Art, in its various forms and uses, permeates everyday life. In its higher manifestations, it expresses the finest aspirations of the human spirit. Yet, only a few schools provided for their students enriching and satisfying experiences commensurate with the importance of the arts in our culture.

The conventional high school curriculum was far removed from the real concerns of youth. The subjects studied in the classroom were the curriculum; the *activities* of the students were the extracurriculum. These activities, initiated and developed by students, were recognized as significant educational experiences, but they were outside the curriculum. There was little realization that much of the work of the classroom was meaningless to students and that they were doing the work assigned chiefly for the "credit" which would add one more toward the total required for a diploma or admission to college. The molds into which education was poured, rather than its essence and spirit, became the goals of pupils and parents alike. This emphasis upon "credits" blinded even the teachers so that they could not see their real task.

Young people wanted to get ready to earn a living, to understand themselves, to learn how to get on with others, to become responsible members of the adult community, to find meaning in living. The curriculum seldom touched upon such genuine problems of living.

The traditional subjects of the curriculum had lost much of their vitality and significance. The purposes they should serve were seldom realized even in the lives of students of distinguished native ability.

The study of a foreign language did not often lead to extensive or searching reading of the great literature in that language; history usually was quickly forgotten, leaving no great concepts of human society, no deep understanding of the forces which mold man's destiny; science raised few fundamental questions of the nature of man or the universe; mathematics seldom became an effective tool, and even less frequently did it become a challenge to insight and understanding; the study of literature generally failed to heighten appreciation, deepen comprehension, or aid in the interpretation of experience.

Most high school graduates were not competent in the use of the English language.   They seldom read books voluntarily and they were unable to express themselves effectively either in speech or writing.

The Commission found little evidence of unity in the work of the typical high school.   Subjects and courses had been added until the program, especially of large schools, resembled a picture puzzle, without consistent plan or purpose. It was customary for a pupil to patch together all sorts of pieces—two units here, one there, a half unit elsewhere. His chief purpose was to collect enough pieces to graduate. If there was basic unity underlying subjects, few students discovered it; subjects of study were isolated, planned and taught without reference to the student's other studies or to any unifying purpose.

Teachers worked alone or in subject departments. The teacher of English limited his vision and concern to his own field; the teacher of science labored only to teach a certain body of scientific fact and skill. Seldom did they confer, and when they did, the results were usually unsatisfactory because neither understood the other's interests or problems. The division of labor, even in the intellectual field, had been carried so far that common language and community of purpose were in danger of being lost. Specialization in teaching in the secondary school had made it almost impossible for any teacher to become himself a person of broad culture. Teachers' lives were needlessly and unfortunately narrowed and impoverished.

The absence of unity in the work of the secondary school was almost matched by the lack of continuity.   The student jumped from semester to semester, from year to year, seldom going anywhere in particular. His work of one year had little relation to that of the preceding or following year. Because neither he nor his teachers had definite, longtime purposes for his work, he had no clear road to follow or compass to guide him in finding his way through the tangled underbrush of the curriculum.

Complacency characterized high schools generally ten years ago. Elementary education had been revolutionized since the beginning of the century, but the high school was still holding to tradition. It was rather well satisfied with itself. Minor curriculum changes were frequently made, but there was little serious questioning of purposes, practices, or results. Lavish financial support and blind faith on the part of the people encouraged schoolmen to conclude that all was right with their world.

Teachers were not well equipped for their responsibilities. They lacked full knowledge of the nature of youth—of physical, intellectual, and emotional drives and growth. They understood little of the conditions essential to effective learning. Relation of the school to the society it should serve was only dimly perceived. Democracy was taken for granted, but teachers seldom had any clear conception of democracy as a way of living which should characterize the whole life of the school. Very few were capable of leading youth into an understanding of democracy and its problems, for they themselves did not understand.

Only here and there did the Commission find principals who conceived of their work in terms of democratic leadership of the community, teachers, and students. Usually the principal was a benevolent autocrat or a "good fellow," letting each teacher do as he pleased as long as neither parents nor pupils complained. Most principals were constantly busy just "running the machine." They seldom stopped long enough to ask themselves, Why are we doing this or that? What are we driving at? Where are we going?

Principals and teachers labored earnestly, often sacrificially, but usually without any comprehensive evaluation of the results of their work. They knew what grades students made on tests of knowledge and skill, but few knew or seemed really to care whether other objectives such as understandings, appreciations, clear thinking, social sensitivity, genuine interests were being achieved.

The high school diploma meant only that the student had done whatever was necessary to accumulate the required number of units. Graduation from high school found most boys and girls without long-range purpose, without vocational preparation, without that discipline which comes through self-direction, and without having discovered for themselves something which gives meaning to living. Youth knew its rights and privileges, but often missed the rich significance of duty done and responsibilities fully met. Unselfish devotion to great causes was not a characteristic result of secondary education.

Finally, the relation of school and college was unsatisfactory to both institutions. In spite of the fact that formal education for five out of six of our youth ends at or before graduation from high school, secondary schools were still dominated by the idea of preparation for college. The curriculum was still chiefly "college preparatory." What the college prescribed for admission determined, to a large extent, what the boys and girls of the United States could study in school.

In large city high schools there was a wide range of fields of study, many of them designed for those who were not going to college; but parents and students looked upon the "college preparatory" subjects as the most "respectable." Thousands who had little or no aptitude for the work leading to college were engaged in it simply because it was the traditional thing to do. In the small high school of five or six teachers, with a necessarily limited offering of subjects, college prescriptions shaped the curriculum. When we realize that 60 per cent of all high school students are in schools of 200 or less, the importance of the influence of the college upon secondary education becomes apparent.

Most communities still judged the success or failure of the high school upon the basis of the school's standing with the colleges. When a student failed in his work in college and returned to his home community branded as a failure, the prestige of the school suffered severely in the eyes of its patrons. The failure of one student in college did more harm to the reputation of the school than its failure to adjust a hundred students who did not go to college to the work and responsibilities of life in the community. Because of this, the school placed undue emphasis upon preparation for college, to the neglect of its responsibility to those who were entering directly into the life of the community.

It was in no spirit of sweeping condemnation that the members of the Commission viewed the work of the secondary school in the United States. Their criticism was not so much of others as of themselves. They realized that many shortcomings were due to the amazing growth of our schools, to the necessity of employing inadequately prepared teachers, and to lack of time to adjust the work of the school to new responsibilities. But understanding of the conditions which produced weaknesses in our schools did not lessen the Commission's conviction that earnest attempts to remove them should be made at once. The cooperation of more than 300 colleges and universities was sought and secured in 1932.

SCHOOLS AND COLLEGES JOIN HANDS

The plan of cooperation between schools and colleges provided that a small number of representative secondary schools, to be selected by the Directing Committee [3] of the Commission, would be released from the usual subject and unit requirements for college admission for a period of five years,[4] beginning with the class entering college in 1936. Practically all accredited colleges and universities agreed to this plan. Relatively few colleges require candidates to take College Entrance Board Examinations. In such cases, these examinations were waived by all except Harvard, Haverford, Princeton, and Yale. These four men's colleges, with this one reservation, accepted the proposal and agreed to cooperate. The Directing Committee was especially appreciative of the full cooperation of the women's colleges.

It was agreed that admission to college during the experimental period would be based upon the following criteria: [5]

1. Recommendation from the principal of the cooperating secondary school to the effect that the graduating student (a) is possessed of the requisite general intelligence to carry on college work creditably; (b) has well-defined, serious interests and purposes; (c) has demonstrated ability to work successfully in one or more fields of study in which the college offers instruction.

2. A carefully recorded history of the student's school life and of his activities and interests, including results of various types of examinations and other evidence of the quality and quantity of the candidate's work, also scores on scholastic aptitude, achievement, and other diagnostic tests given by the schools during the secondary school course.

It is intended that the tests used will be of such character that the results submitted to the colleges will give a more adequate and complete picture of the candidate than is given by methods now in use. A special Committee on Records is now at work endeavoring to determine:

1. What information the college needs for wise selection and guidance of students
2. How that information can best be secured
3. In what form it should be recorded and presented to the colleges.

The cooperating colleges will not be obliged to admit under this agreement all such students as meet the new requirements. However,

[3] The Commission had become too large to work effectively. The Directing Committee was charged by the Commission with the responsibility of conducting the Study to its conclusion. For membership of Directing Committee, see introductory pages. (*The Story of the Eight-Year Study*)

[4] This period was later extended to eight years.

[5] A Proposal for Better Coordination of School and College Work. For complete document, see Appendix, pp. 140–146. (*The Story of the Eight-Year Study*)

during the experimental period and from the limited group of cooperating schools, the colleges agree to accept students under this plan without regard to the course and unit requirements now generally in force for all students, and without further examination. The colleges, for this period, agree, also, that students applying for admission under the new requirements will be considered without discrimination in comparison with students applying from other schools where present requirements are in effect.

The participating schools agreed that the following principles should guide their work during the eight years of the study: emphasis upon exploration and experimentation, a search for a valid reason for the existence of the secondary school, unity of the curriculum, the relevance of the curriculum to concerns of the students, the relationships of education to democracy, better knowledge about each pupil and better guidance based on that knowledge, improved mutual understanding between secondary schools and colleges, better evaluation, and doubt of the validity of college entrance requirements. All these characterized the beliefs of the schools as they began their work.[6]

THE SCHOOLS PLAN FOR THE USE OF THEIR NEW FREEDOM

In 1933, shortly after the participating schools were chosen, the principals met with the Directing Committee to plan together for eight years of difficult work. Everyone had a strong sense of sharing in a great adventure; few anticipated fully the hard work, the problems, the discouragements, and the eventual satisfactions which were to come. No one present at that first conference will ever forget the honest confession of one principal when she said, "My teachers and I do not know what to do with this freedom. It challenges and frightens us. I fear that we have come to *love our chains.*" Most of use were just beginning to realize that we were facing the severest possible test of our initiative, imagination, courage, and wisdom. No one of the group could possibly foresee all the developments ahead, nor were all of one mind as to what should be done.

Members of the Commission and representatives of the Thirty Schools continued to meet annually to think and plan together. Although each school would decide for itself what to do with this new

[6] *Ibid.,* pp. 16–24.

freedom, everyone was eager to have the benefit of the thinking and experience of all the others. The reader should keep in mind always that the principals and teachers of the Thirty Schools were striving, groping, searching constantly in their attempts to decide what to teach and how to teach. The schools did not all start from the same place or go in the same direction. It is difficult, therefore, to report their purposes and plans both briefly and accurately. However, it can be stated that they became convinced in the course of reconsideration of their own work, that two major principles should guide their efforts at reconstruction.

The first was that the general life of the school and methods of teaching should conform to what is now known about the ways in which human beings learn and grow. Until recent years learning in school has been thought of as an intellectual process of acquiring certain skills and of mastering prescribed subject matter. It has been assumed that physical and emotional reactions are not involved in the learning process, but if they are, they are not very important. The newer concept of learning holds that a human being develops through doing those things which have meaning to him; that the doing involves the whole person in all aspects of his being; and that growth takes place as each experience leads to greater understanding and more intelligent reaction to new situations.

Holding this view, the participating schools believed that the school should become a place in which young people work together at tasks which are clearly related to their purposes. No longer should teachers, students, or parents think of school simply as a place to do what was laid out to be done. Nor should schooling be just a matter of passing courses, piling up credits, and, finally, getting a diploma. The school should be a living social organism of which each student is a vital part. It should be a place to which one goes gladly because there he can engage in activities which satisfy his desires, work at the solution of problems which he faces in everyday living, and have opened to him new interests and wider horizons. The whole boy goes to school; therefore school should stimulate his whole being. It should provide opportunities for the full exercise of his physical, intellectual, emotional, and spiritual powers as he strives to achieve recognition and a place of usefulness and honor in adult society.

The Thirty Schools realized that many changes in ways of teaching, as well as in organization and curriculum, were necessary if attendance at school was to become the stimulating, meaningful experience it could be for each student. They knew that the classroom should become a place of cooperative activity in which teacher and students would seek together to achieve results which they believed important. Only as society's demands and student concerns were united in school objectives could education become an experience of vital significance. Only then would eager outreach for knowledge and understanding supplant credit accumulation. Only then would earnest, hard work be done gladly and intelligently. For then the student would be seeking the essence and substance rather than the forms and husks of education.

The second major principle which guided the work of the participating schools was that the high school in the United States should rediscover its chief reason for existence. It is not enough to create better conditions for learning. It is equally necessary to determine what American youth most need to learn. Out of their searching study the Thirty Schools came to realize that the primary purpose of education is to lead our young people to understand, to appreciate, and to live the kind of life for which we as a people have been striving throughout our history. Other things are important but only relatively so. It is necessary to teach the three "R's," science, language, history, mathematics, the arts, safety, vocations, and most of the other subjects that now crowd the curriculums of the schools; but unless our young people catch the vision which has led us on through all generations, we perish.

Year after year the conviction became clearer and deeper that the school itself should become a demonstration of the kind of life in which this nation believes. The Commission and the schools said that the most important service the school can render youth is to give them understanding and appreciation of the way of life we call democracy, and that the best way to understand and appreciate is to live that kind of life at school every day.

It was soon discovered that application of principles of democracy to the life of the school would cut deep. To develop a sense of worth in each individual, to promote full participation by each one in the affairs of the school, and to lead everyone to think for himself would demand radical change in many aspects of the curriculum and ways of teaching. Nevertheless, the Thirty Schools, holding these ideas, set to work to put them into practice.

They were quite sure that the spirit and practice of experimentation and exploration should characterize secondary schools in a democracy. The schools in the Eight-Year Study came to be called "experimental" schools. Most schools were fearful of such appellation. The term had come to connote foolish, careless, haphazard changes made without serious study and concluded without painstaking evaluation of results. The Thirty Schools entered the Study to make honest attempts to find better ways of serving their students. Thoughtful investigation and planning preceded each innovation, and careful measurement of results followed. If results were not satisfactory, further change was made in the light of fuller knowledge. In this sense the Thirty Schools were and are "experimental," and they believe that every school in a democracy should be also. No aspect of any school's work should be so firmly fixed in practice or tradition as to be immune from honest inquiry and possible improvement. It is only in this way that life and vigor are maintained and progress achieved.

Many in the Study thought that fundamental revision should be undertaken only after thoughtful, cooperative reconsideration of the high school's function in the community it serves. They believed that no change in any part of the curriculum should be made without consideration of its effect upon the whole program of studies. They realized that this would require time, organization, and leadership.

As the schools began their studies preparatory to revision of their work, they were sure that the curriculum of the secondary school should deal with the present concerns of young people as well as with the knowledge, skills, understandings, and appreciations which constitute our cultural heritage. There was no disposition to undervalue or eliminate from the curriculum the accumulated, well-organized experience of civilization. But there was widespread recognition of the fact that much of the conventional high school curriculum had become inert and of little value and that many vital needs of youth were not being met effectively. Many of the schools thought that the problems common to young people growing up in the United States should constitute the heart and center of the curriculum for all, whether they are going to college or not.

Every school in the Study sought from the start to develop greater unity and continuity in the curriculum. They realized that artificial barriers, which separated subject from subject and teacher from teacher, had been erected in schools generally. In all the proposals for change submitted by the schools in 1933, there were devices for bringing subjects together and for teachers to plan and work cooperatively. It was thought that these changes would enable students to see the relationship of one subject to another, teachers and students would begin to glimpse the underlying unity of all knowledge.

Continuity was to be found by arranging courses in better sequence. In a few of the schools it was realized at the beginning that really significant continuity of experience cannot be achieved by any fixed prearrangement of courses alone. This year's work must build upon last year's, but no two groups or individuals are the same. Therefore, some schools with unusual insight and understanding attempted to secure continuity of growth by enlisting the students in the work of planning each unit of study in relation to the experiences which had gone before.

Because of their concern for the individual as well as for the whole group, the schools realized that they must know each student well and guide him wisely. They said they should know each one as a person, not just as a student of English or mathematics or as halfback on the football team. Some teacher should know him in these and all other phases of his life, including his home. That teacher should be sensitive, understanding, and wise enough to bring all the appropriate resources of the school and community to bear upon the task of guiding the student in meeting his personal, educational, and vocational problems.

From the beginning the Commission and the schools recognized their responsibility for measuring, recording, and reporting the results of their work. They knew this would be difficult. They realized that neither they nor any other schools really knew much about the results of school experiences in the lives of their students. They had means of measuring accretions of knowledge and development of skills, but they could not be sure of the achievement of other equally important but less tangible purposes. They expected that fuller appraisal of results would facilitate curriculum revision, revealing weaknesses and strengths and providing a sound basis for further change.

As the Study got under way, the Thirty Schools hoped that more satisfactory relations with colleges and universities would be developed. Some schools were sending almost all graduates to college; from others only one in five or six continued his formal education. All the schools were eager to improve their service to both groups. Theoretically, secondary schools were free to meet the needs of the noncollege-going student in any way they wished; but, as has been pointed out, college requirements fixed in most schools the program of studies for all. It was acknowledged that high schools did have a limited range of freedom, but it had to be admitted that they did not use the freedom they possessed and that college prescriptions were often only an excuse for stagnation and inaction.

Now that these requirements were no longer binding on the Thirty Schools, they were under the necessity of proving that they could use freedom creatively and wisely. They were eager to do this, for they believed that the larger measure of freedom which they now had should characterize school and college relations generally. They doubted that success in college depends upon the study of certain subjects for a certain length of time. They questioned the basic assumption upon which college-school relations were based: that only by the study of English, foreign language, mathematics, science, and history could a student be prepared for the work of the liberal arts college.

The schools believed that there are many different avenues of study and experience by way of which young people could develop the skill, understanding, and intellectual maturity necessary for satisfactory achievement at the college level. They were convinced that work in school should have meaning for each student because of its pertinence to his concerns and that such work would develop the powers needed in college. In the formal proposal to colleges and universities, the Commission stated, "We are trying to develop students who regard education as an enduring quest for meanings rather than credit accumulations." The schools were confident that this could be done by basing the secondary school curriculum upon the needs of youth in our society. If the high school helped students to find the meanings of their life experiences, they would go on to college to seek deeper and broader meaning in their maturing experiences. To this end traditional studies would have to be revitalized and reoriented; much new content would have to be included in the curriculum of school and college.

The schools involved in the Study were quite sure that they could really prepare students for the life and work of college. Most "college preparation" consisted of doing what was necessary to get in. Little thought was given by the student or his teachers to the real purposes in going to college or to the problems of living and working there. These schools took their eyes off the college gates and looked to the fruitful fields beyond.

Everyone involved in the Study was convinced that some means should be found by which teachers in the schools and professors in the colleges should work together in mutual respect, confidence, and understanding. Unless this could be done, the Thirty Schools knew that honest, realistic coordination of school and college work would not be achieved.

And so the adventure in pioneering was begun. To some teachers even in the participating schools the Study was an unnecessary and dangerous innovation; to some college professors, "Progressive Education now had enough rope to hang itself;" and to some parents the Study was a source of uneasiness and dissatisfaction. But to most of the teachers in the Thirty Schools and to thousands of educators and parents throughout the nation, it held great promise for the future.

During the eight years of the study, the schools learned that their pupils could succeed in college without having followed the tradi-

tional pattern of requirements set up for college admissions. But out of their experiences they learned other things, too. They learned that competent secondary schools can be trusted with the responsibility for their own program of education. They came to comprehend the waste of time and resources that occurred when school and college do not work together in mutual respect.

They learned that all teachers, and parents, too, must be involved if meaningful change in secondary school programs is to take place. They learned that desirable change is a process of the whole school and does not come about through piecemeal efforts. They learned that modifications in a school must go hand in hand with appraisal and evaluation. They learned, too, that responsible change is a painstaking process.

These and other products of the eight years of work and study are recounted in the following section.

This We Have Learned [7]

What can be said now at the end of the Eight-Year Study? What has been learned through this experience? Have the hopes and expectations of those who inaugurated the project been fulfilled?

It should be recalled that the Commission had two major purposes:

1. To establish a relationship between school and college that would permit and encourage reconstruction in the secondary school.
2. To find, through exploration and experimentation, how the high school in the United States can serve youth more effectively.

Let us consider now the findings of the Study in the realm of school and college relations.

MANY ROADS LEAD TO COLLEGE SUCCESS

The proposal for cooperation, which was approved by colleges and universities generally in 1932, established an effective cooperating relationship between them and the Thirty Schools for the period of the Study. It permitted and encouraged the participating schools to go ahead with their plans for revision of their work. As already stated the Commission and the schools held that

> Success in the college of liberal arts does not depend upon the study of certain subjects for a certain period in high school.
>
> There are many different kinds of experience by which students may prepare themselves for successful work in college.

[7] *Ibid.*, pp. 116–139.

Relations more satisfactory to both school and college could be developed and established upon a permanent basis.

Ways should be found by which school and college teachers can work together in mutual regard and understanding.

The study of the college experience of the graduates of the Thirty Schools was made to secure evidence which would confirm these beliefs or show them to be unwarranted. The evidence is reported briefly in Chapter V and in detail in Volume IV of this Report. A careful examination of the findings can leave no one in doubt as to the conclusions that must be drawn:

1. The graduates of the Thirty Schools were not handicapped in their college work.
2. Departures from the prescribed pattern of subjects and units did not lessen the student's readiness for the responsibilities of college.
3. Students from the participating schools which made most fundamental curriculum revision achieved in college distinctly higher standing than that of students of equal ability with whom they were compared.

These facts have profound implications for both school and college.

First, the assumption that preparation for the liberal arts college depends upon the study of certain prescribed subjects in the secondary school is no longer tenable. This assumption has been questioned for some time. Earlier studies threw some doubt upon it. The results of this Study disprove it. Success in college work depends upon something else. Real preparation for college is something much more important and vital than the accumulation of 15 prescribed units.

School and college relations based upon this untenable assumption are neither satisfactory nor sound. The relationship is an unhappy one. Colleges criticize the schools saying that students come to college unprepared for their work, that they are deficient in even the most rudimentary academic skills, that their habits of work are careless and superficial, and that they lack seriousness and clarity of purpose. Schools, on the other hand, charge that colleges regiment students, treat them too impersonally, counsel them inadequately, and fail to stimulate them intellectually. Teachers in secondary schools say that college professors are unwilling or unable to see the great problems of the high school, thinking of it only as a place of preparation for college and forgetting the school's obligation to the 80 per cent who stop their schooling at or before graduation from high school. Whether these criticisms are warranted or not, they reveal an unsatisfactory relationship. It does not seem that there can be much more happiness in either group until a sound basis of relationship is established.

The customary relations of school and college are unsound in that emphasis is placed upon outworn symbols—units, grades, rankings, and diplomas. To stand well with its patrons the high school must meet college requirements. If those requirements are not essentials, both school and college are forced into false positions. The college is placed in the position of saying that certain subjects, grades, and units are essential when it knows that they are not; and the school is placed in the false position of forcing students through work which may be of little value to them.

The conclusion must be drawn, therefore, that the assumption upon which school and college relations have been based in the past must be abandoned. It is evident that the liberal arts college has not examined its work thoroughly and realistically and based on that examination its prescription of what is essential in preparation. This Study has proved that some knowledges and skills heretofore generally assumed to be necessary are not needed. It has established, also, that necessary disciplines of mind and character may be achieved through many other subjects than those formerly assumed to be the only effective ones.

It does not follow that it is useless or impossible to describe what preparation is actually required for success in college. Indeed colleges need to know—teachers, pupils, and parents need to know—what knowledge, what skills, what habits, what attitudes constitute the foundation for satisfactory achievement in college. When these are determined, colleges should then require them for admission; schools could then be intelligent in their important task of preparation.

But this is more easily said than done. The college cannot state what preparation is essential unless it knows its own purposes. It must be said here that liberal arts college faculties seldom state clearly what they mean by liberal or general education. Perhaps they do not know. Individual professors often have clearly defined purposes. Sometimes departments such as English, history, economics have set up goals for their work. Rarely, however, have whole college faculties cooperatively thought their problem through and set forth their purposes and plans.

Although cooperative faculty study of liberal education is not usual in colleges, in some the faculty as a whole is attempting to redefine general education and to revise its work in the light of clearer purpose. One college, Columbia College, Columbia University, which has been studying this problem seriously, turned last year to the question of preparation for college. Dean Herbert E. Hawkes gives this encouraging report of their deliberations:

A few weeks ago I called a conference of all the instructors of freshmen in Columbia College in order to talk about this important topic. In the course of the conference I asked them what kind of students they really wanted in their courses, what kind of intellectual background, what pattern of preparation, what areas of competency. The replies were interesting. They reported with one accord that they wanted boys who could read with good speed and comprehension, and who knew how to gauge their reading to the various types of material that they were called upon to master. They wanted boys who had a reasonable facility in self-expression, both orally and in writing. So much for English. Then they wanted boys who knew how to tackle a hard intellectual job and carry it through to completion—a boy who had acquired the habit and zest for work. You may call this discipline. Furthermore they wanted boys who knew an idea when they saw one, who were accustomed to dealing with ideas, in short, who had reasonable intellectual maturity.

These three points were mentioned again and again in one form and another. The amazing fact was that very little was said about the specific pattern of subject matter preparation. If the students had gained these fundamental qualities and attitudes they did not care where they got them. In fact, many of the instructors in the various freshman courses in social studies, in humanities and even in science said that they could not tell from the way in which a boy took hold of his college work whether he had passed this or that entrance examination except insofar as it was reflected in these qualities. To be sure, in the humanities it appeared that the boy who had good grounding in Latin had a head start in the reading of the Greek and Roman classics that are included in this course. But in this course, those who had received such training could not be distinguished from those who had not after a few weeks, provided they knew how to work. The corresponding fact held true in the sciences.

Here is a college faculty declaring that success in college depends upon skill in the use of the mother tongue, readiness and ability to work hard, and "reasonable intellectual maturity." Similar conclusions have been reached by other faculties. As more colleges reexamine their own purposes and procedures, and as they reconsider the problem of preparation for higher education, agreement may be reached upon some such essentials as those stated by the faculty at Columbia.

To go further and to conduct such cooperative study among many institutions is a most difficult task, as the Thirty Schools have discovered. Yet, if this were done, it would make possible a sound basis of relationship with schools. Until colleges and secondary schools know and agree on what they are trying to do, there is no intelligent way for them to unite their efforts on behalf of those who expect to go to college.

It should be emphasized here that it is already possible for colleges to establish adequate admission requirements that do not prescribe the content or organization of the secondary school curriculum. Prescription of subjects, units, and requirements of entrance examinations based upon predetermined subject matter have undoubtedly fixed the pattern of secondary education for the great majority of young people in the United States. Without intending to do so, the colleges have handicapped schools in their attempts at fundamental reconstruction. To move ahead schools must have encouragement from colleges. To give that encouragement colleges must abandon their present admissions policy.

No one questions the right of colleges to set up requirements for admission of students. Quite properly colleges desire only those students who are equipped to do the work the college expects. They may justly require evidence of the candidate's fitness. It is the school's responsibility to provide that evidence. But all colleges and universities, whether tax supported or privately endowed, are public institutions and, therefore, they have a public responsibility. Accordingly, no college can be justified in setting up requirements for admission which have been shown to be unnecessary in preparing students to do college work.

For the Thirty Schools many colleges waived the customary entrance examinations, and all colleges granted freedom from subject and unit prescriptions. The schools, however, gave colleges abundant significant evidence of the student's readiness for college work. Upon the basis of this evidence colleges selected candidates from the participating schools. The findings of the Commission's follow-up study show that the colleges were able to select students intelligently on the basis of the information provided by the Thirty Schools. These students did their college work at least as well as others of equal ability, failed no more frequently, stayed in college and graduated in equal numbers, and won distinction more often.

The Eight-Year Study has demonstrated beyond question that colleges can secure all the information they need for selection of candidates for admission without restricting the secondary school by prescribing the curriculum. For this purpose, evidence from such sources as the following would provide ample data:

1. Descriptions of students, indicating qualities of character, habits of work, personality, and social adjustment. Many of the record forms prepared by the Commission's Committee on Records and Reports are helpful and suggestive in this connection.
2. The results of the use of instruments of evaluation:
   a. Such standardized tests as are applicable to the school's work
   b. Other types of tests appropriate to the objectives of the school,

such as those prepared by the Evaluation Staff of this Study.

c. Scholastic aptitude tests that measure characteristics essential to college work and are independent of particular patterns of school preparation.

3. For colleges that require tests given by an outside agency, records of achievement in examinations that do not presuppose a particular pattern of content. An example is the Comprehensive English examination of the College Examination Board.

An admission plan such as this would not fix the content or organization of the high school curriculum.

If such a plan were adopted generally by colleges, the secondary schools of the United States could go about their business of serving all youth more effectively. Uniformity would be neither necessary nor desirable in the work of the school. One student would develop the essential skills, habits of mind, and qualities of character through studies appropriate to his abilities, interests, and needs; another student would develop the essentials of mind and character through quite different studies. The secondary school would then be encouraged to know each student well and to provide experiences most suitable to his development. This, in turn, would lead to dynamic school curricula. The static, frozen pattern of subjects and credits would disappear and secondary education would move ahead with other dynamic forces toward the achievement of a greater democracy.

The second major implication of the results of the Eight-Year Study is that secondary schools can be trusted with a greater measure of freedom than college requirements now permit. The Thirty Schools, representing secondary schools of various kinds in many sections, have not abused their greater freedom. On the contrary, many college authorities wonder that these schools did not use their freedom more extensively. It may be thought that the participating schools were restrained from wild experimentation by the college members of the Directing Committee, but such was not the case. In fact, they have constantly urged the schools to greater adventure. However, custom is deeply embedded in secondary education. It is not easy to break down traditional patterns of thinking and acting, nor do teachers create new ones readily.

Perhaps the chief reason for confidence in the schools' use of freedom is to be found in the genuine sense of responsibility which most teachers feel. They are conscious of the far-reaching consequences of their work. Because of this sense of duty they do not turn lightly from practices of proved worth to engage in irresponsible experimentation. If some in the colleges feared that the Thirty Schools would use their freedom recklessly, they now know that their fears were without foundation.

Without exception the colleges involved state that this Study has been very much worthwhile. Although there may be doubt concerning some of the innovations in the schools, the colleges are unanimous in recognizing the growth which the schools have achieved through participation in the enterprise. The Thirty Schools fervently hope that their new work can be continued and developed more fully. This can be done only if their present freedom is not taken away from them.

The existing agreement between the Thirty Schools and the colleges expires in 1943. "What will happen then?" the schools are asking. Will it be necessary to give up the new work, which the schools are eager to carry on, and return to prescribed courses and a static curriculum? Perhaps the colleges would be willing to extend the agreement with the Thirty Schools beyond 1943, but neither the schools nor the Directing Committee favors continuing an arrangement involving only these schools. They hope for extension of the freedom which the member schools now have to competent schools everywhere.

This can be done. As has been suggested in these pages, three steps should be taken:

1. Until the purposes of general education in the liberal arts colleges are clearly defined and plainly stated, subject and unit prescriptions and entrance examinations that prescribe the content or organization of the secondary school curriculum should be discontinued.

2. The knowledge, skills, habits, and qualities of mind and character essential as preparation for college work should be ascertained by colleges and schools cooperatively.

3. A plan of admission should be adopted which provides the college with needed information concerning candidates, but which does not prescribe the content or organization of the secondary school curriculum.

Should these three steps be taken great progress would surely come in both secondary and higher education throughout the country. Upon this new and sound basis schools and colleges would develop relations which would bring them together in mutual respect and understanding. Professors from the colleges and teachers from the schools would sit down together often to think and plan for the education of American youth. They would learn from each other. They would understand better one another's purposes and problems. Theirs is a common task, the teachers at one level, the professors at another. By deliberating together they would see that task more clearly and perform it more effectively.

During the eight years of the Study many school-college conferences have been held. They have always resulted in increased mutual regard and confidence. For many college professors and school teachers it was a new experience to spend two days together in an atmosphere of friendly cooperation around the conference table. This sort of experience should not be rare; it is as necessary as any other conference with one's colleagues. Neither the school nor the college can understand fully or render adequately its service to youth apart from the other.

The failure of schools and colleges to coordinate their work has resulted in enormous waste of time, effort, and money. The tragic consequences to thousands of boys and girls are beyond all measurement. But wastage of the nation's material and human resources need not continue. By taking time to know each other and by seeking together for solutions of common problems our institutions of secondary and higher education can bring their united strength to the service of the nation.

THE SCHOOLS COUNSEL FROM THEIR OWN EXPERIENCES

Early in the Eight-Year Study the member schools and the Commission promised to give a frank account of their experiences when the project came to its end. They said they would tell of mistakes and failures as well as successes, and they agreed to reveal the difficulties and problems they encountered along the way. Anyone who has followed the story of the Study in this volume or delved more deeply into the other four volumes of the Report must be aware of the frankness and sincerity of the hundreds who have been engaged in this attempt to find better ways of serving American youth. Although the schools' experiences have differed in many ways, it is possible to record some that have been fairly common and to draw out of them some lessons which may be helpful to other schools about to undertake the difficult task of reconstruction.

Before summarizing the experience of the Thirty Schools, let it be said again that they do not pose as model schools. They do not claim to have solved all problems, nor do they think they "know all the answers." They realize that many other schools, not included in this Study, have been engaged in the same task and that their contributions to the improvement of secondary education probably are just as important as the achievements of the schools which have participated in this project.

The members of the Directing Committee and the teachers and administrators in the Thirty Schools have learned from the experiences of these eight years that effective secondary school reconstruction requires thorough preparation.

This takes time. The schools which plunged into change without taking time to think their problems through often found it necessary to go back to the beginning and start over. This caused confusion and uneasiness which might well have been avoided.

Thorough preparation demands cooperative deliberation. Piecemeal revision by individual teachers or subject departments usually is disappointing. Every teacher's work is significant in its relation to the whole effort of the school. Therefore, any important change in any part of the school's work should be made only as one move in a comprehensive plan. Administrators, teachers, parents, and students should unite in the thinking and planning which should precede any revision of the school's work.

All teachers should participate. When the Eight-Year Study was started, some schools selected a few members of the faculty for the new work; the others, who were not consulted, felt left out. This resulted in division and misunderstanding. In some schools it led to jealousy, bitterness, and sabotage of the new work. This unhappy state of affairs has long since disappeared in almost all of the schools, but it is a danger which can and should be avoided by giving every teacher an opportunity to share fully, to advocate or oppose change, to voice his convictions whatever they may be. Complete agreement is desirable and is sometimes reached by means of thorough discussion. However, unanimous decision is not essential. New work may be developed satisfactorily and without faculty dissension if every one shares in the deliberations which lead to change.

Parents, too, must share in preparation for high school changes. The schools which did not draw patrons into the planning which preceded revision encountered parental misunderstanding. Unwarranted criticism and opposition were the results. In some instances worthy innovations had to be abandoned because of censure. This could have been avoided if these schools had taken pains to secure parental participation in the thinking which led to change in the curriculum. Moreover, these schools did not have the good counsel that many thoughtful laymen can give. Others of the member schools took parents into their confidence, consulted with them as plans were developed, and gained the strength of their support in new undertakings. Out of these happy and unhappy experiences the Thirty Schools have learned that no school is fully prepared for reconstruction unless the cooperation of parents has been secured.

Adequate preparation involves research. Before any school revises its work the faculty should study the community the school serves and the needs of youth in that community. The results of research elsewhere should be studied carefully for their application to the local situation. The services of specialists and experienced curriculum consultants should be secured if possible. Above all, the faculty should reexamine the democratic tradition, clarify its meaning, and consider its implications for the school in every phase of its work.

No teacher or school is fully ready for constructive change until plans for appraising results are carefully formulated. The school should find out whether changes in curriculum and methods of teaching achieve purposes more effectively. The Thirty Schools emphasize the necessity of taking time to secure all possible evidence of student progress and to study that evidence searchingly for clues to further action. Equally important are adequate means for recording and reporting all significant aspects of pupil development. Evaluating, recording and reporting are inextricably interwoven in the whole fabric of education. Therefore, they cannot be ignored in any sound preparation for educational reconstruction.

The Thirty Schools have learned that thorough preparation for revision requires honest belief in exploration and experimentation as a method of educational progress. This means that principals and teachers must have an abiding faith in the possibilities of youth. They should be able to see in each boy or girl the potential self-supporting, well-adjusted man or woman of individual dignity and worth. It means, also, that the school believes sincerely in the possibility of continuous improvement of its own work—that nothing is so well done that it cannot be done better. No teacher is ready to contribute to educational progress unless he is willing and able to reconsider and call in question whatever has been taken for granted. Open-minded analysis of assumptions is a strong stimulant to vigorous, constructive thinking.

Constructive thinking requires the capacity to break up one's customary patterns of thought and to create new ones. This is especially necessary in those who would see education afresh. Usually education is thought of in patterns of school buildings, classrooms, classes, textbooks, courses, grades, credits, diplomas. It is only when these paraphernalia of education can be pushed into the background of one's mind that realistic thinking becomes possible. Only then is the teacher able to see the student as a young human being growing up in a very complex and difficult world. And only then can the teacher begin to see clearly and constructively what the school should be and do.

Experience has taught the participating schools that no school is ready to advance until teachers have a sure sense of security in adventure. They are safe in following tradition; they must be sure that they will be equally secure in departing from tradition. Only then can they maintain their personal and professional integrity and grow into the fullness of their stature as teachers and personalities.

Pleasant surroundings and favorable working conditions facilitate preparation for secondary school reconstruction. A modern, commodious, well-equipped building, spacious grounds, freedom from traffic noises, adequate libraries, laboratories, studios and shops, small classes, a homogeneous student body—these are all much to be desired. But it has been learned that they are not essential. Some of the most significant contributions coming from the Eight-Year Study have been made by schools where few of these advantageous circumstances exist. Without strong conviction on the part of teachers that youth must be better served, no important changes will be made. With that conviction, with leadership, cooperation, imagination, initiative, and courage teachers will move forward no matter how unfavorable the physical environment and working conditions may be.

Out of their experience the Thirty Schools counsel others about to revise their work to take time to see where they are going, to "look before they leap." The high school which cooperatively reexamines, in an open-minded and realistic spirit, its service to its students and community always reaches the conclusion that many important needs of boys and girls are not being met satisfactorily and that something should be done. Then these questions always arise: What part of our work should we surely retain? What part should be discontinued? What new work is needed? Shall we adopt this proposal or another? In what direction shall we move?

Asking these questions, a school faculty might choose an easy solution by copying what some other school had done. They might turn, for instance, to this Report and adopt a revised curriculum which had been developed in one of the schools. Such a procedure would be a serious mistake and the results would certainly be unsatisfactory. Genuine reconstruction does not come that way. All teachers, all faculties must go through the hard experience of thinking their own problems through. The experiences of other teachers and schools can be useful in pointing the way, but no teacher or school can travel for others the hard road of reconstruction. Schools must find their own answers to their most puzzling questions.

These questions cannot be answered intelligently until objectives are determined and clearly stated. Therefore, this difficult task must be attempted. Statements of objectives often have little meaning. Sometimes they are couched in such general terms that they provide no guidance. On the other hand, so many detailed, specific objectives are often listed that no sense of direction is indicated. The member schools encountered both of these difficulties early in the Study. Later when they were asked to restate their objectives in terms of desirable changes in pupils—changes which could be observed or discovered objectively—meaningless generalization and multiplicity of purpose were much less in evidence in the revisions. But this searching question remained largely unanswered: What changes in pupils are desirable? Thus the problem of purpose continued to thrust itself into the forefront of the thinking of the schools. They have learned that it cannot be escaped and that sure progress in reconstruction cannot take place in any school until unity and clarity of purpose are achieved.

The purposes of the school cannot be determined apart from the purposes of the society which maintains the school. The purposes of any society are determined by the life values which the people prize. As a nation we have been striving always for those values which constitute the American way of life. Our people prize individual human personality above everything else. We are convinced that the form of social organization called democracy promotes, better than any other, the development of worth and dignity in men and women. It follows, therefore, that the chief purpose of education in the United States should be to preserve, promote, and refine the way of life in which we as a people believe.

This, then, is the conclusion which grew out of the continuing search for guiding objectives in the Thirty Schools. This great, central purpose gave direction. What part of the school's curriculum should be retained? That part which promotes the kind of life we seek. What changes in young people are desirable? Those which lead in the direction of democratic living.

But what is the American way? What are the principles of democracy? These are the questions which individual teachers and school faculties sought to answer. They had to answer them clearly in order to know what the school should be and do, for they had become sure that the school should be a demonstration of democracy in action. This search for purpose and meaning was the turning point for many of the participating schools.

The schools affirm that this concept of the chief purpose of education in the United States leaves no room for provincialism or narrow, selfish nationalism. Our unique privilege as a nation is that of working out here, on this rich and pleasant land, the kind of life of which men of vision, good will, and noble character have long dreamed. Our roots go deep into the past. Our present and future are closely interwoven with the fate of all men and nations. Therefore, if our youth are to know and prize the American way of life, their studies should take them back to its origins and on to the great issues before us in a world in which we cannot live apart.

Because their struggle to achieve clear purpose has proved to be of inestimable value to them, the Thirty Schools urge every school to search the democratic ideal for principles to guide thought and action in any attempted revision of administration, curriculum, or ways of teaching. That ideal, they say, sets up the guideposts which point the sure way to reconstruction of every phase of American secondary education.

The school which has prepared itself thoroughly and established its central purpose is now ready to proceed confidently with the arduous task of reconstruction. The Thirty Schools have learned that effective democratic leadership is essential. The principal is the one who would be expected to lead. That school is fortunate whose principal has the capacity and skill to be the educational leader. Some principals cannot carry this responsibility. They are excellent executives rather than leaders of thought. Usually such principals recognize their limitations and turn to others for the kind of strength they do not possess. That is often found in some member of the faculty. By close cooperation the principal and faculty leader are able to unite the school in thought and action.

Whatever the conditions are, educational leadership there must be. Although the leader must be a thoughtful educator, he does not do the thinking for the faculty; he stimulates and challenges their thinking. He respects their worth, believes in their integrity, welcomes their best thought, and unites them in the great common cause of making education more fruitful for every boy and girl in the school. He keeps all eyes constantly upon the students.

The pupils, too, have an important part in school reconstruction. To those who have been working with the schools during the eight years of the Study, it seems that the most profound change is the shift in emphasis from subject matter to the boys and girls themselves. Curriculum content is still important, but only as it helps young people with their problems of living in our democracy. Whatever the school does, finds its value in service to youth. It follows, then, that they should share in making the curriculum. Experience has taught that high school students are well able to share effectively in school reconstruction. Many of them have surprised and delighted their teachers by the mature and constructive thought which they have brought to the problem when they were invited to think with teachers and parents about the work of the school.

Therefore, the participating schools advise taking students into partnership in changing the general life of the school and in revising the curriculum. Their ability to share responsibility in school organization and government has been demonstrated in schools everywhere, but their readiness and capacity for participation in curriculum making have only recently been discovered. In many of the member schools students are now habitually consulted concerning curriculum problems, and teacher-pupil planning is becoming an established practice.

The reasons for pupil participation are compelling. The schools have taken the position that the source of the curriculum is to be found in the concerns of youth and in the nature of the society which the school serves. Therefore, youth should have opportunity to ask that the schools heed their needs and to tell what some of those needs are. An even more vital reason for their sharing is that the kind of life we seek in America can be achieved only by full participation in planning for the common welfare and in meeting common responsibilities. School is the place for youth to develop the habit of cooperative thought and skill in group action.

Even with competent leadership and effective student cooperation, no school can go very far along the road of reconstruction without freedom to act according to its best judgment. The schools in the Study have had that freedom for eight years. A plan is proposed earlier in this chapter by which all schools may have the freedom essential to progress. When it comes, schools will learn, as the Thirty Schools did, that greater freedom entails greater responsibility for wise guidance of youth. But young people cannot be counseled wisely by the school unless each individual is well known by some teacher. Ways by which each boy and girl can be known intimately have been suggested in these pages. However, intimate knowledge of a student does not of itself bring intelligent guidance. Teachers must have time and opportunity to use that knowledge to the student's advantage. The wisest teachers should have the largest measure of responsibility for counseling. Sometimes specialized, professional advice is needed, but of one thing the schools are sure: that guidance cannot be divorced from the everyday work of the classroom. All teachers share this responsibility.

But who shall give teachers wisdom sufficient for guidance of youth? To that question there is no answer, but the teachers who have become wise through experience say that preparation for teaching should be quite different from that usually provided by colleges of Education. Preparation for teaching in the high school that is emerging should lead to understanding of young people—their urges, drives, concerns, and problems. At the same time it should develop a clear concept of the democratic ideal and insight into the social problems that must be solved if American society and education are to approximate the ideals which our people hold.

Each teacher needs competence in his own field, of course, but he needs a broader competence. Fusion courses, broad fields, culture epochs, career-centered courses, core curriculums—all these are designed to meet youth's needs more directly. They require teacher collaboration. This unity of teacher effort demands the breaking down of artificial barriers which have separated teacher from teacher and subject from subject. It also calls for the removal of the limitations which have prevented teachers from becoming truly educated persons themselves. When they work together, they learn from each other. When they consider the whole responsibility of the school, they gain insight into the implications and relationships of their fields of work. Whatever the form of curriculum organization, teachers should work together for common purposes, clearly understood and constantly kept in mind. The Thirty Schools agree, therefore, that narrow subject specialization by teachers, which stands in the way of their cooperation with others and blinds them to youth's needs, should disappear from secondary education.

With the best possible preparation, the teacher will still have to learn through experience how to know, understand, and guide young people. As he works with them day after day in the classroom, his relationship with his students becomes, more and more, that of friendly counselor. To have that relationship, the work of the classroom must be vital to students. Therefore the content of the curriculum becomes extremely important.

What have the Thirty Schools to say now about the curriculum? They have five conclusions to report:

1. Every student should achieve competence in the essential skills of communication—reading, writing, oral expression—and in the use of quantitative concepts and symbols.
2. Inert subject matter should give way to content that is alive and pertinent to the problems of youth and modern civilization.
3. The common, recurring concerns of American youth should give content and form to the curriculum.
4. The life and work of the school should contribute, in every possible way, to the physical, mental, and emotional health of every student.
5. The curriculum in its every part should have one clear, major purpose. That purpose is to bring to every young American his

great heritage of freedom, to develop understanding of the kind of life we seek, and to inspire devotion to human welfare.

This report of lessons learned by the Thirty Schools could be extended indefinitely, but that would be of doubtful value to other schools. However, one other result of the Eight-Year Study should be reported as this record of adventure is brought to a close. Participation in the Study has brought renewed vitality to every school. Whether the school altered its curriculum and ways of teaching markedly or not, whether its contributions to the improvement of secondary education are small or great, each one brings enthusiastic testimony to the extraordinary value of the experience. Out of their attempts to meet a challenge, out of searching study of their own work, out of their struggle to serve youth better, the Thirty Schools have grown immeasurably in educational stature and wisdom.

Throughout the nation there are thousands of high schools, large and small, in city and country, still following tradition. In these schools, faithful teachers are increasingly aware that their boys and girls are facing urgent problems of living with little help from any source. These teachers are beginning to see that much of the help which youth seeks must come from the high schools; this means that education must take on new responsibilities.

To fulfill these wider obligations schools must have a considerable measure of the freedom that the Thirty Schools have had during these eight years. This freedom was a challenge to the best that was in them. Who can doubt that other schools would respond equally well to the same challenge? As hundreds of teachers in the participating schools discovered in themselves unknown creative powers, so would thousands of others develop new vitality and strength in their attempts to perform new duties. Surely the freedom which produces such results will not long be denied.

The ten million boys and girls now in our high schools cannot carry the nation's burden in this hour of world conflict. That burden is ours. We are determined that the earth they inherit shall not be in chains. Theirs will be the task that only free men can perform in a world of freedom. It will be an even greater task than ours. To prepare them for it is the supreme opportunity of the schools of our democracy.

Those interested in a fuller account of the various ways the Thirty Schools went about the business of reorganizing the curriculum will find a summary in Chapters 2, 3 and 4 of The Story of the Eight-Year Study *and a much more complete account, school by school, in* Thirty Schools Tell Their Story.

As the Commission knew when they launched the study, the pos-
sibility of accomplishing significant changes in the secondary schools
was linked with the ability of the schools to demonstrate that they
could change their practices without jeopardizing the future success in
college of those who chose to continue education beyond high school.

The account of what happened in college to those pupils who went
there from the Thirty Schools is found in the following section.

What Happened in College? [8]

Among the important purposes stated by all high schools "preparation for college" is always to be found near the top of the list. Even
though a small minority go to college, the school is vividly aware of
this objective. All of the Thirty Schools stated that they expected to
send young men and women into college well ready for the responsibilities they would meet there. The schools in the Study, believing
that there are many different kinds of work through which students
may develop the skills, habits, and qualities essential to satisfactory
achievement in college, made such changes as are reported in Chapters
2 and 3. Many of these innovations were marked departures from the
conventional pattern prescribed as preparation for college. These
changes were made to meet more fully the present, as well as future,
needs of students. School work was brought much closer to students'
lives; their concerns while in high school became content of the curriculum for all, whether they were going to college or not.

It has long been assumed that adequate preparation for the work of
the liberal arts college depends upon proficiency in certain studies in
high school. The colleges and universities have been saying something
like this to prospective college students: "To be ready for the work
that will be expected of you here, you should study English during
your high school course. If you do well and secure good grades, you will
have 3 or 4 credits to present for admission. You should also study
algebra for at least one year, preferably two, and geometry for one
year. That will add 2 or 3 admission credits. It is necessary for you to
know at least one foreign language; therefore you must spend at least
two years in the study of a foreign language. But we advise you to
spend two more years in the study of that language, or two or three
years in studying a second foreign language. That will provide from
2 to 5 more entrance credits. You must study history, preferably ancient
history, for one year, and science, preferably physics or chemistry, for
one year. There you have 2 more credits. You now have accumulated
at least 9 entrance credits which we require; but if you have followed

[8] *Ibid.,* pp. 102–115.

our recommendations, you have 14 of which we heartily approve. We require for admission a total of 15 credits. To secure the required number you may present other subjects which you have studied in high school, but we advise you to present additional credits in those fields of study we have recommended. If you wish to offer credits in some other subjects—such as mechanical drawing, art, or music—your school must have its courses in these subjects approved by this college."

Colleges differed, of course, in the rigidity with which they adhered to these prescriptions. Some prescribed more, some less. A few colleges imposed no credit prescriptions whatever, but required entrance examinations in at least the four subjects studied in the senior year of high school.

The Thirty Schools set out upon their explorations with the consent of practically all colleges and universities. From many the schools received sympathetic understanding. Taken by and large, the institutions of higher education have kept the agreement in letter and in spirit. In all cases the participating schools were freed from subject and credit prescription and in most cases from entrance examinations. Hundreds of young men and women entered college from the Thirty Schools without having studied all of the usual required subjects. Some had taken such subjects, but for shorter time than is usually required.

THE COMMISSION AND THE SCHOOLS ASK QUESTIONS

It seemed to the Commission and the schools that an attempt should be made to learn whether departures from the conventional pattern of college preparation handicapped students in their work in college. The relation of school and college in American education was based upon the assumption that the skill, knowledge, discipline, habit of mind, and understanding essential for success in college depend upon the study in high school of certain subjects for certain periods of time. Here was an opportunity to test that assumption. If the graduates of the Thirty Schools were not ready for college work, it would indicate that the assumption is sound; if they did well, there would be evidence that the assumption is untenable and that a sounder and more realistic basis of school and college relations should be established.

Other related questions called for answer. Will these secondary schools use their new freedom wisely? Can they be trusted? Will their standards of work suffer? If these Thirty Schools prove that they can be trusted to use freedom sanely and creatively, will it be safe for colleges to extend such freedom to other schools? Is it possible to give more attention to present concerns of all high school pupils without sacrificing adequate preparation for those going on to college? Can practicable ways be found for colleges and schools to work together more effectively for common purposes?

According to the agreement made with the colleges, the first class to be included in this plan would enter college in September, 1936. Therefore, preparations were made to study the graduates of the Thirty Schools as they pursued their careers in college. Volume IV of the Commission's Report, entitled *Did They Succeed in College?* gives a detailed, complete account of this investigation and of the findings that resulted. Here, in this overall report of the Eight-Year Study, the way in which the college study was conducted and the findings thereof are reported in summary only.

The college investigation was made under the immediate direction of Dr. Ralph W. Tyler, Chairman of the Department of Education for the University of Chicago. Responsible, impartial members of college faculties who knew how to work with college students were chosen to make the study.[9] It should be understood that this college staff approached their work without prejudice and without commitments to the Progressive Education Association or to the Commission.

Their task was a challenging one, for the first questions they had to answer were these: What does success in college mean? Upon what basis shall judgment be rendered? What are the significant aspects of the student's life at college? How can we discover and record the important evidences of his growth and development?

After spending the summer of 1936 in conference among themselves, with members of the Commission and the Commission's Staff, with teachers and principals in the Thirty schools, with college deans, professors, and graduates, they drew up this set of criteria for their guidance:

1. Intellectual competence
2. Cultural development; use of leisure time; appreciative and creative aspects

[9] John L. Bergstresser, Assistant Dean, University of Wisconsin, representative for the state universities, July, 1936 to July, 1937; Dean Chamberlin, Assistant Dean of Freshmen, Dartmouth College, representative for the eastern men's colleges; Enid Straw Chamberlain, Instructor in English, Wellesley College, representative for the eastern women's colleges; Neal E. Drought, Assistant Dean, University of Wisconsin, representative for the state universities from July, 1937 until the end of the Study; William E. Scott, Assistant Dean of Students, University of Chicago, representative for the endowed coeducational colleges; Harold Threlkeld, University of Denver, special representative for colleges in the Denver area.

3. Practical competence; common sense and judgment; ordinary manual skills; environmental adaptability
4. Philosophy of life (pattern of goals)
5. Character traits (pattern of behavior)
6. Emotional balance (including mental health)
7. Social fitness
8. Sensitivity to social problems
9. Physical fitness (knowledge and practice of health habits).

As the staff making this College Follow-up Study explains, "Each of these criteria was broken down into more detailed and specific subdivisions, and opposite each criterion were listed suggested possible sources of evidence." [10] For example, the first criterion, intellectual competence, was subdivided as follows: [11]

Criteria	*Sources of Evidence*
1. Intellectual competence of the student	
A. Scholarship Formal measurement of academic achievement	1. Official college records 2. Honors, prizes
B. Intellectual curiosity and drive Manifestation of interest and activity in intellectual matters beyond course requirements	1. Questionnaires, reading records 2. Interviews, interests—number, quality, and variety 3. Samples of written work 4. Reports from instructors
C. Scientific approach Degree in which his work and thinking conform to the usually accepted characteristics of the scientific attitude	1. Tests 2. Interviews 3. Reports from instructors

D. Study skills and habits
Willingness and ability to employ the tools of learning
	1. Subject matter placement tests
	2. Oral reading tests
	3. Silent reading tests
	4. Other tests (library use, study techniques, etc.)
	5. Samples of written work
	6. Reports from instructors
	  a. Research ability
	  b. Accuracy, thoroughness, and organization
	  c. Facility with examinations
	  d. Request for special aid

[10] Vol. IV, *Did They Succeed in College?* Chap. I.
[11] The other criteria with suggested sources of evidence may be found in *ibid.*, Appendix.

Criteria	*Sources of Evidence*
	7. Interviews and questionnaire
	a. Time distribution
	b. Study environment
	c. Student's own evaluation
	8. Official records
	a. Excuses and cuts
	b. Late papers
	c. Remedial records

About 2000 graduates of the Thirty Schools entered 179 colleges in the fall of 1936. It was obviously impossible for the college study staff to go to all these colleges to follow all students. Selection had to be made. This was done on the basis of three factors: (1) the number of graduates of the Thirty Schools enrolled; (2) types of colleges; (3) the degree of cooperation offered by the colleges to the Follow-up Staff. The colleges that were agreed upon as centers for intensive study are:

State Universities
Ohio State University
Oklahoma A. and M. College
University of Michigan
University of Oklahoma
University of Wisconsin

Men's Colleges
Amherst College
Brown University
Columbia University
Dartmouth College
Harvard University
Massachusetts Institute of Technology
Princeton University
Williams College
Yale University

Coeducational Endowed Colleges and Universities
Cornell University
Swarthmore College
University of Chicago
University of Denver
University of Pennsylvania
University of Tulsa

Women's Colleges
Bennington College
Bryn Mawr College
Mount Holyoke College
Smith College
Wellesley College

Many other colleges cooperated in the study by distributing questionnaires and by supplying the college observers with grades, instructors' reports, and other materials. Among the colleges thus assisting were: Iowa State College, University of Iowa, Antioch College, Drake University, Colgate University, Johns Hopkins University, Lehigh University, Wesleyan University (Connecticut), Barnard College, Connecticut College for Women, Mills College, Pembroke College, Radcliffe College, Sarah Lawrence College, and Simmons College. One hundred and twenty other colleges willingly supplied grades and other information to the Follow-up Staff upon request.

It was necessary to establish some just basis of comparison if the work of the graduates of the Thirty Schools was to be judged fairly. Since it was expected that they would be somewhat above the average college students in native ability, it would not do to compare their achievement with average performance. Therefore, a basis of comparison was established by matching, with utmost care, each graduate from the Thirty Schools with another student in the same college who had taken the prescribed courses, had graduated from some school not participating in the Study, and had met the usual entrance requirements. They were matched on the basis of sex, age, race, scholastic aptitude scores, home and community background, interests, and probable future. For example, here is a boy—the son of a lawyer and a graduate of one of the large, public schools in the Study—eighteen years of age, from a home and community which afford cultural and economic advantages, unusually able in mathematics and planning to become an engineer. As his "matchee," the Follow-up Staff selected in the same college a boy, eighteen years of age, who had a similar background, the same vocational interest and scholastic aptitude, but who had met the customary entrance requirements.

THE STAFF STUDY THE STUDENTS

The members of the College Follow-up Staff did their work with painstaking care. They learned all they could about each student, treating alike the students from the Study and their matchees. Their sources of information were official college records, lists of honors or prizes won, reports from instructors, samples of written work, results of various types of tests given by the college, and the student himself. Each student was asked to reply to three questionnaires a year. After the first, which was filled out early in the school term, interviews lasting from fifteen minutes to two hours were held with each student.

The conversation usually began with a discussion of the questionnaire, which asked about the student's academic, social, and personal problems; his health; his activities, athletic and otherwise; his reading, attendance at lectures and concerts, radio listening, and movie attendance. Also, the student was asked to discuss his preparation for college and his reaction to college life as he found it. The conversation soon shifted to all sorts of topics: from raising puppies to world affairs. In most cases students welcomed the chance to talk freely with a friendly person who showed interest in them. From these written replies to questions, from long, informal talks, and from information secured from college records and college instructors, deans, and other personnel officers the college staff came to know each student well. Upon this intimate and abundant knowledge they base the report of their investigation.

Altogether, 1475 pairs of students were studied—those entering college in 1936, for four years; those entering in 1937, for three; those entering in 1938, for two; and the class entering in 1939, for one year. A vast amount of data was accumulated, and the staff gave their summers and most of 1941 to analysis of the collected information.

What did they discover?

THE GRADUATES OF THE THIRTY SCHOOLS SUCCEED

In the comparison of the 1475 matched pairs, the College Follow-up Staff found that the graduates of the Thirty Schools

1. Earned a slightly higher total grade average
2. Earned higher grade averages in all subject fields except foreign language
3. Specialized in the same academic fields as did the comparison students
4. Did not differ from the comparison group in the number of times they were placed on probation
5. Received slightly more academic honors in each year
6. Were more often judged to possess a high degree of intellectual curiosity and drive
7. Were more often judged to be precise, systematic, and objective in their thinking
8. Were more often judged to have developed clear or well-formulated ideas concerning the meaning of education—especially in the first two years in college
9. More often demonstrated a high degree of resourcefulness in meeting new situations
10. Did not differ from the comparison group in ability to plan their time effectively
11. Had about the same problems of adjustment as the comparison group, but approached their solution with greater effectiveness
12. Participated somewhat more frequently, and more often enjoyed appreciative experiences, in the arts
13. Participated more in all organized student groups except religious and "service" activities
14. Earned in each college year a higher percentage of nonacademic

honors (officership in organizations, election to managerial societies, athletic insignia, leading roles in dramatic and musical presentations)

15. Did not differ from the comparison group in the quality of adjustment to their contemporaries
16. Differed only slightly from the comparison group in the kinds of judgments about their schooling
17. Had a somewhat better orientation toward the choice of a vocation
18. Demonstrated a more active concern for what was going on in the world.

The College Follow-up Staff has this to say about these findings:

Some of these differences were not large, but wherever reported, they were consistent for each class. It is apparent that when one finds even small margins of difference for a number of large groups, the probability greatly increases that the differences cannot be due to chance alone.

It is quite obvious from these data that the Thirty Schools graduates, as a group, have done a somewhat better job than the comparison group whether success is judged by college standards, by the students' contemporaries, or by the individual students.[12]

When these results began to emerge, the Directing Committee and school Heads asked whether this creditable showing might be due to the graduates of those of the Thirty Schools which had not departed greatly from traditional patterns and ways of college preparation. To answer this question the college staff analyzed the records of the graduates of the six participating schools in which least change had taken place and the records of the graduates of the six schools in which the most marked departures from conventional college preparatory courses had been made. Each of these groups was studied in relation to its respective comparison group. This investigation revealed that

The graduates of the most experimental schools were strikingly more successful than their matchees. Differences in their favor were much greater than the differences between the total Thirty Schools and their comparison group. Conversely, there were no large or consistent differences between the least experimental graduates and their comparison group. For these students the differences were smaller and less consistent than for the total Thirty Schools and their comparison group.[13]

12 Vol. IV, *Did They Succeed in College?* Chap. 10.
13 *Ibid.*

The College Follow-up Staff comments on these facts as follows:

If the proof of the pudding lies in these groups, and a good part of it does, then it follows that the colleges got from these most experimental schools a higher proportion of sound, effective college material than they did from the more conventional schools in similar environments. If colleges want students of sound scholarship with vital interests, students who have developed effective and objective habits of thinking, and who yet maintain a healthy orientation toward their fellows, then they will encourage the already obvious trend away from restrictions which tend to inhibit departures or deviations from the conventional curriculum patterns.[14]

In order to refine this particular analysis still further, the graduates of two of the most experimental schools were selected for a separate study. One of these schools is a relatively small private school, the other is the experimental section of a large public school in the Study. In the private school were small classes, intimate knowledge of each student, close contact with his parents, and a fairly homogeneous economic and social background. In the public school many of these favorable conditions were lacking. The graduates of these two schools were contrasted with their matchees. As a result, the staff reports that "the superiority of these progressive graduates over their comparison group was greater than any previous differences reported." [15] The graduates of these two schools surpassed their comparison groups by wide margins in academic achievement, intellectual curiosity, scientific approach to problems, and interest in contemporary affairs. The differences in their favor were even greater in general resourcefulness, in enjoyment of reading, participation in the arts, in winning nonacademic honors, and in all aspects of college life except possibly participation in sports and social activities.

Concerning the different conditions prevailing in these two schools, the college staff has this to say:

The products of these two schools are indistinguishable from each other in terms of college success. Good teaching obviously was characteristic of both these schools. But good teaching alone was not responsible for the superiority of the product—good teaching, after all, was characteristic of most of the Thirty Schools, as well as most of the schools from which the comparison group was drawn. The other important characteristics of both schools were: their willingness to undertake a search for valid objectives; organizing curricula and techniques and setting them in motion in order to attain the objectives;

14 *Ibid.*, Chap. 7.
15 *Ibid.*, Chap. 10.

and, finally, measuring the effectiveness of curricula and techniques by appropriate evaluation devices. These are basic processes; their utility in any type of school is proved.[16]

The Directing Committee asked a group of distinguished college officials to examine the findings of this investigation and to draw any conclusion which in their judgment the data warrant. This committee prepared a report which was presented by the chairman to various regional meetings of the Association of American Colleges early in 1940. Their report concludes with these two paragraphs: [17]

The results of this Study seem to indicate that the pattern of preparatory school program which concentrates on a preparation for a fixed set of entrance examinations is not the only satisfactory means of fitting a boy or girl for making the most out of the college experience. It looks as if the stimulus and the initiative which the less conventional approach to secondary school education affords sends on to college better human material than we have obtained in the past.

I may add that this report to you has been approved by a Committee of the Commission on School and College Relations consisting of the following membership: President Barrows of Lawrence College, President Park of Bryn Mawr, Dr. Gumere of Harvard, Dean Speight of Swarthmore, Dean Brumbaugh of Chicago, and myself.

HERBERT E. HAWKES, Chairman.

The major findings of the investigation of the success of students in college were presented to the colleges in a series of regional, round-table conferences in the spring of 1940. The results of the Study, as presented, were not seriously questioned by anyone. What changes in school and college relations these conclusive findings will produce remains to be seen. Many colleges are now giving serious consideration to their relations with the schools from which their students come. There is reason to expect that the schools and colleges of the country will soon draw more closely together in a mutually satisfying relationship.

16 *Ibid.*, Chap. 8.
17 For complete report, see Appendix of *The Story of the Eight-Year Study*, pp. 147–150.

YOUTH TELL
THEIR STORY

Excerpts from a Survey by the
American Youth Commission

The American Youth Commission, ap-
pointed by the American Council on
Education, began its work in 1935. The
major accomplishment of the Commis-
sion was the survey conducted in the state of Maryland in the
1930's. The results of this study were reported in a single
volume entitled Youth Tell Their Story,[1] *published in 1938.*
It bore the subtitle "A Study of the Conditions and Attitudes
of Young People in Maryland between the Ages of 16 and 24."

The stated objective of the American Youth Commission,
identifying the major needs of youth, was a formidable one.
But to go beyond this and investigate attitudes of youth toward
home, school, work, leisure, and institutionalized religion as
does Youth Tell Their Story *represents an even more difficult*
task.

Data from the more than 13,000 Maryland youth sampled
indicated cultural, social, and economic problems of deep
severity, if the attitudes and life conditions reported by the

youth were in any sense reflective and accurate. A nation, fearful of "alien" ideologies such as Communism and Nazism, and struggling to recover from economic depression, became aware of the discontent of its own youth. Some of society's most revered institutions, the schools and the economic structure especially, were perceived by youth as failing to meet their needs. By far the most pervading attitude reflected was one of discontent and discouragement.

Homer P. Rainey, Director of the American Youth Commission, in the Foreword of Youth Tell Their Story *provides some background information for the survey and an overview of the social problems facing the youth of our nation in the middle and late 1930's. His analysis is reprinted in its entirety.*

It will be noted that there is a great deal of correspondence between this report and the report of the Regents' Inquiry.

YOUTH TELL THEIR STORY

The following excerpts are taken from the Introduction. The first three sections give some indication of the motivation for the study and the procedures followed. The last three paragraphs are taken from the end of the Introduction. These reveal the general tone of the discussions that will follow.

Introduction

Since Adam, there have been but two generations—the young and the old. And one of the most ancient and venerable human pastimes is the business of one of these generations looking with a quizzical and none too sympathetic eye upon the activities and the philosophies of the other.

The essential character of this younger generation of Americans has been so variously interpreted by adults that the student who seeks to understand it is likely to experience considerable difficulty in arriving at any sound conclusions. While some adult spectators are inclined to see our youth going hell-bent to perdition, other observers will see them as developing into a freer, stronger, more intelligent, and self-reliant generation than has ever appeared upon the stage of human affairs.

In this babel of confusing and contradictory voices, one might well wonder where to look for the truth. Those responsible for the present study have proceeded on the assumption that the best single source of authentic information about the essential character of this younger generation is the young people themselves. So, through the agency of trained and experienced interviewers, the American Youth Commission of the American Council on Education has gone direct to youth—has given them a chance to reveal the conditions under which they are living, to speak their minds on significant issues, and generally to bare their souls.

The present inquiry is one of the most comprehensive of its kind ever undertaken. Its scope is as wide as the activities of youth, and its range as broad as society itself.

THE YOUTH PROBLEM

Almost lost behind the fog of the immediate reasons for such a study, and the insistent demands by socially minded people that such a study be made, is the first and primary reason—the recognition of what has emerged during the past few years as distinctly a youth problem.

The genesis of the problem probably goes back to the days when the more or less indiscriminate employment of children in business and industry was generally accepted with casual indifference, and to the unfortunately dead past when circumstances assured every normal youth, willing to make the effort, a place under the sun. The physical frontier with its undeveloped resources of agricultural land, minerals, and timber made unemployment unheard of and idleness a disgrace. A rapidly growing population, boomed by heavy immigration as well as by high birth rates, created constantly increasing demands for professional services in teaching, medicine, and law.

But now what have we? A brave, new world? Well, perhaps. Yet, with all its glitter of newness and the fanfare of its often dubious bravery it is hardly a place of rejoicing for great numbers of the youth who live in it. How many, on looking back, will feel impelled to exclaim with the romantic poet of another day, "Ah, then 'twas glorious to be alive, but to be young was very heaven!"

If there is somewhat less rejoicing among our modern youth over the blessings of being young, it is quite likely because they have found themselves caught in the meshes of a complicated social machinery for which they have neither the background of experience nor the benefit of sufficiently realistic instruction to enable them to understand. If there is anything at which to wonder, it is not that they are befuddled and bewildered, but that they are not a good deal more befuddled and bewildered than they are. Along with the problems that are historically and traditionally those of every generation and every age, the youth of this modern generation find themselves facing a problem that is uniquely and increasingly their own: what to do with themselves during the ever widening period between the time when schools are through with them and jobs are ready for them. Here is the crucial element in the Youth Problem.

In addressing itself to the amelioration of the difficulties of young people, and in devoting its efforts to the business of pointing the way to a practical solution of their fundamental problem, the American Youth Commission is quite alive to the size of the job it has undertaken. It fully realizes that if any effective solution is to be worked out and any effective program is to be adopted, they must grow out of the concerted and purposeful action of all agencies, both public and private, dedicated to the service of youth.

As one of these agencies, the first move of the American Youth Commission was to embark on a cruise of exploration, determined to discover the essential needs of youth and, once these discoveries were made, to recommend how these needs might best be met. Between the day when, for whatever reason, the young person sees the last of his schoolroom and the day when he experiences the gusto of his first job, there has developed what, for him, is a veritable "no man's land of final futility." If we care to avoid the social and economic penalties that must inevitably come from a continued indifference to the needs of our young people, it is altogether fitting and logical that we make every effort to discover and adopt the best ways and means of filling these wasted years with healthful and constructive activity.

Such, in general, is the Commission's primary reason for making studies like the one we are about to consider. It has been indicated that a clear understanding of this reason is essential to an intelligent appraisal of the following report. Equally important, however, is an understanding of how these studies are made.

PROCEDURES

The whole body of data, gathered over a period of seven months with a field staff of thirty-five interviewers, can well be divided into two kinds—facts that reveal conditions and expressed opinions that indicate attitudes.

Of the general accuracy of the factual data that were recorded we feel there can be little reasonable doubt, as there seldom existed any inclination or motive on the part of a young person to give false information. As for the responses to the questions designed to elicit attitudes and opinions, they can, taken together, be accepted as an indication of the extent to which our young people between the ages of sixteen and twenty-four are thinking about the significant issues of our time. It was not assumed, of course, that every youth had even the most naïve opinion about many of the issues raised in the course of the interview. When a subject stated that he had never given any thought to this or that matter, the interviewer recorded a "no opinion" and passed on to the next question. When the subject did have an opinion and wished to express it, the interviewer recorded this point of view with a detached and impersonal objectivity. The result was the acquisition of a body of information which, with a measure of generosity, can quite reasonably be interpreted as the philosophy of modern youth. . . .

If the following pages will reveal anything, they will reveal the activities and the thinking of a generation that is still making an effort to adjust itself to the educational, social, and vocational realities of an era that is past. With what looks very much like a pathetic docility, youth are trying somehow to find adequate satisfaction in such things as a secondary educational system that too often persists in preparing them for colleges they will never enter, a system of vocational training that too frequently trains them for jobs they will never find, and colleges of "liberal" arts that develop cultural tastes that quickly become atrophied in a chaotic society which denies the means of their satisfaction.

If there is anything in the nature of the present situation for sober adults to view with alarm, it is not that youth will rise in revolt against the programs and policies of antiquated institutions that are intended to serve them, but that they will, with a supine meekness, continue to accept these programs and policies exactly as they inherit them.

At a time when there is so much talk about the dangers of reactionary oldsters, it might be an excellent idea to give a little thought to the dangers of developing a generation of apathetic youth. In the old a smug conservatism may be a menace, but in the young a listless apathy can quite easily become a national calamity.

Foreword

When the American Youth Commission began its work in October 1935, it was faced with the necessity of identifying the major needs of our youth population. Because there was a serious lack of adequate and reliable information about the conditions that were surrounding our young people it was impossible for the Commission to do any constructive long-range planning until it had a more complete picture of youthful needs. The Commission therefore set aside approximately two years of its allotted time to the task of identifying and defining the major factors in the youth problem. In this process it brought to its aid all the information that it could obtain from an analysis of the many surveys of youth that had been made in recent years. In addition, it carried on a series of comprehensive studies on its own responsibility, sinking sample shafts at various levels and in different parts of the country in an effort to discover what the needs of youth are and how those needs are being served by present institutions. It sampled the youth population of two states (Pennsylvania and Maryland), one large middle sized city (Dallas, Texas), one smaller municipality (Muncie, Indiana), and forty rural villages scattered throughout the country.

This survey in the state of Maryland represents one of the major accomplishments of the Commission to date. In attempting to ascertain true conditions, representatives of the Maryland study went directly to youth themselves, and, by means of personal interviews, secured first-hand information and opinions from more than 13,000 individuals. Great caution was taken to assure the reliability of the data which should be gathered. Much care was exercised in the preparation of the schedule of questions and the manual of instructions which accompanied it. The interviewers were given a special course of training before undertaking their work. Furthermore, the sampling technique used was scientifically developed and rigid controls were employed to guarantee strict adherence to the standards that were adopted. The statement of the statistician called upon to review the techniques being employed in the investigation is of interest. Dr. Bruno Fels, nominated, at our request for a disinterested evaluation, by the Central Statistical Board of the United States government, says in his report to the Commission: "I do not hesitate to state that in my opinion there can hardly be found a more thorough and well planned way of taking such a sample. . . . After all, it seems to me that quite apart from the method of sampling or from the degree to which this sample may be representative of the youth of the United States as a whole, the full importance of this study is to be seen in the results obtained from youth of every social and economic background, of different race, parentage, and over a definite range of ages, et cetera. This analysis of the differential within the group of youth included in the sample appears to have been attained to a full one hundred per cent."

The Commission is indebted to Dr. Owen R. Lovejoy, the general supervisor of the Maryland, Dallas, and Muncie studies, and to Mr. Howard M. Bell, who was immediately in charge of the Maryland investigation, for their efficient leadership. These men and the staff which was recruited and trained under them have produced for us an invaluable picture of a cross section of our American youth population. This investigation brings into sharp relief certain urgent social problems that must be faced. It seems desirable in this foreword to identify several of the more important issues set forth:

1. Certainly one of the paramount problems which this study reveals is the necessity of equalizing educational opportunities. The facts bearing upon this situation are disturbing. Almost a constant inverse ratio exists between the birth rate for any given group and its economic status. The social classes who have the fewest children possess the highest per capita wealth. In general, those who enjoy the richest cultural resources are failing to replace themselves, whereas those who have the lowest income have the highest number of children per family. Profound consequences for the future of the country are inherent in these facts. It has been argued that a democracy can exist only among equals and that in every society hitherto the inevitable inequality between economic classes has nullified every democratic program. The facts in this study indicate that our present secondary school is still a highly selective institution adapted to the needs of a small minority of our population. The public schools of this country have been supported on the theory that they serve as an instrument for the maintenance of equality of opportunity. In view of the very great inequalities in educational opportunity that exist at the present time, one may well question whether this end is, in fact, being accomplished. There is grave danger that the public school system, if present tendencies persist, may become a positive force in creating those very inequalities in the condition of men that it was designed to reduce.

2. The second need identified by this study is that of finding employment for youth as they emerge from their school experience. The gap which now exists between school and employment is reaching ominous proportions. It is established in this study that the percentage of out-of-school and employable youth who had not obtained any full-time employment at the expiration of a year after leaving school falls within the range of 40 to 46 per cent. The average period of delay for the youth who dropped out of school before the age of 16 was three and a half years, and the average duration of the unemployment of all these youth was a year and eleven months. Twenty-six per cent of all of them have never been employed. It is imperative, therefore, that ways be found of bridging this gap.

3. A very large percentage of youth assert that economic security is their most urgent personal need. The problem of unemployment is very great, but even employed youth face serious difficulties. Rates of pay tend to be low; hours tend to be long; a majority of youth with jobs must contribute to the support of families. Many youth are in

blind-alley jobs. Some are in jobs which they will shortly lose because of advancing age. Many more aspire to enter professional and semi-professional fields than are at all likely to be accommodated, and the majority are forced into unskilled or only slightly skilled occupations. Youth face an occupational future in industry that is becoming more mechanized, less concerned with highly developed mechanical skills, less given to practical instruction outside the industrial plant, and more insecure for one with a single vocational skill. In a word, *mobility* has taken the place of *fixity*, and *uncertainty* the place of *security*.

4. Guidance is one of youth's most pressing necessities. Under present conditions only a small minority of youth are receiving anything that could be called adequate vocational guidance. The increasing complexity and tempo of modern life demands a more effective system for the induction of youth into appropriate channels of employment than now exist.

5. This study also reveals the lack of appropriate and adequate vocational training. At the present time there is too little relationship between the types of jobs which youth enter and the training which they have received. The need for vocational training is especially acute for rural youth. The occupational training facilities for trade employment in rural areas are practically nonexistent. Education and training as at present organized are deficient both for those youth who will remain in rural territories and for those who will migrate to the cities.

6. The program of general secondary education for youth is in serious need of thorough reorganization. There is abundant evidence that the secondary schools as now operated are ill suited to a large percentage of youth attending them. We seem to be rapidly approaching the time when something approximating one hundred per cent of our youth are going to remain in school up to 18 years of age or through what is now the senior high school. Since the majority of youth cannot get jobs until after 18 years of age, and since the vast majority of them can be trained for their specific jobs in short-term courses, it is clear that the high school period is going to be free for training of a more general character. The time has come when we must think of providing a common education for practically all of our youth up through the senior high school. This is a new responsibility for our secondary schools and one which no society at any time has ever been called upon to face. The meeting of this problem will tax all the educational statesmanship that we possess.

7. Because of the lack of employment opportunities and the reduction in hours of labor, the matter of leisure time emerges as a social problem

of real significance. The training of youth and adults alike for a constructive use of their spare time is surely one of the major objectives of modern education. Recreation and education are parallel needs.

8. If we are to have happy and effective citizens, it is clear that a great deal of attention must be given to health education, including social and personal hygiene.

9. Any listing of the problems raised by this study would be seriously deficient that did not bring to our notice the implications for citizenship that arise out of the attitudes which young people hold. Youth's indifference to the ballot and to other civic responsibilities and privileges is worthy of serious attention on the part of those who are called upon to provide a program for the training of our future citizens.

10. These studies also reflect the need for community planning for youth. The present organization of social service work in the United States is very complex. Made up of a network of agencies—local, county, state, and federal; public, private, and semipublic; religious, philanthropic, and profit making—the social organization has been motivated largely by individualism and laissez faire. It has evolved with little conscious social planning. Whenever needs arose, institutions and agencies arose to provide for those needs. The result is that we have hundreds of agencies but no well-integrated program for the handling of community problems. These studies reveal wide gaps in our services to youth, particularly for those in the older age groups. Community disorganization constitutes a major difficulty in planning a program to meet the needs of youth. Each agency works with little or no regard for the others, with the result that the treatment of social problems is undertaken by institutions or agencies acting in their individual capacities rather than from a unified approach.

We need therefore a comprehensive program which must first of all develop a sociological approach to the problems and find ways of focusing all the efforts which society can make upon the individual youth and his needs. This is the starting point and no amount of work is going to be of much value unless there is effective coordination at the point of operation, which is the individual youth. In the "community approach" we must find the natural unit which touches the lives of individuals most directly and start building our programs there. An essential step in the care and education of youth is for each community which has its own distinctive pattern to make its own inquiry to ascertain what are the present needs and wants of its young people. Continuous investigation should be carried on to seek out the class of youth who are either overlooked or willfully excluded from the service of existing agencies for various reasons of institutional policy.

I commend this study to all groups and individuals who are interested in young people and who have responsibility for the development of programs that relate to youth and their needs.

Homer P. Rainey, Director

American Youth Commission

If the study had described young people who were unique to the state of Maryland, it would have been of limited value. However, Chapter 1, National Implications of the Maryland Data, is devoted to establishing the general applicability of the findings reported in later chapters. Note that an effort was made by the investigators to sample various strata within the state, urban, and rural population of the relief–nonrelief, opulent–impoverished, educated–relatively noneducated, public–parochial students. It is further argued that Maryland is somewhat representative of the United States, geographically, socioeconomically, and culturally. The entire chapter is included below.

Chapter 1: National Implications of the Maryland Data

Probably no fact or condition is more basic in an intelligent evaluation of a social survey than the representativeness of its sample. In a study like the present one, it is neither possible nor necessary to reach 100 per cent of all the subjects concerned. Small percentages are interviewed on the assumption that the characteristics of the part will be essentially the same as the characteristics of the whole.

In Maryland, 13,528 young people between the ages of sixteen and twenty-four were interviewed by the agents of the Commission. In the state, the total youth population between these ages is about 250,000. In the United States as a whole, there are more than 20,000,000. Therefore, it was of vital importance that every possible effort be made to justify the assumption that the 13,500 young people who were to be interviewed could speak with some degree of authority, not only for the quarter of a million young people of Maryland, but for the 20,000,000 young people of the nation.

In so far as the persistent exercise of scientific controls can be made to insure the integrity of a sample, the 13,528 Maryland youth who were interviewed can be definitely accepted as representative of the young people of Maryland. The first precaution consisted in choosing representative areas in the state. On the basis of pertinent social and economic criteria, eleven census areas were chosen from the city of Baltimore's seventy-eight. From the general standpoint of socioeconomic level, these areas ranged from the most opulent to the most impoverished neighborhoods. Exactly the same principle was observed in the selection of ten of the state's twenty-three counties.

There is a need for still further precautions if a representative sample is to be obtained. In Maryland these further precautions consisted in determining the approximate state ratios for such important groups as youth in and out of school, youth from relief and nonrelief families, from farm and nonfarm families, employed and unemployed, white and Negro, male and female, married and single, and youth in each separate age group from sixteen to twenty-four. Once the best available estimates of these state ratios were determined, the next step was to make certain, by means of periodical counts, that a proper representation from these social and economic categories was being reached.

In view of the precautions that were taken and the constant checks that were made, the staff succeeded in eliminating any serious doubt as to the representativeness of their group so far as Maryland is concerned. Every kind of neighborhood or area, every social and economic stratum, and every educational and intellectual level was proportionately represented in the final sample. Youth from cities, towns, villages, and the open country; young people from exclusive country clubs, middle class neighborhoods, and blighted areas; students from colleges, high schools, vocational and parochial schools, along with young people who have never gone to school—all these were given their place in the composite picture of the younger generation of Maryland.

IS MARYLAND A "TYPICAL" STATE?

The degree of authority with which these 13,528 youth of Maryland can be said to speak for the 20,000,000 young people between the ages of sixteen and twenty-four in the United States depends largely upon the answer to this question: To what extent, and in what essential respects, is Maryland a "typical" state?

For a considerable time before the study was launched, the staff of the Commission pondered this question. That Maryland was finally selected as a state laboratory was due to a number of reasons. Although its history is in some respects unique, it has shown during the past half century an unusual capacity to reflect national trends of thought.

Moreover, Maryland seemed quite clearly to present a great variety of characteristically "American" situations and conditions. First of all, there is the essentially metropolitan area of Baltimore, differing more in such intangible things as atmosphere than in the fundamental social and economic problems that every large city must meet. Again, there is the suburban area of Prince Georges County, serving the city of

Washington as a populous and inadequately organized hinterland, in the manner of most suburbs.

To a sensitive observer, the counties of Maryland comprise a little world that has within its relatively narrow borders a diversity that is not usually found in other states. In the northern and central counties of Carroll and Howard there are stretches of slightly rolling farm lands, dotted here and there with patches of uncleared forest, that differ only superficially from other agricultural areas in the Central Atlantic and Midwestern states. In such southern counties as Calvert, where life is predominantly rural, tobacco culture and a large proportion of Negroes tend to give the area a flavor that is essentially southern. Garrett County, in the extreme northwestern corner of the state, has a topography as well as a social and economic character that stamp it with the peculiarities of the places where "hill people" live. The mountains to the east of Garrett are scarred with small mining settlements, such as those in the Georges Creek district of Allegany County. Some eke out a precarious existence on what is left of the soft coal market, while others reflect the spiritless resignation of industrially disinherited towns.

Farther to the east, between the hill county of Garrett and the rolling farm lands of the central part of the state, there is Cumberland, an industrial city of factories and mills. And finally, across Chesapeake Bay and to the south, there is Maryland's Eastern Shore with its truck farms, fishing fleets, and oyster houses.

To a Marylander these are counties or areas of Maryland, but to a stranger they seem more in the nature of different slants at this infinitely varied spectacle we call the American scene. To the extent that the areas of Maryland are stamped with the social and economic characteristics of the nation as a whole, it can reasonably be said to be a "typical" state, and to the degree to which its youth are molded and conditioned by pressures that are essentially national, its young people can be said to be "typical" Americans. So far as those responsible for the Maryland study are concerned, Maryland is such a state, and its youth are such Americans. It is because of this that they consider it neither improper nor unreasonable to present the young people of this study, not merely as young Marylanders, but as young Americans.

DO THE MARYLAND DATA REFLECT NATIONAL CONDITIONS?

To urge that this sample of 13,528 Maryland young people constitutes a perfectly representative sampling of America's 20,000,000 youth between the ages of sixteen and twenty-four would be as presumptuous as it is unnecessary. It is, after all, a sample study and not a national youth census. We are therefore impelled only to suggest that in many essential respects the Maryland sample exhibits, within reasonable limits, the characteristics of the national youth population.

The answer to the question, "What makes a representative sample of young people?" is to be found in the answer to another question, "From what social material is a younger generation made?" Without attempting a comprehensive sociological analysis, let us accept, if we can, the basic premise that in the generation we are considering, as with all generations, there are present varying numbers of individuals from different social, economic, and educational levels, living in communities or areas with different social, economic, and educational standards or backgrounds. In more specific terms, we are called upon to recognize the existence of social, economic, and educational inequalities and diversities—to recognize, for example, the existence in our society of such socially underprivileged groups as the Negro, such economically depressed groups as the families on relief, and such educationally retarded groups as the illiterate.

Any acceptable sample of young people must include therefore a reasonably accurate number of representatives from the essential elements from which the larger group, or generation, is made. It must include a fair representation from youth living in cities, towns, villages, and on farms. It must come reasonably close to the national ratios with respect to such fundamental divisions as youth in and out of school, youth from relief and nonrelief families, of foreign and native-born parents, from Protestant, Catholic, or Jewish homes, male and female, white and Negro, and all the ages between sixteen and twenty-four.

Table 1 reveals the similarity in the characteristics of the Maryland youth sample and the national youth population. The vertical column under "United States youth" shows the distribution of American youth within specified categories. The second column, under "Maryland sample," shows the distribution of the youth interviewed with respect to these same social groups. The right-hand column shows the degree of difference between the national and the sample percentages.

These differences between the national and the sample percentages are generally too slight to justify or demand an exhaustive analysis. The only instance in which there appears a substantial difference between the national percentage and the percentage interviewed is in the distribution of youth of native and foreign-born parents. The number of youth of foreign-born parents is undersampled to the extent of 16.8 per cent. As it is often assumed that the foreign element in our population tends to depress economic standards, and as it is somewhat

TABLE 1 Characteristics of the Maryland Sample Compared with Characteristics of the National Youth Population

Primary group	Percentage of each group		Difference between Maryland sample and United States youth **
	United States youth *	Maryland sample	
Age			
16	11.8	11.2	—0.6
17	11.4	10.5	—0.9
18	11.7	11.0	—0.7
19	11.1	12.2	+1.1
20	11.0	12.1	+1.1
21	11.0	12.0	+1.0
22	10.9	10.4	—0.5
23	10.6	9.2	—1.4
24	10.5	11.4	+0.9
Sex			
Male	49.4	50.9	+1.5
Female	50.6	49.1	—1.5
Marital status			
Males married	16.1	13.1	—3.0
Females married	35.7	33.4	—2.3
Race			
White	87.2	84.6	—2.6
Negro, other	12.8	15.4	+2.6
Farm, nonfarm			
Farm	25.5	21.0	—4.5
Nonfarm	74.5	79.0	+4.5
Parentage			
Native	70.1	86.9	+16.8
Foreign, mixed	29.9	13.1	—16.8
School status			
In school	19.0	19.4	+0.4
Out of school	81.0	80.6	—0.4

* Based on youth 16 to 24 years of age. *Fifteenth Census of the United States* (1930), Population, Vol. III, General Report, pp. 593–601, 845, 1180–81.
** Minus differences mean that the sample did not meet United States percentages, while plus differences mean that the sample exceeded United States percentages. (The differences in the above table are within the allowable errors due to sampling, with the exception of those associated with the parentage and the farm groups. Both these departures, however, are in the direction in which these factors are operating in the United States.)

popularly believed that "furriners" tend to lend a pinkish glow to our national thought, the only practical effect of this quite inadvertent undersampling will probably be one of raising the economic level of the group as a whole and, perhaps, to add a slightly unwarranted touch of "100 per cent Americanism" to the group philosophy as revealed in expressed attitudes.

The only other groups that would seem to demand explanation are two that were not included in the distribution table because of the difficulty in getting unchallengeable census data regarding them. These groups are the relief–nonrelief and the employed–unemployed.

As everyone realizes, the number of persons in the United States who are on work relief projects or who receive direct relief through government agencies varies from month to month. The same thing, of course, is true with respect to the number of persons who are gainfully employed. The recognition of these variations forced us, therefore, to accept the most reasonable estimates available for both of these categories.

For the purposes of uniformity of interpretation, a "relief family" was defined as a family that had received economic assistance from a public or private agency at some time during the year preceding the interview. Using the best available information as a guide,[2] we estimated that during the course of the year preceding June 1936, when our interviewing began, about one person in eight at one time or another had received some kind of public or private relief. In the Maryland sample, we reached slightly less than one in eight. For the Negro, our percentage for the relief group was the same as that for the nation —one in four.

For the percentage of youth between the ages of sixteen and twenty-four who were employed, there was almost no reliable information available. Estimates released by the United States Office of Education in November 1935 indicated that the percentage of employment was about 40. In view of the increased industrial activity that had taken place by June 1936, we estimated that the percentage of the employed had increased to somewhere between 40 and 45. The percentage of the Maryland sample is 46.4.

Chapter 3, Youth and the School, is a discussion of relationships between youth and the school. An underlying dissatisfaction with

2 *On Relief*, a publication of the Federal Emergency Relief Administration (October, 1935), Chart I.

schools was apparent. One may be required to infer the central factors producing this dissatisfaction. One central factor may be that public education was failing to be a significant vehicle for social mobility. As the report indicated, the father's occupation was the best predictor for school completion. The low income father had more children and fewer of these completed school. Thus the youth were forced to enter the occupational level of the father. Economic pressures forced many of these youth out of school, and for many others in this low income group motivational characteristics and interest patterns precluded their continuance. The poorer the family, the less likely was the youth's motivation and interests to be in consonance with the school activities. Thus the cycle of deprivation was repeating itself from generation to generation in many instances. The investigators were forced to conclude that equality of educational opportunity did not exist. Another underlying factor related to the dissatisfaction was the current economic condition. The lack of employment opportunity for the youth leaving the schools was the primary concern of the youth. It is natural that the youth would judge the school according to whether or not it would help them economically. Thus their judgment had economic overtones. Over two thirds felt that their schooling was at least of some economic value. Those who had the greatest economic problems—older youth, Negro youth, and farm youth—thought schooling of less economic value than did the remainder of the population. The education provided seemed to be irrelevant in terms of the needs of the youth at that time.

The report data indicated a need for technical training and vocational guidance. The schools had not included vocational and specialization training to any large extent. Public secondary education in the United States has never assumed a significant role in vocational training. It has been and continues to be most successful in academic and nonvocational training. Thus, it has less appeal for those who are nonacademically oriented.

One fourth of the youth gave as a reason for leaving school either lack of interest or inability to adjust to the school program. The 25 per cent figure was believed to be an understatement.

"Our data reveal that with several groups of youth, unsatisfactory school adjustment—by which is meant a combination of lack of interest, disciplinary difficulties, and too difficult subjects—is a more general reason for leaving school than a lack of family funds. So far as the youth's own statements of why he left school can be accepted as the real reasons, all of this indicates that, for large groups of youths, the schools simply have failed to function as a genuine force. The fact that relatively high percentages of youth giving lack

of interest as their reason for dropping out were found among those who left school at the upper high school level, as well as among those who left at the elementary level, indicates that all along the line the schools, as they are now set up, are adapted to neither the needs nor interests of large numbers of our young people," the Commission reported.[3]

The findings of *Youth Tell Their Story* are consistent with the other studies and reports included in this book. The secondary schools had not succeeded in adapting their programs or their philosophies to the needs, capacities, interests, and ambitions of a school population which had expanded to embrace almost all in the high school age group. For far too many, school was not a meaningful, productive experience.

The opening paragraphs set the stage for the analysis. They note the primary areas of interest to the investigators. The second selection summarizes the factors influencing the amount of schooling youth receive and then provides information about the reasons youth leave school. It may be noted that none of these reasons which the youth gave can be totally divorced from economic factors in the light of relationships between socioeconomic class and scholastic motivation, health care, scholastic attainment, and age of marriage. The data reflect a resounding "No" to the question of whether or not equality of educational opportunity exists. The need for vocational training and guidance is indicated. The authors address themselves to the question of who is responsible for these conditions. The youth's appraisal of the economic and cultural value of schooling is reported. The comments of students are especially interesting.

The third section presents data about the relationship of the father's occupational level to grade attainment. The final excerpt is a summary of the chapter.

Chapter 3: Youth and the School

There are many kinds of educational surveys, differing primarily in the manner of approach. Among others, there is the survey that studies educational programs by going to the schools, to the teachers and superintendents. And there is the one that approaches education from the angle of those who are going, or who have gone, through the educational mill.

A Commission-sponsored survey of the Baltimore and the Maryland school systems has already been made by Frank W. Wright and Payson Smith, who adopted the first approach. They went direct to the schools, talked with teachers and superintendents, and studied school records

[3] *Youth Tell Their Story*, p. 67.

and reports. The result was an interesting and valuable report on the educational program in the state, followed by sympathetic evaluations and pertinent recommendations.

The present study of the educational program follows the second approach. It is believed that such an approach yields results that are less distinctly local in character, and uncovers conditions more likely to be found elsewhere in the United States. Provided always that the sample of the youth studied is essentially national in character, the facts uncovered can be accepted as having national implications. And, as previously indicated, it is with the national implications, and not the local peculiarities, that the staff of the Commission is primarily concerned.

So, in approaching this vitally important area of the youth's school life, we went, as usual, to the youth themselves. A glance at Table 1 (page 216) will show that, when the last Federal census was taken in 1930, 19 per cent of the youth of America between the ages of 16 and 24 were in schools or colleges. In our sample, the percentage of school youth was 19.4, a difference of only 0.4 per cent. While going through these school data, it will be well to remember therefore that about four out of every five youth considered were permanently out of school.

So far as these out-of-school youth are concerned, our interest will be to discover what the schools have done, what the youth's reactions to their past education have been, and what, if anything, there was in the economic, domestic, or social conditions under which they lived that tended to affect, for better or worse, the quality and quantity of the education they received. . . .

SUMMARY OF FACTORS AFFECTING THE AMOUNT OF SCHOOLING YOUTH RECEIVE

In what appears to be the order of their importance, the outstanding factors that affect the amount of schooling youth receive are enumerated below :

The occupation of the father. The largest variations in the schooling youth had received were found to be associated with the father's usual occupation. This held true for the Negro as well as the white youth, as well as for each sex group within the races.

Race is placed second and above sex. An accurate evaluation of the importance of the race factor is complicated because Negro youth, especially in the rural areas, have fathers whose usual occupation is either farm laborer, farm tenant, or unskilled laborer. Thus it is impossible to determine exactly how much of the relatively low grade attainment of Negro youth is due to some "race difference" and how much is the result of the fact that a large proportion of Negroes are in economically weak occupations.

Sex. Sex differences appear regardless of how the data are analyzed. Within the races, within occupations, within the different age groups, and within the various localities, the female youth in general have higher median grades.

WHY DO YOUTH LEAVE SCHOOL?

So far, we have been concerned chiefly with an analysis of the factors that seem to influence the youth's school progress as measured by the grade he has attained. Our purpose has been to discover these factors, and to attempt to measure their relative potency. At this point, we consider briefly the factors operating to terminate a youth's formal education, as revealed by the reasons for leaving school that were given by the youth themselves.

YOUTH'S REASONS FOR LEAVING SCHOOL

The following table presents an analysis of the reasons given by young people for leaving school.

TABLE 18 Reasons Given by Youth for Leaving School

Reason given	Percentage of youth
Economic reasons	54.0
Lack of family funds	34.1
Desire to earn own money	15.7
Needed to work at home	4.2
Lack of interest in school	24.6
Lack of interest	20.6
Disciplinary trouble	2.2
Subjects too difficult	1.8
Feeling of completion upon graduation	13.2
Poor health	3.2
To marry	3.0
Other reasons	2.0
Total	100.0
Number of youth	10,858

The responses analyzed in Table 18 indicate that, for every twenty-five youth who have left school,

Ten left because of economic need
Six left because of lack of interest or because of maladjustment
Four left because they wanted to earn their own money
Three left because they considered their education completed upon graduation
Two left for other reasons such as marriage, health, etc.

The outstanding reason given by the youth for leaving school was the financial inability of their parents to keep them there. In fact, almost four out of every ten (38 per cent) of the out-of-school youth indicated that they would have preferred to remain in school, but that lack of family funds, or the need for their services at home, prevented their continuing.

It is also significant that a fourth of the youth said they left school because of a lack of interest or because of their inability to adjust themselves to the school program. This 25 per cent is probably an understatement, as undoubtedly a large proportion of those who said they dropped out because they wanted to earn money for themselves did so because the attraction of economic independence was greater than that of the school program.

The fact that 13.2 per cent said they had left school because they considered their education complete upon graduation does not mean, of course, that only 13.2 per cent actually completed the grades in the various school levels. All it means is that this proportion left school at the completion of the elementary, secondary, or college level because they felt that the education they had received was adequate to meet their needs.

DOES "EQUALITY OF EDUCATIONAL OPPORTUNITIES" EXIST?

In so far as the matter of leaving school at undesirably low levels is the direct result of inadequate funds, it is obvious that the remedy lies deeper than any improvement or extension of the educational programs. If society is interested in broadening and deepening the educational backgrounds of all its young people, it seems quite clear that the first move is to make further schooling possible for them by some local, state, or Federal subsidizing program, a beginning of which has already been made by the National Youth Administration.

As indicated above, about 40 per cent of our youth would go farther in school if the opportunity were provided them. An analysis of the responses of the twelfth grade graduate suggests that almost half (46.8

per cent) failed to proceed to a higher educational level because of a lack of family funds. Almost as large a proportion (42.7 per cent) of the youth employed on relief projects gave the same reason.

It seems obvious that before the schools can effectively participate in any solution of the national youth problem opportunities for attending them must be provided. In other words, it would seem that society's first job is to change the nature of "equality of educational opportunity" from that of a noble jingle to an established and effective reality.

ARE SCHOOLS ADAPTED TO THE NEEDS AND
INTERESTS OF YOUTH?

Four out of every ten youth assert that they leave school because their parents cannot continue to send them. For them, the solution is primarily a matter of providing opportunities that don't exist. For a large proportion of the remainder, the solution is more definitely a matter of so adjusting our school programs as to make them sufficiently attractive to compete with other things. Our data reveal that, with several groups of youth, unsatisfactory school adjustment—by which is meant a combination of lack of interest, disciplinary difficulties, and too difficult subjects—is a more general reason for leaving school than a lack of family funds. So far as the youth's own statements of why he left school can be accepted as the real reasons, all of this indicates that, for large groups of youth, the schools simply have failed to function as a genuine force. The fact that relatively high percentages of youth giving lack of interest as their reason for dropping out were found among those who left school at the upper high school level, as well as among those who left at the elementary level, indicates that all along the line the schools, as they are now set up, are adapted to neither the needs nor the interests of large numbers of our young people.

For youth who are preparing for professional vocations, it appears that the holding power of the schools is exceedingly strong. Less than 5 per cent of young people found to be engaged in professional work stated that they left school because they lacked interest. Somewhat the same situation is true for youth discovered in office and sales work, as only 14 per cent of the youth so engaged gave lack of interest as their reason for dropping out.

Three hundred and forty-two (about 3 per cent) of the out-of-school youth gave marriage as their reason for leaving. Of this number, a substantial proportion dropped out of school at relatively low levels. In fact, over half the married boys (52.4 per cent) and almost half the married girls (42.3 per cent) were found to have received no more than an elementary school education. This naturally raises the question as to what schools are doing to help these youth meet the obligations and problems which marriage is certain to force upon them. If there is an economic justification for providing vocational training for youth who will have to earn their own living at a comparatively early age, there would seem to be an equally sound social justification in providing young people with at least a basic knowledge of the obligations and problems of marriage. That youth themselves consider this a part of the school's job is indicated by their opinion that sex education should be made a regular part of the school program.

WHAT TO DO ABOUT IT

An analysis of the reasons given by youth as to why they left school tends, in a general way, to support the conclusions that grew out of our analysis of the data on the school progress they had made. The first move should be one of providing adequate educational opportunities for all the youth who are capable and who are desirous of taking advantage of them.

The second step in increasing the extent to which the schools can effectively participate in the solution of the youth problem concerns those youth who, though provided by their parents with adequate opportunity, chose to leave school at relatively low levels. For these, the approach is clearly one of adapting school programs to their interests and needs. Youngsters, like horses, can be led to water, but only thirst will make them drink. . . .

DO OUT-OF-SCHOOL YOUTH WANT VOCATIONAL TRAINING?

This question was asked only of youth who had left school. They were asked if they would take vocational training if it were made available. As used by the interviewer, the term "vocational training" meant training for any job. It included training in the professions and arts, as well as in business and trades. For the majority (60 per cent) the answer was "yes."

As suggested in one of our introductory paragraphs, the questions asked of our young people were generally such as to exclude any temptation to make false or inaccurate responses. In this particular question, however, there is clearly an encouragement of wishful thinking. That six out of every ten of the out-of-school youth are, in fact, genuinely desirous of further vocational training is, we suspect open to question. We doubt, therefore, if this 60 per cent can be taken as an indication of the potential demand by out-of-school youth for free public vocational training.

It is believed, however, that these data reveal that there is a real demand for more vocational training. Many young people have learned, especially during the past few years, what usually happens when, to a prospective employer's question, "What can you do?" they answer, "Anything." What usually happens is that they get no job. These and similar experiences have led them to believe that training for a specific type of work is very often not only desirable but necessary.

TYPE OF VOCATIONAL TRAINING DESIRED

An element of wishful thinking is also apparent in many of the responses to the second half of the question: If so, for what kind of job would you like to be trained?

An examination of Table 20 will reveal that out of every twenty-five youth expressing a desire for vocational training,

TABLE 20   Types of Vocational Training Desired by

Out-of-School Youth

Classification of youth	Professional	Business and secretarial	Trades and crafts	Domestic or personal	Agriculture and related fields	Other types; uncertain
All out-of-school youth	36.4	24.8	23.5	8.2	1.7	5.4
16-year-olds	22.0	27.0	30.2	11.0	2.0	7.8
18-year-olds	33.3	28.9	23.6	8.3	0.9	5.0
20-year-olds	38.3	25.1	21.8	8.3	1.5	5.0
22-year-olds	41.4	24.1	20.7	7.7	1.8	4.3
24-year-olds	42.4	21.8	20.7	7.7	3.0	4.4
Farm	25.4	19.6	26.8	9.5	7.5	11.2
Village	36.1	26.7	22.6	8.1	0.7	5.8
Town	41.9	28.1	15.7	6.8	0.9	6.6
City	39.2	25.0	24.7	8.1	0.3	2.7
Employed	36.2	23.4	26.4	5.5	2.6	5.9
Unemployed	34.3	26.3	24.8	8.8	0.6	5.2
Homemakers	38.5	28.9	6.9	21.6	0.3	3.8
Youth's occupation						
Professional–technical ...	82.8	11.3	2.9	1.1	0.4	1.5
Managerial	40.8	24.6	16.2	—	9.9	8.5
Office–sales	38.3	39.2	13.5	3.2	0.8	5.0
Skilled	38.2	12.7	44.0	0.6	—	4.5
Semi-skilled	35.6	19.7	33.3	5.3	0.6	5.5
Unskilled	19.3	9.3	49.6	2.5	8.0	11.3
Domestic–personal	34.3	27.1	10.8	23.2	1.0	3.6
Relief projects	23.1	18.7	46.2	7.7	1.4	2.9
Father's occupation						
Professional–technical ...	63.0	18.9	9.4	4.0	1.7	3.0
Office–sales	47.2	31.8	13.0	4.8	0.4	2.8
Skilled	33.8	27.5	26.7	7.4	0.8	3.8
Farm owner–tenant	27.7	22.3	22.0	8.5	7.3	12.2
Unskilled	27.0	20.8	34.4	13.3	1.0	3.5

Nine desired training for one of the professions
Six desired training for business or commercial work
Six desired training in trades and crafts
Two desired training in domestic and personal service
Two desired training in other unclassified fields.

About all that some of these data show is that vocations, like the grass that grows in pastures, usually look greener on the other side of the fence. This is somewhat dramatically illustrated by the responses of farm youth. About one out of fourteen wanted training in agriculture.

Yet, even when due weight is given to human nature's ancient enthusiasm for variety and change, there still remain in these expressed preferences for vocational courses some implications that are worthy of sober consideration.

More than five out of every six out-of-school youth who wanted training wanted it in one of the professions, in business, or in the skilled trades. For the out-of-school group as a whole, 36 per cent wanted training in the professions. It will be remembered that the median grade attainment of this group was the completion of the ninth grade.

These two facts—the outstanding preference for professional training, and the generally low grade attained—can, and probably do, mean two things. They mean that this younger generation aspires in the traditional manner of all younger generations. It wants to do bigger and better things. They also mean that, for some reason or other, there has been precious little realism injected into the thinking of a large proportion of our young people about the jobs that are available and the services they are qualified to perform. In view of the almost complete absence of vocational guidance from their school experiences, at least a part of the responsibility for this dearth of realism can justly be laid at the doorstep of the schools.

Among the hopeful and constructive facts that the data in Table 20 reveal is the very real demand for training in trades and crafts. In spite of the denials from certain labor leaders, there is a considerable body of evidence to suggest that, if there is such a thing as an unfilled labor demand, it exists in certain kinds of skilled trades. The fact that half of the 1,000 youth who were found to be employed on unskilled jobs desired some kind of vocational training, and that half this number (49.6 per cent) wanted training in some trade or craft, is not only a refreshing item of realism, but a definitely hopeful sign.

Youth Evaluate Their School Experiences

VOCATIONAL GUIDANCE—FACT OR MYTH?

As used by the interviewer, the term "vocational guidance" was understood to mean vocational advice given by someone reasonably well acquainted with the various occupational fields. This person might be a school counselor, teacher, principal, official in a public or private employment agency, or any other qualified person, exclusive of the youth's family or his close relatives. As used, the term further presupposed that the person giving the advice had made a reasonably careful study of the youth's aptitudes, limitations, and interests, and that he had given his advice accordingly.

YOUTH WHO HAVE RECEIVED VOCATIONAL GUIDANCE

About the only encouraging implication of the data presented in Table 21 is that a larger proportion of youth now in school reported that they had received vocational guidance than was the case with those who had permanently left.

TO WHAT EXTENT DO YOUTH RECEIVE
VOCATIONAL GUIDANCE FROM SCHOOLS?

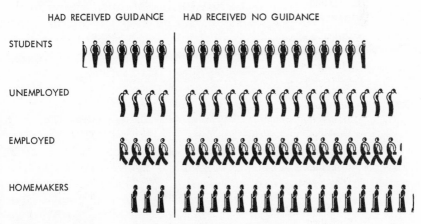

HAD RECEIVED GUIDANCE   HAD RECEIVED NO GUIDANCE

STUDENTS

UNEMPLOYED

EMPLOYED

HOMEMAKERS

Each Complete Figure Represents 5% of The Youth In Each Group

An examination of the first column of Table 21 will give one an idea of the extent to which youth in various groups have received vocational guidance. Some of the factors that seem to exert an influence over

**TABLE 21 Extent to Which Youth Have
Received Vocational Guidance**

| | Percentage who received | |
Classification of youth	Guidance	No guidance
All youth	22.7	77.3
Students	34.3	65.7
Nonstudents	19.9	80.1
Farm	12.7	87.3
Village	16.4	83.6
Town	17.5	82.5
City	31.8	68.2
Male: white	23.7	76.3
Male: Negro	17.6	82.4
Female: white	22.9	77.1
Female: Negro	21.1	78.9
16-year-olds	27.9	72.1
18-year-olds	24.5	75.5
20-year-olds	22.6	77.4
22-year-olds	20.4	79.6
24-year-olds	16.9	83.1
Youth's occupation		
Professional–technical	33.3	66.7
Managerial	22.6	77.4
Office–sales	25.4	74.6
Skilled	22.8	77.2
Semi-skilled	20.1	79.9
Domestic–personal	16.1	83.9
Unskilled	10.8	89.2
Father's occupation		
Professional–technical	32.5	67.5
Office–sales	27.6	72.4
Skilled	26.2	73.8
Farm owner–tenant	13.5	86.5
Unskilled	17.8	82.2

228

whether or not a youth receives this important service are set down below:

School status. It will be seen that almost twice as large a proportion of youth now in school stated they had received guidance as those who had left school (34.3 per cent as against 19.9 per cent).

Area. It will also be seen that the amount of guidance youth receive, like the median grades they attain, is closely associated with the population density of the areas in which they live—the least for youth living on farms, and the most for youth living in cities.

Race. One finds almost equal proportions of white and Negro youth who have received vocational guidance.

Age. One next finds an inverse relationship between guidance received and the age of the youth. Starting with the 24-year-old group (with 16.9 per cent), there is a progressive increase for all ages, reaching a maximum of 27.9 per cent for the youth who were 16 years old.

Youth's occupation. While one out of every three youth found to be engaged in professional work had been given vocational advice, less than one out of every nine working as unskilled laborers had received such service.

Father's occupation. One sees again the apparently inevitable relationship between the services youth receive and the occupation of their fathers. Almost twice as many of the youth whose fathers were in the professions had received guidance as was found to be the case with the youth whose fathers were unskilled laborers.

As a finally significant fact, the following condensed table reveals that, of the youth who had left school, more than two thirds of the high school graduates, and almost two thirds of those who had obtained some college education, had never received any vocational guidance from any source.

TABLE 22 Proportions of Youth in Specified Grade Levels Who Had Received Vocational Guidance

Grade completed	Received vocational guidance
7th grade	1 out of 10
9th grade	2 out of 10
12th grade graduate	3 out of 10
4 or more years beyond high school	4 out of 10

SOURCES OF VOCATIONAL GUIDANCE

Although our primary purpose in asking this question was to discover the extent to which youth had received vocational guidance, we
also wanted, if possible, to arrive at some conclusion as to how this
need was being met by schools, employment agencies, and other sources.

In so far as the youth of our sample were getting any vocational
advice at all, it may quite definitely be stated that they were getting
it from the schools. In fact, more than 90 per cent (93.3) of the vocational advice was given by these institutions. Only one youth in a
hundred was found to have received vocational guidance from officials
in public and private employment agencies.

YOUTH'S EVALUATION OF VOCATIONAL GUIDANCE RECEIVED

An effort was also made to get the youth's own evaluation of whatever guidance he may have received. In view of the fact that practically
all guidance was provided by the schools, these evaluations will necessarily refer to the school guidance programs. The first column of Table
23 shows the percentages of youth in various groups who considered
that the vocational counseling they had received had been, or would
be, of real value to them in determining a job for which they were
fitted.

HOW YOUTH EVALUATE THE VOCATIONAL
GUIDANCE THEY ARE RECEIVING OR HAVE
RECEIVED FROM THEIR SCHOOLS*

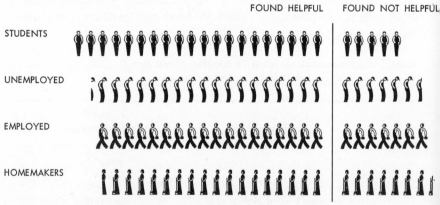

*Only 2762 or 20% Had Received Guidance From Schools

Each Figure Represents 4% of The Youth of Each Group Who Had Received Guidance From The School

TABLE 23   Source and Youth's Evaluation of
Vocational Guidance Received *

	School		
		Not	*All other*
Classification of youth	*Helpful*	*helpful*	*sources*
All youth	69.0	24.2	6.8
Students	75.3	18.8	5.9
Nonstudents	66.6	26.4	7.0
Employed	65.7	26.0	8.3
Unemployed	69.0	26.0	5.0
Farm	77.9	15.3	6.8
Village	77.1	16.0	6.9
Town	72.2	19.5	8.3
City	64.9	28.8	6.3
Male: white	69.8	22.0	8.2
Male: Negro	72.0	22.6	5.4
Female: white	68.1	26.3	5.6
Female: Negro	68.4	27.7	3.9
16-year-olds	76.6	19.6	3.8
18-year-olds	69.6	25.3	5.1
20-year-olds	67.8	27.9	4.3
22-year-olds	63.3	25.6	11.1
24-year-olds	67.7	22.9	9.4
Father's occupation			
Professional–technical	71.6	20.2	8.2
Office–sales	68.9	25.6	5.5
Skilled	67.5	25.9	6.6
Farm owner–tenant	77.4	16.5	6.1
Unskilled	65.5	28.3	6.2

* This table covers only the 22.7 per cent who had received guidance.

Of the out-of-school youth who had received guidance from the schools, over 70 per cent (71.4) reported that they had found it helpful. It would seem to require an unusually critical mind to find anything very unfortunate in this record. In so far as youth themselves are capable of passing intelligent and unbiased judgments on the services they receive, this indicates that, so far as it functions, the vocational counseling service of the schools has been better than 70 per cent efficient.

The unfortunate thing, of course, is that for the great majority of young people the schools simply haven't functioned at all, so far as this very important service is concerned. When all the youth including those now in school are considered, one still finds that only sixteen out of every hundred have received what they consider helpful vocational guidance from their schools.

RELATION OF GUIDANCE TO YOUTH'S EVALUATION

OF THEIR SCHOOLING

Later on we will discuss briefly youth's estimate of both the cultural and economic value of their school experiences. Table 24 suggests

TABLE 24   Relation Between Vocational Guidance Received
and Youth's Appraisal of the Economic Value
of Their Schooling

Economic value of schooling	Employed youth		Unemployed youth	
	No guidance	*Helpful school guidance*	*No guidance*	*Helpful school guidance*
No help	12.1	5.3	16.0	6.0
Little help	19.7	9.1	21.4	15.2
Fair amount of help	22.3	14.2	20.5	16.3
Considerable help	20.0	26.1	20.4	26.3
Great help	25.9	45.3	21.7	36.2

the extent to which their receiving, or not receiving, vocational guidance may have affected their estimates of the economic value of the schooling they have had.

This table reveals two interesting facts: For both the employed and the unemployed groups, the proportion of youth who asserted that schooling had been of great economic value to them was substantially higher among those who had received helpful guidance from the schools than it was among those who had received no guidance at all. Over 45 per cent (45.3) of the employed youth who had had the benefit of helpful vocational counseling felt that their school experience had, in general, been of great economic value. For the employed youth who had received no guidance, the percentage who felt the same way was only 26. The difference is significant.

Here are a few responses quoted to indicate what young people say when they think about vocational guidance:

Principal of high school was very helpful to me.

It got me my job.

The greatest problem is finding a career that suits.

That's a weakness in all schools.

Young people are wondering what they are going to do when they get older.

I just advised myself.

I done all my own planning.

I wish I had had some help.

I'd have been better off if somebody had helped me.

Teachers influenced me very little.

Most everyone can get enough education. The real trouble is finding out what to do with it.

They [in high school] had vocational guidance teachers, but we never paid any attention to them.

They led me wrong.

They don't know their stuff. People get misguided by them.

Vocational teachers call the girls in about three times a year, but it doesn't help much.

I had my palm read.

WHOSE RESPONSIBILITY?

No one who is close to the realities of this situation will have the notion that the schools can be expected to provide vocational guidance to all the youth who have been exposed to their influence. When it is remembered that half the youth between the ages of 16 and 24 drop out of school at various levels between the early elementary grades and the completion of the ninth grade, at least one of the reasons for the scarcity of vocational counseling becomes obvious. We know, in fact, that as youth go farther in school the probability that they will receive guidance increases accordingly. In terms of exact percentages our data indicate that, while only 4 per cent of the youth who had left school before the completion of the sixth grade stated they had received vocational guidance, 38.7 per cent of the college graduates made the same report. Thus, even when just allowance is made for early drop-outs, the fact still stands that two out of every three youth finishing high school, and almost the same proportion finishing college, had never enjoyed the benefit of what, to them, might have been a most valuable service.

If this vital need of providing adequate vocational guidance is to be met, the first step is obviously one of increasing and improving the service to the youth who are still in school. The proportion of high school graduates who had received no vocational guidance indicates that even when the schools have adequate time and opportunity they do little about providing this kind of service. The next step should consist either in expanding the sphere of the school's influence, in order to reach the large numbers who drop out at early levels, or in creating some new agency to meet the problem.

Further along in the course of the interview, each young person was asked, "Regardless of available opportunities, what kind of work would you most like to do?" The large majority thought they knew. How they came to their decisions, and how much cold realism had entered into the thinking that produced them, we are in no position to know. All we do know is that about four out of every five had to decide without the benefit of the schools or other agencies.

At a later time, we will also discuss the relationship between the jobs which employed youth preferred and the work they were actually found to be doing. The reality of vocational maladjustment stands out like a bump.

Probably as good a remedy for this situation as has so far been suggested is a comprehensive and effective vocational guidance program. Effective vocational guidance involves a "casework approach" and is based upon three fundamentals: a sound understanding of the aptitudes and limitations of the individual, a general acquaintance with the technical requirements of specific jobs, and a realistic knowledge of available employment opportunities.

So far as young people are concerned, what is clearly needed are techniques and procedures that can uncover not only the aptitudes but also the potentialities of the individual. What is also needed is a reliable method of determining actual labor demands, such as an adequate employment–unemployment census. Before we can presume to guide our young people, it would be well to know what there is for them to be guided into.

In the provision of this much needed service the schools, through a vigorous and intelligent administration of vocational clinics, can play a considerably more important part than they have played so far. Once the schools, within their limited sphere of influence, have done all that can reasonably be expected of them, perhaps society, more keenly conscious of its responsibility to its youth, will provide appropriate agencies to assume what remains of the job. The agency probably best equipped to serve the large majority of youth who are out of school is a more thoroughly developed junior employment division of the public employment service.

DOES EDUCATION PAY?

The difficulty of adapting our education programs to the needs and interests of modern youth is aggravated, not so much by a dearth, as by a diversity, of qualified opinions on what should be done. We have no impulse to assume that one of these sources is more authoritative or reliable than another. The truth, if there is any, lies buried in various places, and one of these places, we suspect, is in the opinions and suggestions of the youth themselves.

In bringing about the long delayed and vitally needed adjustment of school programs to the realities of modern social and economic life, responsible people will find much that is valuable in the reactions and the evaluations of the youth themselves. There is hardly any danger that the evaluations of young people will be taken too seriously. There is a far greater danger that they will be ignored.

A number of our questions were designed to elicit the opinions youth have about certain subjects to which they could reasonably be expected to have given some thought. One of these was worded as follows: "Do you feel that your education helped or will help you to earn a living?"

As source material upon which to base our conclusions as to the opinions young people have on certain issues, we have what might be defined as both quantitative and qualitative data. In other words, we have both the statistical analysis of the youth's answers, and cards on which are recorded some 15,000 verbatim responses. In our effort to present the picture of how youth have reacted to the education they have received, we shall draw from both these sources of information.

It will be clear, from an acquaintance with the procedure observed in presenting other data, that it is not enough to analyze findings with respect to the total group and stop at that. It is usual that only in the disclosure of differences between facts or opinions, as they are related to important groups, can the real meaning and implications of data be revealed.

WHAT YOUTH THINK ABOUT THE ECONOMIC VALUE OF THEIR SCHOOLING

Table 25 brings together significant data on this question as related to specific groups. For those who may prefer not to risk losing themselves in the "whelming brine" of such an array of percentages, the outstanding implications are listed below:

Students–nonstudents. Three out of every ten youth (30.7 per cent) who had permanently left school were found to have the feeling that the schooling they had received had been or would be of little or no economic value to them—but less than one out of ten (7.9 per cent) of the youth in school felt that the education they were receiving would, in the future, be of little or no value. This seems to indicate that for a substantial proportion of young people education fails in later years to fulfill its original promise.

All youth. Stated in other terms, these data disclose that, for every thirty young people, both in and out of school,

Three consider their education of no economic value
Five consider their education of little economic value
Six consider their education of some economic value
Six consider their education of considerable economic value
Ten consider their education of great economic value.

In short, twice as many young people made the two highest appraisals as made the two lowest.

TABLE 25   Youth's Appraisal of the Economic Value
of Their Schooling

| | Percentage of youth in each group | | | | | |
| | Amount of help | | | | | |
Classification of youth	No help	Little	Some	Considerable	Great	No opinion
All youth	10.4	16.0	18.6	21.7	32.0	1.3
Male	10.8	17.6	20.2	21.9	28.7	0.8
Female	10.0	14.2	16.9	21.9	35.8	1.2
White	10.6	13.5	17.8	22.1	35.1	0.9
Negro	9.3	29.9	23.3	20.1	15.8	1.6
16-year-olds	7.0	13.4	14.8	23.2	39.6	2.0
18-year-olds	9.6	15.4	18.9	24.0	31.4	0.7
20-year-olds	11.5	16.3	18.8	21.7	30.8	0.9
22-year-olds	12.7	18.1	18.6	19.5	30.8	0.3
24-year-olds	12.3	17.7	21.1	18.3	30.1	0.5
Employed	10.9	17.8	20.6	21.0	28.8	0.9
Unemployed	14.4	19.7	19.3	21.3	23.7	1.6
Students	2.3	5.6	10.4	25.1	55.2	1.4
Nonstudents	12.3	18.4	20.6	20.9	26.5	1.3

Age. The older and more experienced the group, the less favorable their judgments. For example, the proportion of 24-year-olds who consider their schooling of little or no economic value was one and a half times the proportion of 16-year-olds.

Race. The white youth were more favorable in their appraisals than were the Negro youth. More than twice as large a proportion of whites considered their education as having great economic value than was the case for the Negroes. The percentages are 35.1 for white and 15.8 for Negro youth.

Locality of residence. Farm youth were less generous in their appraisals than city youth, and young people from the relief families of both races were more critical than the youth from families who had not been on relief during the year preceding the interview. Nearly four out of every ten from white relief families and more than eight of every ten from Negro relief families considered their schooling of little or no economic value.

DOES EDUCATION PAY?

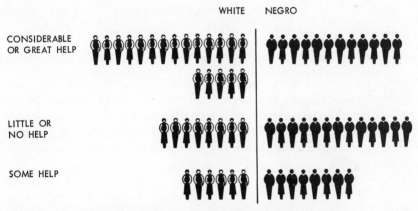

Each Symbol Represents The Evaluations of 3% of Each Racial Group

The table above sets forth the evaluations of all youth. It includes the responses of the young people who were in school as well as those who were out of school at the time of the interview. Figure 8 deals only with the youth who are out of school—with those to whom school is no longer an everyday reality, but an experience that calls up memories that seem to be as varied as the youth themselves.

The outstanding implication of Figure 8 is a decidedly constructive one so far as the schools are concerned. Nearly nine out of every ten (88 per cent) young persons who had gone through college looked back upon their school years with the feeling that their education had been of considerable or great economic value, while only 36 per cent of those who had left school at the completion of the eighth grade recalled their schooling with a similar sense of value received. When one combines the "little" and "no" value groups, one sees that as the

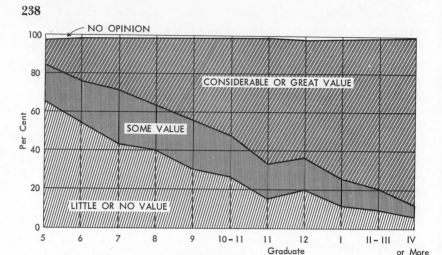

OUT-OF-SCHOOL YOUTH ESTIMATE
THE ECONOMIC VALUE OF THEIR SCHOOLING

Figure 8

grade attainment of the youth increases these unfavorable appraisals decrease accordingly. It is significant that the proportion of out-of-school youth who regarded their schooling as of little or no economic value is higher in all of the four lowest grade groups than the proportion who estimated the economic value of their education as considerable or great.

It will be remembered that for the whole group a little more than half the young people felt that their education had been, or would be, of considerable or great economic value. A few of the comments made by young people who were so classified are quoted below:

You have to have at least a high school education to get along.

If you haven't got a high school education, you can't get anything.

If I hadn't a had the education that I did, I couldn't have even applied for the position.

Without school you're no good. My mother and father had none, and I know what that has meant to them.

You have a pretty tough time without an education. It seems nowadays the more education you have, the better chance you got.

I wish I'd a went higher. You can't get a job lots of places without a high school education. (This from a young man, 20 years old, who had completed the sixth grade and two years at night school. He is now employed as a laborer in a steel mill.)

If I hadn't taken up dressmaking, I wouldn't have gotten the job I have

now. (This girl had had a two-year course in a vocational school. She is
now employed in a dress factory.)

All they ask is 'how much education do you have?'

I only wish I had more.

Yes, indeed. Department stores won't take you unless you're a high school
graduate.

It trains your mind to think.

Don't know what I'd do without it.

A little more than a fourth of the young people interviewed felt that
their education had been of little or of no economic value to them.
Here are a few of the things the youth in this group had to say:

I wish I hadn't went. I hated school. I liked only shorthand and typing.
(This 22-year-old girl is a high school graduate. Her only job so far has
been that of an operator in a pants factory. She is now unemployed.)

The trouble with high school education is that it gives you a bit of everything, but you can't get a job with it, better than a laborer.

I'd give anything to have more education, because you can't get ahead
without it. I'll probably be a maid all my life.

Private schools for girls are a fizzle and a flop.

They teach you the same thing over and over again in Catholic schools.
For some years, I learned nothing new.

It was the biggest waste of time in my life. They didn't teach anything
useful to me.

The jobs that I've had have been where you don't need to use your brains
at all. You just work.

I've always worked on farms, and that don't take no education.

DOES EDUCATION MAKE LIFE MORE WORTH LIVING?

There has been no inclination on our part to suggest that the primary function of the schools is to provide vocational education. Our
purpose has rather been one of disclosing the fact that considerable
numbers of young people feel quite strongly that at least one of the
functions of our educational programs should be that of preparing
them to earn a living.

THE CULTURAL VALUE OF SCHOOLING

Once the interviewer had obtained the youth's appraisal of the economic value of his schooling, the next step was to get his evaluation
of his education in terms of the contribution it had made to his capacity
to "enjoy life more." Had his school experience made the business
of living a richer and pleasanter thing?

The answer was quite generally "yes." Youth seem to take the cultural value of an education as a matter of course. A very common reaction to the inquiry was an expression of good-humored sympathy for people who ask obviously silly questions.

A glance down the first column of Table 26 will suggest how rare an experience it is to find a young person who feels that his schooling has been of no cultural value. It is quite clear that the great majority feel that without their school experiences living would have been decidedly more meaningless and drab.

TABLE 26 Youth's Appraisal of the Cultural Value of Their Schooling

	Percentage of youth in each group					
	Amount of help					
Classification of youth	*No help*	*Little*	*Some*	*Consid-erable*	*Great*	*No opinion*
All youth	3.8	8.0	15.5	25.1	46.5	1.1
Male: single	4.4	9.1	17.2	25.6	42.8	0.9
Male: married	6.4	13.2	21.0	26.0	32.8	0.6
Female: single	2.2	5.2	11.5	24.6	56.0	0.5
Female: married	4.4	9.1	16.5	25.3	43.7	1.0
White	3.4	6.3	14.0	25.0	50.6	0.7
Negro	6.2	17.6	24.1	26.2	24.8	1.1
Farm	3.1	11.7	23.6	27.9	33.7	—
Village	2.9	7.8	16.7	29.1	43.5	—
Town	2.9	7.0	10.9	24.1	55.1	—
City	5.0	6.9	12.6	22.7	52.8	*
Students	1.1	2.5	8.7	26.0	60.6	1.1
Nonstudents	4.5	9.4	17.1	24.9	43.0	1.1
Employed	4.0	9.1	17.0	25.2	43.9	0.8
Unemployed	5.9	10.9	18.1	23.7	40.0	1.4
Homemakers	3.9	8.2	16.6	26.9	42.9	1.5
Father's occupation						
Professional–technical .	1.3	1.8	8.4	20.3	68.2	—
Office–sales	2.1	3.9	11.2	22.6	59.6	0.6
Farm owner–tenant ..	2.2	9.5	21.8	28.8	36.8	0.9
Unskilled	8.3	14.4	19.9	25.9	30.3	1.2

* Less than 0.05 per cent.

A few of the comments made by the great majority of youth who felt that their schooling had been of considerable or great value are listed below.

If I hadn't gone to school, I couldn't ever read. (A grateful tribute to a sixth grade "education.")

It develops somewhat of a personality.

My college education has been everything in my life.

My father picks up a paper and can't read a word.

Immeasurably.

Wished I could have went to high school.

I got a little more polish and refinement in junior college than I got in high school. In other words, it taught me to be a lady.

If I didn't get no learning, I couldn't get along very good.

Without the education I have received, life wouldn't be worth living.

I read a lot and know the poets and that sort of thing.

I'd be as dumb as an ox if I didn't know how to read or write. (Another grateful tribute to the elementary school.)

My mother can't read or write. I feel for those who can't read or write.

All the help in the world.

If I hadn't got a little literature in my hide, I'd have been satisfied to read western stories all my life.

It has given me what is known as a personality, which is helpful in meeting the public.

And then, as a sort of brash interlude in this paean of praise, you hear the mumbled grumbling of the few malcontents.

It only made me feel disgusted with life. It has made me feel the inadequacy of the education I have had. (With a ninth-grade education this 23-year-old youth apparently feels that a little learning is a useless thing.)

In our school it's strictly technical, nothing cultural—except a pool table.

It don't do you no good. (This blast from a 16-year-old girl who had to leave school at the age of 14 after completing the tenth grade. One of eight children of a coal miner, this girl, whose income is needed at home, had been unemployed for two years and three months.)

I doubt if it helps to enjoy anything.

IMPLICATIONS

These appraisals of the economic and cultural value of schooling bring to mind the old French proverb which, if our memory serves us right, translates into something that means "the appetite grows with eating." Certainly, if these data mean anything, they mean that the more schooling youth receive the more likely they are to consider it valuable. They further suggest that many of the destructive judgments that young people have passed upon the schooling they have had may quite as logically have arisen from a sense of incompleteness as from a conviction that the schools have failed to meet their needs. We suspect, in fact, that their evaluations have been quantitative as well as qualitative, and that in both their censure and their praise the sense of completeness or incompleteness has tended to color their thought.

However, the question of whether an ex-student's sense of futility arises from a consciousness of the inadequacy of his education or whether it comes from a conviction that his school has failed to give him the kind of training he needed is somewhat beside the point. The discontent that springs from a youth's sense of educational incompleteness can be faced only by increasing the quantity of his education. The dissatisfaction that grows out of a youth's belief that the schools have failed to prepare him to cope with the bewildering complexities of his out-of-school world can be faced only by so changing the quality of our educational offering as to adapt them to his interests and needs.

This means that provisions should be made that will result in larger numbers of youth staying in school for longer periods of time. Besides thus increasing the quantity of education a youth receives, steps should also be taken to so adjust educational programs to the youth's interests and needs that larger numbers will derive deeper satisfaction from their school experiences.

Our data suggest that many schools are so organized at present that young people have to go through the whole school program before they can be led to see any genuine value in it. This inevitably creates a sense of inadequacy among the majority of young people who drop out shortly after the completion of the elementary school. The answer is the development of educational programs so closely related to everyday living that each school year, instead of being a means to some more or less remote end, becomes in fact an end in itself.

All of which adds up to the conclusions that the consideration of other data has forced upon us: A more genuine equality of educational opportunity should be provided for all groups of youth, and more realistic and satisfying programs should be devised to meet their needs. . . .

The Social Significance of Low Grade Attainment

RELATION OF THE FATHER'S OCCUPATION TO THE
YOUTH'S GRADE ATTAINMENT

In a previous section of this chapter, we considered how the social and economic background of the youth and his family was related to his educational progress. We said something about the apparent existence of social and economic forces that tend to freeze social levels and to hold young people in the grip of the same restrictions to which their parents had been subjected.

From a glance across the horizontal lines of Table 28, it will be seen that the out-of-school youth, whose grade attainment was relatively low (the completion of the ninth grade or less), were largely recruited from families whose fathers were employed in the low income occupations. Over 93 per cent of the youth who had left school before they had completed the sixth grade had fathers who were either skilled, semiskilled, or unskilled laborers, or who were farm owners, farm tenants, or farm laborers. At the other extreme, the majority (84.8 per cent) of the college graduates were the children of fathers who were in the professional–technical, managerial, sales, office, or skilled labor groups.

A comparison of the unskilled and semiskilled groups with the professional–technical and managerial groups clearly indicates the extent to which the youth's grade level has been influenced, if not in a large measure determined, by the occupation of his father.[7]

RELATION OF THE YOUTH'S GRADE ATTAINMENT TO THE
OCCUPATION HE WILL FOLLOW

With the fact established that the youth's grade attainment is influenced by the nature of his father's job and the amount, therefore, of

[7] Supplementing these data from another source, it is worthwhile to examine the findings of a Commission sponsored study of 30,000 Pennsylvania students. Using the Chapman-Sims Socio-Economic Scale as an index of the family's socioeconomic background, Harlan Updegraff, the director, discovered a clear-cut relationship existing between the grades youth complete in school and the socioeconomic level of the families from which they come.

Grade Completed	Median Score
6th grade	1.9
7th grade	2.3
8th grade	2.8
9th grade	2.9
10th grade	3.8
11th grade	4.9
12th grade	5.0
13th grade (Freshman)	7.5
14th grade (Sophomore)	7.2

While the median score (as indicated by the Chapman-Sims Socio-Economic Scale) of the youth who had reached the college level was well above 7, the median score of those who had dropped out at the completion of the sixth grade was less than 2.

TABLE 28 Out-of-School Youth Who Completed Specified Grades, According
to the Occupations of Their Fathers

					Percentage of youth in each group				
Grade completed	Prof.-tech.	Managerial	Sales	Office	Skilled	Semi-skilled	Un-skilled	Farm laborer	Farm operator
Below 6th	—	2.1	0.8	0.6	9.1	7.0	26.0	24.9	26.1
6th grade	0.4	5.6	0.6	1.0	18.2	13.5	22.7	11.5	21.9
7th grade	0.5	4.6	1.3	1.1	19.3	12.6	16.6	9.8	31.8
8th grade	1.9	9.9	2.2	2.0	29.3	18.6	15.3	3.4	14.4
9th grade	1.8	9.8	3.4	2.9	32.2	16.4	11.0	2.0	17.1
10th or 11th	3.1	14.8	4.2	4.8	32.1	14.9	8.8	2.0	11.1
11th graduate	2.5	15.1	3.7	6.1	22.2	5.0	4.1	0.7	39.1
12th graduate	6.5	21.9	6.4	7.8	27.7	13.2	4.5	0.6	8.6
1 year*	12.4	31.0	6.8	9.1	20.0	3.8	2.4	0.3	13.0
2 or 3 years*	15.2	28.2	8.4	9.8	12.8	4.9	3.2	—	12.8
4 or more years*	23.7	34.8	5.7	8.8	11.8	3.1	1.0	—	9.0

* Beyond high school graduation.

TABLE 29 Occupational Distribution of Out-of-School Employed Youth
According to the School Grades They Had Completed

| | | | Percentage of youth in each grade group | | | | | |
Grade completed	Prof. or tech.	Office or sales	Managerial	Skilled	Semi-skilled	Domestic	Un-skilled	Percentage base
Less than 6th	—	1.3	2.2	1.8	14.6	17.8	61.8	398
6th	—	6.5	1.9	4.8	27.8	15.8	43.2	310
7th	0.4	6.2	5.4	5.2	28.9	16.9	37.0	698
8th	2.0	12.4	2.8	6.0	40.2	15.8	20.8	564
9th	2.2	23.1	4.6	4.2	41.5	9.2	15.2	499
10th or 11th	1.6	28.3	3.4	7.3	34.0	15.1	10.3	803
11th graduate	1.6	48.6	7.7	2.0	17.7	10.0	12.4	549
12th graduate	5.7	47.2	4.2	3.5	25.8	9.3	4.3	1,059
1 year beyond*	5.6	68.2	4.5	2.5	11.6	5.1	2.5	198
2 or 3 years*	45.0	35.2	3.8	3.8	7.0	3.1	2.1	287
4 or more years*	59.4	23.1	10.6	2.2	2.9	1.1	0.7	273

* Beyond high school graduation.

his father's income, another trip around our vicious circle is begun. We dig a litle deeper and we discover that young people who had relatively little schooling have usually gone into the low wage occupations. The data presented in Table 29 deal only with the youth who were found to be employed at the time of the interview. A cursory examination of this table will reveal how clearly the youth's grade attainment is associated, not only with the nature of his father's job, but with the kind of work which he himself will follow.

SUMMARY

The employment of the youth's father in one of the lower or higher income occupations profoundly affects the amount of schooling the youth is likely to receive. The amount of his schooling will, in turn, determine to a marked degree the kind of job he will get and, therefore, the income he will earn. Out of school for a longer period, youth leaving at the lower levels tend to marry earlier and have larger families. All these factors threaten, in their turn, to impose similar restrictions on the opportunities of the youth's children. Though often upset by the force of individual effort, the tendency seems to be toward social and economic stratification and the strengthening of social barriers.

There are cogent social, as well as political and economic, reasons for making every effort to break up this conspiracy of forces that tends to keep certain groups more or less permanently submerged. A decent social conscience demands that equality of opportunity be made more real. The enduring health and efficiency of a democracy demands an awareness of fundamental issues without which the vote must eventually become a meaningless gesture and the pawn of demagogues. Then, too, the weight of the national burden of unemployment could be substantially decreased by the elimination of large numbers of school-age youth from the labor market.[8] All this adds up to the desira-

---

8 It is not intended to assume that total employment is a fixed quantity of persons and that additional persons cannot be absorbed as wage workers. It is recognized that when circumstances in the economic system favor the extension of investments and the exploitation of new resources a period of substantially full employment may arise. In the twenties the amount of unemployment was comparatively small. However, the present situation is characterized by acute unemployment, and efforts to restore employment to normal proportions have shown only partial success. Resort to work-spreading through shorter hours and partial employment has been widespread. Under such circumstances the introduction of additional workers could be successful only in those areas of skilled employment where there might be a scarcity of labor. The greatest unemployment tends to be in groups of unskilled persons. Consequently, the early employment of youth under such circumstances will tend to depress a labor market which is already depressed and create unemployment among older persons who will be thrown out of work or

bility of society's taking a hand in the development of a national program of constructive and profitable activity for its youth.

In such a program, the schools can make a much larger contribution than they are now making. Before they can be expected to exert their maximum influence, steps should be taken to insure a more genuine equality of educational opportunity. Far too many youth, who are both capable and desirous of further education, are out of school and in the labor market for the simple reason that the low economic status of their families made continued schooling impossible.

A start in the direction of making further schooling possible for all youth has already been made by the student aid activities of the National Youth Administration. The effect of these activities has been to provide educational opportunities for a limited number of youth in the economically submerged groups.

There still remains, however, the substantial number of young people for whom the present school programs have little or no appeal. Their dropping out of school at undesirably low levels is the result, not so much of economic necessity, as of sheer indifference. For them, the obvious solution is the development of school programs that are more realistically adapted to their interests and needs.

The steps suggested would result in a larger number of youth remaining in school for longer periods, and their ultimate effects would, in all probability, be the elevation of the national educational level and a reduction of unemployment.

The dangers in any superficial, hit-or-miss program for a younger generation of any country may be subtle, but they are very real. There is ample evidence in the governments and social systems of certain nondemocratic countries to suggest the possible consequences of continued indifference. Only a pathetic smugness can lead one to suspect that anything that has happened elsewhere cannot happen in America. An efficient democracy, like a certain philosopher's idea of immortality, is an achievement, not a bequest, and only a people that strives mightily for it will ever attain it.

Some of the disenchantment about the schools was economically based. This seems timely at a period when economic problems were

---

forced to accept very low wages in some other occupation than the one in which they are accustomed to work. If the youth can be kept in school and prepared for more skilled work they may be absorbed by industry at a later time in occupations where there is a relative scarcity of employees without tending to depress a labor market already oversupplied with workers.

paramount. The central theme of Chapter 4 is one of discontent with the economic and employment situation and with future prospects.

The question could be asked: How could a nation hardly beginning to solve its unemployment problems after a bitter depression provide employment for its youth? Employment was inadequate for the major work force. Employment of a young and untrained emerging work force is certain to be problematic during such a period. Available work is likely to be less than desirable in both the type of job and the number of jobs available. In the light of the depression it is not surprising that the most overwhelming problems noted were economic in nature. The recession of 1937–38 did nothing to reaffirm the employer's faith in the economy. Thus, the prospects for youth were poor indeed.

Six excerpts have been selected from Chapter 4, Youth at Work, in which the author discusses youth and their concerns about employment. The introductory paragraphs set the stage. Following this, a summary of wage-influencing factors is reported. A brief discussion of the reasons for the discontent among the young people of the nation is presented in the third excerpt. This is followed by a summary of the findings related to the age at which youth begin work. Some of the social consequences of unemployment are examined in the fifth selection and a brief general summary completes the chapter.

Chapter 4: Youth at Work

If one hundred American youth were selected at random, and each one were asked if he or she believed there was a youth problem, our data indicate that sixty-five would not only recognize the existence of such a problem, but would also define it. Twenty-five would assert that there was no problem, while ten would state that they didn't know whether such a problem existed or not.

If a hundred of these youth who recognized the existence of a youth problem were each asked to state what, in his or her opinion, was the crux of the problem, our data further indicate that sixty-five would characterize it as basically economic. To many, this would mean jobs— any jobs. To some, it would mean wages that would permit the enjoyment of a higher standard of living. To others, it would mean jobs that provided a deeper sense of security and a more hopeful promise of vocational adjustment. And to still others, it would mean an income sufficient to make marriage or further education possible.

The general problem of economic security is particularly acute for young people for the reason that they so often lack the background of training and experience so necessary to both placement and vocational progress. Hundreds of thousands who are now in the labor market could better serve their own and society's interests by remaining longer in school. But, through a lack of interest or opportunity, they have left their classrooms, and are in active competition with adults for the jobs which in our most prosperous times are hardly enough to go around.

We have indicated elsewhere that there are sound economic reasons for making it possible for larger numbers of our young people to remain in school for longer periods. To us, a general expansion of educational opportunity for all our youth promises to yield substantial economic as well as cultural returns.

Yet, for better or worse, millions of youth are now in the American labor market. Constituting, as they do, a very considerable part of the national youth population, it is appropriate that we make an effort to find out something about them—the kinds of jobs they hold, how old they are when they start to work, the wages they receive, and what they think about the work they do. . . .

SUMMARY OF FACTORS AFFECTING WAGES YOUTH RECEIVE

In the foregoing sections, we have analyzed the various factors which influence the median weekly wages that young people receive. Without regard to ranking, the seven that were found to affect a young person's income in one way or another are listed below:

> Sex
> Race
> Age
> Hours worked
> Locality of residence
> School grade completed
> Youth's occupational field.

Over the first three of these factors, the youth, as an individual, can exert no control whatever. By no exercise of will can he change his race, his sex, or his age. Over the last four, there is a possibility that he can exert sufficient control to better his general condition. By the exercise of will and the aggressive application of his native ability, he might, for example, find a full-time instead of a part-time job. If he is rarely endowed with both determination and talent, he may make his educational opportunities and attain a higher grade level. He can, moreover, move to a different locality, and in some instances he can shift to a more lucrative occupational field. In so far as the total effect of the factors above can be said to influence a young person's income, it is clear therefore that he is partly the master of his economic fate. No effort to measure the relative strength of these factors will be made, for the reason that the result of such an effort would be open to serious question. For example, it would appear on the surface that the most potent single factor in determining the wages a young worker will receive is that of the occupational field in which he works. One doesn't have to scratch very far beneath this surface, however, to discover that the occupational field in which a youth finds himself is usually related to the amount of schooling he has received. This amount of schooling has, in turn, often been the direct result of the income level of his father. Thus the occupational field in which the youth works is quite as logically the ultimate result of the economic status of his parental home as it is the cause of his relatively high wages.

The higher income fathers, with their smaller families, provide their children with relatively adequate schooling, which tends eventually to place them in the more highly paid jobs. The lower income fathers, with their large families, provide their children with less schooling which, in turn, tends to route them into the more poorly paid jobs. Thus the observation, "For whosoever hath, to him shall be given, . . . but whosoever hath not, from him shall be taken away," still retains, in our modern life, much of its literal meaning. . . .

WHY THIS DISCONTENT?

Exactly what is at the root of all this discontent, we are not in a position to say. Doubtless a good deal of it is the direct result of serious vocational maladjustment. Much of it, however, is probably a reflection of a healthy desire to work in more socially and economically desirable occupations. For better or worse, it has been a part of our national tradition to encourage the idea that there is something essentially superior about working with white collars on. Along with the social stigma associated with various kinds of manual work, there is the even more potent factor of wages. From data already submitted, it is known that the average weekly wage of the youthful unskilled workers was $8.53, while that of the proprietary and managerial workers was well over twice that much. Thus both reality and tradition contribute something to the general discontent. To decrease it, what is clearly needed, along with the continued trend toward higher wages, is a revived faith in the dignity of working with one's hands.

At the bottom of this general dissatisfaction, there is more, however, than a desire for a more socially acceptable and better paid job. There is often the feeling of being lost in a bewildering world of machines. To this is added the policy of some individuals and corporations of hiring young people almost exclusively, and releasing them as soon as they have passed a certain age limit. A study of the average age of the employees of some of our large factories and stores would uncover some very significant things. All of this, of course, inevitably leads to a sense of futility and frustration, and encourages a quite understandable "don't care a damn" philosophy.

When a young person is led to suspect that his job will be over as soon as his briskness and zest have begun to wane, or as soon as his employer decides that he can save money by replacing him with another worker at a lower wage, perhaps he will be forgiven if his attitude toward his vocational future is not too cheerful. His education has usually been insufficient to develop anything like vocational versatility, and his actual work experience has often been confined to a few routine, mechanical tasks. Thus he is denied the chance to grow up vocationally and deprived of the hope and optimism that often spring from the assurance that his present job will lead to a better one.

Much has been said in previous sections about the social and economic dangers inherent in any indifference to the general welfare of a younger generation. When one considers this personnel policy of hiring young people and firing them as soon as they have passed beyond a relatively early age limit, one comes to suspect that the "waste of human resources" is more than a popular current phrase. It becomes, in fact, a definitely ugly reality. As a personnel policy, it is as vicious and as socially nearsighted as any waste of natural resources that one can imagine. We become disturbed at wanton destruction of oil and coal. When economists tell us that we waste four barrels of oil for every one we produce and that we fritter away some 9 billion tons of coal for every 7.5 billion that we consume, our sensibilities are outraged and we clamor for restrictive laws—forgetting, the while, that the waste in human resources, though perhaps less tangible, is no less real.

Unpleasant stories are told of operators of coal properties who, in their frantic haste to get their coal from the ground, mine only the richer veins and leave the smaller ones to cave in. This coal, it is said, is forever lost. Somehow this sort of thing reminds us that youth, too, never comes again. . . .

SUMMARY

An analysis of our findings on the age at which youth secured their first full-time jobs forces upon us the conclusion that the relatively early age at which large numbers start to work is as definitely opposed to the best interests of our social and economic system as it is unfortunate for the young people themselves.

As we have seen, more than half the youth who at some time had had full-time jobs had secured them before they were 18 years of age. We have further seen that over a fifth (21.9 per cent) of these youth had worked on some full-time job before they were 16 years old. It was also discovered that by holding young people in schools their entry into the labor market was substantially retarded.

Even a superficial consideration of the data so far presented will suggest how generally related is the amount of schooling a young person receives to the standard of living he later enjoys. There are, of course, noteworthy and dramatic exceptions, but if we are to keep our social thinking on the ground, we will recognize them as the exceptions and not the rule.

The total effect of the data uncovered with respect to the age at which youth start to work has been to support our suspicion that an investment of time and thought and money in the development of purposeful programs for young people will yield gratifying social and economic returns to both the youth who are affected by them and the society that makes them possible. Once in a while a person happens along who is strong enough to make his opportunities. But most of us do well if we can take advantage of the opportunities that circumstances provide us. . . .

Social Consequences of Unemployment

About half the unemployed youth had never worked on full-time jobs. At the time of the interview, this group had already been out of school an average of more than a year and a half (1.6 years for the males and 2.1 years for the females). Exactly how much of this continued idleness was the result of the failure of communities to provide work, and how much of it was the result of the youth's indifference, is, of course, problematical.

When due allowance is made for the failure or the inability of communities to provide adequate employment opportunities for their youth, the facts seem to indicate that, among large numbers of our youth population, an apathy and indifference has developed that can hardly be said to be in keeping with what are generally accepted as the traditional qualities of a younger generation.

There is every reason to believe that the bulk of unemployment among young people is directly traceable to inadequate employment opportunities. Yet, whether long periods of idleness are voluntary or enforced, the final result for the individual is very much the same. Such periods are veritable breeding grounds for the "don't care a damn" philosophy. They retard mental and social growth, and they are quite often as packed with unfortunate consequences to the individual as to society and the community.

The average person can be told only so many times that his community has no use for what he has to offer. Sooner or later, by the force of sheer repetition, he will come to believe it. And one result is the development of a tendency to look to the super-community, the government, to take things over and set things straight.

As we shall see in our later discussion of attitudes, the contemporary youth's conception of the sphere of national government seems to have widened considerably beyond that of preceding generations. Matters which rightly or wrongly have been more or less traditionally accepted as responsibilities of the individual, or the local community, are becoming increasingly accepted by young people as responsibilities which should properly be laid at the doorstep of the national capitol. This apparent impulse of young people to add item upon item to the total responsibility of government can hardly be said to be growing out of a ripe knowledge of the deficiencies of our social order, however obvious and glaring these deficiencies may be. Nor is it growing out of an enlightened and mature conception of the sphere of government in a modern state. It is growing out of a suspicion that, somehow, the world they have inherited is a cockeyed world, and that the only agency wise enough and big enough to do anything about it is an ever expanding national government that can and will set the crooked straight.

At a later time, we will show that the attitude of large numbers of this younger generation toward the effectiveness of the suffrage, which is the very spine of a democracy, has already been hardened with skepticism. Thus we have an electorate of tomorrow that, while calling for expanded government activity and responsibility, seems to have a definitely limited faith in the ability of democratic institutions to achieve the ends they desire.

It would be idle to suggest that youth, as such, entertain any recognized enthusiasms for any nondemocratic forms of government. Without giving it a name, what they seem to want is a government that will do more and more of their thinking and planning for them. So far as they are concerned, that government is best which governs most.

All this is pertinent, at this point, because we are dealing with apathy and indifference. Whether it is the apathy and indifference of large numbers of our youth toward the opportunities that exist, or whether it is the hardbitten callousness of communities that make little effort to provide opportunities, is beside the point. They both lead to waste. Both are loaded with consequences that are unfortunate for the youth themselves, the economy of our social system, and the ultimate destiny of our democracy. And the only effective way to avoid these consequences is to make it quite clear to youth that they too have a place in our social and economic scheme of things. . . .

SUMMARY

An analysis of the data submitted in the preceding sections has led us to the following general conclusions:

1. The ultimate effect of a "youth program" should be the general improvement of the social and economic level of all young people. The first and basic step in this direction must, of necessity, be something that approaches more closely the universal provision of opportunities for all youth.
2. Once an effort is made to provide something more closely resembling a general equality of opportunity for all youth, existing agencies should be expanded to the end that the wasted years between school and employment will become periods of profitable activity.
3. Along with the expansion of such existing agencies as full-time and part-time schools, employment offices, and community recreation centers, new agencies, such as vocational "clinics," should be created. These should be especially adapted to serve the needs of youth for whom formal school education is no longer desirable.

It is obvious that these three approaches can be followed concurrently. The first is equivalent to a more comprehensive program of student aid along the lines already explored by the National Youth Administration. The second calls for an enlargement of the sphere of influence of agencies which already exist in some communities. The third consists in the creation and development of instrumentalities capable of providing services that are not being provided by existing agencies. The total effect of an aggressive prosecution of these three objectives would ultimately lead to a "youth program" that would yield high social and economic returns to both the younger generation and our national life.

Chapter 5: Youth at Play

An overview of Chapter 5, Youth at Play, can be obtained by perusal of three sections—an introduction to recreational and related problems, a summary of the data, and a summary statement from the end of the chapter.

An American who stays a while in Jerusalem is likely to come home with mixed feelings about the people and places he has seen. It is quite possible that he will recall his first surprise at the passionate interest of its people in mosques and holy ground, and the apparent indifference of these same people to the anemones that throw a colorful blanket of soft beauty over the scars of the Mount of Olives.

An Arab who remains a while in the United States might, with even better reason, return to his country somewhat perplexed by the nature of a people that can give itself over, with such wholehearted passion, to the veneration, or the damnation, of a political idea, and yet remain unmoved by our tragic waste of human resources. The anemones that "waste their fragrance on the desert air" and young people for whom the art of dawdling has become an unwanted career have, it seems to us, a good deal in common.

Another vivid impression that an American in certain parts of the Near East is apt to bring home with him is the apparent indifference of the average person to the prevalence of blindness. Trachoma has been accepted, in many quarters, with a truly oriental submission to what appears to be the will of God. Blindness just comes—it is written in the stars, and, having come, it is the business of the blind to accept their darkened world with quiet grace.

Social, as well as physical, ills are quite as likely to be accepted with such "oriental" resignation. Let us consider, for a moment, the matter of crime in the United States. It seems that our very familiarity with criminal and delinquent behavior has bred an attitude that is more closely related to indifference than contempt.

The United States has, with more or less justification, acquired the doubtful distinction of being the "most criminal" of all the civilized nations of the world. In 1930 there were three times as many homicidal deaths per 100,000 people in the United States as in Italy, more than four times the number in Germany, and ten times the number in Great Britain.[9] And in 1933 more than 40 out of every 100 of the criminals committed to federal and state prisons and reformatories were between the ages of 15 and 24.[10] The national bill for this incredible extravaganza is variously estimated at from $4,000,000,000 to $16,000,000,000 a year, and a low estimate would probably put the annual loss to each family in the nation at about $160.

And, to make matters worse, anybody who reads the newspapers knows that "only a small proportion of our people who commit crimes are caught. Of those arrested, only a few are convicted; and of those convicted, only a few are imprisoned."[11]

[9] Statistical Bureau, Metropolitan Life Insurance Company.
[10] *Prisoners in Federal and State Prisons and Reformatories in 1933*, Bureau of Census, U. S. Department of Commerce, 1933.
[11] "Crime in the United States," *The National Forum*.

What might be called the "Age Curve of American Crime" reaches its peak between the ages of 20 and 24. From that point on it progressively decreases with every age group. No qualified student of delinquency and crime believes that there is anything peculiarly "criminal" about these ages. A far more plausible explanation is the fact that these years generate physical and nervous energies that are often as disturbing as they are superfluous. If the youth's total environment is not adapted to the effective and productive absorption of these energies, antisocial conduct is very often an inevitable result.

This general theme about the kind of work the devil finds for idle hands to do has been developed so often and so effectively that it needs little elaboration from us. Innumerable studies have been made, and reports written, on the subject of the relationship between idleness and delinquent behavior. A careful study, made by the Baltimore Criminal Justice Commission, of a police district where delinquency was unusually high revealed that of 592 boys arrested only 5 per cent had any supervised recreational activities, while 82 per cent were forced to resort to street play and corner gangs. Yet in this district there were 39 vacant lots of varying size which could have been converted into playgrounds.

The best answer to this particular challenge of youthful delinquency and crime is the same as the answer to the whole youth problem: programs of constructive activity.

When we have referred, in previous sections of this report, to developing national "programs of constructive activity" for young people, we have naturally included, in our thinking, programs of recreation. Even if the activities of the schools were so expanded and so revised as to absorb and hold a larger proportion of our idle youth, and even if effective vocational programs would result in placing larger numbers of our youth in profitable employment, there would still be a gap that only constructive recreational programs could fill.

It is probably unfortunate that, in our efforts to "sell" recreational programs to the people of America, we have laid such stress on the value of recreation as a sponge to absorb the superfluous energies that might otherwise seek an outlet in antisocial channels. By our emphasis on this negative phase of the value of play, public recreation, in some minds, has acquired the character of a kind of medicine—a social prophylactic. It is, of course, exactly this. But it is also a great deal more.

Recreation has positive as well as negative values. It not only tends to translate human energy into socially desirable conduct, but it adds to the social and spiritual stature of the person who indulges in it.

There is a good deal of basic sense in the belief that one can arrive at "strength through joy," as there is also something sound in the conviction that "the days that make us happy make us wise."

The need for more effective and comprehensive recreational programs in most of the urban and rural areas in the United States reminds us of Mark Twain's observation that everybody talks about the weather, but nobody seems to be doing much about it. So far as our data are concerned, this seems particularly true in farm areas, where one out of every five young men interviewed reported that his principal leisure time activity was loafing. . . .

How Youth Spend Their Leisure Time

Trying to find out exactly how people have spent their leisure time during, say, the past year, is like trying to discover how they have spent their last year's earnings. As a rule, they can't tell you because they don't know.

Even more difficult, however, is the task of discovering the one leisure-time activity in which the most time was spent. If a youth is asked this question in January, he will be tempted to say "skating." If it is put to him in July, he is more likely to name "swimming."

Also, when we speak of the youth's principal leisure-time activity, it will be understood that the choice of any youth's activity will, of necessity, be influenced and limited by the recreational opportunities and facilities available in his community. For large numbers of young people, especially those living in the less populous areas, this activity amounts to little more than a choice among what, to them, is the least of various evils.

LEISURE-TIME ACTIVITIES OF YOUNG MEN AND WOMEN

So, with these suggestions as to the limitations of such data, we present Table 64. This table reveals the responses of young men and women to the question that was designed to uncover the one type of activity in which each youth spent most of his leisure time during the year preceding the interview.

Perhaps attention should again be called to the fact that the field work of the present study was carried on during the summer and fall months. The nature of these seasons doubtless had the tendency to increase the number of youth who named some kind of outdoor sport as the type of recreation in which they most frequently indulged.

Probably the most significant item in Table 64 is the 13.1 per cent of the young men who reported that their chief leisure-time activity was loafing. There are obvious subjective factors that would operate to reduce the number of such admissions below what is probably the actual number. Thus the number of young people who had spent most of their free time doing nothing is probably much larger than this 13.1 per cent would indicate.

It is also of some significance, perhaps, that over a third (35 per cent) of the young women named reading as their most time-consuming leisure-time activity. An analysis of these data revealed that, for the girls, reading was the most popular pastime for all ages.

**TABLE 64   Principal Leisure-Time Activities of Youth,
According to Sex**

	Male youth			Female youth	
Rank	*Activity*	*Percentage*	*Rank*	*Activity*	*Percentage*
1	Individual sports	21.6	1	Reading	35.0
2	Reading	16.7	2	Dating, dancing	13.7
3	Team games	15.7	3	Handicrafts, hobbies ..	13.4
4	Loafing *	13.1	4	Movies	12.0
5	Dating, dancing	10.9	5	Individual sports	11.1
6	Movies	9.4	6	Loafing *	5.4
7	Hobbies	5.5	7	Listening to radio ...	2.2
8	Listening to radio	1.8	8	Team games	1.1
9	Quiet games	1.5	9	Quiet games	0.8
10	Other activities	3.8	10	Other activities	5.3
	Total	100.0		Total	100.0
	Number of youth ..	6,872		Number of youth .	6,635

* This includes idling, sitting on front steps, talking on street corners, pleasure driving.

SUMMARY

Probably the most significant revelation that has come out of this analysis is the need, and the demand, for various types of social recreation. That the need exists is unfortunate, but the demand can well be accepted as a source of satisfaction by those who are concerned with the development of more effective and comprehensive programs for young people.

A careful consideration of these findings has forced upon us the conviction that communities would do well to explore the possibilities of community youth centers. Such organizations could be initiated as recreation centers, and could, in time, be expanded to meet other phases of the youth problem.

There is considerable evidence to suggest that once youth become conscious of the fact that an organization exists in their community which is dedicated to the single purpose of meeting their needs, the basic problem of reaching them will have been solved. The people who are responsible for the development of the recreational programs of these centers should build upon what is known about what young people want. This general enthusiasm for social recreation is a force that should not be suppressed. It should rather be directed into channels that are as beneficial to the social life of a community as they are satisfying to the youth themselves.

Once a youth center has established itself as a source of satisfying recreation to the young people in a community, and, without stooping to the level of a glorified roadhouse, has generated sufficient power to hold its youth, the time to expand its activities will have arrived. The first step in this expansion might well be to develop, within the framework of the center, what might be known as a vocational clinic.

Adequately staffed with trained workers, the chief concern of this clinic would be the problems of the great majority of young people who are out of school. Its special interests would be the problems of the unemployed and the vocationally maladjusted. Its general character would be that of an advisory council, its techniques that of an informal, but no less efficient, case work agency.

The primary purposes of this clinic would be guidance and placement. Its function would be to place young people where they belong. To some, this would involve placement on available jobs. To others, it would mean placement in a vocational school for further training. To all, it would mean sympathetic and realistic guidance, and its total effect would be to cultivate a more general feeling among youth that they have a place in our social and economic scheme of things.

There are doubtless many sympathetic and socially minded people to whom this proposal to develop community youth centers will seem to involve an expense that cannot be met. About the only answer to this is the promise that such a center would, in all probability, yield an ultimate return to the community which would quite surpass its cost. It is quite possible that a satisfactory policy of financial participation among local, state, and federal agencies could be worked out. It is also possible that such centers could be made to pay a substantial part of their way. All of this would, of course, have unfortunate consequences for at least some of the operators of pool halls, roadhouses, cabarets, and "pinball joints." But the rest of the community would stand to gain.

There are many cities in the United States that are well known for the beauty and the cost of the monuments they have built in memory of their heroic dead. While one is impressed, there come times when one wonders if an honest expression of gratitude and appreciation really needs so many blocks of stone. In these unguarded moments, one is led, in fact, to wonder if it is not as noble to serve the living as honor the dead. In fact, one is led to suspect that perhaps the most effective way to honor the dead is to erect monuments that most effectively serve the living. It is quite possible that no better choice for such a monument could be made than a community center dedicated to the single task of directing into profitable channels the years and energies of our young people that are now going to waste.

The role which organized religion played in the lives of the young people is examined in Chapter 6, "Youth and the Church." Two short selections—three introductory paragraphs and a very brief summary— are reproduced below.

Chapter 6: Youth and the Church

To arrive at sound conclusions as to the part the church is playing in the lives of young people is not a simple task. The obvious difficulties are aggravated by the fact that it is impossible to isolate the church as a single factor in a youth's experience and background. It is quite possible, of course, to discover the conditions under which the youth of different church groups are living, and also to find out whatever differences may exist in the ways they react to current problems. However, to presume to measure the extent to which these differences are due to dissimilarities in religious backgrounds and affiliations is not only unscientific but highly dangerous.

It is one thing to suggest that certain variations in conditions and attitudes are associated with such religious groups as Protestants, Catholics, and Jews, but quite another thing to insist that these dissimilarities are directly the result of different church affiliations. For example, almost 20 per cent of the youth from Protestant homes were Negroes. Thus, what may appear on the surface to be a distinctly religious factor turns out to be influenced by the factor of race. Either the mother or the father, or both, of 35 per cent of the youth from Catholic homes were foreign born. This means, of course, that ethnic, as well as religious, backgrounds contribute to whatever differences may appear in the Catholic and non-Catholic groups. Similarly the attitudes and the conditions of the Jewish youth are, without doubt, considerably influenced by the facts that 84 per cent of their parents were foreign born (over half of them from Russia) and that their median grade attainment was about two grades higher than that of the youth in any other religious group.

Thus it is that differences which, on the surface, may appear to be basically religious in character are, in fact, profoundly affected by such factors as race, nationality, locality of residence, and educational attainment. As it is impossible to dissociate completely the youth's religious background from all these other factors, it will be well, therefore, to interpret the variations about to be disclosed as related to, rather than caused by, differences in church affiliations. . . .

SUMMARY

Although it would be unwise, perhaps, to make any general statement about the extent to which the church is affecting the living and the thinking of our young people, the data we have just analyzed clearly indicate that, for all its alleged decadence as a vital social force, the church still retains a substantial measure of its original appeal. It will be remembered that three fourths of the youth considered themselves church members. Six out of every seven reported that they had attended services at some time during the preceding year, and about half of this group stated that they were in the habit of going to church once a week.

Even though an actual check of these reports might reveal that church membership and attendance is somewhat less general than our findings indicate, the fact would still stand that the majority of young people want to be identified as church members and like to have it known that they participate in its devotional activities.

In the minds of the great majority of youth, the church is neither a public forum nor a recreational center. It still retains its original character as a place of worship.

A rather comprehensive study of attitudes and opinions of American youth about several important social issues is reported in Chapter 7. The general method of analysis is discussed in the opening paragraphs and a terse statement of the findings on each of the issues appears in the summary.

Chapter 7: Attitudes

It has been our primary purpose, thus far, to study the social and economic conditions under which young people are living. At times, we have set down their evaluations of certain institutions and policies, but, in the main, we have dealt with such tangible things as the wages they received on their jobs and the grades they attained in school. Far less tangible, but, to many observers, quite as important, are the attitudes and opinions young people have on some of the significant issues and problems of our time.

In analyzing the responses that our 13,500 young people have made to the various attitude questions, we do not assume the position of judge or critic. It is our business to report, not to evaluate.

So far as our knowledge goes, in no other study of young people has a similar effort been made to ascertain the apparent relationships between so comprehensive a number of attitudes and facts. This somewhat unusual fusion of an attitude and factual study grew out of the conviction that the real meaning of our attitude responses could be disclosed only when they were studied in relation to the fundamental groups that constitute our youth population.

The procedure of studying responses in relation to basic social groups is, of course, a commonplace of social research. It is a principle that we have observed with what, to some, may have seemed excessive zeal, throughout the analysis of all the factual data already considered.

The social analyst who earns his salt sees himself in the position of an examining doctor—a diagnostician. A patient doesn't go to a diagnostician to be told that he is sick. He is painfully aware of the fact that he is sick. What he wants, and what he has every right to expect, is an analysis of his condition that will tell him, with at least a measure of precision, what and where his trouble is.

We recently heard a distressed person remark, in resounding terms, "There's something wrong with our social order!" This, we suggest, is not news. Most of us realize that there are quite a few things wrong with our social order. We realize that the ills of society are almost as varied and, in some cases, quite as dangerous as any of "the thousand natural shocks that flesh is heir to." What we particularly want is a more definite idea as to what and where these social ills are.

So far as the social analyst is concerned, the task of locating and identifying these "natural shocks" of society consists, among other things, in determining the extent to which they are related to fundamental social and economic groups. We have already seen how such matters as low grade attainment and inadequate wages are related to such basic groups as male–female, relief–nonrelief, and white–Negro. In precisely the same manner, we shall attempt to analyze the reactions of certain groups of young people to such currently significant issues as the functions of government, the effectiveness of the suffrage, the role of the church, indulgence in alcoholic beverages, the gainful employment of children, and going to war. . . .

SUMMARY

In summarizing the attitudes and opinions of young people, as revealed by the present study, we would stress the fact that most of the youth interviewed had opinions on the various topics discussed, and that they were willing, and often anxious, to express themselves. If space permitted, we could have included many times the number of verbatim quotations in which the youth colorfully and vigorously presented their points of view.

Wages. On the matter of wages, we found the majority of the youth of the opinion that wage rates generally were too low, and that governmental action was the best means of raising them. When asked directly if the government should set minimum wage and maximum hour standards for business and industry, three fourths of them said that it should.

Relief. Ninety per cent believed that the provision of relief for the needy unemployed was a responsibility in which the Federal government should participate. They were equally emphatic in their opinions that the relief provided should be on a "health and decency" level, and that it should be given for labor performed, not as a direct grant.

Child Labor. Again the young people were almost unanimous in favoring government regulation of the gainful employment of children 14 and 15 years old. Less than 5 per cent said the government should "keep hands off." The others were divided equally, half believing in the complete abolition of child labor, while the other half considered it permissible under certain circumstances, largely economic in character.

The Suffrage. Taking up the matter of the suffrage, we discovered that slightly more than half of the 22- to 24-year-old group had availed themselves of the privilege of voting when they last had the opportunity. Indifference stood out as the chief reason for the youth's failure to vote. When asked if, in their opinion, candidates were usually elected to public office because of their capability to fill the office, somewhat more than half the youth thought they were. Almost a third, however, felt that this was infrequently or never the case.

Employment of Married Women. In considering the question of gainful employment of married women who want to work, one sixth of the youth voiced no objection whatever, one eighth would completely exclude them from the labor market, and more than two thirds would permit their employment under certain conditions.

Drinking. More than half the youth admitted that, with varying degrees of frequency and moderation, they indulged in some kind of alcoholic beverage. One fifth were unqualifiedly opposed to drinking, and somewhat more than a fourth, though not drinkers themselves, were not opposed to others drinking. Drinking was indulged in by large numbers of boys and girls under 21, more than half the boys and almost two fifths of the girls admitting that they drank.

War. The majority of the youth voiced the opinion that war was both needless and preventable. Few showed any enthusiasm for war, but only one in six said that he would refuse to go. The majority would follow the course of least resistance and go if they were drafted.

The Youth Problem. As youth themselves see it, the "youth problem" is largely a matter of economic security. In many respects, their conception of the basic problems that confront their generation has been reflected in the conclusions that have been set down in various sections of this report.

It seems to us, as apparently it seems to them, that the most pressing problems, involving the need for the most vigorous social action, fall into three general areas:

1. Employment. For hundreds of thousands of youth in America, this means getting a job. For as many others, it means a wage that will provide both an acceptable standard of living, and an opportunity to provide for future years.

2. Education. For large numbers who have been forced out of school for economic reasons, this means the creation of a less fictitious equality of opportunity, and, for many others who are still in school, it means an educational program that is more clearly in harmony with their interests and needs.

3. Recreation. For no less than millions of young people in America, this calls for an awakening, on the part of communities, to the social as well as the personal values of healthful and satisfying recreation, and a determination to develop leisure-time programs that will not only absorb energies that often lead to delinquent behavior, but which will add something valuable to the spiritual stature of those who participate in them.

CHARACTER AND COST OF PUBLIC EDUCATION 7

*Selections from the Regents'
Inquiry in the State of
New York*

 *The Regents' Inquiry was carried out in
the late 1930's. The results of the studies
were published in 11 volumes. The gen-
eral report is set forth in Education for
American Life, A New Program for the State of New York,
written by Luther Gulick. The supporting studies are reported
in the following volumes: High School and Life, by Francis
T. Spaulding; Preparation of School Personnel, by Charles H.
Judd; State Aid and School Costs, by Alonzo G. Grace and
G. A. Moe; Adult Education, by F. W. Reeves, T. Fansler, and
C. O. Houle; Motion Pictures and Radio, by Elizabeth Laine;
When Youth Leave School, by Ruth Eckert and Thomas O.
Marshall; Education for Citizenship, by Howard E. Wilson;
Education for Work, by Thomas L. Norton; The School
Health Program, by C. E. A. Winslow; and School and Com-
munity, by Julius B. Maller.*

*The New York Board of Regents is comparable, insofar as
its responsibility for the public schools is concerned, to the*

state boards of education in other states. Its 14 members are appointed by the legislature and serve 14-year terms.

Some indication of the motivation for the Inquiry and the types of personnel involved can be gleaned from the following passage taken from the Foreword of Education for American Life.

No one can look at the world situation today without recognizing the unique function of education in a democracy where the wisdom, the morality, and the vitality of the state and the freedom, well-being, and happiness of the population rest so directly upon the education of all the people. It may well be doubted if there can be democracy without free education, or anything else but democracy where education is free.

Under the constitution of the State of New York, central responsibility for the leadership, but not the detailed management, of the entire educational system is placed with the Regents of the University, a body created in, and maintained since Revolutionary days. Recognizing that great changes have come into the life of the boys and girls and men and women of this State, especially since the World War, the Regents determined in 1934 that the time had come to review broadly again the whole educational enterprise of the State. The Regents' Inquiry Into the Character and Cost of Public Education in the State of New York is the result of this decision.

Though this Inquiry has been made directly under the Board of Regents and not under any informal or unofficial survey body, the Regents have scrupulously maintained a policy of noninterference. The Regents selected the Director and Associate Director, passed upon the outline of the Inquiry as a whole, and insisted that the educational specialists for the staff be drawn primarily from outside of the State so that their appraisal of New York's educational system might not be influenced unduly by their prior participation in the development of New York's schools. The Regents desired an independent outside audit of New York's policies and administration. Beyond this, the conduct of the Inquiry, the presentation of its results, the formulation of this report, Education for American Life, and of the supporting studies, rest upon the unhampered work and the full responsibility of the directors of the Inquiry and their colleagues.

On behalf of the Regents and of the people of the State of New York, it is appropriate to acknowledge the debt owed to those who have made this Inquiry possible. The study as a whole was financed by a generous grant of the General Education Board, which has done so much to advance the cause of education in America. Columbia University and the Institute of Public Administration released to the Regents for a three-year period the Director; the University of Buffalo furnished the Associate Director. Other major members of the staff were made available for periods of from one to two years by the following universities: Chicago, Purdue, Princeton, Harvard, New York, Rochester, and Minnesota.

On briefer assignments the Inquiry drew upon staff members of Teachers

College, Columbia University, Ohio State University, the University of Michigan, Rutgers University, Wesleyan University, Iowa State Teachers College, the State Teachers College at Macomb, Illinois, and the State Teachers College at Montclair, New Jersey.

A special committee of Certified Public Accountants formed from members of the firms of Haskins and Sells; Peat, Marwick, Mitchell, and Company; Boyce, Hughes, and Farrell; and Lybrand, Ross Brothers, and Montgomery rendered an invaluable service in advising on a new school district accounting system.[1]

Further background information is reported in the Preface of Education for American Life.

The Inquiry was organized late in 1935, under the direction of a Special Committee of the Board of Regents, consisting of John Lord O'Brian, William J. Wallin, and Owen D. Young, Chairman. Thomas J. Mangan, the present Chancellor, and James Byrne, the former Chancellor, have sat with the Committee as ex-officio members from its inception.

The work of the Inquiry has been divided into three major undertakings: first, the examination of the educational enterprise of the State and the analysis of its outcomes, methods, and costs; second, the critical appraisal of the work now under way; and third, the formulation of policies and programs for dealing with the immediate problems and issues, and long-range objectives of the educational system of the State. The procedure of the Inquiry has not been to gather great masses of statistics, to devise numerous questionnaires, or to present meticulous statistical descriptions of every phase of education within the State. Rather, the Regents' Committee and the staff of the Inquiry have been interested in isolating major issues and in hammering away at the chief problems discovered in order to find a reasonable comprehensive solution which would commend itself to the forward-minded people of the State of New York. Though the staff of the Inquiry have made extensive studies in New York City with the aid of New York's school authorities, and though certain of the findings and recommendations are applicable to the City, the major focus of the Inquiry has been outside of the City of New York, which is, after all, primarily responsible for its own schools.[2]

Luther Halsey Gulick served as Director of the Inquiry, Samuel P. Capen was Associate Director, and Sterling Anders became Executive Officer.

What were some of the principle problems underlying public education in New York at the time of the Regents' Inquiry?

---

[1] Luther Halsey Gulick, *Education for American Life.* New York: The McGraw-Hill Book Company, Inc., 1938, pp. ix–xi.

[2] *Ibid.,* pp. xiii–xiv.

1. The educational system has not yet adjusted its program to carry the new load imposed by the coming into the schools, particularly into the secondary schools, of all the children of all the people, with their many new and different needs.
2. The school work for boys and girls has not been redesigned to fit them for the new and changing work opportunities which they must face in modern economic life.
3. The school program does not sufficiently recognize the increased difficulties of becoming and of being a good citizen.
4. The educational system has not caught up with the flood of new scientific knowledge about the natural and social world which has been made part of life in recent decades, and fails to give boys and girls a scientific point of view and an understanding of the world.
5. The educational system has not been replanned to meet the new conditions of modern life and new ways of living, in which the family, the church, and early work now exercise less influence, and in which increasing leisure in later life calls for, and makes possible, a rich and growing inner life.
6. The citizens and the school leaders of the State of New York do not have a specific, agreed-upon goal. Both groups are going ahead in many directions, but without a destination toward which all may bend their energies.[3]

Portions of Education for American Life, High School and Life, *and* When Youth Leave School *were selected and are included herein. These represent the principal findings of the Inquiry.*

One of the focal points of the report was the problem of the dropout. Three out of five secondary students dropped out prior to graduation. The Commission felt that these students, as well as those who graduate, should be considered in the evaluation of the secondary school. The school could not adequately train a large segment of its population for work, citizenship, and leisure without retraining the dropout. The investigators felt that the school should train in all of these areas.

One of the more profound aspects of this report is the recommended diversification of the roles which the secondary school should perform, as conceived by the investigators. The reader will note that in addition to the school's function in the "physical and mental growth of all children," the school should teach the student social skills, democratic processes, how to deal with his own personal problems, leadership, citizenship, leisure skills, and work skills.

The following excerpts are taken from the first and last chapters of

[3] *Ibid.,* p. 5.

When Youth Leave School. The first selection provides background information about the problems facing education in the late 1930's. The approach to the study, the assumptions upon which it was based, the types of persons investigated, and the aims of the study are discussed in these introductory pages. The final selection provides a concise summary of the findings of the study.

WHEN YOUTH LEAVE SCHOOL

The Nature of the Approach

No educational philosophy has faced a more rigorous test than is being given the democratic theory in the secondary schools of America today. In a very real sense these schools constitute a laboratory for appraising the validity, not only of a unique educational plan, but of a whole social scheme.

Even more striking than the unprecedented increase in attendance, which in New York State in 1938 has brought eight pupils to the secondary school for each one entering in 1900, have been the changes in the character of the population enrolled. Whereas a few decades ago the secondary school devoted attention almost exclusively to the college preparation of boys and girls, today it is being called upon to provide suitable training for a relatively unselected group of young people, the majority of whom will not go on to college. Less than one boy or girl in five who now begins ninth grade work in New York State will enter any institution of higher learning.

Whether the present secondary school can meet the challenge presented by such a widened range of talent and interests, or whether it will be superseded by an educational unit more responsive to social pressures, cannot yet be determined. What has become increasingly clear is that school experiences must be planned in terms of the life goals of adolescent boys and girls, rather than of traditional academic patterns, and that these goals must be suited to the astonishing diversity that exists with respect to abilities, needs, and interests. Some years ago the success of the secondary school might have been estimated from the subsequent college careers of its students; today the criterion must be sought in the relevancy of high school offerings to the needs of the entire population.

TASK OF THE SECONDARY SCHOOL

Although the problems involved in extending educational opportunities to all youth of a democracy possess important implications for the elementary school and the college, it is in the secondary school that these issues must be faced most directly. To the elementary school is committed the responsibility of providing forms of pupil experiences that will contribute significantly to the physical and the mental growth of all children and that will at the same time ensure a reasonable mastery of basic skills and knowledges. Sociological changes that have altered fundamentally the objectives of secondary education have therefore left the elementary school relatively undisturbed. Although the college has experimented with many significant curriculum reorganizations, designed to meet the needs of less able students, higher education must retain to a large degree its selective character. So long as many vocations require only a limited number of carefully chosen individuals, and the economic resources are not available to extend the period of training for all youth, responsibility rests squarely on the college to be discriminating in its choice of students.

Upon the secondary school, therefore, devolves the task, begun by the elementary school, of insuring command of socially useful processes and of promoting sympathetic acquaintance with democratic aims and procedures. Since few students will have further educational contacts, the secondary school must also lead each boy or girl to think realistically concerning his own personal problems and to make constructive plans for the future. Whatever the secondary school fails to do in developing general competence for living will, for the most part, remain undone.

Current plans to provide more adequately for youth who must immediately face the problems of out-of-school living must not eclipse, however, the responsibility of the secondary school for training leaders. As the social scene is surveyed, it is strikingly evident that competent and broadly trained leaders are lacking in almost every field of endeavor. There is an abundance of specialized knowledge and technical skill, which the college or professional school is well fitted to supply, but the intellectual balance and social perspective essential to leadership in a democratic society remain conspicuous by their absence. While the secondary school alone cannot supply these qualities, it is exceedingly important that able students be given adequate opportunities to discover their talents and to develop an active concern for social goals.

PROBLEM OF EVALUATION

The question of how well the secondary school is adjusting its program to the needs of adolescent boys and girls on the one hand and to the demands of contemporary civilization on the other, has been approached from a number of angles. Analyses of aims have occupied an important place in such appraisals, and rightly so, for first of all there must be conscious recognition of changing functions of the secondary school. The vigorous self-questioning that this approach involves is wholesome, and has disclosed in arresting fashion the unplanned nature of many of our educational developments.

Because of the subjective and intangible character of most of the goals, appraisals have more commonly been based on a close examination of school materials and procedures. By careful analysis of curricula, instructional plans, and final tests, certain of the more specific objectives of secondary education have been identified. While these are usually much less pretentious than are the goals outlined in current philosophies, they possess the advantage of approximating actual working objectives. This method is chiefly of value in revealing the *status quo;* it almost invariably serves to throw into sharp relief the "cultural lag" of the schools. Although the school has been commonly viewed as a directive force in social reconstruction, it is often difficult to establish any clear relationship between classroom experiences and present-day problems.

No single approach can be expected to yield a completely valid appraisal of the success of the secondary school. That increasing recognition is being given to the importance of civic, vocational, and leisure-time training is distinctly encouraging, but no evidence is provided that boys and girls are actually being better fitted for these imminent responsibilities. Likewise, the time studies and frequency counts that tend to dominate investigations of current practice are impotent to yield any really adequate measure of how well the high school is meeting the peculiar problems of our democratic culture. Such investigations can only indicate that pupils and teachers have gone through certain motions; whether the hoped-for modifications in thinking and in behavior have occurred remains unknown.

ONE SIGNIFICANT APPROACH

That the field of inquiry be extended to include direct examination of the boys and girls themselves—their abilities and interests, their home background and school experiences, their present outlooks and future intentions—seems a reasonable proposal. Instead of making the easy assumption that the objectives of the teacher or the content of the textbook result in desirable patterns of thinking and living, this more realistic procedure makes the pupils the test of the system. Attention is shifted from process to product. A vital and relatively objective means is thereby provided for evaluating secondary education, revealing the strengths of current systems and indicating in no uncertain manner the areas in which the outcomes have fallen far short of the "adaptation to individual needs," which is so familiarly re-echoed in the philosophies of the day. Application of this method does not result in a set of ultimate goals for education; it simply suggests the character of the contribution made by the secondary school of today to the education of youth.

Studies that have adopted this point of view have usually considered only those students who have graduated and, in most instances, gone on to college. Only the "flower" of the system is analyzed, so that the institution is judged by its successful students and not by the members who have fallen along the way. Such concentration of attention on a selected or élite group may be justifiable in certain social orders. In a professedly democratic scheme, however, every pupil who has entered the secondary school ought to constitute an indication of the worth of the educational experiences offered. Thus in New York State where fewer than two boys and girls in every five remain to graduate, those who drop out are just as important in revealing the pattern of secondary education as those who remain.

That academic tasks will be completed with success by all pupils is not to be expected, for training during adolescent years will not compensate entirely for the blunders and misfortunes of heredity or of early nurture. Thousands of influences have been exerted on growing boys and girls, some unconscious and others with the definite aim of indoctrination. These have served to shape points of view and to determine the specific interests, attitudes, and abilities shown at the conclusion of secondary school training. The school remains, however, as the only agency in contemporary life, outside the home, which is charged with direct responsibility for training these young people and which has the potential resources for doing so. As a result, the years spent in school should be definitely and measurably profitable to each pupil, whether or not he remains sufficiently long to receive a formal certificate or diploma.

AIMS OF THE PRESENT STUDY

This investigation rests on the two basic assumptions outlined above, that the character of the students who leave the secondary school constitutes a valid measure of the quality of the school's contribution to effective living and that this test should rightfully be applied to each leaving pupil and not simply to the minority who receive diplomas. In accordance with these assumptions, the type and character of students who left secondary schools throughout New York State during a single year, June 1936 to June 1937, have been investigated. All classes of leaving pupils were included: those who withdrew prior to graduation, those who were awarded final certificates or diplomas, and those who left after they had completed some postgraduate work. While a survey of pupils who had left school at a much earlier period would have had certain advantages, the present group may be more legitimately studied as the "products" of the school. Such varied outside experiences have confronted the young people who have been working, loafing, or pursuing advanced study for several years, that secondary school training could not be accurately judged by studying their present characteristics. Recent graduates and withdrawing students appeared to offer better subjects for testing the adequacy of secondary education, for contributions too nebulous to be detected at the time youth leave school will hardly exert a marked influence on their later activities.

The primary aim of this study has been to outline the characteristics of pupils leaving the secondary school, and thereby to secure material which would reveal the clues needed to modify school practices. Of all the possible traits and qualities that might have been investigated, a selection was made of those that appeared to contribute most directly to social competence, or the ability of young people to meet successfully the problems of out-of-school living. Since school marks and other academic measures yield only very partial and imperfect indications of the character of pupil development, data were included on family background, the students' possession of socially useful skills and information, their interests and attitudes in other areas than purely bookish ones, and their educational or work status some months after withdrawal from school.

Another objective has been to find out how the school views its leaving pupils. An exploratory study of the character of the school's knowledge was made possible by the fact that teachers and principals furnished much of the necessary information. Aside from the traditional academic judgments passed on students, do school officials, who have been associated with these boys and girls for several years, consider them really competent to assume the responsibilities of citizenship? Do they frankly believe that these leaving pupils can encounter the problem of earning a living with reasonable hope of success? Have the years of intimate association indicated to the school the types of homes from which these pupils come, and revealed particular talents or handicaps that ought to be considered by the student in laying plans for the future? Expressions of opinion on these points represent judgments concerning leaving pupils, but they also constitute indirect evaluations of the accuracy with which the school knows its students and of the confidence it has in them after years have been spent in formal instruction.

SUMMARY

It has been mentioned that comparisons were made of the responses of pupils from communities of various sizes, of pupils enrolled in different curricula, and of employed and unemployed pupils. However, the comparisons of the responses of boys and of girls, and of graduates and of withdrawals seemed to have the greatest significance. The responses from city, small-town, and rural youth were strikingly similar, especially among the girls.

Some of the problems discussed in this study were encountered almost by accident, and were not carefully investigated. The most important of these incidental problems is the apparent need for the education of the parents of school children. In attempting to discover how the guidance programs of high schools were working, pupils were asked who advised them in regard to their curricular choices. Among those who had had any advice, the important source of advice had been the parent. Undoubtedly this response should lead to further study of the problem.

The one general problem which seems of most importance is the need for a realistic evaluation of the program of the high school in terms of the aims of education to which New York State educators have already given lip-service. Most of these educators are ready to agree that the functions of secondary education have changed, but few have made comparable changes in the program of their schools. Experimentation with the school program in an attempt to come closer to the aims of education is urgently needed. Such experimentation would probably be more economical and more effective on a local basis than it would on a state-wide basis. Every encouragement should be given to local schools which attempt to modify school programs in terms of local needs.

The following summary is a review of the most important findings of the study. The evidence on which conclusions are based, is found in detail in earlier chapters. The present summary is intended to point out the most striking facts and impressions, and some of their educational implications:

1. The former pupils, especially those in the larger communities, had few contacts with adults.

It was almost impossible for the interviewers to find adults who knew anything about the activities of the pupils. In at least five places during the interview, pupils were asked for names of adults connected with various activities, or to whom the pupils might go for advice, or who might be used as references. Many pupils had no such names to supply, even as references, except those of teachers and school officers.

The adults who were selected as those who would know the pupils best proved to know so little of the life of the pupils that their testimony was practically worthless. Many of the adult contacts of pupils were of only a few weeks' standing, and were taken much more seriously by the pupils than by the adults.

2. The young people just out of school had little home life.

Especially in the cities, interviewers had difficulty in finding pupils in their homes. Parents frequently said that the young people were at home only at mealtime and bedtime, and that they did not know where their children spent their time.

Large numbers of pupils did not consider their homes as places in which recreation is possible. Even with the most liberal interpretation of their responses, it would appear that a quarter of the sample group had no recreational activities at home.

3. Lines of educational and recreational activity started in school were usually discontinued immediately after the pupils left school.

Even though the school had an extensive club program, most of the pupils did not belong to clubs of any sort after leaving school nor did they continue the activities which these clubs intended to promote. Schools seldom made any provision for contact between in-school and out-of-school groups. Adult organizations made little attempt to enlist young members just out of school. Communities rarely provided club activities as a continuation of the in-school activities.

The reading activities of the former pupils were meager. Few of them read books of any kind. The books read were usually fiction, much of it an inferior type. More pupils read magazines, but confined their reading to fiction, mostly of the sort written by hack writers and found in the cheaper magazines. A large share of the stories were detective and mystery, adventure, true story and love, or sports fiction. The nonfiction reading was apparently done mostly in women's, motion picture, and popular science magazines. The weekly miscellanies such as *Liberty* and *The Saturday Evening Post* were very popular, perhaps because they cost little. A more expensive magazine which seemed to be popular with all types of the former pupils is *The Reader's Digest*.

Except for newspaper reading (on which it is almost impossible to get detailed information) little attempt was made by the former pupils to find out about and understand current events. They did not read about current events in magazines, read few of the new books about national or international affairs, and did not listen to radio commentators. The radio was used almost entirely for recreation.

4. After the pupils left school, they had very little contact with it. Most schools made little or no attempt to find out about the activities of their graduates and withdrawals. Few attempted to act as agencies for advice and help for out-of-school youth. Few provided any activities for the former pupils.

Teachers and school officers generally knew almost nothing about the homes of the pupils, or about their parents, or about the out-of-school activities of former pupils.

Former pupils did not consider the school to be an agency for advice, and seldom returned to the school to seek it.

Many pupils questioned the ability of the school officers to give dependable advice on nonscholastic problems.

The exception to these generalizations is to be found in the responses of the boys who graduated from the specialized vocational schools.

5. Although graduates seemed to be better adjusted than the withdrawals, they also needed help after leaving school.

6. Hundreds of high school graduates and withdrawals later attended proprietary schools. Some of these schools are legitimate educational institutions, but it is apparent that many of them exploit youth in various ways.

7. The guidance program for pupils in the schools was decidedly inadequate.

Most of the former pupils stated that they had no advice about curriculum at the time they made a curricular choice.

Elective choices were usually made by pupils with no guidance.

School officers frequently gave misinformation with regard to the value of courses given by proprietary schools.

The schools had little direct influence on the vocational choices of the pupils. Pupils had little information about various occupations, the required aptitudes, necessary training, the possibilities for advancement, the salary scales, the working conditions, or the opportunities for employment, on which to base their choices. Not unnaturally many of the pupils made poor decisions.

In many communities, the relationship between the school and industry was not cooperative. It was not unusual for school people to know very little about their local industries.

In general there had been consistent selection in the kind of pupils enrolled in the various curricula. The brightest pupils generally were found in the college-preparatory group, less intelligent pupils in the commercial group, and the least intelligent in the industrial group.

Various selective factors, all related, may have caused this classification. Home background, occupation of parent, wealth, interests, and other factors may have been influential, but it seems from the interviews that in general only one factor, intelligence, had received specific attention by the schools. As a result many of the pupils who had no money for college, or who did not wish to go to college, had received college entrance diplomas, merely because they were able to pass the work for these diplomas. Commercial diplomas were given frequently to pupils in communities where there were few clerical jobs. Industrial courses were given to pupils who were not able to pass any of the other courses, regardless of their aptitude for industrial work.

8. High school diplomas were not at all descriptive of the individuals who received them, although they may roughly indicate differences among the large groups of pupils enrolled in different curricula.

Many graduates apparently had not developed sufficient resources to continue their education independently.

The leisure-time activities of the graduates did not indicate that the school had affected them much.

The award of a diploma affords no prediction of good citizenship. Many of the graduates felt no concern for their civic responsibilities. Some had actually been recognized as offenders against society, within a few months after leaving school.

Many of the former pupils felt that they were not ready to begin work when they left school, that they had neither the information nor the skills which would help them to begin work. Employers agreed with these statements and added that the attitudes of many of the pupils were such as to handicap them on their jobs.

The weaknesses of the diploma were paralleled by the other recommendations by school officers. Employers frequently mentioned that the schools' recommendations of applicants for positions were almost worthless.

Nevertheless, employers frequently utilized the fact of graduation and the selection operating by means of the various curricula. Some took only college-preparatory graduates, not because of the particular values of the work, but because they thought they would thus get bright pupils.

9. Pupils left school with certain attitudes which made it difficult for them to adjust themselves to the out-of-school situation.

No matter what type of community these young people lived in, or what occupations their parents engaged in, former pupils wanted white collar jobs, and were discontented and unhappy if they found it necessary to take some other kind of job.

Pupils left school under the impression that it is wrong and weak to seek advice.

Pupils were not at all realistic about their plans for the future. Many looked forward to entrance into the professions, even though there was little chance that these hopes might be realized.

The following selection from pages 46–49 of Education for American Life, the general report of the Regents' Inquiry, provides a summary statement of recommendations for secondary education programs. You may note a statement of intent to establish general vocational education in the high school. This represented a recognition of the need for somewhat specialized training. Heretofore little had been done to prepare youth to enter into specialized work life. Another important aspect of these recommendations was the statement of need for vocational guidance services. The American Youth Commission isolated the same need as reported in Youth Tell Their Story. The American Youth Commission cooperated with the Regents' Inquiry during the course of its study.

EDUCATION FOR AMERICAN LIFE

Outline of New Educational Program

(Secondary Education)

The secondary schools should recognize the needs of youth today by offering in addition to the college preparatory program, which has been so much overemphasized, more specific courses and work to fit boys and girls for useful citizenship, for self-support, and for a growing individual life. This is to be accomplished in such ways as the following:

Begin the secondary school program with the seventh grade in all school districts.

Make general education the central objective of the secondary school program by devoting the greater part of the time up to the end of the twelfth grade to the study of general science, human relations, community life, world history, general mathematics, and the arts—subjects which touch many now divided academic topics, and which cover matters of direct value and interest to the average American citizen. Present these broad fields of knowledge in the ways in which they are generally encountered in life and work, and not as semester hours for college entrance. Introduce more "review" in basic skills, such as reading and writing, particularly for those whose elementary school work is deficient.

Recognize that the school has a distinct responsibility for character education, not by multiplying rules and discipline, but by establishing student activities, developing a knowledge of the great ethical literature and standards of mankind, and above all, by furnishing inspiring leadership in school. Make understanding and enthusiasm for the democratic system part of character education.

Make all high schools large enough, but not too large (300- to 1,200-pupil capacity if possible), so that there can be electives without too small classes, and so that pupils may really experience student government, intramural sports, group music, and clubs—activities which should be greatly expanded as part of the school program. Make possible easier cooperation among school systems to handle the more specialized subjects economically.

Establish a guidance service in each school system equipped to give educational and vocational help to boys and girls in high school and to those who have finished but have not found a satisfactory first job.

Permit a pupil to leave school at sixteen years of age, if he has a real job. If he is unemployed and is not attending an educational institution, require him to continue under the supervision of the school and to pursue the kind of educational program thus worked out until he is eighteen, unless he gets a job in the meantime. This program may be in school or not, as the boy and his advisers may determine. Discontinue continuation schools.

Include general vocational education in the program of every comprehensive high school. In high school vocational courses lay chief emphasis on broad vocational training and not on the development of specialized skills.

Gradually add to the secondary school program beyond the twelfth grade new cultural courses and new subprofessional courses which will prepare boys and girls to enter the technical and semiprofessional occupations—surveying, laboratory work, junior engineering occupations and the like—wherever such courses are not now available. These new high school courses beyond the twelfth grade should qualify for state aid only on the approval of the local expanded educational plan by the state.

Base high school graduation on readiness to leave school, as judged by local school officers in accordance with rules and regulations to be approved by the State Education Department, and discontinue the Regents' Diploma. The local diploma should specify the work done and the competence achieved.

End the Regents' Examinations as graduation tests, and transform them into examinations designed to discover the weak spots in curriculum or teaching. Make available to the schools a variety of examinations through which the schools themselves can measure pupils' achievement.

Emphasize in the school health and physical education program mental, emotional, as well as physical health. Protect pupils and teachers against persons within the school exercising a destructive emotional influence. Expand sports and activities in which all can join which have adult carry-over values; abandon the perfunctory but expensive annual "physical examination" now required by law and have in its place one examination on school entrance, one on entering seventh grade, one on entering ninth grade, and one at the end of twelfth grade.

Give more attention specifically to gifted youth and to handicapped youth, not only for their sake and the future of society, but also as a means of improving instruction for the average group of students.

Improve libraries and increase reference, research, field work, and report-writing assignments; increase emphasis on English expression and broad reading.

The school authorities cannot undertake the whole responsibility within each community for the development of an intelligent handling of the problems of youth, but the school authorities should join with other interested groups in seeing that the work of all local agencies which deal with youth in the area is coordinated and is in some way meeting each of the basic problems of youth.

The following excerpt from Chapter 14 of High School and Life includes the statement and discussion of nearly 20 proposals for improving high school programs. The type of curriculum provided, the school's responsibility for individual pupils, the policies and procedures for appraising pupils' work, and the school organization are all considered within the selection. Practically every aspect of schooling and life is discussed. Recommendations are made with respect to the role of the school in developing general adjustment, enhancing social life, developing citizenship skills, developing work skills, and teaching more rewarding use of leisure time. Several forward-looking recommendations presented were increasing counseling services, expanding schooling beyond the twelfth year, and early identification of potential dropouts.

There is a great deal of correspondence between the problems found by the Regents' Committee and the American Youth Commission investigators as well as the recommendations pursuant to those problems. This is not surprising since the two studies were conducted at about the same time. The agreement of the two studies attests to their depth of understanding of the problems.

In some instances the recommendations are radical departures from traditional schooling, and some even seem advanced in terms of the current situation. For example, it was recommended that some subjects may need to be dropped to make the time available to train for citizenship. It was admitted that some academic subjects provide little training in this area. Another departure is the concern that students should be equipped with skills to "learn independently" during their years of formal schooling as well as afterwards. A second radical departure is the recommendation that every student be prepared for social and vocational adjustment on leaving the secondary school or be prepared to continue his education. A third unusual recommendation is in the area of follow-up. It was recommended that the student should be helped after he finished his schooling, for at least a few months. The rationale for this was that it would not only help the individual but would also help to evaluate the school programs. Included within this concept was the recommended provision of recreational contacts for students who have left school.

HIGH SCHOOL AND LIFE

The Secondary School Curriculum

Analysis of the present high school curriculum has made evident one paramount reason for a lack of social competence among young people just out of high school. That reason consists in the schools' failure to give boys and girls a chance to acquire many of the abilities and attitudes which the out-of-school world will almost certainly demand of them. In any better program of secondary education a prime essential must therefore be a curriculum more directly focused on the kinds of competence which young people out of school will surely need.

To set forth all the details of a curriculum which will effectually prepare high school boys and girls for out-of-school living is at present impossible. Any thoroughly effective curriculum must grow in considerable measure out of planning on the part of each school that is to use it—planning which takes into account each school's resources in its plant and in the local community, which pays particular attention to the backgrounds of the school's pupils, and which capitalizes the special interests and abilities of the school's teachers. Moreover, the changes which need to be made in the curricula of most of the New York State high schools call for the introduction of methods and materials of teaching which have thus far been tried in only a few of the schools. Before these new methods and materials can be widely used there needs to be further experimentation with them under varying conditions. The comparative effectiveness of different plans for producing the same results needs to be carefully tested; subject matter needs to be systematized and put into a form in which it may be used by other teachers than those who first developed it; additional teaching materials need to be devised in fields in which present efforts have gone only far enough to show definite promise. Many of the details of an improved curriculum must therefore wait on progressive development over a period of years.

Furthermore, some of these details, once worked out, will undoubtedly have to be changed as conditions outside the schools change. Though a large part of any well-devised curriculum may be relatively permanent, a curriculum which is to center its attention on out-of-school problems and needs must be thoroughly responsive to new conditions. On this account also no complete prescription for a new curriculum can be offered.

Nevertheless, the broad outlines of a better curriculum can be fairly clearly distinguished.

As a major part of such a curriculum, every secondary school ought to provide for those subjects of study and those forms of pupil experience which promise fullest preparation for citizenship in the broad meaning of that term. Education for citizenship is no less important in the case of boys and girls who are to go on to higher institutions than in the case of those who will complete their full-time schooling in the secondary school. In its provision for education of this sort the high school probably ought not to distinguish between the two groups of pupils. Both groups need to be made as ready as their abilities will allow, not merely for their formal duties in relation to government but for their informal day-by-day association with family, neighbors, and fellow workers.

The secondary schools cannot be expected to make boys and girls completely ready for citizenship in the sense that young people leaving the high school will possess all the knowledge and understanding and insight that an adult citizen may need. The schools can, however, inform their pupils both thoroughly and broadly about important phases of American community life: about the physical resources of the nation, the arts and occupations characteristic of America, the institutions on which American life depends, the agencies for ministering to human needs and raising the level of human wants, the means by which public opinion is shaped and used for individual or social ends. Furthermore, the schools can help boys and girls to understand something of the origin and significance of the major social problems which now confront America. In so doing, the schools can awaken the interest of boys and girls in current efforts to solve such problems, and can foster in these boys and girls an active concern to make democracy work. Through a program designed to achieve these purposes, young people may be prepared, by the time they leave school, to take advantage of the opportunities which adult citizenship offers them for becoming increasingly responsible and intelligent participants in American democracy.

The preparation for citizenship that is most likely to achieve these ends cannot be accomplished through teaching from books alone. Much of this preparation must be gained through young people's direct observation of the way in which government operates and the way people get along together, or fail to get along together, outside the school. It must include as much attention to social problems and social needs in the pupils' own communities as to the more remote problems of national and international affairs. And in order that this preparation may not be a mere talking about social problems, it must give young people immediate experience in dealing with problems of personal and group relationships within the school—experience of such a nature that the pupils may learn from their own success or failure in group enterprises which they themselves manage and which are important to them.

Nor can adequate preparation for citizenship be left entirely to teachers of current events, civics, and American history. It must grow in part out of teaching in fields that are now only occasionally dealt with from a social standpoint. For boys as well as girls, and for all pupils rather than a few, adequate preparation will include a realistic consideration of the problems of establishing and maintaining a home —problems now considered in only a few of the broader courses in home economics. It should draw upon the courses in science for an appreciation of the part which science plays in collective living, and for an understanding of the major applications of science to the problems both of the individual and of society. It should provide for study of certain economic problems—not the techniques of bookkeeping and formal business operations, but problems of earning and saving, investment, wise spending, and economical buying as these problems may affect the individual citizen and the social group. And it should include the development of habits of healthful living, and the study of fundamental problems of personal and social hygiene. Teaching which is to cover so broad an area plainly cannot be entrusted to a few members of the high school staff, but must be shared by teachers in various fields.

Perhaps most important, the schools' effort to prepare young people for citizenship should not stop with seeing that boys and girls "know the facts." Facts are essential to any constructive citizenship in a democracy. At least equally necessary, however, are respect for the rights which democracy guarantees, and a concern that democratic government shall succeed. Hence the schools' attention must be directed at the same time both to teaching young people the facts with which they need to be acquainted, and to awakening in them an active desire for social progress and a willingness to sacrifice immediate personal comfort or gain in the interests of justice and the general social good.

Thoroughgoing preparation for citizenship will demand more teaching time than most schools now give to academic history and civics. Some subjects may need to be dropped from pupils' programs, or the schools' emphasis on certain subjects lessened, to make this time available. In the small high schools particularly, the schools' whole program of studies may need to be readjusted on this account. There can be little question that time may more justly be given to education for a citizenship in which all boys and girls must eventually play a part, than to training in purely academic subjects which will be valuable for a few only. If a school cannot provide effective training for citizenship and at the same time supply a full program of academic work, it may well sacrifice those academic subjects which seem to be offering least educational return to its pupils in general.

Beyond preparation for citizenship the secondary schools need to concern themselves with their pupils' readiness for continued learning. As a part of its basic curriculum every high school ought to provide whatever teaching of reading, oral and written expression, and arithmetic may be necessary to give all its pupils at least enough command of the tools of learning so that they are able to learn through independent study.

Merely because a boy or girl has been promoted from the elementary school, the high school cannot safely assume that he has adequately mastered the skills which he ought to possess in oral expression and in the three R's. Association with older pupils is often better for an average elementary school pupil than is continued work in the elementary school environment; so that elementary schools may sometimes be justified in promoting to the high school pupils who have not mastered the tool skills.[4] Again, pupils who enter the high school with a minimum command of these skills may slip back unless they are given continued teaching which will make that command permanent. For both these reasons the high school needs to be continuously alert to provide such elementary instruction as may be appropriate for certain of its pupils. It may do so in part through special coaching or remedial teaching; but every high school teacher ought to recognize his responsibility for teaching the special learning habits or skills that his particular subject may require.

Moreover, every high school ought to see to it that each of its pupils knows where and how to go on learning most profitably after he leaves the high school. For pupils who are to continue their education in higher institutions, this means that the school should actively help each boy or girl both to choose the higher institution most appropriate for him, and to decide tentatively on his program of further study in that institution. For boys and girls who are to end their full-time schooling with the high school, the high school ought to provide realistic information about chances for part-time study. Such information can probably best be given just before individual boys and girls are about to leave school, rather than early in the high school program. In many instances it may perhaps better be furnished as a part of the guidance which the school offers to individual pupils than as a phase of any formal "subject." However it is given, the information should acquaint every boy and girl with the kinds of education that may be open to him after he leaves school; it should put him on his guard against exploitation by unscrupulous salesmen of proprietary courses; and it should help him to see what sort of further education is most likely to be profitable for him in particular.

The high school should assume responsibility, furthermore, for its pupils' growth in ability to learn independently. Only a minority of

---

4 This fact does not warrant the abandonment by elementary schools of all standards of attainment. In the matter of reading especially, methods of teaching have been brought to a level of effectiveness at which it is entirely possible for an elementary school to guarantee a reasonable minimum of skills by the time even a somewhat dull pupil has spent six or more years in school, provided the school is willing to make a particular point of teaching its pupils to read. The tool skills are so important as a basis for continued learning that it is to be strongly urged that elementary schools make a systematic and determined effort to see that on reaching the end of grade six every boy and girl of normal mental ability has reached an agreed-on minimum of competence in reading, English expression, and arithmetic. Failing to develop this minimum in the case of any pupil, the elementary school ought to inform the high school of that fact, so that the high school may provide for special teaching.

high school pupils need be limited by their meager scholastic aptitude to a mastery of the minimum skills of reading, expression, and arithmetic. The majority can, and should, make steady progress beyond any such minimum, in their command of the tools of learning. During each year of their stay in the high school they should become more proficient in obtaining for themselves information that may be useful to them; they should grow more skillful in analyzing what they read or hear or see; they should become increasingly aware of the part that studying may play in adding to particular kinds of individual competence. Above all, they should grow more and more accustomed to learning without having a teacher supervise all the details of their work. Pupils' growth in these respects is not likely to be achieved merely by introducing a required course in how to study, or by insisting that pupils work without help. It must come largely through the teaching done by individual teachers, in their particular fields. To teach each boy or girl how to learn for himself, and to interest him in learning to such an extent that he will want to use some of his own time for learning, should be as important a part of every teacher's task as to teach any formal body of subject matter.

The secondary schools must concern themselves with their pupils' use of their leisure time for other purposes than studying. If secondary education is to have as much constructive influence as it may well have on the way young people spend their leisure, every secondary school should provide teaching which will lead its pupils to enjoy the best types of recreation open to them after they leave school.

To do what needs to be done in preparing boys and girls for a more wholesome use of their leisure, schools will need in part to modify their present teaching. Instead of teaching English literature with an eye chiefly to giving boys and girls an analytical knowledge of certain "standard" works, the schools will need to start with boys' and girls' present tastes in reading, and by introducing pupils gradually to better and better books—always making the reading of these books a pleasant experience—lead the pupils as far as possible toward a liking for the kind of reading that the schools would have them habitually do. Instead of paying little attention to pupils who have no talent for drawing or painting, the schools will need to awaken the interest of all their pupils in the art which they may have a chance to see and enjoy. And instead of placing chief emphasis on the coaching of bands and orchestras, the schools will need to give at least equal effort to fostering less formal musical activities, and especially to developing their pupils' appreciation of music from the listener's point of view.

In addition, the schools will be obliged to introduce some entirely new teaching. They cannot remain blind to the fact that moving pictures are quite as much a subject for enjoyment and appreciation as are the plays printed in books. Nor can they safely ignore young people's tendency to listen to the radio much more often than to listen to formal concerts or to go to the theatre. In the field of athletics the schools will need to recognize that small-group or individual sports—tennis, golf, swimming, hiking, and the rest—offer more frequent opportunities for out-of-school recreation than do football, baseball, track, and soccer. The recreations which boys and girls are practically certain to indulge in anyway will have to be definitely represented in any curriculum that is to do its full share in giving direction to young people's out-of-school living.

As with preparation for citizenship, the schools' attention to preparation for leisure-time activities may come into conflict with the teaching of purely academic subjects. The conflict must again be resolved in terms of the kind of teaching which will yield greatest returns to all high school pupils. A school too small to offer both a sound program for the majority of its pupils and specialized academic training for a few ought not on that account to shape its whole program for the few. Though it ought to protect the interests of the pupils who need intensive academic training by seeing that they have a chance to get such training elsewhere, the small school's first attention should go to the greater number of young people for whom it is responsible.

Finally, the secondary school curriculum should take positive account of the need on the part of most high school pupils to get and hold jobs once they are through with their schooling. For every pupil who is to complete his formal education in that school, each secondary school ought to provide a necessary minimum of definite preparation for a vocation. In the case of girls who do not expect to earn their livings outside the home, this minimum may perhaps be restricted to training in the management of a household. For other pupils it ought properly to include experience with the basic operations of various kinds of jobs, through which these pupils may become used to adapting themselves to differing requirements and accustomed to learning on the job; experience in getting along with fellow workers and superiors under job conditions; and enough specific training in a salable vocational skill to give each leaving pupil the chance for a foothold at the bottom of a recognized occupation. In addition the high school ought to provide young people with some fundamental understanding of the social problems inherent in vocational employment. No boy or girl ought to leave school without knowing, for example, about organized labor and the part which it plays in various occupations, or about the working conditions created by the growth of large-scale corporations and combinations of employers. With respect to skills and understandings both, the high school curriculum ought to furnish each boy and girl who is going immediately to work with the background which is clearly necessary for every beginning worker who is to be in any sense a master of his own vocational fate.

High schools ought not, however, to try to make boys and girls who have never had successful vocational experience into highly skilled craftsmen. The school's responsibility to vocationally untried young people is to give them a start, not to make them immediately ready to compete with experienced workers. Moreover, the school needs to recognize that, for beginners particularly, vocational adaptability is likely to be more important than highly developed specialized skill. It should therefore not train young people who have never held jobs to be electric welders, for example, though it may train them as electricians' helpers; nor should it try to make them into cafeteria or tearoom managers, though it may train them for counter service or as waitresses; nor should it attempt to make them full-fledged stenographers, though it may give them the basic skills in shorthand and typewriting; nor should it try to train them as specialists in horticulture, though it may make them competent to support themselves as general agricultural workers. Its training program for beginners should resemble in general the broader courses in industrial arts now offered in certain of the academic high schools rather than the specialized courses toward which most of the separate vocational schools have been tending.[5]

[5] The degree of specialization which should be aimed at in the high school vocational courses must obviously be determined by the abilities required of beginning workers in particular fields. Requirements may differ from time to time, from one occupation to another, and even to some extent from one city to another. The vocational training program ought therefore to be developed on the basis of continuous surveys of local needs. For a more detailed discussion of these matters, see T. L. Norton, *Education for Work*, Regents' Inquiry, 1938.

It is to be understood that the proposal here made that the secondary school program should not aim at highly specialized training for vocationally untried pupils is not intended to rule out the provision of specialized training for experienced workers. The state's educational program ought to include more schools than at present, geographically well distributed and probably organized as separate vocational schools, which offer specialized vocational training. Specialized training should be restricted, however, to persons who have demonstrated initial vocational competence under adult working conditions. Training in electric welding or cafeteria management or stenography or horticulture may properly be offered as a part of this advanced program, even though such training should not be open to the vocationally inexperienced pupils who are receiving initial

At the same time the secondary schools need to recognize the present lack of educational opportunities for young people who may properly enter various semiprofessional occupations. Every secondary school whose resources permit it to do so should provide needed preparation for vocations requiring a more extended period of initial schooling than can be completed by the end of the twelfth grade, but demanding less training than that offered by established higher institutions. The training in question should prepare students for beginning employment in such occupations as those of the laboratory assistant, the dental hygienist, the secretary (as distinguished from the typist or stenographer), the surveyor, the architectural assistant, the dietician. Admission to training of this sort should be restricted to pupils who have successfully completed a secondary school program extending through the twelfth grade, and who show definite aptitude for semiprofessional education. The work which the secondary school offers these pupils should not be merely a collection of technical courses piled on top of an undergraduate program. Neither should it be a program duplicating that of the first year or two of four-year higher institutions. It ought properly to consist of a carefully planned program in its own right, calling for from one to three years of training beyond the twelfth grade, as the nature of each occupation for which it prepares may require, and including continued general education as well as attention to specialized knowledge or skill.[6]

These various phases of the secondary school curriculum—prepara-

---

vocational education. Training for experienced workers has been recognized in the Inquiry as a phase of adult education rather than of secondary education. See Floyd Reeves, T. Fansler, and C. O. Houle, *Adult Education,* Regents' Inquiry, 1938.

[6] It will be noted that this proposal does not contemplate any upward extension of the high school program in the form of an academic junior college. The desirability of establishing junior colleges has been canvassed in the study of higher education conducted by the Inquiry. The results of that study make it clear that high schools in New York State ought not to attempt to duplicate the work of the early years of the liberal arts colleges. New York is liberally endowed with colleges of high standing, so distributed throughout the state as to be geographically accessible to practically all young people. Boys and girls who can profit by a college education but who cannot afford the cost of college work can accordingly be better provided for in New York by an extension of the present plan of state scholarships than by the establishment of public junior colleges. Recommendations with respect to desirable increases in the number of state scholarships and in the stipends which they carry are presented in the Inquiry's general report. See Luther H. Gulick, *Education for American Life,* Regents' Inquiry, 1938; see also the recommendations with respect to scholarships in Chapter 15 of the present report.

tion for citizenship, for continued out-of-school learning, for recreation, and for jobs—include the fields of teaching most in need of improvement in New York State high schools at the present time. They do not include formal preparation for college. That part of the high school program has received so much emphasis in the past that it needs less immediate attention than do the nonacademic phases of the high schools' work. The young people who are preparing for college are nevertheless vitally concerned in the proposals here made. Many of these young people, like the boys and girls who will not go to college, are leaving the high schools deficient in the knowledge and interests and abilities which a sound general education ought to have given them. The most clearly necessary improvement in the high school program, for them as for the pupils who will have no further full-time schooling, lies in the development of a curriculum which will prepare all boys and girls for out-of-school living as successfully as the present curriculum prepares a minority for academic work in the liberal arts colleges.

Responsibility for Individual Pupils

Changes in the curriculum alone, however, will not enable the secondary schools to do all that is necessary in preparing boys and girls for social competence. Young people now leave school unready for what lies ahead of them partly because the schools have paid little attention to their individual needs. Beyond improving the high school curriculum, the secondary schools must therefore undertake far more systematically than at present, to recognize their pupils as individuals and to see that each pupil gets the kind of education appropriate for him.

If it is to do more than run its pupils through a mill, a secondary school cannot consider its work accomplished until it knows that each of its pupils who is on the point of leaving school is prepared as fully as his abilities allow for one of two alternatives. Either he should be ready to make a successful social and vocational adjustment to out-of-school conditions, or he should be prepared to continue his schooling successfully in an appropriate higher institution. The school's responsibility for insuring one or the other outcome for each individual boy and girl may occasionally need to be qualified in the case of pupils who present problems of delinquency or of inability to learn with which the public secondary school cannot properly deal. Such pupils will obviously have to be referred to other institutions. For the rest of its pupils the school's responsibility should be direct and positive.

In order to exercise this responsibility adequately, every secondary school must necessarily undertake certain duties which only a few schools now systematically perform. First, and most obviously, every school must make it a point to learn as much about its individual pupils as may be necessary for a sound estimate of their abilities and needs. No school ought to be content with what it discovers about its pupils merely from their class records or from the information that pupils and their parents volunteer. It ought to find out for itself, particularly in the case of boys and girls from the less privileged homes, about each pupil's general home background, about his interests and special abilities, about his major out-of-school activities and his hopes and plans for the future. Certain designated members of the staff should ordinarily be responsible for directing the collection and use of information of this sort. The school can probably learn most about individual boys and girls, however, not by assigning to one or two members of its faculty the task of trying to find out all that needs to be known about large numbers of pupils, but by making it a part of every teacher's responsibility to know certain pupils well. Dividing this responsibility among its teachers, the school may at the same time pool the judgments of various people as to each pupil's needs, and encourage greater sensitiveness on the part of teachers to young people's individual differences.

In the second place, each secondary school ought to use its information about its pupils as a basis for systematically adapting its teaching to individual pupils' particular needs. Most boys and girls probably gain more from having to learn in a group than they would gain from purely individual instruction, even though group teaching necessarily results in some slighting of individual interests. Group teaching, however, ought not to mean almost complete disregard of individual pupils, as it does in many high schools at the present time. The plans of homogeneous grouping and of differentiated teaching which certain schools have adopted may go far to prevent this disregard. Some such plan ought to be a part of the program of every school which enrolls pupils of widely varying abilities—not merely in order to prevent the slighting of pupils who have less ability than the average, but in order to hold the ablest pupils to a standard of work commensurate with their abilities. Especially in the case of teachers who have pupils of widely differing abilities in their classes, such plans should provide for relieving teachers as far as possible from purely clerical duties or routine administrative assignments, to allow the time that is necessary to make definite provisions for pupils' individual needs.

Every secondary school ought, moreover, to give its pupils positive educational guidance. Schools cannot rely on informed educational choices by most pupils or their parents. The schools themselves must take the initiative in seeing that pupils get the kinds of education most suitable for them.

If the guidance which the schools offer is to be dependable, each school will need to know more about its pupils' potential abilities than most schools now know or try to discover. On this account each school ought not merely to keep a systematic record of its pupils' school work and to use all its information as to pupils' out-of-school circumstances and interests, but it ought thoroughly to test its pupils' capacity to learn. In particular, it ought to give pupils a chance to try themselves out briefly in special fields of study before it requires them to choose among these fields in planning their specialized programs.

In the light of the information about each pupil which it may thus secure, the school ought to direct individual boys and girls away from programs which do not promise to lead to their social and vocational adjustment. Its concern should be quite as much for pupils who choose below the level of their abilities as for pupils who aim too high. Though it obviously cannot be sure of what may constitute the best educational choice in each individual case, it can certainly identify many of the seriously mistaken choices which pupils without guidance are likely to make. These it ought to use all its persuasion and influence to prevent.

Not every high school can offer a comprehensive program of secondary education. The best interests of certain boys and girls may require, therefore, that these boys and girls be directed to other schools in which they can secure a kind of education more appropriate to their needs. Individual high schools ought to have a conscience about all such pupils. No school ought, if it can help it, to allow a pupil to continue in a program which is clearly not the one that he needs. With young people who might better be transferred to other schools quite as much as with the rest of its pupils, every secondary school should take the initiative in seeing that each boy and girl discovers his own educational needs and finds a way of meeting them.

Each secondary school ought likewise to give those boys and girls who do not go on to higher institutions direct help in making their first out-of-school adjustments. If it is to assure itself that young people make effective use of what they have learned, the school will need to provide pupils who are about to leave school with realistic vocational guidance. It will need also to see that each boy and girl leaving school has a chance to make the out-of-school contacts which he most needs to make.

Vocational guidance which is to be thoroughly meaningful to high school pupils must deal with the vocational problems that boys and girls face at the time those problems are crucial. Eighth grade or ninth grade surveys of occupations or of the problems involved in choosing a vocation are not likely to be meaningful for many pupils. Most boys and girls in these early grades are looking forward to staying in school. From their point of view the problem of getting a job is as yet a matter to be merely casually considered rather than a matter of vital and immediate concern. That problem becomes crucial for the majority of pupils only when they realize that they are on the point of leaving school. It is at this latter point that the vocational guidance which the school may offer is likely to make the most lasting impression, and it is here that the school's guidance can be of most direct assistance to individual boys and girls.

Each school, therefore, ought to single out as early as possible in every school year the young people for whom that year is likely to be their last of full-time schooling. For these pupils it ought to provide a survey of chances for jobs—not a remote study of occupations in general, but a canvassing of the actual job opportunities which are open to these particular boys and girls. It ought not to stop with talking about how to choose a job; beyond any such general discussion, the school should see that each boy or girl has a tangible plan for finding a job for himself, that he knows how to interpret help wanted advertisements and how to approach a prospective employer, that he is familiar with local nonschool agencies—particularly government placement and welfare agencies—which may help him to find employment, and that he makes definite use of all this knowledge in getting work.

The school ought also to follow pupils for at least a few months after they leave. It should do so not merely in order to give much needed help to individual boys and girls, but in order to gain a pragmatic measure of the value of its own teaching. From the latter standpoint it will do better to ask all its teachers to share in the task of discovering what happens to individual pupils than to assign this task to one person; though one person ought, no doubt, to be primarily responsible for directing each school's general follow-up program. In this program the school should not restrict itself to watching its former pupils' vocational success only. It should properly be concerned with all the activities of its pupils toward which the school has tried to contribute, namely, the pupils' relations with other people, the share they take in civic affairs, their recreations, and their further studying, as well as their work on their jobs.

Wherever possible the school should work through and with other agencies in its follow-up program. In many communities there are already organizations—state and federal employment agencies, welfare agencies of various sorts, and groups of citizens actively interested in helping young people—which are directly concerned with boys and girls outside of school. The school ought neither to duplicate the work of these agencies nor to compete with them. The school is, nevertheless, the only social agency now actively in contact with all boys and girls, and it is thus the only agency which can make sure that individual young people who are badly in need of help are not lost or forgotten. The school's responsibility should be to see that boys and girls who need assistance from other agencies get such help as those agencies can afford. Only when no organization exists or can be established in a community to furnish assistance to boys and girls outside of school ought the school to undertake the whole task of meeting these young people's needs.

Schools may properly undertake, however, to supply certain activities for out-of-school young people which are now all too infrequently provided. For one thing, every school ought to make a systematic effort to supply wholesome recreational contacts for pupils just out of school. Through clubs, dances, and organized sports, schools furnish such contacts for boys and girls still in school. Nevertheless most schools let their pupils leave school without any assurance that outside of school these pupils will have a chance to exercise the interests which the schools have been trying to develop. The experience of numerous schools has shown that out-of-school young people welcome the opportunity to continue at school the kind of recreation which the school can readily provide. Even though a school may not be able to open all its recreational facilities to former pupils, it may at least allow them to attend school dances, to use the school's playing fields when the fields are not occupied by boys and girls still in school, and to share in the school's dramatic and musical activities. Unless some such opportunities are made available to out-of-school young people, the schools' efforts to develop habits of wholesome enjoyment are destined to be largely futile.

Furthermore, every school, so far as its resources permit, ought to see that work opportunities are provided for beginners whose need for jobs cannot be met through normal employment. Again the schools ought not to compete with established organizations—the National Youth Administration and the Civilian Conservation Corps in particular. The schools ought to make certain at the outset that all the young people who are eligible for the help which these agencies can give are brought in touch with the proper authorities. But the Youth

Administration and the Civilian Conservation Corps provide for relatively limited numbers and kinds of young people, and are obliged to provide for them in ways which do not always meet individual circumstances. As a practical answer to the needs of many boys and girls in times when jobs are scarce, the schools can and should actively supplement the work of these agencies. They should assume responsibility, when there is the need, for enlisting the cooperation of local employers in providing opportunities for young people to do useful work. They should use to the full such possibilities for fruitful vocational experience as the operation of the school itself may provide: experience in routine clerical work, the keeping of records, the operation of the school cafeteria, the servicing of school buses, the making or repair of school apparatus, the decoration of the school building and grounds. Their faculty members may cooperate, as faculty members in various schools have done in recent years, to provide employment in the care of automobiles, the serving of lunches, or minor jobs about their homes. The work thus furnished should supplement that ordinarily done by adult workers, instead of making the employment of adults unnecessary. It should nevertheless be real work, and it should be paid for in terms of pocket money, at least—both because it ought to be worth paying for, and because paid jobs rather than busy work represent the real need of boys and girls who are through with their schooling.

For the school to take responsibility for finding such work for young people will not mean any change in the school's chief obligation. The school is primarily an educational institution and not a custodial or charitable institution, and it should remain so. With respect to jobs as well as to recreation, however, the education which the school provides may often be wasted if boys and girls who are through with their schooling get no chance to use what they have learned. In doing its utmost to discover temporary jobs for young people who cannot find work elsewhere, and particularly in bringing to the attention of the public the need for such jobs on the part of individual boys and girls, the school will be doing no more than must be done to make its educational program effective.

These various proposals as to what every secondary school should do for individual boys and girls are not based on mere idealistic theory. Neither are they based on any sentimental conception of society's "debt" to young people. They grow directly out of a consideration of the maladjustments of young people under an educational system in which schools pay little attention to individual needs, and of the harm to society as a whole which these maladjustments threaten. The school obviously cannot be a cure-all for social ills. But if it will acquaint itself with its pupils' individual needs, if it will see that each boy and girl chooses an education as much as possible in keeping with his particular abilities, and if it will help pupils who are leaving school to make the best practicable out-of-school adjustments, the school may at least make a direct and positive contribution to the betterment of a social situation which is at present none too happy.

Appraisal of Pupils' Work

As a part of their responsibility for their pupils as individuals, the schools ought properly to assume certain new responsibilities for the appraisal of pupils' work. In particular, the schools' requirements for promotion and graduation ought to be determined more largely than at present by the individual secondary schools.

Exactly what standards any given school should use for promoting its pupils from one grade to the next can hardly be determined from outside that school. The size of the groups of pupils with which the school has to deal, the plan of teaching which the school has adopted in the light of its pupils' educational needs, special circumstances which may make it more profitable for individual pupils to be assigned to one class-group rather than to another, all need to be considered in deciding either on a general promotion scheme or on the promotions of individual boys and girls. Any one of these factors may clearly be of greater importance in a particular situation than pupils' formal "credits" in a specified list of academic subjects.

Accordingly, each secondary school ought to assume responsibility for its own promotions. Though the promotion plans which will result from this assumption of responsibility may not be different from the plans heretofore used, each school, as it modifies its general program, should be free to adopt whatever new plan best meets the needs of its pupils.

Each secondary school ought to be responsible likewise for the granting of diplomas. The present system of state-awarded diplomas, valuable as it has been in giving prestige to high school graduation, makes almost impossible the recognition of anything but formal scholastic achievement as a basis for graduation. It pins every pupil's fate, moreover, on his success in a series of written examinations, a measure which may be quite inappropriate for certain kinds of ability and for certain pupils. Though examinations should continue to be used in appraising each pupil's readiness to graduate from high school, they ought to be regarded as supplying only partial evidence of the pupil's accomplishment. The rest of that evidence, and the final decision as to each pupil's achievement, properly ought to be supplied by the school itself.

Eventually, individual secondary schools ought to establish a new type of high school diploma. The diplomas now in use in New York State, like most of those awarded by high schools elsewhere, consist of little more than summary reports on pupils' work in courses. Schools may properly continue to issue transcripts of credits to pupils who want such summary reports. The diploma itself ought to be a statement of what the pupil has gained from his high school education, and not just a record of the scholastic motions he has gone through. If a school has been seriously attempting to make its pupils ready for higher education or for out-of-school living, its diplomas ought to indicate that fact. They can do so most straightforwardly if, instead of certifying merely that a pupil has passed certain courses, they attest that the pupil has attained the goals which the school has been seeking for him: that in the judgment of the school faculty he is prepared either for entrance into a specified vocation or for admission to a specified type of higher educational institution, and that he can be positively recommended as likely to take an acceptable part in the out-of-school social groups to which he will perforce belong.

Serious practical difficulties clearly stand in the way of awarding any such diploma at the present time. Few schools are either well enough acquainted with the conditions which individual young people must face outside of school, or sure enough of the qualities that are likely to make for successful out-of-school accomplishment, to be able to award a diploma of this kind with confidence. Parents and high school pupils are attached to the conventional diploma; any immediate shift to a radically different measure of pupils' achievement would undoubtedly meet with strong resistance, especially from parents whose sons or daughters were entitled to the conventional diploma but could not fairly be recommended for the new one. The very strength of these obstacles, however, indicates something of the task which confronts the secondary schools if they are to achieve any fundamental reform in the nature and direction of their work. A school which is not ready to warrant the competence of its graduates is in all probability either shooting wide of the mark at which public education ought to aim, or leading its pupils through a round of activities whose value the school itself is hard put to justify. A public which conceives it to be no part of the school's duty to judge the actual competence of boys and girls is far from appreciating the part which secondary schools at their best may play in preparing young people for out-of-school living. If social competence is to be an aim of secondary school work, each school's final judgment of its individual pupils ought to be in terms wholly consistent with that aim. Each secondary school should, therefore, move as rapidly and effectively as its particular circumstances allow, against the obstacles which now keep it from a realistic appraisal of its work.

School Organization

Changes in the high school curriculum and in the attention which schools pay to individual pupils will be difficult to make as long as the schools hold rigidly to the conventional four-year high school organization. Provision of tryout courses on which a dependable program of educational guidance may be based will require the downward extension of secondary school work into the seventh and eighth grades. The establishment of new programs of semiprofessional training will make it necessary for certain secondary schools to add one or more grades beyond the twelfth. If it is to be effectively planned and coordinated, the work of these lower and higher grades ought to be under the same supervision as that of the four grades now included in most of the high schools. Accordingly, the seventh grade through the twelfth grade, and in addition such higher grades as may be organized in connection with the needed upward extension of secondary school work, should be recognized in each school system as secondary grades, and instruction in all these grades should be directly supervised by the local school officer or officers primarily responsible for the program of secondary education.

The proposal that grades above the sixth should be recognized as secondary grades does not mean that special barriers should be erected between the sixth grade and the seventh. As with promotions from one secondary grade to another, responsibility for advancing pupils from the elementary school to the secondary school should rest with the local schools. In general, pupils should be admitted to the secondary grades whenever, in the judgment of the local school authorities, the needs of these pupils can be served better by association with older pupils or by a program emphasizing vocational preparation than by a continuance of elementary school work.

Nor does the proposal that all the secondary grades should be under unified supervision mean that a single pattern of grade organization should be adopted by the secondary schools of the state. It is probable that an approximation of the six-year junior-senior high school plan offers the most effective scheme of organization for the majority of secondary schools at the present time, and most school systems will do well to adopt some such plan. Systematic experimentation with other forms of organization is highly desirable, however—especially with forms of organization which make semiprofessional training above the twelfth grade a unified part of the secondary school program. The essential condition for improvement would seem to be not the adoption of any one particular scheme, but the substitution for a conventional plan which no longer fits educational needs, of whatever plans may lend themselves best to the educational programs and the educational facilities of individual school systems.

The proposal as a whole does mean, however, that separate vocational schools (including continuation schools) for pupils who have not completed the twelfth grade should be given up as rapidly as possible. Separate schools may appropriately be used for offering "upgrading" vocational training to young people who have had initial vocational experience, or for supplying technical courses to students who have successfully completed an appropriate high school program of twelve grades. The initial nonspecialized vocational training which needs to be given to pupils below the twelfth grade can be both economically and effectively provided in general high schools. Such training, instead of being set off by itself, ought to be an integral part of the program of secondary education which each general high school offers.

Inauguration of the Proposed Program

The changes in secondary education here proposed will affect the high school curriculum, the high schools' methods of guiding their pupils and providing for pupils' individual needs, the means by which the schools appraise their pupils' achievement, and the general organization of the secondary schools. In order that the proposed changes may be seen in due relation to one another, it may be well to recapitulate them briefly.

The high school curriculum should be reorganized to give first place to subjects of study and forms of pupil experience which promise fullest preparation for citizenship in a democracy. In addition, the basic curriculum should provide whatever training in fundamental skills and whatever information about opportunities for further schooling may be needed by individual pupils, to allow each pupil to go on learning in ways appropriate for him after he leaves the high school. The curriculum should also include teaching which will lead pupils to enjoy the best types of recreation open to them outside of school. Finally, the curriculum should give each boy and girl who is not going to college the minimum of practical preparation that he may need to allow him to make a successful beginning at a kind of employment appropriate to his particular interests and abilities. The high school curriculum should not furnish training in specialized craftsmanship, but it should provide such general understandings and skills, including those necessary as preparation for semiprofessional occupations in the case of young people capable of entering such occupations, as will assure each of its pupils a foothold at the bottom of a recognized field of employment.

To make its curriculum thoroughly effective, each high school should assume more responsibility than schools in general now assume for what happens to its individual pupils. It should learn as much about each of its pupils as may be necessary for a sound estimate of his abilities and needs. It should systematically adapt its teaching to its pupils' major differences in interest and ability. It should furnish its pupils with positive educational and vocational guidance. It should follow the young people who do not go on to higher institutions for at least the first few months after they leave school. It should make a systematic effort to supply wholesome recreational contacts for boys and girls just out of school, and to see that opportunities for work are provided for beginners whose need for jobs cannot be met through normal employment.

In the case of all its pupils, the high school should take independent responsibility for their promotion from grade to grade, and for the award of high school diplomas. If its appraisal of its pupils' work is to be consistent with its educational aims, the high school must eventually grant diplomas not in terms of formal credits or hours of work, but on the basis of the competence which its pupils achieve.

The organization of each high school should take whatever form best lends itself to that school's educational program and to the plant and equipment which the school has available. In most schools, the four-year high school organization should eventually be displaced by a form of organization which recognizes the grades above the sixth as secondary grades, and which places those grades under unified supervision. Separate vocational schools should not be maintained for secondary school pupils, but the high school organization may properly include grades above the twelfth, as a means of providing semiprofessional training of a type not now readily available either in the secondary schools or in higher educational institutions.

Stated as they have had to be in terms of general needs, these proposals are intended not so much to furnish a set of explicit directions for individual schools as to suggest the basis for a long-term program of improvement in secondary education. It is apparent, nevertheless, that most of the changes which will be necessary to put such a program into effect will have to be made in individual high schools, by the men and women who are in immediate charge of those schools. The changes can obviously not be made quickly, nor can they be brought about by the efforts of administrative officers alone, or of teachers alone. To introduce them successfully will call for a genuinely cooperative attack on major educational problems by each school faculty as a whole. Teachers and principal, working together, will need to make of the school a laboratory in which the educational needs of individual boys and girls are given the time and thought which they rightly demand. Whether a given school becomes that sort of laboratory, rather than chiefly a smooth-running organization for providing drill on facts called for in examinations, is likely to depend most of all on the vision of its principal. There can be no escape, therefore, from the fact that the test of this program will eventually be found in the ability of the principals of the secondary schools, first of all to see what most needs to be done for high school boys and girls in local communities, and then to unite the teachers in their schools in an actively interested effort to plan, experiment, and measure the actual gain from each new undertaking.

EDUCATION FOR ALL AMERICAN YOUTH ⑧

Reports of the Educational
Policies Commission and the
Harvard Committee

 *The key word in the title of Education*
for ALL American Youth is "all." The
Educational Policies Commission said:

When we write confidently and inclusively about education for all
American youth, we mean just that. We mean that all youth, with
their human similarities and their equally human differences, shall
have educational services and opportunities suited to their personal
needs and sufficient for the successful operation of a free and demo-
cratic society. . . .

Each of them is a human being, more precious than material goods
or systems of philosophy. Not one of them is to be carelessly wasted.
All of them are to be given equal opportunities to live and learn.

This Commission believes that, in the main, educators and lay
citizens alike want the schools to extend their services so as to meet
all the educational needs of all youth. Tradition, to be sure, and some
vested interests impede change in education, as in every other insti-
tution. But, for the most part, these impediments do not arise from
any active opposition to educational advancement. They will largely

be swept away by a vigorous movement to shape education to the needs of all youth, when once that movement gains momentum.

The book was written as World War II was nearing its end. The Commission imagined two hypothetical histories of the postwar period. One was "The History That Should Not Happen;" the other, "The History That Must Be Written." The former recounted the take-over by the Federal government of the education of the youth of the nation, following the unwillingness of the government to help provide the financial assistance needed by local and state educational systems, and because of doubt that the local and state systems would reorganize their traditional programs, thus perpetuating a "profound discordance between purpose and program, between promise and performance," and failing therefore to provide for large segments of the secondary school population. Too late, years later, the people discovered the dangers of a centrally controlled education for the youth of the nation.

The second history, by contrast, recorded the provision of funds to states and localities to equalize educational opportunity, and the willingness of the public, teachers associations, and state and local school officials to devise and operate an educational program suitable to all American youth.

The two histories are reprinted in the following pages.

The Commission also described a theoretical program for rural and city schools, "The Farmville Secondary School" and "Schools for Youth in American City."

The Commission listed the differences that distinguish young people —differences in intelligence and aptitude, in occupational interests and outlooks, in availability of educational facilities, in types of communities in which youth live, in social and economic status and race, in parental attitudes and cultural backgrounds, in personal and avocational interests, and in mental health, emotional stability and physical well-being.

Running through the entire volume of Education For ALL American Youth were the needs youth have in common. The National Association of Secondary School Principals made a summary of the Educational Policies Commission report. This summary was published in 1944 under the title Planning for American Youth and featured a list of ten "Imperative Educational Needs of Youth":

1. All youth need to develop salable skills and those understandings and attitudes that make the worker an intelligent and pro-

ductive participant in economic life. To this end, most youth need supervised work experience as well as education in the skills and knowledge of their occupations.

2. All youth need to develop and maintain good health and physical fitness and mental health.
3. All youth need to understand the rights and duties of the citizen of a democratic society, and to be diligent and competent in the performance of their obligations as members of the community and citizens of the state and nation, and to have an understanding of the nations and peoples of the world.
4. All youth need to understand the significance of the family for the individual and society and the conditions conducive to successful family life.
5. All youth need to know how to purchase and use goods and services intelligently, understanding both the values received by the consumer and the economic consequences of their acts.
6. All youth need to understand the methods of science, the influence of science on human life, and the main scientific facts concerning the nature of the world and of man.
7. All youth need opportunities to develop their capacities to appreciate beauty, in literature, art, music, and nature.
8. All youth need to be able to use their leisure time well and to budget it wisely, balancing activities that yield satisfactions to the individual with those that are socially useful.
9. All youth need to develop respect for other persons, to grow in their insight into ethical values and principles, to be able to live and work cooperatively with others, and to grow in the moral and spiritual values of life.
10. All youth need to grow in their ability to think rationally, to express their thoughts clearly, and to read and listen with understanding.

The following represents excerpts from Education for All American Youth. Included are portions of Chapter I, Could it Happen?, Chapter III, The Farmville Community School, Chapter IV, Schools for Youth in American City, and Chapter VI, The History that Must be Written.

EDUCATION FOR *ALL* AMERICAN YOUTH [1]

Foreword

This volume stems from a firm conviction on the part of the Educational Policies Commission that the extension, adaptation, and improvement of secondary education is essential both to the security of our American institutions and to the economic well-being of our people. Such a development in secondary education can and should be brought about within the framework of the local and state educational systems. If the Federal government will help to finance and encourage such a development, and if the local and state leadership will do its part, it will be neither necessary nor desirable for the Federal government itself to operate educational services for the youth of the nation.

In the nearly three years in which it has been developing these policies for secondary education, the Commission has tried to dig beneath statements of general principles and to suggest in some detail how approved principles can be carried out in practice. It should be emphasized, however, that the programs of education described in this volume are not intended to be blueprints for local school systems. On the contrary, they are merely samples of the many different possible solutions to the problem of meeting the educational needs of all American youth. These samples are offered in the hope that they will stimulate and aid the planning and action which are already under way in many states and communities and which soon must be undertaken in all.

Plans for postwar education are too complex to be improvised in a few months after the problems are already upon us. Now is the time, the one and the best time, for citizens and educators in thousands of American communities to join forces in planning the kinds of schools which America needs and must have.

Could It Happen?

Educational change is bound to come, and to come swiftly. Only the nature and direction of change may be controlled.

No one can surely foretell the future of American education, for no one knows what American educators, boards of education, and legislatures will do during this critical period. We can, however, foresee the alternatives. And, by a study of our past experience, we can predict

[1] Educational Policies Commission, *Education for ALL American Youth,* Washington, D.C.: National Education Association and American Association of School Administrators, 1944. Reprinted by permission.

the general consequences of each of the lines of action—or inaction
—which the public schools may pursue.

The alternative possibilities, very briefly stated, are these:

1. A federalized system of secondary education may be created, at
first to compete with and ultimately to replace the traditional American
system of state and local control of education.

2. A wisely planned and vigorously implemented program for the
improvement, adaptation, and extension of educational services to
youth may be developed by the local and state educational authorities.

The Commission strongly and unanimously favors the second alternative and rejects the first.

Nevertheless, the Commission firmly believes that if local and state
planning and action are lacking, a Federal system of secondary education is scarcely less certain to occur than the succession of the seasons.

In order to compare and contrast the two possible lines of development, this volume contains two hypothetical histories. One "history,"
constituting most of the remainder of this chapter, is written on the
assumption that the first alternative occurs. The other "history," presented in Chapter 6 of this volume, relates what can happen if we
follow the second alternative.

In order that the reader may be constantly aware that the two
"histories" in this chapter and in Chapter 6 are projections of the
future, they have been printed in a type face which sets them apart
from the rest of this volume.

The remainder of this opening chapter, then, consists of quotations
that may possibly be found in the concluding pages of some standard
history of education published some twenty years from now. This is
a sequence of events which the Commission fervently hopes will not
happen. But they will happen unless effective planning and action
occur to direct educational developments in more desirable directions.

Here, then, is:

The History That Should Not Happen

The end of the second World War marked a turning point in the history
of youth education in the United States.

The complete victory of the United Nations, after a long and bitter
struggle, was followed by the demobilization of our armies and the rapid
conversion of the bulk of the war industries to the pursuits of peace. Although the United States government made strenuous and, on the whole,
successful efforts to administer the process in an orderly fashion, the demobilization and readjustment of some 30,000,000 persons placed a severe
strain upon economic, social, and educational institutions that had been
geared for years to the demands of a total war.

EDUCATIONAL NEEDS FOLLOWING THE SECOND WORLD WAR

Many of the demobilized soldiers were in their late teens or early twenties. Their civilian education had been interrupted by military service; few of them had enjoyed extensive experience in normal community living or in earning a livelihood by civilian pursuits; all of them needed guidance and training in order that they might find a place in the ongoing life of the nation. They were grown men and women, yet they needed education in the attitudes and activities of civilian life.

Similar educational needs were found among the men and women who had been employed in the war industries. In many cases their wartime vocational skills were no longer useful. For many of the younger workers, as for many soldiers, employment in a war industry had meant an interrupted educational career.

The boys and girls in their middle teens who were still in school at the end of the war were greatly disturbed. They had been diligently preparing themselves, by means of preinduction training and vocational preparation, to take an active part in the armed forces or on the production fronts. With the end of the war, their vocational outlook was rendered profoundly different and difficult, their future status uncertain. While the war continued, their services had been desperately needed. They had been urged and assisted to prepare themselves as rapidly as possible for full-time employment in civilian or military pursuits. But now the opportunities for work in war industry were few, and the labor market was flooded with returning soldiers and displaced war industry workers, many of whom had priorities on jobs and previous working experience. Even the great program of P. W. P. W. (Postwar Public Works) at first gave preference to the war veterans and offered relatively little opportunity for youth employment.

Youth were therefore urged to remain longer in school. This was certainly sound advice, not primarily because it was one method of limiting the labor supply, but chiefly because the vast and complicated responsibilities of adult citizenship in the postwar world clearly required extended civic, vocational, and cultural education.

The secondary schools of the country, with the exception of those in a very few localities, had no comprehensive plan available to meet this situation. They had given little thought to what they ought to teach or how they ought to teach it, either to returning soldiers, to demobilized war industry workers, or to the young people already in their schools who now changed their objective from immediate wartime employment to extended preparation for living in a strenuous period of national and world reconstruction.

The result of this situation, if we may compress the educational history of nearly a decade into a single phrase, was the establishment and entrenchment of our present National Bureau of Youth Service (N. B. Y. S.) as the only important agency of secondary education in this country.

This development is so important that the next few pages will be devoted to a more careful review of its causes and consequences.

WHY THE SCHOOLS WERE UNPREPARED

We who live in the second half of the twentieth century may find it quite difficult to understand why the schools of an earlier day were so ill prepared to meet the contingencies which must certainly have been expected, at least by the educational leaders of that time. But while we may be justified in regarding their failure with wonder, we should refrain from censure. Hindsight is always easier than foresight, and we must remember, as we review the history of those trying years, that there were at least four reasons for this apparent lethargy, this inability to cope with the new situation.

For one thing, the secondary schools had devoted themselves with amazing energy to a series of highly successful efforts to help win the war. In view of the extremely narrow margin which, at the outset of the war, separated victory from defeat, we can certainly approve their industry and understand their anxiety.

The schools made some far-reaching changes in the very midst of war. They showed themselves not only resourceful but flexible. The preinduction training for young men and the programs which trained over five million workers for the war industries are but two examples. The locally controlled public school systems showed that they could react promptly, vigorously, and effectively when confronted by a national war emergency. This ability of the local schools to react to a national wartime crisis was not equally evident with respect to the long-range planning for the peace.

The published records of the professional meetings held in those years show us clearly how engrossed the schools were in the immediate war problems. Even a cursory examination reveals that while the records abound with eloquent references to postwar education and reconstruction, they are almost barren of specific suggestions as to how the educational system would be changed in order to accept the responsibilities which everyone knew would devolve upon it in the event of a victory for the United Nations. On the contrary, it seems to have been assumed that, when the war ended, the schools would simply collect the fragments of their prewar program which had been put in storage for the duration and fit these elements back into the familiar prewar pattern. No one seems to have noted that the pattern, too, was shattered and beyond repair; that the end of the war was the end of an epoch to which there could be no return, in education or in any other aspect of life.

We must remember also that many secondary schools were poorly organized to meet a suddenly emerging national problem. There were at that time about 28,000 high schools in the United States. The median high school had only 140 students and six faculty members. Each of the thousands of smaller high schools was controlled by a local board of education which, within certain very general and broad requirements, acted as a law unto itself. Many of the state departments of education were weak and not legally constituted to meet such a critical situation. Almost all of them were understaffed and overworked.

In the third place, the local funds available to education, even when supplemented as they were in a few states, by state school funds, were often quite inadequate to provide the buildings, equipment, and personnel necessary for complete educational service. The one agency that might have improved this fiscal situation, the government of the United States, failed to act effectively.

It must be said on behalf of the educational leaders in that day, that they used their utmost talents of persuasion and strategy to secure the appropriation of Federal funds (pitifully small requests they now seem to us, by comparison with our Federal school expenditures) to equalize educational opportunities. They made vigorous representations before one Congress after another, both prior to and after the entry of the United States into the war. They called for action in the name of fair play and democracy; they engulfed the Congress in oceans of convincing statistics; they could summon to their support all the logic, the evidence, the common-sense reasoning, and the appeals to high motives. Their efforts were hampered, not only by the active opposition of certain influential minorities and the lack of vigorous support from the current national Administration, but also by the relative disunity and weakness of the professional organizations of teachers as compared with other occupational groups in the population. They were, therefore, unable to awaken the public from its apathy on the issue and to arouse widespread public support for Federal aid to education.

Still, they might have succeeded in obtaining Federal funds had it not been for a formidable psychological obstacle. That barrier was the now almost incomprehensible fear that harmful Federal control of education would inevitably follow Federal aid to the states for education. These fears seem strange to us at present, not only because the Federal government now controls practically all of our secondary education, but also because we see clearly that failure to strengthen the financial basis of local education inevitably led to Federal operation and control of large segments of our school system. It was the lack of Federal assistance to the local and state school systems that created the necessity for our present system of Federal control. But that fact, so obvious now to the historian, was apparently quite invisible to the contemporary statesman.

Meanwhile, the Congress and the Administration, hearing no strong demand for action from the American people as a whole, refused to grant any funds whatever for education, except certain earmarked emergency funds for wartime vocational training and other special purposes.

The fourth, and last, reason for the incapacity of education during postwar years was the tremendous pressure of the traditional educational program. We have seen in earlier chapters of this history that the American high school began as a means of preparing youth for college and for cultural pursuits. Although its enrollment doubled, redoubled, and redoubled again, during the first four decades of this century, and although its declared purposes had been broadened far beyond college preparation, equally fundamental changes in the secondary school curriculum and in the preparation of teachers were not made. The heroic efforts and revolutionary changes in procedure which the secondary schools made in the national crisis of war could not be sustained in the peace that followed. The slow prewar processes of minor piecemeal adjustment were quite inadequate for a situation requiring extensive changes and prompt, unified action.

In times of peace, this profound discordance between educational purpose and program, between promise and performance, meant that nearly half of the youth of secondary school age left school before graduation and many of those less adventurous spirits who remained on the rolls were able to profit but little by the instruction afforded. Once a young man or young woman left school, the school ordinarily took no further substantial interest in him. It was generally supposed that any youth who was not absolutely feeble-minded could, if he would "apply himself," learn the information and skills which had for generations been the substance of precollegiate education. It was assumed that in some way, not clearly understood, this knowledge would be useful to him in later years. And it was taken for granted that, even if the knowledge so acquired should be valueless or forgotten, the process of acquiring it was, in itself, a wholesome experience. It followed, therefore, that any young person who "dropped out" of school was so clearly at fault that the school could only wash its hands of further responsibility.

This is a severe picture; too severe, no doubt—for even in those schools, there were multiplied thousands of devoted teachers who understood the needs of young people and who succeeded admirably in giving many of them an excellent education. Yet these and other adaptations, made by individual teachers or occasionally by an entire school system, were too slow and too "spotty" in view of the heavy demands which a period of world reconstruction was bound to impose upon the secondary schools of the United States.

The need for public education in the postwar period on the part of large groups of persons who could profit but little from the conventional "courses" which were the chief peacetime offerings of most schools, together with the failure of the state and local school systems to meet the situation, led the Federal government to move into the vacuum.

THE NATIONAL BUREAU OF YOUTH SERVICE

We have seen how the Federal government experimented, in the decade 1933–1943, with various youth-serving and youth-educating agencies. None of these agencies survived during the war, but their experience and precedent made it easy and natural for similar programs to be revived on an expanded scale. The National Bureau of Youth Service was at first created to provide employment for youth, largely on public works projects. To move from work to work experience, from there to vocational training, and from there to related instruction was a series of easy steps. Within a year, so rapidly did the new influence expand, citizenship training, health education, family-life education, and other aspects of comprehensive developmental programs were taken over by the National Bureau. These new national institutions were, for the moment, relatively free from the dead hand of inertia. They announced themselves as ready and willing to provide an educational service to youth in terms of the demands of contemporary life. Being under Federal control, these agencies enjoyed substantial Federal support. This was an asset of no mean importance in the postwar years and, as we have seen, it was an asset stubbornly denied to the state and local school systems.

The new N.B.Y.S. schools soon attracted many recruits to their wide-open doors. There were, besides young demobilized soldiers and war workers, many out-of-school youth, unable to find employment and often rejected or unwanted in their small local high schools. Even many of the "regular" high school boys and girls, especialy those whose families had small incomes, shifted over to the new Federal institutions. Meanwhile, the local taxpaying groups rejoiced to think (as they erroneously supposed) that the school tax burden was correspondingly reduced, because the Federal government paid the bill.

For a short time, the local and state school systems did retain control of the remnants of the war production training program. This activity, which had successfully trained several million workers for the war industries, was converted, on a somewhat reduced scale, to retraining for the industries of peace and the vocational rehabilitation of wounded veterans. Two years after the end of the war, however, these two programs were transferred by executive order to the N.B.Y.S., taking with them also the "Smith-Hughes" program established in World War I.

In vain the then leaders of secondary education pleaded that the establishment of these Federal agencies resulted in the creation of class systems of education, that they involved Federal control over curriculum, personnel, and teaching methods, and that they endangered the very existence of that system of universal secondary education which had so long been one of the characteristics of the American democratic way of life. They could point out all the defects of the new Federal program, but they had, for the most part, nothing sufficiently definite to offer in place of it.

The public psychology that permitted and even encouraged these developments would be a fruitful topic for extended discussion. There was a strange mixture of confusion, indifference, impatience with the slow adaptations of the local public schools, and inability to see the ultimate and inevitable result toward which public policy in education was moving. The ordinary "average citizen" wanted better education for young people. A Federal system seemed to be an easy way to obtain what he wanted, quickly and painlessly. It made little difference to him, he said, how this education was controlled or administered. He was most confused with reference to the effect of Federal financial aid on the local and state school systems. He was inclined to accept uncritically the glib slogan that "Federal aid means Federal domination of schools," although, as we have already seen, just the opposite was really the case. He shrugged off the warnings of the educators by ascribing their opposition to simple professional jealousy. He wanted action in a hurry, and even though getting the job of educational change done with dispatch meant giving up things of great value, he was not inclined to protest. Indeed, he was not even able to see clearly just what the long-term values of local and state control of education were. Each added bit of Federal activity in education seemed desirable and, taken by itself, quite harmless. He was beset by many economic and political problems which seemed, at first glance, far more important than the issues of educational control. When Federalization of education had run its full course, many of these same people were amazed that a series of small concessions could add up to such great and fundamental changes in the whole purpose and conduct of education and in the American way of life itself.

SOME EFFECTS OF FEDERAL CONTROL OF EDUCATION

It is too early as yet to appraise fully the results of the development that has been described in the preceding paragraphs. Some contemporary students of education believe that great harm has been done to education and to democracy. These critics declare that, after the first short period of pioneering and flexibility, the Federal youth program has assumed a rigidity of pattern and procedure that far exceeds the bad effects of traditionalism in the state and local system that it replaced. They say that the old system, with all its shortcomings, could be changed, improved, and adapted to local conditions by means of local experiments and local freedom to try out promising innovations. It is certainly true that local freedom cannot be permitted to exist within the vast and orderly reaches of a single Federal educational system.

These critics also declare that the present system has created unfortunate class distinctions with respect to the education of youth and that it offers a constant and open temptation to the invasion of youth education for partisan political purposes. They point to the alleged scandals of the presidential campaign of 1956 as one of many examples of this danger. They accuse the political party then in office of misusing the power which lay in its hands through control of the education of the majority of American youth. It is officially admitted that courses of study in all matters relating to history, government, and economics were quietly revised, immediately after the 1952 election, by the experts of the N.B.Y.S. in Washington. These new courses were prescribed for nationwide use in the Federal secondary schools, junior colleges, and adult classes in 1954. Strict inspection was established by the Washington and regional offices of the N.B.Y.S. to see that all teachers and youth leaders followed the new teaching materials exactly. Critics of this procedure were curtly informed that the preparation and prescription of such material is an entirely legitimate function of the Federal government. It has, of course, been impossible for the teachers themselves to combat the trend of the times when the Federal government prescribes their qualifications, administers their eligibility examinations, and issues their pay checks.

As the closing pages of this history are being written, this same group of critics is initiating a campaign to restore the former system of decentralized secondary education. It may not be the function of a historian to predict the future, but this writer believes that it is highly improbable that their endeavor will succeed. Great opportunities rarely return, and it would now require tremendous efforts to recover what the majority of educators, school board members, and other citizens of that time let slip from their hands less than a generation ago. Furthermore, the few remaining local high schools of today have returned to their original function of preparing a selected minority of our youth for strictly cultural pursuits. The history of education, like that of all other social services, is punctuated by the ruins of institutions that would not or could not adapt to new and urgent needs. It now appears almost certain that the locally administered high school, for so many years the center of the American dream of equal opportunity through education, has joined the Latin grammar school of the seventeenth century and the academy of the nineteenth in the great wastebasket of history.

The book from which the above paragraphs are quoted has not yet been written.

Whether such paragraphs ever will be written depends upon the effectiveness of educational planning and action, now and in the months immediately ahead. In no area of our life is leadership more greatly needed.

It may be that the future historian will make an entirely different report. He may say that the schools of the nation had anticipated the youth needs of the postwar years; that they were ready to move to meet these needs as they developed; that every state and every large locality had a definite plan for doing so; that the Federal government was at last persuaded to supply adequate financial aid to make this service possible; that the teaching profession was prepared to make the necessary changes in curriculum and administration; that the local organization of education was sufficiently flexible to permit the establishment of secondary schools adequate to the tremendous educational job that waited to be done; and that the secondary schools of America, under state and local control, were transformed into agencies serving all American youth, whatever their educational needs, right through the period of adjustment to adult life.

If, as this Commission firmly believes, the American system of education based on local control and initiative is worth saving, we must begin to save it now. We cannot successfully improvise a program when the war is over. We must plan and act at once or never. If we say to the challenge of the present moment "Not yet," we shall be obliged to say at some future time "It is too late now."

The Farmville Secondary School

A SINGLE INSTITUTION SERVES THE ENTIRE
PERIOD OF YOUTH

In the end, it was decided that the secondary school should include eight grades, from seven through fourteen, and that it should also provide educational services for out-of-school youth and adults. Plans for the educational program were fashioned, taking account—as we shall see in a moment—of the differences between the early and the later years of adolescence. Moreover, it was decided that the new school should serve as the community recreational center and that space should be provided to house other needed community services, particularly a library and a health center. Only after these matters had been agreed upon did the board proceed with plans for the building and for financing the construction.[2] It is four years now since the new secondary school was opened, with Mr. Evans as its principal.

Some 360 pupils in the Farmville Secondary School are in grades 7, 8, and 9. About the same number are in tenth, eleventh, and twelfth grades; for school attendance is now required until the eighteenth birthday.[3] There are eighty students in grades 13 and 14—chiefly boys and girls who expect to remain in Farmville and become farmers, merchants, homemakers, mechanics, office workers, and salespeople. In addition, many young people are served by the school through its program of adult education and recreation.

The entire period of youth is thus encompassed within a single institution. Within the school, one finds no hard-and-fast divisions, but rather a continuous program suited to boys and girls from twelve to twenty, changing with the changing needs and interests of maturing youth, and sufficiently flexible to permit adaptation to students who differ somewhat from the average.

MEETING COMMON AND DIVERGENT NEEDS

Grades 7, 8, and 9 might be called the period of the common secondary school. The educational needs of boys and girls from twelve to fifteen are, on the whole, common to all. Hence the curriculum for these three years is, in its broad outlines, the same for all pupils, though with ample opportunity within each class for the teacher to take account of differences among individuals.

During these early years of adolescence, the pupil continues to grow

2 Plans for the building were subject to approval by the state department of education, since the state law required the state department of education to prescribe and enforce the observance of certain minimum standards in the construction of school buildings. The program of instruction, particularly in the thirteenth and fourteenth grades, was likewise required to meet the minimum standards set by the state department of education.

3 The state law now requires attendance until the eighteenth birthday or the completion of the twelfth grade, whichever is earlier. Productive work outside the school may be counted as school attendance, when it is a planned part of the youth's educational program, and when the school staff supervises the work.

in knowledge and understanding of the world in which he lives; in ability to think clearly and to express himself intelligently in speech and writing; in his mastery of scientific facts and mathematical processes; and in his capacity to assume responsibilities, to direct his own affairs, and to work and live cooperatively with other people. At the same time, he is introduced to a wide range of experiences in intellectual, occupational, and recreational fields, so that he may have a broad base for the choices of interests which later he will follow more intensively. He is helped to understand the processes of physiological and emotional maturing, characteristic of these years, and to develop habits of healthful living. He gains greater insight into his own abilities and potentialities.[4]

In the later years of adolescence—from sixteen to twenty or thereabouts—some of the important interests of individual students diverge. Most striking are the differences in occupational interests. Some youth look forward to farming, some to business, some to mechanical occupations, some to medicine, teaching, nursing, or engineering, some to military service, and some to homemaking. Whatever the interests may be, whether the time of employment be near at hand or still remote, a youth rightly feels that he wants a part of his school experience to advance him on his way to entering the occupation of his choice.

Among older youth, morever, one frequently finds diverse intellectual interests, which are of great significance for education. Here is a boy who enjoys mathematics for its own sake, and another fascinated with literature. Here is a girl who spends many extra hours in the science laboratory because of sheer intellectual curiosity, and another no less devoted to music.

Marked differences also appear in recreational interests, which run the gamut from athletics to reading, from art to woodcraft.

In these three fields—occupations, intellectual pursuits, and recreational interests—the curriculum of grades 10 through 14 is differentiated to suit the needs of individuals. Each student, aided by his counselor and teachers, develops an educational program consistent with his purposes and capacities.

In other fields, however, educational needs continue to be predominantly common to all youth. Most notable is the common need of all youth for education in the responsibilities and privileges of citizenship. Youth also have common needs for education in family living, in health, and in understanding and appreciation of the cutural heritage.

---

[4] Since this volume is a description of the education of youth in their later teens, our references to education before grade 10 will hereafter be only incidental.

In these areas, the curriculum of the upper grades is substantially the same for all students, and adjustments to individual needs and abilities are made within the classes.

Normally the first half of the tenth grade is the time when a student moves on from the common curriculum to the partially differentiated program. As we shall see shortly, this is a time of intensive guidance and planning. No student is compelled, however, to make choices before he is ready to do so, or to postpone his decisions until he reaches tenth grade. Within a flexible program, continuous from grades 7 through 14, it is possible to suit the time of transition to the varying ages at which students mature. There are some youth who, at fourteen or fifteen, are already well started on courses preparatory for occupations or for college. And occasionally one finds a student who, at seventeen or eighteen, has not yet "found himself" and is still pursuing a course designed to help him reach an intelligent decision regarding his future.

Attendance at school, as we have noted, is now required until the completion of twelfth grade.[5] Up to this point, the Farmville Secondary School endeavors to provide educational services for all its students, whatever their plans for the future may be. In grades 13 and 14, however, and in its program of education for out-of-school youth, the school attempts to serve only those youth who expect to remain in Farmville or other rural communities, and who do not intend to study in colleges or universities. All others—those who plan to work in the cities and those who look forward to education in colleges and professional schools—are advised to leave the Farmville School at the end of the twelfth year, and to continue their education in one of the state's eleven community institutes [6] or in a college or university.

Boys and girls in grades 10, 11, and 12 have reached the age (fifteen to eighteen) when youth are thinking seriously about their vocations and their plans for becoming self-supporting. On the basis of careful studies of the local situation, the school staff knows that approximately 40 per cent—fifty youth in each class—should leave the Farmville dis-

---

5 Or the eighteenth birthday, whichever comes earlier.

6 Here, and elsewhere in this volume, the term "community institute" refers to a free public educational institution, offering two years of education beyond the twelfth grade, in a variety of fields, both vocational and nonvocational. For most students, the course in the community institute is "terminal," that is, it marks the end of full-time attendance at an educational institution. Some students, however, move on from the community institute to professional schools or to the upper two years of liberal arts and technical colleges. The community institute also conducts the program of part-time education for out-of-school youth and adults.

trict to continue their education and find their work in the cities. Farmville simply cannot support them. Furthermore, they should leave soon, preferably after completing the twelfth grade, for Farmville has little to offer them in the way of work or education after they are eighteen—and they should not waste precious years in aimless efforts.

But human beings, especially American boys and girls, cannot be expected to conform exactly to desirable statistical patterns. Here is what the boys and girls in the new Farmville Secondary School's three graduating classes have actually done. Of every hundred who have completed grade 12,

18 have continued at the Farmville school through grade 13 only.

24 have continued or expect to continue at the Farmville School through grades 13 and 14.

16 have dropped out of full-time schooling, but have remained in the Farmville district.

16 have gone away to university, agricultural college, teachers college, or liberal arts college—some to return later to Farmville, some to remain away.

17 have gone away to one or another of the state's eleven community institutes, for one or two more years of education before going to work in cities.

9 have gone directly to work in cities, dropping out of full-time schooling.

Who should go to the cities to stay? Who should go away to college or university and come back into rural America to be teachers, doctors, dentists, lawyers, pastors, librarians, nurses, county agricultural agents, home demonstration agents, foresters, farmers, and farmers' wives? Who should stay on in Farmville? And how is this Farmville Secondary School, forty miles from the nearest city of any size, to offer an educational program that will be equally helpful to those who are going to be farmers and village merchants; those who are going to the cities to find jobs in industry, commerce, and transportation; and those who are going on to professional schools of law, engineering, medicine, education, and agriculture? These are some of the questions which the school staff, the board of education, and the parents of the Farmville district have been trying to answer through the program of their school.

The description of the Farmville Secondary School continues, with guidance as the keystone of the school system—". . . personal assistance to individual boys and girls in making their plans and decisions

*about careers, education, employment, and all sorts of personal prob-
lems." The program is one of education suited to individual needs,
preparing youth for occupations, education for civic competence, and
the personal development of youth in such areas as health, family life,
leisure activities, democracy, economic processes, science, and literature
and the arts. The program described also takes into account such things
as general intellectual achievement and character growth. The scheduling of courses and activities is flexible so that different amounts of time
are allocated for different courses and activities, and following joint
planning by the staff. "The schedule is reviewed once each month, and
changes are made as needed."*

*The program is also a continuing one. The responsibility of the
school toward the community does not end when students graduate
from grades 12, 13, or 14. All services of the school continue to be
made available both to out-of-school youth and to adults.*

*Administrative considerations and organization are discussed. The
school plant is a community center. Finally, concern is shown for the
financial burden of public education on the individual student, and
provision is made for equalizing the educational opportunity from a
personal, financial standpoint by an elaborate program of financial
aid to the students administered through the guidance program of the
school.*

*The description of the Farmville Secondary School is brought to a
close with the following narrative.*

Retrospect and Prospect

This completes our review of the activities of the Farmville Secondary School. We have seen that the keystone of the school program is
guidance, a process whereby boys and girls are helped to plan their
own lives in the light of all the facts that can be mustered about themselves and the world in which they live and work. Within this process,
the Farmville school seeks to provide for each youth a program of learning experiences—a curriculum—which in his judgment and in the
judgment of the staff of the school is most likely to meet his particular
needs, abilities, and plans. This program includes preparation for a
useful occupation, education for citizenship, and personal development
for every boy and girl. The entire life of the school is so organized
that the fullest cooperation in the education of youth exists between
the activities of the schools and activities of other agencies in the Farmville community.

It is time now to leave Farmville in order to examine the schools of
a quite different kind of community—American City. Before we move

on, however, there is one fact about the Farmville situation that is of supreme importance. The school staff and the community in Farm-ville are not satisfied with what they have done. They feel that they are making progress, but they know that many problems remain to be solved. They do not look upon their program as the summit of perfection, nor do they regard the Farmville Secondary School as an institution which cannot be altered quickly whenever it may be desirable to do so. This continuing discontent, this lack of com-placency, this eager, forward facing philosophy is perhaps the best summary of the point of view of the Farmville Secondary School, the best explanation for its success so far, and the most hopeful augury for its continued growth and improvement.

A program of education in a city school system is depicted in Schools for Youth in American City. The opening statement follows.

Schools for Youth in American City
(Written five years after the cessation of hostilities)

American City might be any one of two hundred or more cities in the United States. These cities differ from each other at this point and that, but their common characteristics are far more numerous than their differences. They are the nation's centers of manufacturing, trade, finance, transportation, and government. American City represents the third of the nation that is distinctly urban.[7]

In the pages that follow, we shall begin with an overview of Ameri-can City, noting particularly the effects of the depression, the war, and the five postwar years, and the ways in which they have influenced edu-cation. We shall report the progress which the people of American City have made toward achieving better community life through com-prehensive, long-term planning. And we shall inquire particularly about the present conditions of young people from sixteen to twenty-one.

Then—because this is a book about education rather than the life of cities—we shall turn to the public schools and sketch some striking characteristics of youth education in American City today, calling at-tention to the ways in which education has changed in recent years.

This leads to the question: By what processes were these changes brought about? Many readers may be more interested in the processes

---

[7] In 1940, 34.4 per cent of the population lived in cities of 50,000 or more; in 1930, 34.9 per cent.

of change than the products. Therefore, before describing the details of the present program of youth education, we shall tell the story of how this program was developed and of how teachers, administrators, board of education members, parents, youth, employers, labor officials, and many other citizens all had a part in it.

Finally—and this will constitute the greater part of the chapter— we shall tell with some completeness how the three high schools and the new community institute are endeavoring to provide adequate educational services for all the youth of American City and to serve youth beyond high school for a larger region as well.

A major point of emphasis to be drawn from the subsequent descriptions of the city, as it was affected by depression and war with resultant effects on the schools, is that the program of the school is greatly dependent upon prevailing circumstances in society at large, and more particularly the community in which it is located. Joint planning was illustrated as desirable in the formulation of short- and long-term planning and policy development.

The secondary program itself is described in a broad sense in the following manner.

Youth Education in American City Today: Over-All View

Let us try first to see this program as a whole, lest we become lost in details because we do not understand the main features.

THE SCOPE OF SECONDARY EDUCATION

Secondary education in American City begins with grade 7, continues through grade 14, and includes post-high school instruction for out-of-school youth. It covers the ages from twelve through twenty. Although carried on through three institutions—the junior high schools, the high schools, and the community institute—the program is viewed as continuous, and is planned and operated accordingly.

This simple chart illustrates the thinking of American City's educators on the subject.

SOME FACTS AND FIGURES

The three high schools—Washington, Jefferson, and Lincoln—enroll 7,088 local students—all the youth of American City under eighteen years of age save some seven hundred who attend nonpublic schools.

American City System of Public Education

Grades	*Adult Education*	*Ages* *20+*	To liberal arts colleges, techni-cal colleges, and professional schools

Grades		Ages
14	Advanced Secondary School	19
13	(Community Institute)	18
12	Middle Secondary School	17
11	(Senior High School)	16
10		15
9	Lower Secondary School	14
8	(Junior High School) 8	13
7		12
6		11
5		10
4	Elementary School	9
3		8
2		7
1		6
Kdgn.		5
	Nursery School	—5

Secondary Education (grades 7–14), *Elementary Education* (grades 1–6, Kdgn., Nursery School)

In addition, in the high schools there are 386 students who live in suburban areas.[9]

The community institute has 3,787 full-time students: 2,481 from the city, 1,171 from the twelve town and village high schools in Ameri-

[8] In this report, we are concerned with the education of youth from fifteen to twenty. Hence we shall refer to the program of the junior high schools only when necessary in order to understand education in the later years.

[9] Woodland Park, the populous and prosperous suburban community to the north of American City, maintains a high school similar in most respects to the Washington High School in the city. However, youth from this district may attend one of the American City high schools, in order to take advantage of courses in vocational fields not offered in Woodland Park High School. The suburbs to the south of American City have fewer residents and much less wealth. Practically all their youth of high school age attend schools in American City. In each case, the district of residence pays the local district's share of cost of instruction in Ameri-can City. State and Federal funds for public education follow the students.

can City's tributary area of some 3,000 square miles, 135 from the rest of the state. It also offers a wide variety of daytime and evening classes for adults, among whom are 352 youth under twenty-one, who have left full-time school.

CURRICULUM IN OUTLINE

Numbers, however, are not nearly so important as what youth learn in these schools. When we inquire into that, the most striking fact which we meet is that each of the three high schools and the community institute endeavors to meet all of the "imperative educational needs of youth."

Whichever school a student may attend, he will find a balanced program, designed to help him grow in occupational proficiency; in competence as a citizen; in satisfying relationships in family, school, and other personal associations; in health and physical fitness; in discriminating expenditure of money and of time; in enjoyable and constructive use of leisure; and in understanding and appreciation of his cultural heritage. To understand a program with so many purposes, we shall have to examine it more closely.

The staff of each school first of all endeavors to know its students as individuals. This is fundamental to program planning and to teaching. For while the general needs of youth are common to all, the specific needs of each individual are in some respects unique. Later we shall have more to say about guidance and the adjustment of instruction to individual students.

The curriculum of each school includes four divisions of learning, designated as "Vocational Preparation," "Individual Interests," "Common Learnings," and "Health and Physical Education." In addition, there is a tenth-grade course on science, closely related to the course on "Common Learnings." The first two divisions are referred to as the "area of differential studies," since students elect their programs in these fields from a variety of offerings. The last two divisions and the science course are called the "area of common studies" since here all students follow the same general programs. Each student normally divides his time between these divisions, according to the schedule on page 325.

The content of each of these divisions is summarized on the chart. Perhaps these brief statements will suffice for our present purpose of seeing the program as a whole. Later we shall describe each field in some detail. One point, however, should be underlined, in order to avoid possible confusion. The work on Vocational Preparation may be either (1) study, practice, and work experience, intended to equip a youth to go directly to work from high school or community institute, or (2) the study of sciences, mathematics, foreign languages, and other subjects which are part of the equipment for advanced study in the community institute, a four-year college, or a university.

For a student following the usual schedule, vocational preparation will occupy one sixth of his school time in grade 10, one third in grades 11 and 12, one half in community institute. On Common Learnings he will spend one third of his time in each year of high school, one sixth in community institute. Science will occupy one sixth of his time in grade 10. One sixth of his time will be given to health and physical education throughout the five years and the same to individual interests.

PROVISIONS FOR FLEXIBILITY

At first sight, this schedule may seem to be rigid and unyielding—ill-suited to the purpose of serving youth according to their needs. But that is by no means the case. In practice this curriculum is sufficiently flexible to permit almost any student to follow a program "tailor-made" to his needs.

Take first the possible adaptations in the schedule itself. Suppose a student is not ready to make even a tentative choice of an occupational field in tenth grade. He is not required to do so and may elect two courses, instead of one, in a field of avocational, culture, or intellectual interest. Suppose, on the other hand, that a twelfth-grade student needs more than two periods a day for machine shop practice and related training, to get ready for a job which is awaiting him. He may then use the individual interests period for additional vocational education.

Suppose that a student has a strong interest in aeronautical engineering and wants to go to a university school of engineering immediately after twelfth grade. In his vocational preparation time, he can study physics, chemistry, and three years of mathematics; and he may use his individual interests time, if he so desires, for as many as three more courses related to his major interest. Or, take the case of a community institute student who is already reasonably well prepared for employment or for homemaking but wants to learn more about history, economics, literature, or the arts. It is possible for this student to spend two or three periods a day on these interests, instead of one, with corresponding reduction in time for vocational preparation.

More important than flexibility of scheduling is flexibility of class instruction. One result of the long processes of cooperative planning is that teachers throughout the American City schools now endeavor

		High School			Community Institute	
Grades:		*10*	*11*	*12*	*13*	*14*

	1	**Individual Interests** Elected by the student, under guidance, in fields of avocational, cultural, or intellectual interest.	*
	2	**Vocational Preparation** Includes education for industrial, commercial, homemaking service, and other occupations leading to employment, apprenticeship, or homemaking at the end of grade 12, 13, or 14; education for technical and semiprofessional occupations in community institute; and the study of sciences, mathematics, social studies, literature, and foreign languages in preparation for advanced study in community institute, college, or university. May include a period of productive work under employment conditions, supervised by the school staff. Related to the study of economics and industrial and labor relations in Common Learnings.	

Periods per day (average for the year)

3 — **Science** Methods, principles, and facts needed by all students.

4	**Common Learnings** A continuous course for all, planned to help students grow in competence as citizens of the community and the nation; in understanding of economic processes and of their roles as producers and consumers;
5	in cooperative living in family, school, and community; in appreciation of literature and the arts; and in use of the English language. Guidance of individual students is a chief responsibility of Common Learnings teachers.

**

6	**Health and Physical Education** Includes instruction in personal health and hygiene; health examinations and follow-up; games, sports, and other activities to promote physical fitness. Related to study of community health in Common Learnings.

* Broken line indicates flexibility of scheduling.
** Heavy line marks the division between differential studies (above) and common studies (below).

to suit learning experiences within classes to the abilities and needs of individual students.

COMMUNITY INSTITUTE

Before we move on to a detailed description of the program, we should say a few words about the community institute. Here is a new institution, only four years old, yet already enrolling nearly 4,000 students. It was established because the people responsible for educational planning in American City and in the state of Columbia came to the conclusion that a large proportion of youth needed free public education beyond the twelfth grade, chiefly to prepare them for occupations which require training beyond that which is possible in high school, and also to carry them forward in the general education appropriate to free men in American democracy. That these people judged rightly is shown by the school's enrollment.

WHY DO STUDENTS ATTEND THE COMMUNITY INSTITUTE?

1. Some students want to prepare for various technical and semiprofessional occupations which require all the training that high schools can give and one or two years in addition. In this group, for example, are those who wish to become accountants, draftsmen, laboratory technicians, dietitians, assistants in doctors' and dentists' offices, and managers of various businesses.

2. Some want advanced training beyond that which can be offered in the years of high school in the occupations for which high schools provide the basic preparation. Machine shop, metal trades, retail selling, office management, automobile and airplane mechanics, and the various building trades are examples. In one or two years at the community institute, a student is able to extend his mastery of basic operations, enlarge his knowledge of related science and mathematics, secure more practical work experience, and advance in his understanding of economic processes and industrial and labor relations.

3. Some want to prepare for admission to professional schools and the last two years of technical and liberal arts colleges. For various reasons, they prefer to take the first two years of college or university work while living at home. For them, the community institute provides courses comparable to those of the first two years of the four-year colleges.

4. Some want to round out their general education before entering employment or becoming homemakers. To them, the community institute offers a wide range of elective courses in science, social studies, literature, languages, psychology, home economics, music, dramatics, art, and handicrafts.

5. There is yet a fifth group, composed of adults and older youth, mostly employed, who no longer attend school full time, but who wish to continue their education during their free hours. Their interests are wide and varied. Some spring from their daily work, some from their home life, some from their civic activities, some from their uses

of leisure time, and some from the simple desire to "keep on growing." Some enroll in the regular institute courses. Most attend evening classes which are organized especially for them. These classes may meet anywhere in the city, but they are all a part of the community institute program, for this is the school system's agency of adult education.

WHENCE COME THE STUDENTS TO THE COMMUNITY INSTITUTE

The largest number (65 per cent) come from the city itself. But the community institute serves more than the local community. It is the only institution of its kind in an area of some 3,000 square miles, with a population of some 170,000 people, excluding that of the city. Approximately one third of its students come from the twelve high schools of this tributary area.

A few (135 at the time of writing) come from places still more distant. The state department of education has arranged for each of the community institutes in the state to specialize in a few occupations, each of which, for the state as a whole, employs only a few beginning workers each year. The American City Community Institute is the state's training center for the air-conditioning and refrigeration industry and for air transportation. It is also one of two centers each for training in printing and baking and one of three centers for aircraft maintenance.

Some of these out-of-town students commute to their homes. Nearly five hundred, however, live too far away for daily travel to and from school. Residences for students have been erected with state funds, and are operated by the school system on a nonprofit basis. Later we shall see how the institute staff endeavors to utilize the educational possibilities of residential life.

The community institute is located on some forty acres of ground near the center of the city, convenient to transportation from all parts of the city and its suburbs. A part of the cost of the land and buildings (exclusive of student residences) was borne by the state, the remainder by the American City school district.

The description of the secondary program in American City concludes as follows.

TOWARD THE FUTURE

So we conclude this report. We have told of the ways in which youth education in American City has changed in recent years. We have related the story of how those changes were brought about. We have described the main features of the curriculum in the three high schools and the community institute: the courses in Common Learnings and science, the program of health and physical education, the preparation for employment and for advanced study in universities and colleges, and the provisions for students to develop their personal interests. We have told how the program of these institutions is focused upon the particular needs of their thousands of individual students through guidance, flexible schedules and programs, financial aid to students, special opportunities for the gifted, special provisions for the handicapped, and services following the youth from school into adult life. These things we have seen. But we have seen something more.

We have seen that the people of American City—any American city —have within and among themselves the resources for building the educational program for youth which the times demand. We have seen that great advances can be made in a remarkably short time when people resolutely set their minds and hearts to the task. We have seen that the processes through which these advances have come are sound, for they are the processes of democracy, making full use of leadership, yet enlisting widespread participation among the rank and file of the people. We see now that these processes are still in full operation, that the earnest desire to progress has been nourished by each experience of growth, and that each new step forward has yielded a vision of other steps yet to be taken. So we may look to the future with confidence and be sure that the schools will continue to grow in service to all American youth.

The History That Must Be Written

The opening chapter of this book contained an excerpt from an imaginary "history" of the future of American education. In that chapter we described the course which American education is likely to follow if state and local educational agencies fail to plan creatively and adequately, and to act promptly and vigorously, to meet the emerging problems of secondary education. The Commission, of course, hopes that the local and state educational agencies will plan and act in this manner. It believes that they will do so.

We conclude this report on the education of all American youth, therefore, with a contrasting and more hopeful type of "history." This chapter is a prediction of the kind of educational history which we think can, will, and must be written in the future.[10] Here then, for the quarter century from 1925 to 1950, is

---

[10] As in Chapter 1, the hypothetical "history" will be marked by a distinctive type face.

THE HISTORY THAT MUST BE WRITTEN

In 1925 the world was at peace. Armaments were limited by treaty. The League of Nations was meeting regularly. The nations of the world were soon, in the Pact of Paris, to ". . . renounce war as an instrument of national policy." The United States was enjoying the benefit of an unprecedented and growing material prosperity. Production was high. There was work for nearly everyone. Shrewd or lucky investors could reap fabulous profits upon the rising stock markets. The national income was steadily rising to heights hitherto unimagined. Many Americans congratulated themselves that they lived in a golden era, marked by freedom from want and freedom from war.

PROSPERITY AND EXPANSION (1925–1929)

The secondary schools of this era were in the very center of a tremendous program of expansion. Since 1880 their enrollments had doubled every decade. On the material side, it sometimes seemed as though the school architect and the construction industry could scarcely build the high schools fast enough to contain the ever-growing avalanche of young people seeking secondary education. Schools, built but a year or two before to house perhaps 2,000 pupils, hastily readjusted their programs and went on double shifts with total enrollments of 5,000 and 6,000. The typical secondary school building fairly bulged with the effort to find room for the incoming parade of youth.

The task of training teachers for this multitude was equally great. Universities and teachers colleges flourished all year round with huge summer sessions and intersessions for teachers in service and with preservice training for large enrollments during the rest of the year.

There was little time for anyone to stand aside and ponder what type of educational opportunity should be provided for these millions of newcomers to secondary education. It was a period of wild and almost violent expansion in education as it was in industry and economic life. Size was often regarded as a mark of prestige for a school as for a business. Although a few farsighted educators saw that a new educational program was more urgently needed than a larger one, the citizens generally had neither the time nor the inclination to inquire into the deeper meanings of the great social movements which were occurring before their eyes. The energies of those directly concerned with education were devoted largely to just keeping up with the oncoming flood of new students. To be sure, a number of important and useful adjustments were made to adapt the old program more closely to the new needs. When we look back on the difficulties under which the schools then labored, we do not wonder why a more completely successful educational program was not evolved. Rather, we wonder how the harassed teachers and administrators were able to accomplish as much as they did.

DEPRESSION AND RELIEF (1929–1940)

In November 1929 came the great depression which put a painful period to the era of easy money. Investments and savings were wiped out; production and trade figures tumbled downward; the industrialist shut his factory; the workman left his bench; the banks closed their doors. Millions of men and women who had been self-supporting were now out of jobs and desperately seeking employment that was nowhere to be found. The bread lines wound around whole city blocks; the sellers of apples appeared on street corners; the "bonus" army marched on Washington; and the bitter little song, "Brother, Can You Spare a Dime," became a national favorite.

War returned from its too brief banishment. Japan conquered Manchuria. Italy took Ethiopia. The League of Nations failed to act effectively in either case. There were revolutions in Germany, Austria, Spain. The Pact of Paris became another scrap of paper.

In the United States a new administration launched a great campaign to end the depression and to accomplish social and economic changes through governmental action. The Blue Eagle screamed briefly in a million shop windows. The Agriculture Adjustment Act, the Social Security Act, the Securities and Exchange Act, the Labor Relations Act became the law of the land. Through a series of changing organizations, now remembered largely because of the bewildering rotation of their alphabetical symbols, the Federal government tried to meet the needs of the unemployed. There were FERA, WPA, PWA, CCC, and NYA. For those who could not be given work on public projects, there was direct relief in the form of food, clothing, and small cash allowances. Now millions of American citizens, who only a few years ago had thought of themselves as economically secure, depended for daily bread upon the "security wage" of some public works agency or the "family budget" of some relief agency. Stubbornly the depression held on. Not until the end of the decade, when a war-created prosperity made the nation an arsenal of democracy, did large-scale unemployment disappear.

The secondary schools, and indeed the entire structure of American education, were severely and adversely affected by the depression. The enrollments in these institutions continued to gain. Indeed, in many communities, the depression merely gave a further boost to an already steep rate of enrollment increases. But these schools depended, for the most part, upon local revenues, aided by some grants from the several states. These local revenues, based largely on the general property tax, began to dwindle. Many owners of property were unable or unwilling to pay their taxes. Forced sales for tax delinquency increased at an alarming rate. A demand for tax reduction and for constitutional limitations upon local tax rates became effective in legislation in one state after another. Hundreds of schools closed their doors. Almost without exception, the salaries of teachers were sharply reduced to fit the Procrustean limits of diminished revenues. The teachers in many a one-room school and in many a rich American city went to their classrooms month after month without any pay at all.

FEDERAL EMERGENCY ACTION

As long as these conditions endured, the nation was faced by the disgraceful and risky spectacle of millions of youth out of school and out of work. Many youth, ready and eager to work, could not get a first job. Their needs were urgent, insistent. The Federal government had to act quickly, and it did so. It established two Federal youth agencies, the Civilian Conservation Corps in 1933 and the National Youth Administration in 1935. Through them, it spent in the next ten years well over $3,000,000,000. The concern which the national government thus showed for the welfare of the nation's youth excited all but universal approval. It was often said that the youth services were the most popular of the many agencies created by the New Deal, as the early years of the Roosevelt Administration were called. The President and the First Lady both took a lively interest in young people. The latter, especially, took pleasure in visiting the various Federal youth centers, conferring with youth leaders, and generally giving the entire program the benefit of her untiring energy and abundant goodwill.

And yet, while this action by the Federal government was good, it appears, as we now look back upon it, that it was not altogether the wisest course of action that might have been followed.

The Administration seems to have overlooked the great system of local public schools which the American people, over a period of more than a century, had developed to serve their youth. It overlooked the vast resources of 28,000 public high schools and 200 public junior colleges; 300,000 teachers, counselors, librarians, and administrators; and $2,000,000,000 invested in high-school plants and equipment.

It is true that the record of the schools included some faults and failures. Educators had sometimes been insensitive to youth needs and inept in meeting these needs. But, by and large, in the early thirties the educators of the nation were more aware of the youth problem and more eager to do something about it than any other organized group of people in the country. They lacked the financial resources for doing anything on the scale that was needed. Schools were not able to continue even their normal programs. Under the conditions of those days, only the Federal government could supply the funds required for a vigorous attack on the youth problem.

The prestige and power of the national government might have been used to strengthen the established agencies of public education and to lead them forward into greatly enlarged service to the nation's youth. Had this been done, the advancement of youth services as developed through the thirties would have endured. But the Congress and the Administration did not choose to work through the state and local school systems, or perhaps it might be more accurately and more fairly said that the government had no definite and vigorous policy at all with respect to public education. Men and women of extended experience and insight with reference to the public school system of the nation were seldom called into conference by the higher policy-making officials of the government. These educators were in daily contact with the nation's youth. They had the welfare of youth at heart. They were eager to see youth served more adequately. They would have welcomed leadership from the Federal government, for they knew that the problems which had to be met were nationwide. They wanted to regard their Federal government as a collaborator, not as a competitor. But they were not thus recognized or encouraged.

Meanwhile, the two new Federal agencies concerned with young people enjoyed expanding budgets. They began to add education to their employment and relief functions. At last, in 1939, the President himself gave official recognition to the educational function which the Civilian Conservation Corps and the National Youth Administration had assumed. These new Federal agencies, liberally financed by the Federal government, were able to develop ambitious educational and other programs for the youth of the country—programs which were quite beyond the means of the meagerly financed local and state school systems.

This development did not go unchallenged by those who felt that a Federal system of education, by whatever name that educational system was called, was inimical to the best interest of the American democracy. For example, the Educational Policies Commission, an agency established in 1935 by the National Education Association and the American Association of School Administrators, created no small disturbance in the educational world when, in October 1941, it published a document entitled "The Civilian Conservation Corps, the National Youth Administration, and the Public Schools." [11] Herein it was recommended, among other things, that the National Youth Administration and the Civilian Conservation Corps should be discontinued as separate youth agencies; that their functions as agencies of vocational training, general education, and guidance should be continued but transferred to state and local educational agencies; and that their function as public works agencies should be located with the general agency or agencies of public works.

In this highly controversial report, the Educational Policies Commission was addressing itself to the basic issue in the relationship between the state and the Federal government in matters of education. The Commission said that the Federal government ought to provide money to help the state and local educational systems, strengthening and assisting them without exercising control over the processes of education. The Administration, on the other hand, supported by a small minority of educators, apparently felt that the best way to meet these national problems in the field of education was through direct Federal operation and control of educational programs intended to meet the needs of youth.

Both those who favored the Commission's report and those who opposed it agreed that many of the activities conducted by the Federal youth agencies were in themselves desirable educational developments. They agreed that young people who had finished their schooling and were unable to obtain private employment should be given employment upon public works. They

[11] National Education Association and American Association of School Administrators, Educational Policies Commission. "The Civilian Conservation Corps, the National Youth Administration, and the Public Schools." Washington, D. C.: 1941. 79 pp.

agreed on the necessity of providing part-time work for young people in school and college so that they could earn enough money to meet all or part of their expenses in connection with education. They agreed that substantial values had been derived from the CCC camps and the NYA resident projects, although some thought that the educational values in the life of camps and resident centers had not been fully developed. They agreed as to the importance of work experience as an integral part of the educational process.

It may seem, as we review this controversy and survey the large area of agreement, that the whole affair was nothing but a jurisdictional dispute between the schools and the Federal bureaus. In fact, many of the people defending the Federal programs in education did treat the whole matter in these narrow terms.

Furthermore, any criticism of the existing Federal agencies was sure to be either misunderstood or misinterpreted. No matter how carefully the criticisms might be phrased, whoever argued for any other plan of administration than the existing one was almost sure to be tagged as a penurious reactionary who did not really want the youth of the nation to enjoy adequate educational and other services.

Actually, however, the discussion involved a fundamental Federal policy toward the local and state school systems. Would the Federal government aid and support these institutions or would it establish competitive agencies?

The debate proceeded vigorously through 1940 and 1941. In 1942 the matter came before Congress in the form of the appropriations for the National Youth Administration and the Civilian Conservation Corps. After extended and, in the case of the former agency, bitter debate, Congress finally withdrew both appropriations.

The total effect of the rise and brief flourishing of the Civilian Conservation Corps and the National Youth Administration was unquestionably wholesome. These agencies showed clearly that the Federal government could actually operate educational programs with teachers, curriculums, and policies controlled from Washington. Thus they served to dramatize the possibilities and dangers of Federal control of education.

Their positive values have already been noted. They established the principle that Federal funds could be used to good purpose in order to enable students to remain in school. They explored and greatly enlarged the use of work experience in education. They demonstrated that youth employed on public works projects could perform socially useful work. Undoubtedly they saved many youth from idleness and worse and gave them opportunities which benefited both the individuals and the nation.

These agencies, moreover, gave a powerful stimulant to the work of the regular secondary school. They showed that it was possible to provide educational service for many young people, who, for a variety of reasons, were not being served by the schools. Thus they helped to make school administrators and the general public more keenly aware of the needs of all American youth. They sharply called into question the adequacy of the traditional secondary schools. Indeed, their greatest value, over the long run, proved to be the challenge which they gave to the regular secondary schools of the country—a challenge which the public schools, under local administration and with Federal aid, have now accepted and met so completely that direct Federal programs are no longer necessary.

The actions of Congress in 1942 did not settle the underlying issue. They removed the Federal youth agencies, but they gave no assurance of Federal support for an adequate program of youth education in the schools. The question remained: Would the schools be ready when the war was over to offer a comprehensive educational program for all youth with financial help from Federal sources or would the Federal government then reestablish its youth educational agencies? Several events occurred during the war which helped to answer this question.

Undoubtedly, the most important of these events was the passage of the Federal Aid to Education Act. This legislation had been before Congress in one form or another for many years. As far back as 1931, President Hoover created a committee to advise him on the relation of the Federal government to the states in matters of education. The Committee's report, drafted after two years of study, recommended a system of Federal grants-in-aid to equalize educational opportunities among the states. However, no action was taken by Congress or by the President on this document.

The issue could not be thrust aside. A few years after President Roosevelt came into office, he decided to create an advisory committee of his own to restudy this question. This committee, composed like its predecessor of both educators and other citizens, made an extensive collection of evidence. In 1938 it offered recommendations asserting that equal educational opportunity could not be achieved without action by the Federal government to aid the state educational systems and proposing a modest experimental program of Federal grants to education. This document was submitted to the President in 1938 and was subsequently published, together with no less than seventeen volumes of supporting evidence. Again, there was no definite commitment by the Congress, although the President, in an address that summer at the opening of the World's Fair in New York City, told the National Educational Association that he believed in the equalization of educational opportunity through the use of Federal funds.

Public and private agencies continued to study this problem and to reach substantially the same conclusions. The Educational Policies Commission in 1937, the White House Conference on Children in a Democracy in 1940, the American Youth Commission in 1941, the Committee on Intergovernmental Fiscal Relations in 1942, and the National Resources Planning Board just before it ended its work in 1943—all recommended Federal aid to education. Indeed, careful study of the educational documents of the period has not revealed a single serious inquiry into the financing of public education in the United States between the years 1910 and 1940 which failed to conclude that a wider measure of educational opportunity was necessary for the security of the democracy, that certain sections of the nation were unable to finance such education through their own efforts, and that Federal sharing in the support of education was a national necessity.

THE FEDERAL AID TO EDUCATION ACT

As time dragged by without any action by Congress on the matter, the national necessity grew to be a national scandal. At last, the wartime necessity became so clear and the public pressure so overwhelming, that the skilfully organized opposition of minority groups was thrust aside and the Federal government through appropriate legislation tardily recognized that it had definite and immediate responsibilities with respect to the education of its citizens. The law then enacted has been amended from time to time, but it still contains the original provision that no agent of the Federal government shall in any way control the teaching methods, curriculum, or other aspects of the management of the local and state educational systems. This provision has been scrupulously observed.

Since the basic provisions of this Education Act are still in effect, the two purposes of this legislation are well known to all who have contact with the administration and financing of our schools today. First, it provides that the Federal government should allot funds to the states for the purpose of reducing the extreme inequalities in educational opportunity which had existed among the states. It puts a floor under an acceptable minimum program of education for all American youth. When any state, after making a substantial effort and sacrifice from the resources which it can reach by taxation, is still unable to support an adequate minimum program of education, the Federal government uses its vast fiscal resources to make up the difference. The Federal funds for this type of equalization may be expended by the states for elementary, secondary, higher, or adult education; there is no earmarking at all as far as Federal legislation is concerned.

A second purpose of the Federal Aid to Education Act has been to step up the national conception of the size, scope, and value of a complete and adequate educational program for youth. Our modern programs of secondary education exceed the ability of all but the wealthiest states and localities to finance, tax structures and the centralizing flow of wealth being what they are. Local, state, and Federal funds for the support of secondary education have all been considerably increased. The Federal funds, other than those for equalization in general, were at first earmarked for secondary education and had to be spent by the states for this purpose only. More recently, these earmarked funds have been added to the general equalization grant.

The education of American youth now costs between two and three times as much as did the secondary schools of 1940. The number of youth served has increased about 40 per cent. Where about $800,000,000 a year were spent for secondary education in 1940, the nation now spends approximately $2,000,000,000. Congress, however, has not forgotten the days when it was spending upward of $500,000,000 a year merely to train and care for less than 10 per cent of the nation's youth through the CCC and the NYA. Nor have the American people forgotten that the entire annual cost of education would equal only a few days of the money cost of the second World War.

As already stated, the control of education has remained in the states and localities. During the debate on the Act, there were loud declarations from the opposition that such legislation would inevitably be accompanied by Federal control. However genuine these fears may have been, they have been removed by the course of events. We know now that it is entirely possible to draft legislation which appropriates money to the states for education and at the same time forbids any officer or agency of the Federal government to control the educational program.

OTHER FEDERAL ACTIVITIES (UP TO 1946)

The Federal Aid to Education Act was the cornerstone of a whole series of Federal legislative and administrative decisions which have profoundly influenced the course of education. Within two years, the following further activities were begun. Since most of these are still in effect, substantially as enacted or inaugurated, only a listing of them with brief comment will be necessary.

1. *A Federal system of financial aid to help young people meet the expenses involved in attending high school and college.* Funds are usually paid for useful work done by the youth, incidental to his education. The funds are distributed to high schools, colleges, and universities through the appropriate state educational agencies and the U.S. Office of Education. The selection of students to receive aid and the direction of their work and educational experience are handled by the counselors and administrative staff of the local educational system, subject to minimum safeguards against abuse, formulated by the respective state departments of education. In the cases of youth who are unable to work, for reasons of health or other causes, the local school authorities have authority to grant necessary financial aid outright, without work requirements.

2. *The systematic collection, evaluation, and distribution on a national basis of information concerning occupational trends.* In our closely knit economic life, occupational information is inadequate precisely to the extent that it is less than national in scope. Intelligent vocational guidance and training are not feasible without such data. The use of such information is now so commonplace that it is difficult to realize that, less than a generation ago, millions of youth selected occupations and prepared for them without any solid knowledge whatever about future employment probabilities. Although various government agencies have a part in conducting the necessary studies, the information that is of particular use to schools is adapted to their special educational requirements and sent to them by the U. S. Office of Education.

3. *Expansion and strengthening of the U. S. Office of Education.* All during the war the executive branch of the government was so organized and administered that the schools were badgered by materials, questionnaires, directions, requests, and directives from a score of different government agencies. In 1945, however, all Federal educational services were brought to-

gether in the Office of Education, and that agency was staffed with enough capable people to do a good job. It has turned out that this practice costs far less than the total expenditures arising from the previous chaotic, wasteful, and dispersed Federal efforts in educational leadership. And, what is at least equally important, it gets better results.

The recent history of the U. S. Office of Education exemplifies perfectly the power of professional leadership in a democracy to bring about desirable changes in education and to do so without the exercise of compulsion. Foreign educators who have recently visited our country in such large numbers are always amazed to see the accomplishments of the Office of Education and even more amazed to learn that its powers are not conferred upon the Office by legislative orders but are achieved by reason of the competence of its staff, the sound and far reaching research program on which its recommendations are almost invariably based, and the faith which the Office exhibits in the goodwill and good sense of the local and state educational authorities.

In 1945, the Commissioner of Education placed before the President, the Bureau of the Budget, and the Congress a comprehensive and compelling program of educational leadership, thoroughly supported by evidence. It required about a threefold increase in the staff and in the amount of the budget. The educational profession, through the National Education Association and various smaller organizations, gave valuable help in devising and supporting this program. The teachers and the other interested citizens of the nation saw to it that the program received a sympathetic and favorable hearing.

The principal elements of this new program may be summarized as follows:

a. It utilized all Federal services that could contribute to the continuous research, basic to planning an educational program for all American youth. Among these cooperating agencies were those concerned with public health, public works, employment, social security, apprenticeship, child welfare, labor relations, agriculture, and commerce. The Office requested the appropriate Federal agencies to make such studies in the fields of population, migration, employment, industrial, and agricultural trends, and other broad social problems as are necessary to a realistic educational program. These studies now go forward continuously. The pertinent results of such studies are made widely known to educators throughout the nation through a well-directed program of publications, conferences, research, field services, and experimentation.

b. There was created within the Office of Education a strong division of secondary education to study and report the progress made by the states and localities in developing all aspects of a complete program of education for all youth and to render advisory service in this field.

c. Several studies of special importance to the immediate postwar situation were launched at once. One of these was concerned with converting the great war industry training program to peacetime needs and conditions. Another inquiry determined what demobilization policies were likely to be followed by the Army and Navy and studied the effect of these on the schools and colleges. Changes in employment opportunities and qualifications resulting from the increased mechanization of production were studied intensively. Experiences derived from the Army testing and educational programs were thoroughly examined to see what useful conclusions might be found for application in the public schools. Methods of health education, foreign language teaching, citizenship education, safety education, and other fields were brought under constant review by the Office. Information concerning the findings was regularly channeled to schools at all levels and in all parts of the country.

d. The technical services concerned with school buildings were strengthened. Many hundreds of new school buildings were built soon after the war. The Office of Education rendered service of inestimable value in helping local and state authorities to plan these buildings in terms of the educational programs of the years ahead. As a result, a building program which might have "frozen" outgrown educational programs or outmoded systems of school organization for a generation or more has actually helped to bring about a more modern school by supplying a more modern school plant.

STATE AND LOCAL DEVELOPMENTS (1940 TO DATE)

This cooperation by the Federal government, important though it was, could not have been effective without simultaneous action by many other public and private agencies. In one way or another, directly or indirectly, every citizen was involved.

In the years ahead, historians of American education will doubtless write many important monographs on the various phases of the great educational awakening of the 1940's. This volume cannot attempt a full treatment of the subject, partly because we are living too close to the actual events to see them in good perspective, partly because the movement has not yet run its full course, and partly because the infinite variety of the forms of state and local planning and action renders a complete discussion impractical in a brief and general historical account.

We shall, however, mention five of the groups and agencies which have played, and are still playing, a major role in the sweeping educational changes that characterize recent times. These are:

1. The state education associations
2. The chief state school officers
3. The local educational officials
4. The principals and teachers in secondary schools
5. The teacher education institutions.

In addition to these professional groups, a special word should be said regarding the support of citizens' organizations. The changes which have occurred in American education in the past few years could not possibly have been achieved by the efforts of educators alone. Great credit is due to a number of important citizens' organizations and to the devoted interest of their leaders and of members of lay boards of education. Organizations of parents have been particularly influential, notably the National Congress of Parents and Teachers and the state and local parent teacher associations. These fathers and mothers have rightly felt that they have as much at stake in the schools as educators have, and they have made themselves parties to and collaborators in all of the far-reaching changes that have been described. Many citizens who are not parents or who are not affiliated with the parent teacher organizations have also been actively interested. Service clubs; various organizations of women; civic and patriotic societies; organizations of labor, of business, and of farmers; and many of the church organizations might be mentioned and their work praised in detail, if space permitted.

Neither the list of agencies, however, nor the following accounts of what they did are exhaustive.

STATE EDUCATION ASSOCIATIONS

By 1940 the state education associations had arrived at a position of great potential power in their respective areas. They included in their membership nearly 100 per cent of the nation's teachers. Through their journals, they could speak to these teachers every month in the school year. Through the planning and conduct of conventions and institutes they exercised great influence on the thinking and actions of the teaching profession. Their assistance in reorganizing secondary education was indispensable, and it was given unstintingly. They saw to it that their Senators and Congressmen had a clear understanding of the needs in their respective states for Federal aid to education and, what was equally important, of the most effective methods of meeting those responsibilities. They conducted unflagging campaigns to secure state aid for education in amounts that would lift the entire educational service and remove dangerous educational inequalities within each state. Several states had already adopted such systems of support, even as early as 1930. In every case, these systems were enacted and defended largely because of the efforts of the organized teaching profession.

In addition to the support of sound state school finance legislation, the state education associations began a concerted drive to secure a well-staffed, professional department of education in each state. Even as late as 1944 most of the chief state school officers were dependent for their positions on the ups and downs of partisan politics; their terms of office were too short for effective educational planning; the salaries attached to the positions did not, as a rule, properly reward a high type of leadership; their staffs were always small and often subject to political pressure. The state education associations became convinced that we should never have a secure and satisfactory educational opportunity for all children and youth until that situation was changed.

In a few states the professionalization of state educational leadership had come in the twenties and thirties and even earlier. But the shortcomings of the majority of states in this respect tended almost inevitably to act as a drag on all the others.

Even today there remain a few states which cling to the old plan of a weak, politically centered state department of education. But they are not likely to remain long in this category. The example of the majority of the states, with their new professional state education departments, is showing even the most skeptical citizen and legislator that the proposed reforms are in the interest of economy, efficiency, and good educational service.

In addition to championing the financial and administrative improvements, which have just been described, the state education associations were active in many other fields. In a few states, where the state departments were unwilling or unable to initiate planning for youth education, the state associations took the lead. In all states, the associations have cooperated closely with public officials in drafting the necessary legislation and in securing its enactment. They have been particularly useful in the bitterly contested campaigns to raise the school-leaving age to the eighteenth birthday.

STATE SCHOOL OFFICIALS

The chief state school officials themselves were active in improving their own status and possibilities of service. It happened that an unusually large number of the state school officials during the war years were of outstanding caliber. Whether this fact was due to greater public interest in the election of these officers because of the wartime problems of education, or to the influence of critical times in calling forth great educational leadership, or merely to a fortunate combination of circumstances, is a problem which requires further research. Whatever the cause may have been, these forty-eight men and women seemed to have realized keenly that, under the law, they were the directors of the destiny of American education.

While no fundamental change in the theoretical relationship between states and localities in the control of education was brought about, the state departments of education were greatly strengthened in order actually to perform certain functions (to be described later) which, until then, had been theirs only in theory.

The chief state school officers began by insisting that their offices were professional and not political. They acted that way; they reproved anyone else who did not act that way. They insisted that their staffs be professionally selected and paid. They asked that their own positions be made professionally secure and responsible.

In many states the necessary reforms required the tedious processes of amendments to the state constitutions. By now, however, almost all chief state school officers are appointed by nonpolitical state boards of education for terms of at least four years. Political and residential requirements have been abolished. The salaries compare favorably with those of the superintendents of education in the larger cities. The budgets and staffs of the state departments have been made more nearly adequate to the duties incident to a modern program of public education.

In the past ten years, each of the state departments of education has developed certain minimum standards for the local school systems under its jurisdiction. These minimum standards include such matters as the qualifications of personnel; a minimum salary law for teachers; the effort of the local district to support its schools; the safety, sanitation, and general adequacy of school buildings; length of school term; enforcement of attendance laws; interdistrict transfer of students; and the establishment and consolidation of school districts.

All the state departments now contain two relatively new divisions. One of these gives special and continuous attention to studies in school finance and the organization of school districts. Upon the basis of such studies, recommendations have been made to many of the governors and state legislatures concerning changes needed in the financing and organization of education. The present program of secondary education would have been quite impossible without greater participation by the states in the support of education and without legislation which creates local school districts suited to modern conditions and needs.

The other new division keeps in close touch with the secondary education division in the U. S. Office of Education, surveys the occupational conditions and trends in the state, and plans a comprehensive secondary school program. In some states this program had involved an extension of existing systems of junior colleges under the boards of local junior college districts; in others, the establishment and development of new types of schools for youth, sometimes with an agreed-upon specialization of certain institutions in certain vocational fields; in still others, the development of regional technical schools or institutes under state control. In every state, the program has included the development of a statewide system of guidance for youth, operated by local educational systems, but coordinated by the state department of education.

LOCAL EDUCATIONAL OFFICIALS

The history of the activities of local boards of education and administrators in developing our modern program of secondary education is complex. The outward events can be observed and recorded; the changes in loyalties and points of view which gave significance to these events are extremely difficult to define.

Two concepts which gained currency among local educational officials between 1940 and 1945 played a critical and perhaps a determining role in deciding their courses of action.

One of these was the concept that organized public education is an expression of state policy even though its administration is handled locally. The provision and management of public education in the United States had always been primarily a responsibility of the state department. The Federal Constitution clearly implies this; each of these states recognizes that responsibility in its constitution and statutes.

Local school districts are creations of the state, and local officials have a legal and moral responsibility for the provision of educational opportunity to all the children of the state who need the services of education which the local district can supply. Recognition of this fact did not lessen the responsibility of the local board member to the district whose citizens elected him to office, but it did throw a new light on the way in which that responsibility could be met. Local boards of education and school superintendents began to talk less about the local freedom to manage their own educational programs and more about the local duty to assist in developing and conducting the over-all program of education in the state. This point of view had been in the making for a long time. There was nothing particularly novel about it when at long last it achieved rather general acceptance in the mid-1940's. Nor was it adopted on charitable or humanitarian grounds, for any local board of education could see that it had a direct interest in the education of youth everywhere in the state and, indeed, in the United States as a whole.

The second fundamental concept in the point of view of local school officials was the recognition that their job was not merely schooling, but education. The older conception, which is now being rapidly replaced, is well illustrated by the fact that, although most of the local boards were and are officially entitled "board of education," the common language, up until very recently, used the expression "school board" without regard to the legal title. Nowadays, however, the term "board of education" is coming into more frequent use both legally and in ordinary speech. Likewise, the term "superintendent of schools," although still commonly used, is gradually being replaced by the expression, "superintendent of education."

As changes in vocabulary, these are neither important nor universal. They do represent a fundamental change in American thinking about what a local agency for education should be doing. In other words, local school boards have become public educational authorities, offering a program which includes academic, vocational, and leisure-time activities for people of all ages who may profit by participation in it. They have broadened this program to adapt it to the needs of older youths and adults. They have developed close coordination of schools, libraries, and recreational services under qualified and responsible leadership. They speak of "educational centers" at least as often as they do of "school buildings" and they recognize that schooling is only one part of the total educational experience.

These were certainly not novel ideas. They have been held by many a philosopher, statesman, and educator. It was in the years 1940–1945, however, that they became the accepted currency in the interchange of thinking about the administration and purposes of American education. Not that the great majority of educational officials recognized that their theories were undergoing a profound change. It would be impossible to state in some cases whether the change in practice resulted from a change in theory, or vice versa. In any case, many of those who were quite active in the total program of planning for a better educational system for youth and in putting that program into effect remained largely unaware of the theoretical implications of their own actions. Nevertheless, the climate of opinion was important even though those affected were not fully conscious of it.

The preceding paragraphs may perhaps seem to resemble an educational philosophy rather than a sober account of events suitable to a history of education. However, the widespread acceptance of such new points of view is, in itself, a historical event of first importance. An understanding of these viewpoints is necessary if one is to follow what happened to our local school systems in the late 1940's.

The events themselves are not spectacular. Only when we understand that the developments in each local community were part of a great national revival in education do we sense the importance of the sum total of a series of changes that were made in one educational system after another.

For instance, agitation for larger districts of administration in the rural areas had been going on in the United States for at least half a century. Progress had been slow. Suddenly, the acceptance of the principles enumerated above broke through the barrier of inertia and prejudice. It seems incredible now that even in 1940 there were over 100,000 independent administrative units for education in the United States. The 10,000 districts which we now have are the results of combinations and consolidations. So strong was the influence of example and of the new feeling of responsibility that, even in states where the law did not at first compel the local units to consolidate, much well-considered consolidation occurred. Local boards and educational officials began to see that, as state officers, they could not honestly continue to operate inefficient arrangements for education. Some states adopted the county as the unit of educational administration. In most states, however, natural community areas for educational authorities were created to take the place of the old, arbitrary, political subdivisions which often had little or no meaning for the service of education.

Many of the events and decisions in these local communities were so minor that one hesitates to mention them in a general history of American education. The decision of a local board of education in a small town to hold a special meeting every two weeks for the express purpose of planning youth education and youth service in the commuity does not in itself seem to be a world-shaking event. Yet such little acts, multiplied ten thousand times over, did much to give us the educational system we now possess. It does not seem nowadays that it would require profound insight and imagination for a local board of education to consult with employers, labor unions, business organizations, social agencies, farmers' groups, parent organizations, voluntary youth groups, employment services, veterans' groups, service clubs, professional societies, church organizations, and the local organizations of teachers in planning its educational program. Today we regard such community-wide consultation as a perfectly natural part of the democratic process. Yet only a few years ago such consultation was rare. When it occurred; it was marked by a certain self-consciousness and formality on the part of all concerned. Only a few years ago it would have seemed an exciting novelty for a superintendent of education to make a systematic collection of information regarding employment trends, occupational opportunities, and educational qualifications for employment in the community it was serving. As long as the school was isolated from the life of the community, it would, of course, be natural for the school to be quite unconcerned with the vocational aspects of community life.

Another important result of the change in the thinking of the local educational officials was their attitude toward the financing of education. During the years of the depression, a certain habit had become rather firmly established in the thinking of educational administrators. Whenever they were confronted with a desirable new educational service, they usually asked, first of all, whether the money could be secured. When the answer to that question was not immediately available, the flow of creative ideas was blocked. The experiences of the war, together with the changes in educational theory which have already been described, fortunately broke that habit. The local officials turned the spotlight on the services to be rendered to the youth and on the economic, social, and other values to the community which would accrue from these services. When a desired program seemed to have a cost which put it beyond the immediate reach of the community, that fact alone did not thwart their determination to proceed as far and as fast as possible. Of course, they did not allow themselves to float completely away from reality. Somewhere in the process of their planning, they always made careful estimates of the cost of various parts of the program. But these estimates were not allowed to become the initial or the chief consideration.

As a result of this general change in attitude, many boards of education found that funds were forthcoming for a bold and practical program that gave promise of squarely meeting widely recognized community necessities. They found that public reluctance to supply money for education often arose from a lack of vigorous leadership. They found that, if they spent all the money they had as wisely as they could and then asked for the amount required to finish the job, they could often obtain funds in amounts which had hitherto been quite unavailable.

The building program, of course, occupied a considerable part of their attention. Sites available for new school buildings were located and purchased during the war, or options were obtained upon them for later purchase. Plans for the new buildings were ready for use when the war ended, and these plans were definitely related to the type of educational program for the community which the best educational statesmanship of the time could devise.

One of the most difficult of the local problems, and one which is still far from a complete and satisfactory solution, is that of providing an opportunity for youth to get an experience in the world of productive work. There has been considerable resistance to this idea on the part of both employers and labor leaders. Provision for such experience has meant in some instances a slightly lower productive efficiency. It often requires modifications of employment rules and customs. In spite of all the difficulties, however, both employers and leaders of organized labor are coming to realize that they cannot shut off young people from vocational life without grave personal and social consequences. Some communities have had success with a plan which reserves certain areas of work in which youth should have first opportunity. Gradually, but surely, an adequate supply of work experience jobs, as well as of opportunities for civic experience and participation, is being found for youth in all local communities.

A final comment regarding the local educational leaders must mention the programs for improving the teachers in service. It is estimated that at least a third of our present secondary school staff was employed in educational service during the second World War. In the cities the proportion is perhaps half. Consequently, fundamental alterations in the educational program would have been impossible without continuous improvement of those already on the job. Teachers have been given opportunity to vary from established procedures. Skilled and sympathetic supervisory leadership has been provided. Attendance at university summer schools, which was so general in 1920 and 1930, continued to be popular, but this is now less important in most high schools than the work of active curriculum revision committees and organized professional programs of reading, observation, and discussion. Practically all of the larger city-school systems, and some of the state school systems, have organized summer workshops on specific educational problems.

The institutions for the preparation of teachers have also been helpful. They turned with new vigor after the war to the task of in-service education. They made sure that the members of their own staffs were in constant and stimulating contact with the actual problems of teaching, administration, and research in the public school systems of their region. They made, and are still making, constant effort to adjust their programs of in-service education to meet the problems which teachers and administrators actually face in the secondary schools. This has required in many institutions a rather drastic revision of existing courses and arrangement of schedules. Some institutions have offered instruction off campus and at hours not commonly covered by the traditional school days. There has been a considerable expansion of arrangements in many institutions whereby educational leaders offer instruction to prospective teachers on a part-time basis, and some teachers colleges have even assigned members of their staffs to half-time field work with the school systems in their vicinity.

SECONDARY SCHOOL STAFFS

Principals and teachers in the secondary schools constitute another group to which reference must be made in any account, however brief, of the history of American secondary education since 1940. During the war, the majority of these professional workers came to understand that they were privileged to be serving the nation in one of its great creative periods. They realized that if they resisted all change, that if they spent their energies defending traditional curriculum interests, they could not stop change from coming but could only stop it from coming their way. They decided not to allow the currents of history to bypass them.

One of the first activities in many secondary schools was a careful staff study of the occupational life of the community. The teachers realized that the dominant interest of the great bulk of the youth in their charge was getting a job and becoming economically independent. They therefore took pains to become informed about opportunities for employment in the community, and the schools established definite arrangements whereby young people could secure part-time work experience which would yield both financial and educational returns and which might ultimately lead to gainful employment on a full-time basis.

Second, they became concerned about all the youth of the community—not merely about those who happened to be enrolled in the schools. This change of viewpoint can be illustrated by an example. In 1935, if a student came to a certain high school late some morning, he was asked for an excuse. But if, he did not come to school at all, and if he were beyond the compulsory attendance laws, nothing whatever happened. The school was much interested if he came late; it was usually entirely disinterested if he stayed away completely. Now, in this same school, the teachers make it their business to know why a young person leaves school. Merely to cross his name off the high school register without further reflection, and perhaps even with a sigh of relief, would now be regarded as a distinct lapse of professional duty.

The third line of action was related closely to the second. It consisted of the inauguration of systematic methods for obtaining information about all former students of each high school. Ever since the establishment of the American high school, the typical institution had taken great pride in the college records of its graduates. It seems almost incredible to us today, but it is nevertheless a fact that, before the war, there was scarcely a single high school in the country which had reliable information about the vast majority of its former students who did not attend college. Whether such youth were well adjusted in their occupational and home life; whether they continued their own personal cultural development; whether they were reasonably active in the discharge of their civic duties—all this was absolutely unknown territory to the faculty and administration of the secondary school. Nowadays such information is collected as a matter of course and is used constantly as a key to individual guidance, curriculum adjustment, and public relations.

A fourth line of action, which has been widely developed in recent years, has resulted, in nearly all of our secondary schools, in the establishment of programs which seek to make education completely open and available to all who can profit by it. Some city school systems have special local endowments which are available for meeting the needs of those whose education might otherwise be terminated because of lack of funds. These endowments are, of course, powerfully supported by the Federal and state systems of grants-in-aid to students.

The origin of this line of action goes far back in American educational history, but the chief reason for its almost universal application at present is to be found, more than anywhere else, in the policies adopted by the Federal government with regard to the higher education of soldiers during the war and of veterans afterward. So great was the need for qualified and trained manpower in the war that the Federal government established what amounted to a system of Federal scholarships for training young men for technical and officer's work in the Army and Navy. Hundreds of colleges were enrolled in this program. The selection of students was made without reference to the economic ability of the individual. If a young man could demonstrate his ability to profit by training in a field of national need, all of his college expense was paid for by the government. It was natural and fairly easy, therefore, to make a transition to a peacetime application of the same principle. In fact, this was done by the Federal government during the war by the enactment of legislation to support the education of demobilized service men and women.

A fifth area of operation has been the achievement of a larger amount of unity and cooperation among teachers of the different subjects. If any of us could turn the flight of time backward in order to visit a high school of the early 1940's, he would probably be surprised to see the large amount of time given by members of the staff to the defense of "their" respective subjects. One might even have found instances (not common, it is true, but nevertheless symptomatic) of schools which could not introduce necessary new subject matter into the program because it was impossible to reach an agreement as to the department which should be responsible for giving the instruction. Only in comparatively recent years have the teaching staffs of our great secondary schools set themselves free from this bondage. For example, the close cooperation which now exists between vocational and nonvocational teachers was rarely found, even as recently as ten years ago. False and harmful cleavages have now been largely overcome. A comprehensive effort has been going forward to attach a sense of worthiness and dignity to all forms of socially useful labor.

Along with this change, of course, came a departure from the tradition of the high school as a college preparatory institution. Here again, in order to sense the great shift that has occurred, it is necessary for us to imagine ourselves in what almost amounts to another educational era. It is literally true that, less than a generation ago, the American high school was dominated by the supposed requirements of the colleges, even though only a very small proportion of its graduates then went on to college. Long after most of the colleges had ceased to require detailed subject matter patterns for admission, the practice of giving only book-centered, academic instruction to the great majority of high school students persisted. We have recognized since the beginnings of higher education in America that the students who go on to college are an exceedingly important group whose education must be provided with great care. But we have more recently come to recognize that the larger group which does not take college education has a claim on secondary education equivalent to that of the minority who are college bound.

Still another area of change in the high school has been the educator's growing concern for the total welfare of the young people of the community both during school hours and when out of school. In 1940 the Educational Policies Commission of the National Education Association, in a study of citizenship education, concluded that few, if any, schools have yet erected broad and permanent highways whereby they are inseparably united with their communities.[12] The Commission was able to find only a handful of schools in the entire United States which were not "pedagogical islands" cut off by deep channels of convention from the world which surrounded them.

One of the Commission's staff was amazed to hear the principal of one of these schools say: "In this school, we are really concerned with the total experience of our students. If a student has an unsatisfactory home life, we do not just deplore it; we try to think of some way to help. If his health is bad, we try to arrange to have that improved, either through our school health services or in other ways. If the recreational life of our community is mean and tawdry, we try to provide a better kind of recreation for our young people. If we cannot do that ourselves, we do our best to persuade others to do it. We are not always successful. We have to avoid becoming unwelcome busybodies. But we are absolutely sincere when we say that what affects the happiness and welfare of the young people of our community is of direct and vital concern to our staff."

That such a statement of policy could be regarded as at all unusual, even in 1940, indicates how rapidly our educational philosophy and program have developed in recent years.

THE EDUCATION OF TEACHERS

The institutions for the education of teachers and their staffs were closely connected with the developing program of youth education. Before the war, the teacher education institutions and the public school systems had found themselves caught in a circle which prevented rapid educational progress. The boards of education and school administrators, who employed the graduates of the teachers colleges, declared that the institutions were preparing teachers only for traditional programs of education, and that modern programs could not be developed because the teachers were not available. To this the educational institutions retorted, and with some justice, that they could not be expected to prepare teachers for positions that did not exist. It was evident that this circle must be broken by simultaneous action on the part of both the teacher-training institutions and the school systems in their vicinity. An important influence in this direction was supplied by the Commission on Teacher Education of the American Council on Education, which was active from 1938 to 1944.[13]

---

[12] National Education Association and American Association of School Administrators, Educational Policies Commission. *Learning the Ways of Democracy.* Washington, D. C.: the Commission, 1940. 486 pp.

[13] Commission on Teacher Education of the American Council on Education, Washington, D. C. 1944 and 1945. *Teachers for Our Times,* by the Commission on Teacher Education; *Evaluation in Teacher Education,* by M. E. Troyer and C. Robert Pace; *Teacher Education in Service,* by C. E. Prall and C. L. Cushman; *The College and Teacher Education,* by W. E. Armstrong and E. V. Hollis; *Helping Teachers Understand Children,* by the staff of the Collaboration Center in Child Development, and other volumes dealing with the Commission's all-state programs (by C. E. Prall), with the preparation of college teachers (by E. V. Hollis), and with the Commission's conclusions and recommendations.

The developments of in-service education for teachers have already been mentioned. Some of the changes that have occurred since 1940 in the pre-service education of teachers may be summarized in the following terms:

1. There was a great strengthening of instruction in educational psychology, individual differences, human relations, adolescent psychology, human growth and development, and educational guidance and counseling. The institutions have recognized that the new secondary school must serve all American youth and that the teachers in that school need to understand all youth much better than the ordinary secondary school teacher understood them, say in 1920 or 1930. The constant effort has been that this understanding should spring, not only from a general feeling of goodwill, comradeship, and sympathy, but also from the best insight which science can supply regarding the ways in which human beings differ from one another, the ways in which they grow toward maturity, and the methods by which the teacher can achieve understanding of the individual students in his charge.

2. The study and teaching of school and community relations and of educational sociology were greatly strengthened. Prospective teachers were given more close firsthand contacts with other community institutions as well as with the schools. Since the great task of the new secondary school was seen as the development of good citizens, it was recognized that the teachers would not be effective in this task unless they themselves were active, informed, and effective members of society. Likewise, teachers who are to induct youth into occupational life through work experience should themselves have some work experience in employment other than teaching. Many school systems now give preference in employment to those teachers who have had such experience.

3. The expansion of the school program in the fields of guidance and vocational training has resulted in a parallel expansion of the program for preparing teachers in these fields. Many teacher education institutions immediately after the war gave special types of training to men and women who had been successfully teaching or doing personnel and counseling work in the various war industry training programs and in the Army and Navy. Many of these people have become excellent teachers and counselors in the school of today.

So much for the "history" of what must happen in American education.

The Commission wishes to add a few words of comment. We address these words, not to the teacher, the labor leader, the businessman, the parent, the taxpayer, but rather to all of them in their common capacity as citizens of the United States.

HOW GENUINE IS OUR INTEREST IN YOUTH

In the building of our country's future, the education of our youth comes first. The war has reminded us of many virtues and ideals that we had forgotten. One of them is the duty we owe to our children in the provision of their education, not education merely in terms of books, credits, diplomas, and degrees, but education also in terms of living and of preparation for future living.

Look about you. See what we now, in wartime, find it necessary and proper to do for our young men and women in the armed forces. Every one of them is taught some specific occupation, useful to him and to the nation. The health of all of them is zealously guarded by every resource of medical science. Their diet is ample and nutritious. There is useful work for each one of them. Opportunities for their recreation are provided everywhere. They are well clad and cleanly housed, well fed and carefully educated. We compete among ourselves to see to it that they have books to read, music to hear, space to play. We stay at home that they may travel. We deny ourselves that they may have abundance. Their morale and their civic loyalty are our constant concerns. The uniform which proclaims them Americans is the complete and sufficient guarantee everywhere of just and considerate treatment for all American youth. This all costs time, effort, sacrifice, thought, and a great deal of money. But we would be properly ashamed to consider convenience when their welfare is at stake.

Shall these young people and their successors in the onward moving generations be less precious to us when the firing ceases? Is our concern for their welfare, health, education, merely a selfish reflection of our desperate need for their youthful energies and lives on the field of battle? Are we going to forget youth as soon as we no longer need them to fight in the war which we allowed to happen? Where we now teach them how to work, shall we later tell them that their services are not wanted? Where we now assure them that the future of our nation lies in their keeping, shall we later tell young people, in effect, to keep out of civic affairs? Where we now provide college education for all persons qualified for leadership, shall we later return to college education as an economic privilege? Shall we, as soon as peace comes, declare an end to all hopeful cooperation for the welfare of our youth? Shall we then pinch the pennies for peace where we now deal out dollars for destruction?

The program here proposed will cost much more than the inadequate education of the past. There is no doubt of that. But consider this—if we make our economic system work even reasonably well after the war, we shall have a national income of around 110 billion 1940 dollars. Experts who have studied such matters tell us that, with such an income, we will spend:

25 billion dollars for foodstuffs, as compared with 16 billion in 1936

16 billion dollars for housing, as compared with 9 billion

13 billion dollars for household operations and equipment, as compared with 6.5 billion

8 billion dollars for automobiles, as compared with 4 billion

8 billion dollars for clothing, as compared with 4 billion

3 billion dollars for recreation, as compared with 1.6 billion.

Shall we, under such conditions, refuse to increase the 2.5 billion dollars which we have been spending for schools and colleges to educate children and youth of all ages? Shall we, with the highest per capita income of any nation in all history, use our increased wealth to feed, clothe, and house the adults in comparative luxury and neglect to spend any of our increase for the improvement of the education of our children and our youth?

Would you like your children to attend schools like those of Farmville and American City? They can, if you really want them to. Enough is known about how to operate such schools, there is plenty of timber and stone to build them, plenty of wealth to finance them. Your children, your community, your entire state and nation can have schools as good as, or better than, the schools described in this book as soon as you and enough other Americans demand them and do your own special but essential part in bringing them into existence.

THE HARVARD REPORT [14]

General Education in a Free Society was published in 1945. It was the work of a Committee appointed two years earlier by James B. Conant, then president of Harvard, and named the "University Committee on the Objectives of General Education in a Free Society." The Committee were nine members of the faculty of Arts and Sciences and three members of the Graduate School of Education, and were chaired by Paul H. Buck, Dean of the Faculty of Arts and Sciences and Professor of History.

In the Introduction, Mr. Conant quotes from his communication to the Board of Overseers in which he informed them of the appointment of the Committee.

The heart of the problem of a general education is the continuance of the liberal and humane tradition. Neither the mere acquisition of information

[14] Harvard Committee, *General Education in a Free Society*. Cambridge, Mass.: Harvard University Press, 1945, pp. vii–ix.

nor the development of special skills and talents can give the broad basis of understanding which is essential if our civilization is to be preserved.

No one wishes to disparage the importance of being "well informed." But even a good grounding in mathematics and the physical and biological sciences, combined with the ability to read and write several foreign languages, does not provide a sufficient educational background for citizens of a free nation. For such a program lacks contact with both man's emotional experience as an individual and his practical experience as a gregarious animal. It includes little of what was once known as "the wisdom of the ages," and might nowadays be described as "our cultural pattern." It includes no history, no art, no literature, no philosophy. Unless the educational process includes at each level of maturity some continuing contact with those fields in which value judgments are of prime importance, it must fall far short of the ideal. The student in high school, in college and graduate school must be concerned, in part at least, with the words "right" and "wrong" in both the ethical and the mathematical sense. Unless he feels the import of those general ideas and aspirations which have been a deep moving force in the lives of men, he runs the risk of partial blindness.

This was the substance of the Committee's concern. General education was that provided in common to all, as distinguished from the specialized aspect of education which was different for different persons. In effect, the Harvard Committee was addressing itself to the same problem that others had pondered, and which had been expressed in other reports. The Harvard Report differed in one fundamental respect from most of the others, however. It rejected the crossing of traditional subject matter lines and rested its case on the belief that the conventional subjects could be made to lend themselves to the objectives of general education if they were taught in lively, imaginative ways designed for the purpose.

The Harvard Committee was not in disagreement with others on the destination. The difference lay in the road chosen to reach it.

LIFE ADJUSTMENT EDUCATION

We have not included excerpts from Life Adjustment Education for Every Youth. However, a book such as this would not be complete without reference to it. The origin of the concept of life adjustment education is not generally known, and in fact, the program associated with it was not well defined. It grew more out of the statement of a problem than it did from an attempt to devise a program of education. Part of its importance rests on the fact that the phrase "life adjustment" was seized upon by critics to cast doubts in the public mind about the condition of the secondary schools.

At the time the Harvard Committee was completing its work, another group was also bringing its work to final form. This one, sponsored by the Vocational Division of the U. S. Office of Education, was considering the question of "Vocational Education in the Years Ahead." At the final conference on the question Charles A. Prosser presented a resolution.

It is the belief of this conference that, with the aid of this report in final form, the vocational school of a community will be able better to prepare 20 per cent of the youth of secondary-school age for entrance upon desirable skilled occupations; and that the high school will continue to prepare another 20 per cent for entrance to college. We do not believe that the remaining 60 per cent of our youth of secondary-school age will receive the life adjustment training they need and to which they are entitled as American citizens—unless and until the administrators of public education, with the assistance of the vocational education leaders, formulate a similar program for this group.

We therefore request the U.S. Commissioner of Education and the Assistant Commissioner for Vocational Education to call at some early date a conference or a series of regional conferences between an equal number of representatives of general and vocational education—to consider this problem and to take such initial steps as may be found advisable for its solution.

From this resolution evolved in time the document Life Adjustment for Every Youth, which appeared in mimeographed form in 1947 and as a printed publication of the U.S. Office of Education in 1951. Essentially, it called attention to the fact that the secondary schools were failing to provide a meaningful education for a large segment of young persons who could not manage to succeed either in the conventional college preparatory program as then taught nor in the high-skills program offered in vocational education. The proposal called for a practical approach to a curriculum for such pupils, using everyday problems centered around such objectives as citizenship, home and family life, wise use of leisure, health, consumer education, working competence in the basic tools of learning (speaking, writing, practical arithmetic), consideration of ethical and moral questions, and work experience leading to occupational adjustment and competencies.

Life Adjustment Education, a name that was unfortunate in that it lent itself to ridicule from those who were so inclined, withered under the fire from critics and disappeared as a topic of discussion. All that remains is the problem to which the Prosser Resolution called attention, and which still awaits an answer.

EPILOGUE

 The reports contained in this book reach to the end of the 1940's. If the ideas had died with the reports, the book would have only historical significance, but, as we shall see, the questions raised and the issues defined are still relevant—and, to a great extent unresolved.

Beginning with the late 1940's, the schools began to come under fire from a number of critics who directed their attacks against what they considered to be progressive education. The charges leveled, however, covered a range that far exceeded the limited target of progressivism as interpreted by the critics.

In the early 50's, Arthur Bestor, formerly a faculty member of Columbia's Teachers College and at the time a professor of history at the University of Illinois, wrote among other things Educational Wastelands: A Retreat from Learning in our Public Schools (1953), the title of which speaks for itself. Bestor is representative of the more unrestrained criticism of the era. His theme was primarily a call for return to the "academic disciplines," and a belief in the function of education as "teaching people to think." About the same time Albert Lynd's Quackery in the Public Schools appeared as did Robert Hutchins' The Conflict in Education. Many others, including free-lance writers who recognized a promising field, turned their efforts to taking the schools to task.

In spite of the acrimony of many of the debates of the 50's, and the sting of some of the criticism, the White House Conference on Education called by the President of the United States in 1954 seemed to echo many of the thoughts expressed earlier in the reports included in this book. In making the call, the President invited all people to join in "the most thorough, widespread, and concerted study the American people have ever made of their educational problems."

Preceding the Conference in Washington, sectional and state conferences were held in every state in the Union. In most instances, delegates to the White House Conference were chosen by their peers from among those taking part in the conferences within the various states. It was estimated that half a million persons representing a fair cross section of the population took part in sectional, state, and national conferences. In addition, 283 national organizations with an interest in education were represented at the Washington Conference. The two thousand persons delegated to go to Washington convened on November 28, 1955, and for five days went through concentrated discussions and reporting.

The full report of the Committee on the White House Conference on Education was issued in April, 1956. The Committee took a long look at what it described as the expanding role of education which had developed in the preceding two decades and asked if this broadening of goals should be recognized as legitimate.

"Nothing was more evident at the White House Conference on Education," the Committee reported, "than the fact that these goals, representing as they do an enormously wide range of purposes, are the answer to a genuine public demand. The overall mission [of the schools] has been enlarged. . . . The order given by the American people to the schools is grand in its simplicity: In addition to intellectual achievement, foster morality, happiness, and any useful ability. The talent of each child is to be sought out and developed to the fullest. . . . This new ideal for the schools is a natural development in this country. It recognizes the importance of the individual in a free society." The Committee answered the question it raised as follows: "This great new goal of our schools is unanimously approved."

The following year, on October 7, 1957, Russia launched a metal object, named Sputnik, into outer space. What followed, so far as the *schools were concerned, bordered on the incredible. The country was alarmed at the failure of the United States to be first in the space race. This failure took on the appearance of a national humiliation, as the mass media brought its resources to bear upon the matter. Early criticism was directed at the President, the Congress, the military and the space officials. Suddenly, the accusing finger pointed in a new direction. The failure to be first in space was the fault of the schools—not the colleges and universities where, presumably, space scientists and engineers were trained—but of the elementary and secondary schools. Life (magazine) turned over its pages through several issues to the subject, aiming heavy broadsides at the secondary schools. Reporters and photographers visited the Soviet Union to observe their schools. Official delegations followed with the same purpose in mind. Television produced documentaries. Congress passed the National Defense Education Act in 1958, with a crash program in science, mathematics, and foreign languages. Many persons found it difficult to associate the call for more work in languages, which turned out to be mostly French and Spanish, with national defense, but the times did not favor rational questions.*

A new critic, Admiral Hyman Rickover, appeared and was accorded considerable television time and much newspaper and magazine space. Rickover looked with favor on European secondary education, selective and specialized, and urged the creation of special secondary schools for a special group of American youth.

Demands for aid from the Federal government presumably to strengthen weak areas vital to the space effort, and to national defense, increased, and resulted in a large amount of legislation, almost all of which provided funds for particular kinds or aspects of education. Categorical aid to schools increased. Grantsmanship became a common word as school people scrambled for Federal funds. In a way, for a period of several years, education itself went into orbit, spinning about like the Sputnik and the American counterparts of the Soviet metal which were soon circling the earth.

The period also witnessed efforts by large philanthropic foundations, most notably Ford and Carnegie, joined fairly recently by Kettering, to "reform" education by providing handsome sums to those in the schools willing to demonstrate the reforms. In this shifting emphasis to demonstrations of reform, the foundations departed from what may be their more important mission, namely facilitating the study of educational problems and providing support for the careful, objective appraisal of the many projects under way.

It is yet too early to assess the events that occurred in the decade following Sputnik. That education assumed a greater importance in the view of the public and of political leaders there can be little doubt.

Governors of the various states, members of Congress and Presidents of the United States made prominent mention of the importance of education and in many instances requested additional taxation to support the schools. A great deal was said from the public platform and written in the press about the neglect suffered by the educational system. Public attention, first directed to the academically talented, soon was shifted to the children of the poor in cities and rural areas, with special reference to the Negro. Many agencies of the Federal government became involved in education in one way or another, and programs were devised and administered quite apart from the established educational structure, including Job Corps Centers, Manpower Development and Training programs and programs for preschool children in poverty areas. Nation-wide concern was evidenced for the high school dropout.

Spurred on by the United States Office of Education, large industries began to invest resources in computerized educational systems, and in order to obtain the "software" (content material) to use with the "hardware" (computers and teaching machines) well-known textbook companies merged with industrial corporations specializing in electronics.

From a wide range and variety of proposals, opinions, criticisms, activities, reports, and studies, several designs began to emerge.

James B. Conant wrote *The American High School Today*, published in 1959. Mr. Conant, it will be recalled, appointed the committee of the Harvard faculty that produced *General Education in a Free Society* in 1945. He served as a member of the Educational Policies Commission, and was a member of the commission which issued *Education for All American Youth*. Mr. Conant was in Germany from 1953 to 1957, first as high commissioner, then as ambassador to the Federal Republic of West Germany. The Foreword to *The American High School Today* written by John Gardner, then president of the Carnegie Corporation, explains its origin. "*The preparation for the change [Mr. Conant's return from Europe] had already been laid. Many months before I had asked Mr. Conant whether there was any possibility that he might turn his attention to education after completing his tour of duty in Germany. He responded that a return to the field of education was uppermost in his mind and that the thing he wished most to do was to examine some of the critical problems facing the American high school. His answer was good news for American education.*"

The Carnegie Corporation provided $350,000 to the Educational Testing Service, Princeton, New Jersey, on behalf of Mr. Conant for *his use in preparing his book. Free copies were distributed widely to school board members, school officials and others, through the Educational Testing Service (E.T.S.).*

The book appeared while the controversies generated by the Sputnik furor were at their height. As stated earlier, it was being seriously proposed that the United States re-shape its secondary education after European models, with the academically elite provided for either in separate schools, or in noticeably separate parts of the general high school. Some believe that Mr. Conant's greatest contribution was his stout defense of the comprehensive secondary school, which seemed to silence most of the clamor for specialized schools.

Mr. Conant's prescription for the secondary schools of the United States represented the judgment of a distinguished American. The prescription, however, was almost entirely based on subjects to be studied and the length of time they should be studied, and in this respect bore some resemblance to the Report of the Committee of Ten. Unfortunately, his proposals for the fifteen per cent he considered to be "academically talented" were widely misinterpreted as being applicable to the entire student body. He later turned his attention to the remaining eighty-five per cent, and also dramatized the conditions in the schools in the slums, but in these areas his suggestions were less definite. His reports were largely concerned with the processes of education with less attention to purposes or to appraising the relatedness of his subject prescriptions to the needs or capacities of the learners. His reports, nevertheless, received wide attention, and unquestionably influenced the schools. For many schools, in suburbia particularly, his subject requirements served to reinforce confidence in what was already being done.

It seems certain that Mr. Conant, because of the respect in which he was held, succeeded in stifling much of the more irresponsible and uninformed criticism of the secondary schools which characterized the times.

CHOICE-MAKING IN SECONDARY EDUCATION

We turn now to excerpts from Background for Choice-Making in Secondary Education for further comments on the era.[1]

. . . the postwar reappraisal of education has not all been in one direction. If its first big drive was for pure academic excellence—and,

1 The National Association of Secondary School Principals. *Background for Choice Making in Secondary Education,* Washington: D.C., 1966. pp. 32–46.

by extension, concerned chiefly with the more talented youth—the old problem of the less gifted soon reasserted itself powerfully. It was impossible to ignore phenomena such as youth unemployment and rising delinquency and youthful crime. Rather suddenly, a tremendous concern arose for the dropout, and once more the quest was on for programs to fit the group on whose behalf the life adjustment program had been devised.

Furthermore, it did not prove possible to stick for long to any position that education has to do only with the mind, to the exclusion of character and personality. Thus, even in their work with the abler students, the very academicians who had come in to improve the intellectual content of school subject matter soon began dealing in objectives that had as much to do with personality as with cognition. Starting from a base very different from that of the progressive educator, they nevertheless arrived at some basically similar concerns.

It had been the style of the 30's and 40's to try big, neartotal appraisals of needs and purposes, as in the Orientation Committee's analysis of issues and functions. In the 50's and 60's one does not find quite their equivalent. In this latter period it seems to be events which best reveal how Americans were assessing needs and estimating solutions. Therefore, we shall be looking for a little while at things which happened.

The Scholars Enter the Scene

One line of the new analysis identified the chief educational problem as lying within the several academic subjects themselves, with the first focus upon the sciences and mathematics. The subject matter of the typical course, the argument ran, was just not valid any more, if it ever had been. It probably was not taught very well, either, because the teacher did not understand his field deeply enough; but the salient thing was that the scholarly fields had moved ahead and changed radically while the secondary school subjects had stood still.

Even the critics agreed that this state of affairs was partly the fault of the scholars in the disciplines, who had not worked actively enough with their colleagues at the secondary level. The obvious solution was to intensify their efforts. And, beginning with Zacharias and PSSC physics, they have been coming to such work in large numbers. Backed by impressive funds from the National Science Foundation and other sources, they have been reformulating whole fields, developing and refining instructional materials, and working with teachers in workshops and institutes across the land. The movement has spread from the original centers of science and mathematics to the foreign languages, the social studies, and now to English and the humanities. The result has been change at a pace few would have thought possible.

Important as the movement is, its basis is, nevertheless, simply a way of proceeding, which could be applied to curricula with vastly differing purposes and philosophical bases. Its deeper meanings are hard to assess and easy to oversimplify. Some of "the professors" may have entered the work with a fervent belief that subject matter was all important and pure intellectual cultivation the sole objective. But their work has in fact resulted in a surge of attention to method. More important, they have had great impact upon the real objectives of teachers in the several fields. In general, despite their emphasis upon the intellect and knowledge, they have tended to influence teachers away from mere acquisition of factual information, toward more fundamental goals. Thus they have cried down attempts at total "coverage" of subject matter, the memorization of factual information, the excessive manipulation of numbers, and so on. They have shown a passion for "discovery method," the spirit of inquiry, and the coherent learning of fundamental generalizations. They have switched the foreign languages from a study of grammar to the acquisition of a foreign tongue. In the field of literature they have given a new voice to the ideas inherent in the term "humanities." . . .

In sum, these scholars, working increasingly with school teachers and behavioral scientists, have come to show great concern for the kind of person-as-scientist, person-as-historian, etc., the student becomes. As we have already pointed out, they have a great deal in common (though they may dislike the idea) with what was fundamental in progressive education—in, for instance, their stress on giving great freedom and responsibility to the learner, cutting him loose to follow his nose in independent research. And in their use of selected subject matter as means rather than as end, they have a great deal in common with the old-style liberal educator. It seems a reasonable proposition that they are about as open to conservative counterattack as progressive education was. They have, of course, almost nothing in common with the utilitarianism of life adjustment education—but then they have not really tangled yet with the problem of those masses who were the latter's prime concern.

There are two important distinctions: Though the discipline-oriented scholars may approach the progressive educator's zeal for the individual person, so far as their discipline is concerned with him, they have shown little inclination to consider the impact of the entire curriculum, or how the several pieces can be pulled together for optimum effect. Even more notably, they have as yet shown very little concern for those societal goals which were so central in the thirties and forties. For the most part, even those who are working in the redevelopment of the social studies acknowledge little responsibility for producing democratic citizens.

Since the concerns of this group have not run to broad personal integration or the solving of social problems, they have felt little need to reach beyond their disciplines, to follow problems out across traditional subject lines. The question of broader curricular groupings, therefore, scarcely comes up among them. The cleavage lines of the basic disciplines tend to be taken for granted as marking the boundaries of subject matter organization. . . .

The Vocational Education Act of 1963

Every major legislative act is a crystallization of views as to what the salient problems are as well as to solutions. Several features of the Vocational Education Act are tip-offs in both respects.

1. Raising the annual Federal fund to nearly a quarter-billion dollars, it indicates a new weighing of the general significance of vocational preparation.
2. Breaking through the old rigid allocations to set programs (Smith-Hughes agriculture, e.g.), it recognizes a growing need for flexibility and adaptation in a time of change.
3. The explicit inclusion of out-of-school youth and of previously employed persons in need of retraining gives further emphasis to the changing nature of the situation.
4. Special recognition of persons with "academic, socioeconomic, or other handicaps" runs through the Act, with what amounts to a mandate to fashion appropriate programs for them, even if those programs are greatly different from traditional vocational education.
5. There is explicit provision for work-study programs, including payment of the student workers.
6. The Act provides for the establishment of area vocational schools.
7. The spending of certain funds is mandated for programmatic research and periodic re-evaluation of the curriculum.

The sixth of these features, regarding the area vocational school, has generated considerable controversy because it impinges upon the model of the comprehensive high school. Area vocational schools are being built in various parts of the country (while, at the same time, several large cities are backing away from special vocational schools in favor of comprehensive ones), but the construction is everywhere accompanied by argument as to the best form of organization. Despite this controversy it is intriguing to note how clearly the Act reflects a diagnosis of current need and how carefully it guards the ability to shift as the needs shift, from place to place or time to time. And one can almost see in the legislators' minds a constant preoccupation with the "handicapped" group.

The National Defense Education Act, 1964 Revision

If the original National Defense Education Act of 1958 was an exceptionally explicit expression of curricular priorities, its amendments in 1964 were no less so. To the originally emphasized fields of science, mathematics, and the foreign languages, it added English, reading, history, geography, and civics. Even more significantly, it now made special provision for institutes for teachers of disadvantaged youth. This striking turnabout is a clear indication of a fundamental shift in the diagnosis of the educational situation.

Operation Headstart and the Higher Horizons Programs

In the summer of 1965 a new federal fund made it possible to provide special preschool training for hundreds of roomfuls of children from deprived homes. Operation Headstart took its direction from the exploratory work of Martin Deutsch and others, who had been experimenting with three- and four-year-olds from slum homes. That work had demonstrated that it is possible to raise the level of intellectual functioning of such children and bring them into the first grade much abler to learn to read—and to do other tasks in succeeding years.

Much earlier, in 1965, New York City had launched its Demonstration Guidance Project—later extended and popularized under the name "Higher Horizons"—in a junior and a senior high school. Operating in a difficult part of the city, this pilot program had shown that the educational level of the culturally deprived could be signally raised, that the dropout rate could be cut, that the numbers graduating from high school and going on to a successful college experience could be markedly increased. Those responsible for the project thought they also saw "important differences in the personalities of many . . . a poise, a maturity, and a sense of self-worth . . . a new image of themselves and a much greater certainty that they could make their own futures."

Three-year-olds and adolescents are some distance apart, and a higher horizons program is not the same thing as a preschool program. Yet the two programs have a great deal in common—so much, in fact, that it would not be technically difficult to devise a developing program unfolding through all the school years in place of two spurts of effort at the two ends. Both are based on the belief that "the potential is there" —a belief which is getting increasing amounts of hard data behind it year by year. The problem is not, in this view, that the slum three-year-olds or the slum adolescents were born with lower IQ's and worse attitudes, but that in many cases their environment stifled and warped their development. Furthermore, according to this belief, if the environment can be improved—the earlier the better, probably, but anyway "better late than never"—the child or youth can improve in every important dimension.

Even in their methodologies the two programs share much that is basic. The preschool program may go more at pure cognitive awakening, and the adolescent program more at the self-concept attitudes, and aspirations—though it has not yet been proved that significant cognitive gains cannot still be made at adolescence. But both depend basically upon a vastly enriched input of varied stimulation, the opening up of a wider world of experience and opportunity. Both bank on the youngster's seeing more, feeling more, experiencing more, discriminating better, verbalizing and symbolizing better, and putting himself as a worthy person into the larger scene.

The details do not much matter for our purposes here. Programs for adolescents which might be vaguely described as the "higher horizons type" have proliferated into a large variety of styles and methods anyway. What does matter is that all this represents a radically new diagnosis of an overwhelmingly important problem. And if the diagnosis is sound it leads to radically different styles of solutions. It is a vastly different thing to pound away at a dull, indifferent, or hostile student day after day to improve his reading skills by some bit—vastly different from gambling that if you can help him to change as a person his reading will come along rather easily.

Because of the large funds behind Project Headstart, preschool education is now getting wide attention—though not necessarily all the expertise it needs. The "higher horizons types" of programs, though extended considerably through some of the Great Cities Projects and by small operations here and there, have not yet commanded anything like the same attention. One of the real diagnostic needs of secondary education today is to assess their possibilities.

Education and the Office of Economic Opportunity

Nowadays every older educator has a feeling of "This is where I came in." He may even have trouble learning the right new names and initials because, to him, the Job Corps and the Neighborhood Youth Corps are simply the CCC and the NYA all over again.

For our purposes it may be adequate to leave them with little more definition than that, though there are differences. Some of the smaller Job Corps Centers, engaged in conservation activities, do in fact carry on in the old CCC tradition. However, the other larger centers in urban areas are really residential vocational schools. In both kinds of centers there is also a program of "basic" education (chiefly in the tool subjects) as well as of guidance and assistance in placement. It is noteworthy that this time there are also some centers for young women, with curricula quite different from those for the young men.

Regardless of their exact program content, the centers are, of course, a sign of public recognition of a critical and massive problem: the problem of unemployment among out-of-school youth, and of the factors which cause certain young people to be poor prospects for employment. The diagnosis appears to read that their most pressing needs are for vocational training, basic education in the three R's, guidance, and placement help. Further, the fact that even the urban centers are residential may be taken to indicate a belief that youth from certain homes and neighborhoods need to be removed temporarily from their repressive environments. And the fact that a stipend is attached recognizes a need to be earning income.

Inevitably, the question arises as to whether we are in process of creating a "third school system" (in addition to the public and private schools). The remedial education, vocational training, and placement-guidance services could all be offered within the public schools. Having successfully resisted attempts to set off a special set of schools for an elite, we now face a serious choice as to whether we should go outside the comprehensive school to serve the less successful. If the Job Corps is built large enough to serve the whole out-of-school unemployed group, it will become a large institution. The issue is not academic.

In terms of this issue the Neighborhood Youth Corps is marginal. It operates partly within the schools (with the dropout-prone) and partly through Community Action Programs, City Hall, or other sponsors (with out-of-school youth). As part of the anti-poverty program, it has a strong purpose simply to get money in the pockets of lower class youth by paying them to work. It hopes that in the schools such work will be accompanied by appropriate remedial work, guidance, etc. In school or out, it hopes that the work experience will raise morale and have a healthy effect on work attitudes and habits. But it does not offer vocational training and does not see itself as building skills, except incidentally.

Here the question may be not so much whether somebody else is building a "third system" as whether schoolmen have enough commitment to what is possible in this program to work to incorporate it into a genuinely educative milieu. If we mean to build a natural bridge from school into work—and to use work experience as an educational element in itself as well as to make it an organizing center for other curricular elements—the money and resources which the Neighborhood Youth Corps has to offer may be very valuable to us. Whether the Neighborhood Youth Corps drifts more or less by default into a "third system" posture may be less important than whether it slides into providing mere routine job-holding when it could have been a dynamic educational force.

The Elementary and Secondary Education Act of 1965

If the allocation of funds is a valid indicator of the priority of concerns, then Public Law 89-10 shows the Federal government estimating, in effect, that the salient problem is to raise the quality of the education of the poor. If we add to this the same year's Operation Headstart, focused on the preschool children of those same poor, and the Job Corps and Neighborhood Youth Corps, which also came into operation that year for the youth of roughly the same group, we begin to sense a massive concern with those who have done least well in school and whose prospects outside school are dimmest. When we remember that this same Federal government had geared its earlier programs almost completely to the ablest students, we see that it has swung a long way 'round in seven years.

If we look at the Act less in terms of money and more in terms of ideas, we apparently see a great concern for research and development tied into continuing re-evaluation and improved coordination. Thus, funds are set up for supplementary educational centers and services at the local level, to take leadership in developing services not commonly available and to provide models for the improvement of all schools. Other funds are devoted to strengthening research and development on a larger scale, with special provisions for a series of national or regional educational laboratories, bringing the research abilities of universities, professional associations, and private organizations to bear. Finally, money is allocated to strengthen state departments of education, to facilitate constant re-evaluation and planning, and, in essence, to bring the departments more importantly into the research and development picture.

Those features of the Act which enable the public education agencies and the various centers to assist and serve private schools as well as public schools have, of course, re-opened certain questions as to the relations of church and state.

New Trends in Secondary Education

As we stated earlier, it was not our intention to try to write a history of developments and trends in education during the past decade. Opinions differ about the meanings and accomplishments. To Francis Keppel, U.S. Commissioner of Education during part of the period, the events portend nothing less than a revolution in American education, and one to be desired and hastened. To others, like Harold Taylor, ". . . the direction of educational thinking is conservative, restrictive, reactionary. In terms of public policy and public statement of national policy, education is most often linked to the cold war and considered to be an instrument for increased technical and logistic strength in a military and political competition with the Russians."

We believe that some of the fundamental questions raised in the reports included in this book remain fundamental still and need to be once more examined in the light of today. We believe many of the issues raised are unresolved and, hence, demand thought presently as they did when they were raised. We suggest that many of the problems first defined in the early reports are still acute.

Perhaps the time has come again when we should return to a thoughtful search for purpose, to an attempt to relate the many fragmented approaches to secondary education to objectives that are worthy of the best ideals of our society. Possibly we need to ask ourselves once more if we are creating a secondary education for all American youth. It is not unrealistic to ask again what is necessary to provide an education for citizenship in America, a kind of citizenship which embraces all future citizens, regardless of vocation or academic talent or race or economic position. It may be time again to appraise our schools in the ways of the Regents' Inquiry and the Maryland youth study, in order to discover how youth fares in this difficult age. For those who would like to sit back with the comfortable belief that everything in the house of secondary education in these United States has been somehow tidied up and set to rights, the signs seem to belie the hope. It is just at this period, when education has achieved a prominence never before accorded it in this country, that the best thinking of the profession and the public needs to be directed once again to the enduring questions raised by those who labored during the formative period of the universal secondary schools.

BIBLIOGRAPHY

BELL, H. M. *Youth Tell Their Story*. Washington, D.C.: American Council on Education, 1938.

BRENNER, EDMUND. *Working with Rural Youth*. Washington, D.C.: American Council on Education, 1942.

BUTTS, R. FREEMAN, and CREMIN, LAWRENCE A. *A History of Education in American Culture*. New York: Henry Holt & Co., 1953.

COMMISSION ON THE RELATION OF SCHOOL AND COLLEGE OF THE PROGRESSIVE EDUCATION ASSOCIATION. *Adventure in American Education Series*. New York: Harper & Brothers, 1942.
Vol. I. AIKEN, WILFORD M. *The Story of the Eight-Year Study*.
Vol. II. GILES, H. H.; McCUTCHEON, S. P.; and ZECHIEL, A. N. *Exploring the Curriculum*.
Vol. III. SMITH, EUGENE R.; TYLER, RALPH W. *Appraising and Recording Student Progress*.
Vol. IV. CHAMBERLIN, DEAN; CHAMBERLIN, ENID STRAW; DROUGHT, NEAL E.; and SCOTT, WILLIAM E. *Did They Succeed in College?*
Vol. V. *Thirty Schools Tell Their Story*.

CONANT, JAMES B. *The American High School Today*. New York: McGraw-Hill Book Co., Inc., 1959.

—————. *Slums and Suburbs.* New York: McGraw-Hill Book Co., Inc., 1961.

COUNTS, GEORGE S. *The Social Foundations of Education.* New York: Charles Scribner's Sons, 1934.

CREMIN, LAWRENCE A. *The Transformation of the School.* New York: Alfred A. Knopf, 1961.

—————, and BORROWMAN, MERLE L. *Public Schools in our Democracy.* New York: The Macmillan Co., 1956.

CUBBERLY, ELLWOOD P. *Readings in Public Education in the United States.* New York: Houghton Mifflin Co., 1934.

DAVIS, ALLISON, and DOLLARD, JOHN. *Children of Bondage; the Personality Development of Negro Youth in the Urban South.* Washington, D.C.: American Council on Education, 1940.

DEPARTMENT OF SECONDARY SCHOOL PRINCIPALS OF THE NEA (Bulletin No. 64). *Functions of Secondary Education.* Washington, D.C.: NEA, 1936.

————— (Bulletin No. 59). *Issues of Secondary Education.* Washington, D.C.: NEA, 1936.

DEYOUNG, CHRIS A. *American Education.* New York: McGraw-Hill Book Co., Inc., 1960.

DOUGLASS, H. R. *Secondary Education for Youth in Modern America.* Washington, D.C.: American Council on Education, 1937.

EBY, FREDERICK. *The Development of Modern Education.* Englewood Cliffs, N.J.: Prentice-Hall, Inc., 1952.

EDUCATIONAL POLICIES COMMISSION (Reports). Washington, D.C.: NEA, 1937.
The Purpose of Education in American Democracy. 1938.
The Structure and Administration of Education in American Democracy. 1938.
Learning the Ways of Democracy. 1940.
Education and Economic Well-Being in American Democracy. 1940.
The Education of Free Men in American Democracy. 1941.
Education and the Morale of a Free People. 1941.
A War Policy for American Schools. 1942.
Education and the People's Peace. 1943.
Education for ALL American Youth. 1944.
Educational Services for Young People. 1945.
Education for All American Children. 1948.

EDWARDS, NEWTON. *Equal Educational Opportunity for Youth; A National Responsibility.* Washington, D.C.: American Council on Education, 1939.

—————, and RICHEY, HERMAN G. *The School in American Society.* New York: Houghton Mifflin Co., 1947.

GOOD, H. G. *A History of American Education.* New York: The Macmillan Co., 1956.

—————. *A History of Western Education.* New York: The Macmillan Co., 1960.

GRAHAM, BEN G., *et al. What the High Schools Ought to Teach.* Washington, D.C.: American Council on Education, 1940.

HARVARD COMMITTEE. *General Education in a Free Society.* Cambridge, Mass.: Harvard University Press, 1945.

HOLLAND, KENNETH, and HILL, F. E. *Youth in the Civilian Conservation Corps.* Washington, D.C.: American Council on Education, 1942.

JOHNSON, C. S. *Growing Up in the Black Belt: Negro Youth in the Rural South.* Washington, D.C.: American Council on Education, 1941.

KANE, WILLIAM T. *History of Education.* Chicago: Loyola University Press, 1954.

MEYER, ADOLPH. *The Development of Education in the Twentieth Century.* Englewood Cliffs, N.J.: Prentice-Hall, 1939.

NATIONAL ASSOCIATION OF SECONDARY SCHOOL PRINCIPALS. *Planning for American Youth.* Washington, D.C.: NASSP, 1944.

THE NATIONAL COMMITTEE OF SECONDARY EDUCATION OF THE NATIONAL ASSO-CIATION OF SECONDARY SCHOOL PRINCIPALS. *Background for Choice-Making in Secondary Education.* Washington, D.C.: NASSP, 1966.

THE REGENTS OF THE UNIVERSITY OF THE STATE OF NEW YORK. *The Regents Inquiry Into the Character and Cost of Public Education in the State of New York.* New York: McGraw-Hill Book Co. Inc., 1938.
ECKERT, RUTH, and MARSHALL, T. O. *When Youth Leave School.*
GRACE, A. G., and MOE, G. A. *State Aid* and *School Costs.*
GULICK, L. H. *Education for American Life.*
JUDD, C. H. *Preparation of School Personnel.*
LAINE, ELIZABETH. *Motion Pictures and Radio.*
MALLER, J. B. *School and Community.*
NORTON, T. L. *Education for Work.*
REEVES, F. W., FANSLER, T., and HOULE, C. O. *Adult Education.*
SPAULDING, F. T. *High School and Life.*
WILSON, H. E. *Education for Leadership.*
WINSLOW, C. E. A. *The School-Health Program.*

SIZER, THEODORE R. *The Age of the Academies.* New York: Bureau of Publications, Teachers College, Columbia University, 1964.

—————. *Secondary Schools at the Turn of the Century.* New Haven: Yale University Press, 1964.